A NOTE FROM THE AUTHOR

If you are a high school student enrolled in an AP European History course, your text is probably a fat, 1,000-plus-page college book, and you are facing a three-hour national exam in May. This review book will help you make sense of periods, events, and topics as you move through the course and help you prepare for tests throughout the year. It will provide focused summary and review before the AP exam.

Chapters 1 and 2 offer test-taking strategies specific to AP European History, as well as a Diagnostic Test to help you target areas where you need more study. Chapters 3–30 summarize major European events from about 1450 to the 21st century.

Each unit ends with practice multiple-choice questions, answers and explanations, and sample free-response questions accompanied by essay answers. The book includes two complete exams, each consisting of 80 multiple-choice questions, a document-based essay question, and six free-response questions—all with answers and full explanations.

Success in any AP course requires diligence, discipline, and hard work, but the rewards can be great. You will build vocabulary and critical thinking and writing skills. In addition to the possibility of earning college history credit, students of AP European History also gain an understanding of the basis of Western culture—its art, government, science, religion, and literature.

This is a course in "how we got to be the people we are." You will be surprised by the breadth of knowledge you will acquire and by its usefulness in many future endeavors.

Best of luck,
Martha Moore

Kaplan offers resources and options to help you prepare for the PSAT, SAT, ACT, AP exams, and other high-stakes exams. Go to www.kaptest.com or scan this code below with your phone (you will need to download a QR code reader) for free events and promotions.

snap.vu/m87n

RELATED TITLES

AP Biology

AP Calculus AB & BC

AP Chemistry

AP English Language and Composition

AP English Literature and Composition

AP Environmental Science

AP Human Geography

AP Macroeconomics/Microeconomics

AP Physics B & C

AP Psychology

AP Statistics

AP U.S. Government & Politics

AP U.S. History

AP World History

SAT Premier with CD-Rom

SAT: Strategies, Practice, and Review

SAT Subject Test: Biology E/M

SAT Subject Test: Chemistry

SAT Subject Test: Literature

SAT Subject Test: Mathematics Level 1

SAT Subject Test: Mathematics Level 2

SAT Subject Test: Physics

SAT Subject Test: Spanish

SAT Subject Test: U.S. History

SAT Subject Test: World History

AP® EUROPEAN HISTORY

2014

Martha Moore

KAPLAN

PUBLISHING

New York

© 2013 by Kaplan, Inc.

Published by Kaplan Publishing, a division of Kaplan, Inc.
395 Hudson Street
New York, NY 10014

Printed in the United States of America

10 9 8 7 6 5 4 3 2 1

ISBN-13: 978-1-61865-253-9

Kaplan Publishing books are available at special quantity discounts to use for sales promotions, employee premiums, or educational purposes. For more information or to purchase books, please call the Simon & Schuster special sales department at 866-506-1949.

TABLE OF CONTENTS

About the Author XII

Kaplan Panel of AP Experts XIII

PART ONE: THE BASICS

Chapter 1: Inside the AP European History Exam 3

    Overview of the Test Structure 3

    How the Exam Is Scored 4

    Registration and Fees 6

    Additional Resources 6

Chapter 2: Strategies for Success 9

    General Test-Taking Strategies 9

    Multiple-Choice Strategies 10

    Free-Response Question (FRQ) Strategies 10

    Document-Based Question (DBQ) Strategies 13

    The Scoring Rubric 14

    Tackling Each Core Point 15

    Time Management 17

    Stress Management 18

    Countdown to the Test 18

    Prioritizing What to Study 19

PART TWO: DIAGNOSTIC TEST

Diagnostic Test 25

Diagnostic Test Answer Key 29

Assess Your Strengths 30

Answers and Explanations 31

Sample Document-Based Question 34

Three Sample Essay Responses with Evaluation and Analysis 38

How to Make This Book Work for You Based on the Results of Your Diagnostic Test 40

PART THREE: AP EUROPEAN HISTORY REVIEW

Unit One: Early Modern Europe 1450–1600

Chapter 3: The Renaissance 45

    Pre-1450 History 45

    The Italian Renaissance.................................. 46

    The Northern Renaissance................................ 49

Chapter 4: The Reformation and Religious Wars 53

    Crises in the Roman Catholic Church 53

    Impact of the Renaissance............................... 54

    Martin Luther and the German States 54

    Calvinism and Its Expansion 56

    The English Reformation 57

    Catholic Counter-Reformation........................... 59

    Wars of Religion 1559–1648 60

Chapter 5: Discovery, Expansion, and Commercial Revolution 65

    New Knowledge and Technologies 65

    Portuguese Exploration 65

    Spanish Exploration..................................... 66

    Colonization 66

    Price Revolution 68

    Mercantilism... 68

    Unit One Review Questions 70

    Answers and Explanations............................... 74

Unit Two: The 17th Century

Chapter 6: The Age of Absolutism—Western Europe 79

    Characteristics and Philosophies of Absolutism 79

    Development of French Absolutism: 1588–1643 79

    The Age of Louis XIV.................................... 80

    Wars of Louis XIV 81

Chapter 7: The Age of Absolutism—Eastern Europe 83

    Decline of the Holy Roman Empire, Polish Kingdom, and the Ottoman Empire............ 83

    Characteristics of Absolutism in Eastern Europe 84

    Absolutism in Russia 85

Absolutism in Austria..86

Absolutism in Prussia 87

Chapter 8: Constitutionalism in England and the Dutch Republic 89

England..89

The Dutch Republic 90

Chapter 9: The Scientific Revolution 93

Astronomy 93

Medicine..96

Impact of the Scientific Revolution on European Society 98

Unit Two Review Questions 100

Answers and Explanations..104

Unit Three: The 18th Century

Chapter 10: The Enlightenment 109

Impact of the Scientific Revolution 109

Enlightenment Philosophy 109

Exceptions to Enlightenment Thought 110

The *Philosophes*..111

Impact of the Enlightenment on European Society 114

Enlightened Despotism: Austria, Prussia, and Russia.........................115

Chapter 11: 18th-Century Economics and Politics..................................121

Agricultural Revolution 121

Cottage Industry..122

Mid-Century Wars..122

The Impact of the American Revolution 125

Chapter 12: The French Revolution 127

Long-Term Causes 127

1789–1791 128

1792–1799 131

Impact of the Revolution 134

Napoleonic France 134

Unit Three Review Questions...138

Answers and Explanations 142

Unit Four: The 19th Century 1815–1848

Chapter 13: The Industrial Revolution 149

Why England Was the First to Industrialize 149

Hallmarks: Steam Engine, Iron, and Railroads.............................. 150

Social Impact 150

Reforms.. 152

Industrialism on the Continent 152

Chapter 14: Conservatism (1815–1848) 155

Concert of Europe: 1815–1823... 155

Russia 157

France: 1815–1830 157

German States: 1815–1830 158

England: 1815–1832.. 159

Austrian Empire 160

Chapter 15: The Rise of Liberalism (1815–1848) 161

Characteristics 161

England... 162

France: Revolutions of 1830 and 1848...................................... 162

Chapter 16: The Rise of Nationalism (1815–1848) 165

Greece and Belgium: Independence.. 165

Germany: Philosophies of Nationalism and the Revolutions of 1848 166

Italy: Revolutions of 1830 and 1848 169

Austria: Multiethnic Empire and the Revolution of 1848 170

Summary of the Revolutions of 1848 171

Chapter 17: Romanticism... 173

Characteristics, Contrasts with the Enlightenment, and National Revolution 173

Romantic Literature 174

Romantic Art and Music... 175

Unit Four Review Questions.. 176

Answers and Explanations.. 181

Unit Five: The 19th Century 1848–1914

Chapter 18: The Age of Realpolitik (1848–1871) 189

Aftermath of the Revolutions of 1848.. 189

Crimean War 190

The Second French Empire under Louis Napoleon........................ 191

Unification of Italy 193

Unification of Germany 197

Austro-Hungarian Empire 201

Chapter 19: The Rise of Socialism **203**

Utopian Socialists 203

Marxian Socialism 204

Impact of Socialism on European Politics 1815–1871 206

Chapter 20: The Age of Mass Politics (1871–1915) **209**

Characteristics 209

The Third French Republic 209

The German Empire 212

Great Britain 213

The "Irish Question" 214

Austro-Hungarian Empire 216

Impact of Socialism 216

Realism in Literature 218

Social and Political Reforms 218

Chapter 21: Intellectual Movements (1850–1914) **221**

Science 221

Artistic Movements 226

Chapter 22: The New Imperialism **233**

Characteristics of the New Imperialism 233

Imperialism in Africa 235

Imperialism in Asia 239

Unit Five Review Questions 243

Answers and Explanations 247

Unit Six: Europe 1914–1945

Chapter 23: World War I **253**

Long-Term Causes 253

Modern Warfare 258

Society During the War 262

The Treaty of Versailles 263

Aftermath of the War 264

Chapter 24: The Russian Revolution 267

    Russian Society Since 1850 267

    Revolution of 1905 and Afterward 270

    The February Revolution 271

    The October Revolution 273

    The Russian Civil War 274

Chapter 25: Europe Between the Wars 275

    The "Age of Anxiety" 275

    Totalitarianism in the Soviet Union 277

    Fascist Italy 280

    The Weimar Republic 282

    The Great Depression 284

    Totalitarianism in Nazi Germany 286

    Spanish Civil War 289

Chapter 26: World War II 291

    Failure of Collective Security 291

    German Expansion 292

    Turning Points of the War 296

    Diplomacy During the War 299

    European Society During the War 301

    The Holocaust 302

    Aftermath of the War 303

    Unit Six Review Questions 304

    Answers and Explanations 308

Unit Seven: 1945 to the Present

Chapter 27: Immediate Postwar Issues 315

    European Recovery 315

    The Restructuring of Europe 317

    Truman Doctrine, Marshall Plan, United Nations, NATO 319

Chapter 28: The Cold War 321

    1940s 321

    1950s 322

    1960s 323

    1970s 324

    1980s and the Revolution of 1989 324

    Fall of the Soviet Union 326

Chapter 29: Nationalism **327**

   Decolonization 327

   Nationalism in Western Europe... 332

   Nationalism in Eastern Europe 334

   Yugoslavia 335

Chapter 30: Post–World War II Society **337**

   Class Structure 337

   Gender Issues... 337

   Youth.. 338

   Immigration 339

   Religion... 339

   Unit Seven Review Questions 341

   Answers and Explanations... 345

PART FOUR: PRACTICE TESTS

   How to Take the Practice Tests 352

   How to Compute Your Score 353

Practice Test 1.. **355**

   Answer Key.. 375

   Assess Your Strengths 376

   Answers and Explanations... 377

Practice Test 2.. **397**

   Answer Key.. 417

   Assess Your Strengths 418

   Answers and Explanations... 419

Glossary... **437**

ABOUT THE AUTHOR

Martha Moore has been teaching AP European History since 1988 at Shelby High School in Shelby, North Carolina. She has served as a reader for the AP European History Exam since 1992 and a table leader and consultant for the College Board since 2001.

The author wishes to acknowledge the AP European History students at Shelby High School, who have shared and inspired this journey; her colleagues at the AP European History Reading, from whom she has learned so much; her editor, Ruth Baygell, for her encouragement and guidance; and her husband, Bob, and daughters, Cindy and Susan, for their unending love and support.

KAPLAN PANEL OF AP EXPERTS

Congratulations—you have chosen Kaplan to help you get a top score on your AP exam.

Kaplan understands your goals and what you're up against—achieving college credit and conquering a tough test—while participating in everything else that high school has to offer.

You expect realistic practice, authoritative advice, and accurate, up-to-the-minute information on the test. And that's exactly what you'll find in this book, as well as every other in the AP series. To help you (and us!) reach these goals, we have sought out leaders in the AP community. Allow us to introduce our AP European History expert.

AP EUROPEAN HISTORY EXPERTS

Jerry Hurd has been teaching AP European History for 16 years at Olympic High School in Silverdale, Washington. He has been a consultant to the College Board and an AP reader for nine years and a table leader for the past five years. He regularly attends the AP Premier Summer Institute and leads workshops in AP European History. In 2002, he was voted "Most Outstanding Table Leader."

Anthony "Tony" Jones has taught Advanced Placement courses for the past 10 years, including AP U.S. History, AP European History, and AP World History. He has taught at Houston County High in Warner Robins, GA, and Rutland High School in Macon, GA. He is a member of the World History Association and the National Council for Social Studies. He is a table leader and reader for the AP World History Reading exam. Additionally, he has been a presenter on integrating technology into the social studies and AP classroom at several conferences.

| Part One |

THE BASICS

CHAPTER 1: INSIDE THE AP EUROPEAN HISTORY EXAM

Advanced Placement European History is a course in *modern* European history, which means that it covers a time frame from approximately 1450 (the time of the High Renaissance) through 2001. The approach is thematic, as well as chronological, with emphasis on intellectual, cultural, political and diplomatic, social, and economic history:

- **Intellectual history** includes changes in thought, outlook, and view of the world and of humanity; examples include the scientific revolution, developments in religion, the Enlightenment, romanticism, and existentialism.

- **Cultural history** refers primarily to art, music, literature, and film, all of which reflect the people and times that produce them.

- **Political** and **diplomatic history** covers the development of nation states, wars, treaties, international agreements, and political ideology (such as Marxism).

- **Social history** includes attitudes toward gender and class and the ways people live their lives (their food, dress, housing, family life, entertainment, employment, etc.).

- **Economic history** involves all things related to money and finance, from the price of bread, to wages, to the production of goods and trade.

Of course, these six areas often overlap; for instance, the development of a certain technology might come from intellectual history and affect social and economic history.

Each chronological period should be studied through the six approaches; you are expected to develop skills in analysis and interpretation of evidence, events, and trends in history.

OVERVIEW OF THE TEST STRUCTURE

The exam lasts 3 hours and 5 minutes.

First 55 minutes (PART A):	80 multiple-choice questions; 5-minute break
Next 130 minutes (PARTS B and C):	Essay questions

In the essay section, you will write three essays in response to a document-based question (DBQ–PART B) and two free-response questions (FRQ–PART C). For each FRQ essay, you will select from a choice of three questions in each of two parts. Be careful not to do two FRQs from the same part, or that second essay will not be scored.

Make sure to pace yourself as you work through the entire exam. You may go in whatever order you choose for the essays; all responses are written in the same booklet.

SECTION I: MULTIPLE CHOICE (50 PERCENT)

The 80 multiple-choice questions are drawn from the six thematic areas and cover the entire chronological frame of the course, 1450–2001. Approximately one-half of the questions address the period from the Renaissance up to the French Revolution, and the other half covers the years from the French Revolution and Napoleonic era through the very early 21st century.

No single textbook covers everything on the exam, and students are not expected to know every single answer. Questions reflect varying levels of difficulty, and the levels are mixed throughout the questions.

SECTION II: ONE DBQ (22.5 PERCENT) AND TWO FRQS (13.75 PERCENT EACH)

Students have 2 hours and 10 minutes to read the essay questions and then plan and write the three essays. Pacing is critical and is up to the student. Because not all testing rooms have clocks, having a watch (no alarms) is important. Test takers are required to read and plan (writing in the test manual) for 15 minutes, covering the historical background, prompt, and all the documents of the DBQ and the question choices in Parts B and C. The ideal is then to devote 45 minutes to writing the DBQ essay and 35 minutes each to writing the two FRQ essays.

HOW THE EXAM IS SCORED

The score from the multiple-choice section counts for 50 percent of the total exam score. The other 50 percent is the combined essay score from the DBQ and FRQs. Within the essay half, 45 percent comes from the DBQ, and 55 percent from the two thematic FRQs.

Scores are based on the total number of questions answered correctly. **No points are deducted for wrong answers.** No points are awarded for unanswered questions. Therefore, you should answer every question, even if you have to guess.

Your multiple-choice section is scored by multiplying the total number of correct answers by 1.125 to get your weighted score. The DBQ essay is scored by multiplying the total number of points earned (out of 9) by 4.5. The total points earned on each of the FRQs are multiplied by 2.75. These three weighted scores are added together to get your total weighted essay score.

The Section I and Section II weighted scores are added together to get your composite score. Your composite score is converted to your AP score, on a scale of 1 to 5:

5 = Extremely well qualified

4 = Well qualified

3 = Qualified

2 = Possibly qualified

1 = No recommendation

A conversion chart is provided in the Practice Test section of this guide.

While some college programs accept a score of 3, schools with more competitive entrance requirements will require a composite score of 4 or 5. Others may not give credit but will want to see your scores. Check school websites or contact their admissions offices to understand their AP credit policies.

HOW THE ESSAYS ARE GRADED

After the AP exam has been administered, high school and college teachers from across the country read and evaluate all of the essays. Essays are ranked on a 10-point scale, 0 to 9:

- A good essay is organized. It begins with a relevant introduction and contains a thesis statement. It shows understanding of the required tasks, which means that the writer has followed such directives as "compare and contrast" (tell similarities and differences), "analyze" (examine the component parts and their relationships), or "show to what extent" (explain the scope or magnitude or degree).

- The well-done essay accomplishes all the tasks required by the prompt; it is a good plan to underline each of these and to check periodically while writing to see that you are fulfilling all requirements.

- Above all else, the good essay gives *specific* information (examples) to prove assertions. Certainly, good sentence structure, spelling, and grammar are helpful in making a good impression, but these qualities are not directly assessed.

- The essay is evaluated on how much appropriate information it contains that responds accurately to the prompt directives. Note: Because you are writing about history, events in the past, it is generally better to use past tense verbs consistently.

- The good essay incorporates accurate chronology. Often, the essay questions refer to specific time periods, and questions frequently link two periods for purposes of comparison and/or contrast. (Remember that the 17th century means the *1600s*, the 18th century means the *1700s*, etc.)

> **AP EXPERT TIP**
>
> Remember: in a good essay, the thesis must answer the question.

> **AP EXPERT TIP**
>
> Because this is a historical essay, write in third person and avoid phrases like "I think," "I believe," and "in my opinion." These statements are subjective and don't show an objective historical understanding of the material.

- The document-based question (DBQ) is assessed via the rubric discussed in Chapter 2, and the two other essays are judged by scoring standards established at the reading, based on an extensive sampling of student essays and reviewed for consistency within the process.

REGISTRATION AND FEES

If you are taking AP European History at your high school, registration for the AP exam is done in March. See your teacher or AP coordinator to make sure that your name is on the exam order form that your school sends to the College Board. At the time of printing, the cost of an AP exam was $89, and $117 at schools and testing centers outside the United States. For those qualified with acute financial need, the College Board offers a $28 credit. In addition, most states offer exam subsidies to cover all or part of the remaining cost for eligible students. To learn about other sources of financial aid, contact your AP Coordinator.

If you are homeschooled or not in a school that offers AP courses, you can still take the exam. Call AP services at (609) 771-7300 or 888-225-5427 by March 1 for a list of schools in your area where you can take the exam. Then contact the AP coordinator at one of the schools identified by the College Board to get a place on exam day.

The College Board makes accommodations for documented disabilities. These may include extended time, large-print exams, use of a word processor, and other necessary accommodations. If you have a need for special accommodation, see your AP coordinator.

For more information on the AP program and the European History exam, contact

> AP Services
> P.O. Box 6671
> Princeton, NJ 08541-6671
> (609) 771-7300; 888-225-5427
> Email: apexams@info.collegeboard.org
> Website: collegeboard.com/student/testing/ap/about.html

ADDITIONAL RESOURCES

1. **Textbooks.** Certainly, no one textbook is perfect, but your selection should be a recognized college text of approximately 1,000 pages. In addition to extensive text written at the college level, it should contain good maps, illustrations, art, and documents. Some texts begin with the earliest Western civilization; your study should begin with some brief background in the high Middle Ages but move swiftly to the Italian Renaissance. Your book should be of

fairly recent edition because the exam tests material into the early 21st century. Reading the textbook is a first step to learning the material covered in this course.

Check your textbook for Web support. Virtually all textbook publishers maintain sites with practice questions and review material.

2. **Websites.** You are also encouraged to explore the official College Board AP website (apcentral.collegeboard.com) for information about the course and the exam. Questions and essays with scoring guidelines from the previous year are available for both FRQs and DBQs.

CHAPTER 2: STRATEGIES FOR SUCCESS

Being prepared is the key to success. Aside from engaging in the course-long practice of reading the textbook, taking good notes, and developing writing skills, there are specific things you can do before the exam to help you perform your best.

GENERAL TEST-TAKING STRATEGIES

1. A thorough review of the material is a necessity; allow four to six weeks for this review. This is an exam on which knowing a body of information will have an impact. Save all your tests throughout the course; these make good review material.

2. Study with others, especially if this has proven to be personally helpful in the past. Any study group should have an organized plan and stick to it in order to maximize time use.

3. On the day before the exam and the morning of the exam (AP European History is usually an afternoon exam), it's a good idea to lighten up. Look over and think about the visual elements of your text—maps, pictures, illustrations. It is also good to review the guidelines for the essay questions.

4. Do not stay up late on the night before the exam. Eat a healthy breakfast and lunch and carry a small snack with you (for the break between the multiple-choice and essay sections—no food or drink in the exam room). Avoid other students who are excessively anxious.

5. Know the location of the exam (probably not your classroom and maybe not your school building) and how you will get to it, if it isn't at your school. Arrive early.

6. Do *not* bring a cell phone with you to the exam. Do bring the following:

   - A watch (with no sound)
   - Two #2 pencils with good erasers (for the multiple-choice answer sheet)

- Two dark pens, preferably black (for the essays). Do *not* write essays in pencil, because your writing will smear as the booklets are packaged and transported. It is okay to mark out text neatly, and make changes.

- Photo ID

- Social Security number (or other government-issued ID number)

- A light sweater or jacket and tissues or a handkerchief. Testing rooms are sometimes cold.

MULTIPLE-CHOICE STRATEGIES

For the multiple-choice questions, your goal is to get as many questions correct as possible. Here are some rules:

1. Be aware of the time throughout the test—you have 55 minutes. Do not linger over any questions.

2. On questions where you aren't sure of your answer, try to eliminate at least two choices, or mark the question to return to later, and then guess.

3. Every once in a while, take a split second to make sure that the number of the question in the test booklet matches the number of your answer on the bubble sheet.

4. Take time to read each question carefully. You are looking for the *most correct* answer; sometimes one or more wrong answers may sound correct at first, so you must read all the answer choices on every question.

5. Ignore other test takers who may finish before you do. Use the entire 55 minutes!

6. Do *not* close your test book and sit idly if you finish early. Use any extra time to go over any questions you were unsure of.

7. Experts caution about changing answers, however; your first intuition is more likely to be correct.

8. Be wary of extreme answer choices. The AP will try to fool you with "absolute" words such as **NANA: N**ever, **A**lways, **N**one, **A**ll. An example is "control of all trade with Spain's American colonies."

FREE-RESPONSE QUESTION (FRQ) STRATEGIES

There are two free-response essays on the exam. Generally, these essays are shorter than the essay for the document-based question. You'll be able to choose one question from Part B and another from Part C. The questions in the two parts will be quite different; they'll address different aspects of the course (cultural or social or political),

---

AP EXPERT TIP

Read through and answer the questions you absolutely know. Then, try to eliminate two or three choices, and guess. Do not leave any questions blank.

as well as different time periods, countries, and topics. Often, a question draws from different eras in two different places: "Compare and contrast the Reign of Terror in Revolutionary France with Stalin's Purge Trials of the 1930s." Try to give balanced treatment to both sides of the question; this will be part of the evaluation criteria.

In deciding which questions to answer, you obviously want to select the one about which you can present the most concrete information. Read each question carefully and quickly and, in the test booklet, quickly outline the question you think you can answer. Don't choose a question based on which topic you "like best"; choose the one for which you can produce the most evidence.

Be very careful about chronology. Most questions are time-specific, and the grading tends not to be generous about errors in time period. If the question refers to the "English religious settlement of the 17th century," the topic is the dispute between Anglicans and Puritans and the English Civil War—not the English Reformation of Henry VIII in the 1500s.

On many exam administrations, one of the six FRQs is the "woman question"— something related to specific women in European history (Elizabeth I, Madam Curie, etc.) or to gender roles in general (female factory workers during World War I). Avoid this question unless you are very sure you can answer it with specific, accurate evidence. Readers find that student responses on the woman question tend to be very good or very, very bad. If you are winging it on this question, chances are that your essay will come across as incompetent. On the other hand, if you really know some applicable information, your essay could receive a high ranking in comparison to the hundreds of poor ones other test takers have written.

Pacing is crucial for the FRQs. During the 15-minute reading period, spend 10 minutes reading the question and documents (for the DBQ) and making notes. You'll have 5 minutes left to read the essay choices in the two parts and jot down a few notes. Underline the task words *analyze, compare and contrast*, etc.

In the margin, do a quick outline of your chosen question. Be extremely careful about chronology; giving a wealth of information about the wrong time period will earn no credit. If you find yourself quite short on evidence, jot down what you know about a different question and, certainly, go with the one about which you can write the most.

If you find yourself at a loss on *all* the questions in Part B or Part C, and if one of the questions in that section deals with social issues, choose that one. You are more likely to get credit for general statements on a social issues question.

> **AP EXPERT TIP**
>
> It is critical that you read and answer all parts of the question.

> **AP EXPERT TIP**
>
> Good writing is always good writing. While you are not scored on grammar, sentence structure, or penmanship, solid writing skills will help you make your points more clearly to the reader scoring your FRQs.

Don't write more than two to three paragraphs if you're floundering. Do *not* appeal to the reader's mercy, make personal statements, or offer excuses. Simply try to address the question in the best way you can.

Try to devote about 35 minutes to each FRQ. These two essays should be written either first and third, or second and third. (The DBQ should *not* be left for last.) Handwriting can matter; it is to your advantage to write as legibly as possible—print if necessary.

ORGANIZE YOUR IDEAS EFFECTIVELY

The best FRQs do two things: They address all parts of the question, and they support the thesis claims with specific, accurate examples and information. As you plan the essay, jot down evidence you can use as proof of your claims. If you can't think of any examples, you are attempting to do the wrong question!

Devote a paragraph to each example and make its connection to some part of the prompt. Organize your evidence in a way that matches the question—chronologically, by country, etc. An effective FRQ response should span over a page—ideally, at least two pages. If there is time, proofread. It is all right to make additions if you think of any; you can draw an arrow to where the material is to be inserted.

A POWERFUL THESIS

The ideal location for an effective thesis statement is at the end of the first paragraph, the introduction. It should be a statement of what the essay will show or prove; it should be more than a simple restatement of the prompt.

The following, for example, would *not* be a good thesis if you have been prompted to discuss differing views on slavery in the 18th century. It does *not* take a stand—it says next to nothing and merely repeats the prompt:

> "There were various opinions on slavery in the 18th century."

A better thesis might be:

> "Economic interests defended the sale of slaves, while humanitarian and religious groups condemned it."

The thesis should proclaim the central idea(s) of the essay, and body paragraphs should prove this claim with information, elaboration, and examples.

POWERFUL BODY PARAGRAPHS

There is no magic number of "correct" developmental paragraphs. The most important aspect of a body paragraph is that it illustrates or proves some part of the prompt with *specific* information. It is essential to elaborate on all parts of the prompt, equally well, if possible.

Many prompts will ask for at least two tasks. The highest scores will go to essays that are balanced between the tasks, so don't say a lot about half the question and very little about the other half. The material (evidence) should be presented in a way that meets the prompt's directive. If you're asked to analyze, merely describing the material won't earn you a good score.

Essays are ranked by the amount and quality of accurate evidence they present. Essays that don't get beyond very broad, general statements will receive lower scores.

STRONG CONCLUSION

If you have time at the end of your essay, write a short conclusion—three to five sentences are sufficient. A strong conclusion ties together the strands of the essay in a final, compelling way. Do not merely repeat the thesis or the information from earlier in the essay—you're better off having no conclusion at all.

You will not lose credit for not having a conclusion, though a strong final paragraph can certainly add to the essay's overall effect.

DOCUMENT-BASED QUESTION (DBQ) STRATEGIES

The document-based question (DBQ) assesses how well you can analyze, interpret, and synthesize information from documents, paying attention to the source of each. In a sense, it's a mini research paper for which someone else has done the research and handed you 10 to 12 small bits of information from a variety of sources (speeches, letters, diaries, poems, maps, art, etc.).

Usually, the documents are presented in chronological order. Pay close attention to each source; often, the nature of the source affects how you analyze the document, especially in deciding whether it is to be taken at face value or judged to be biased in some way.

You are asked to analyze and synthesize the information into a critical essay that addresses all parts of the given prompt. As you plan, reread the prompt and mark which documents relate to which parts of the question; organize the material and group documents as they apply to the prompt.

The DBQ essay is judged by a specific scoring rubric that is widely publicized; you should memorize and practice the formula. Writing a superior DBQ essay is a skill that is not difficult to develop with practice.

AP EXPERT TIP

The conclusion should be a synopsis of the points you are trying to make throughout your essay. Often, a stronger thesis statement is found in the conclusion than in the introductory paragraph.

AP EXPERT TIP

You are asked to discuss the author's point of view (POV) for at least three documents. This is a relatively new skill for this exam, and students often find it challenging. As you read each document, remember that every document has a reason behind it. As you read, write these reasons in the margin.

Make sure to use the reading time. This is not time wasted! Read the question and background information carefully. Underline the tasks you are assigned. Each DBQ begins with a paragraph of historical background. Remember that this is *not* a document. It is meant to establish a setting for the question. It is wise not to repeat much of this information or to quote from it in your essay. Your writing will be judged on your use of the documents, not the historical background. Information from this paragraph gives you no points on the scoring rubric.

As you read the documents, make notes beside each. Pay attention to the source of each, especially if it is someone you recognize or if you can connect it to such topics as religion, money, gender issues, or political bias. Try to group the documents into at least two main sides of the question's topic, with possible subgroups within each division.

Do a quick, rough outline. Then write.

Make sure you're covering the six core scoring requirements. You cannot make a score higher than 6 unless you have every one of the basic six.

THE SCORING RUBRIC

The FRQs and the DBQ are assigned scores from 0 to 9. The first 6 points on the DBQ are given for the following elements:

- States a thesis explicitly, which addresses all parts of the question. It does not merely restate the question.

- Uses a majority of documents; that is, uses at least *one more than half* the documents provided. Documents must be used individually and specifically.

- Shows an understanding of the basic meaning of a majority of the documents. Essay misinterprets no more than one of the documents.

- Supports the thesis with interpretations of a majority of the documents.

- Analyzes point of view or bias in at least *three* documents.

- Analyzes documents by explicitly organizing them in at least *three* appropriate groups.

If, and only if, an essay receives all six of the basic core points is it eligible for up to three more points from the Expanded Core. Expanded Core elements would have an especially strong thesis, using the documents very persuasively, showing four or more examples of bias or point of view or four or more groupings, or bringing in *relevant* outside information (not required, but helpful).

Be very aware of covering the six basic core items as you write. Even if you have four or five examples of bias, if you have only two groupings, you'll receive at most a score of 5 on the DBQ.

TACKLING EACH CORE POINT

1. Begin with a careful introductory paragraph. *Briefly* describe the background. Establish a time and place setting by including the "four Ws"—*who, what, where,* and *when*. Include a thesis sentence at the end of the introductory paragraph—this is essential!

   The thesis should announce the stand you will take in the essay, and it should cover all parts of the question. It must not be a simple regurgitation of the prompt. Don't say, for example, "There were various opinions about whether women should participate in science." Tell what those opinions were: "While most men criticized women scientists, the women themselves saw their work more positively."

   Readers are bound to form a first impression from the first paragraph, so its quality is of paramount importance. Your thesis can span more than one sentence; two may be necessary to address all parts of the prompt. Being exact and analytical here is what matters.

2. Think about *why* each document has been included, paying attention to the source of each. Instead of writing, "Doc. 2 says …," it is much more effective to refer to its source: "A French priest, writing to his bishop in 1745, said that …"

   Do not write, "The map shows …" [*What* map?] Write as if the reader can't see the map. Say, instead, "A map of Spain in 1600 shows that …" If you list the document numbers in the margin, it will be easy for both you and the reader to do a quick count of how many documents you have used. Mix up the order of the documents, connecting them as they relate to each other.

3. Try to use almost all documents provided—all, if you can. You *must* use half of the documents *plus one* to get the basic core point. If there is one document that you absolutely do not understand, omit it, rather than make a mistake in interpreting it. Often, the most difficult documents for students are the visual ones—the charts, maps, or art.

4. The core point for three examples of bias or point of view seems to be the most difficult for students to accomplish. Think about *why* a speaker would say what he says or why he would hold a certain opinion.

   Often, bias hinges on issues of gender, wealth, or religion. A clergy person in a document, for instance, might condemn or approve some behavior on the basis of morality. In that case, you can write, "It is expected that a priest like _____ would condemn prostitution …" or "… would approve of the giving of charity." You can write, "Madam _____ showed bias because she was a member of the aristocracy, who looked down on the poor," or, "Because she was a woman, Jane Doe spoke out in favor of education for girls." For you to receive credit for understanding bias, the bias interpretation must be reasonably accurate.

Not every document shows bias; a government report on infant mortality might be considered to contain accurate statistics. But even neutral documents like these can be used to demonstrate a point of view. You can write, "Because this was a government report, it could be accepted as factual." The type of bias is often shaped by the type of document: In a public statement, an official might say what others expect, while a personal journal entry or private letter might be judged as representative of the speaker's true sentiments.

5. Think about how to organize groups effectively. At least three groupings of documents are required to receive the basic core point; a "group" consists of two or more documents. Grouping is based either on the documents, content, or on their sources.

   In the initial reading period, note in the margin similarities and differences between documents. Groupings may show either one of those. Example: "The lawyer in doc. 3 argued that...; however, the judge in doc. 7 took the opposite view, saying that..." Example: "The German astronomer in doc. 5 and the Italian professor in doc. 8 seemed to agree that..."

   Groupings may be assigned based on a number of factors: gender, profession, social status, economic status, nationality, type of document (two journal entries, two speeches in Parliament), similarity or difference of opinion, or time period, to name a few. Be specific in noting groupings. It is better to say, "Both John Wesley (doc. 4) and George Whitfield (doc. 6) said...," than to write, "Documents 4 and 6 said..."

6. Do not write about the documents in their original numeric order. A deadly approach is to write, "Doc. 1 says... Doc. 2 says... Doc. 3 says..."

   You must interpret and analyze the information from the documents rather than simply paraphrase it. You are trying to prove a point, or points, that you have made in your thesis statement. Use the documents to establish the proof you want to show.

   If you quote, and that is not required, keep the quotations *short* and *few* in number. Never quote an entire document; use phrases and pieces of sentences to make your point. And never quote without immediately following up with your interpretation of the quoted words.

   Keep your personal opinions out of the essay. The pronoun *I* should not appear anywhere. Similarly, don't insert any personal bias or judgment of the sources or the information. This is a presentation of the material and opinions of others, not a personal essay.

   Do not bring in outside information unless you're truly sure that it is accurate and applicable. Remember, outside information isn't required on the exam.

AP EXPERT TIP

Do not write about the documents in their original numeric order. This is often referred to as a "laundry list." This will not earn you the point for discussing the majority of the documents, nor does it demonstrate understanding of the documents.

TIME MANAGEMENT

Because there's no way to know if there will be a visible clock in the testing room, bring a watch and monitor your time. Read all the material in the essay booklet in the 15-minute reading time, making notes in the booklet. Try to choose your FRQs then. Remember and observe the time limits—doing so is up to you. The proctor will not tell you when to begin a new essay. Do what seems to be the easiest essay first; this should be either the DBQ or one of the FRQs.

Do the DBQ first or second. If you leave it for last, you may run out of time, and if you are well prepared, the DBQ is an essay on which you should be able to do well. Leave some blank space after each essay in case you end up with a few extra minutes and you think of something else to add.

The absolute best preparation for AP essay writing is long-term practice. Hopefully, your course has required essay questions as part of tests and ample numbers of DBQ practices, evaluated by the core scoring rubric. Besides knowing the course content, there are steps you can take to write better essays.

Know the prompt words:

- To *analyze* is to define components, especially in terms of their relationship to each other and to their meaning and importance. *Describe* is often connected to *analyze*; you're expected to give an account of some event or situation and, from the description, produce conclusions regarding its importance, relationships, possible consequences, etc.

- To *assess* or *evaluate* means to determine a judgment toward something, to appraise positives and/or negatives, to take a stand on an issue.

- To *compare and contrast* are opposite instructions frequently used in combination; they ask you to show similarities and differences, respectively.

- To *discuss* implies presenting different aspects of something by examining various sides or opinions.

- To *explain* means to give clarification by presenting details.

Some questions include the term *to what extent*, which also calls for a judgment regarding the scope, depth, or limits of the topic.

> **AP EXPERT TIP**
>
> You should answer the question you feel most comfortable with first. There is no requirement to answer the questions in any particular order.

STRESS MANAGEMENT

The high school AP program is intended to provide rigorous, college-level instruction. AP European History demands higher-level thinking and analytical skills. The course is not easy, but the rewards are worth the effort. This course can become basic to the study and understanding of many, many other areas of endeavor. And above all, it helps us understand our world and society; it explains much of "how we got to be who we are."

Motivated students taught by competent instructors can do well on the national exam. If this is your situation, this book is a useful supplement to your textbook, class notes, essays, and tests. The review chapters will help you focus on what is important to study for tests throughout the course, and the sample multiple-choice questions and essays will help you target areas of weakness. The two full-length exams at the end of the book will give you a sense of timing, coverage, and expectations of the "real thing."

But what if your class and/or teacher, for whatever reason, may be less than excellent? Certainly, this is a disadvantage, but it doesn't mean that you can't succeed. Thousands of students are successful on AP exams, despite having below average classes or even no AP class at all. In this case, success requires much work, self-discipline, and independent study on your part.

Whether or not you are enrolled in an effective European history course, you may want to create a study group with other students who are in the same situation as you are. Divide up the review tasks and share review notes. Use the European history themes listed in Chapter 1 and the division of the course by centuries. Have a fixed agenda when the group meets so that the gatherings are productive.

COUNTDOWN TO THE TEST

Exam preparation is a course-long process, but you will want to begin a more intense review about six weeks before the exam—that is, beginning in late March or early April. Go back to the early chapters of the course and move forward chronologically, refreshing your mind on people, issues, and events. Prepare a study plan by dividing the material. One approach is to look at each century and make lists of major events, wars, treaties, cultural developments, social and economic changes, scientific advancements, and intellectual trends. Try mentally to assimilate the connections of events into their time periods.

PRIORITIZING WHAT TO STUDY

Making study lists by topics, as mentioned, can be useful. About two weeks before the exam, fill in gaps in your preparation. For instance, major developments and changes in the French Revolution, or in the events of 1848, are complex and may require extra attention. This review book, along with your textbook, will help provide missing content, as well as highlight what is important throughout the course. Be reasonable; late night study is probably not beneficial. Plan your schedule to coordinate other demands on your time with your needs to prepare for this exam.

PRACTICE WITH MULTIPLE-CHOICE

Hopefully, you will get experience answering multiple-choice questions throughout the year in class. The questions in this book will also help you become familiar with question types. All of the FRQs can be found at the College Board's website. In the weeks before the test, spend some time going over the background and writing of these essays.

One style of question the College Board uses is this:

> **"All the following statements are true about _____, EXCEPT"**

Another style has the correct (or incorrect!) (E) answer:

> **(E) All of the above**

Extensive practice also hones the higher thinking skills of analysis, synthesis, and evaluation. It will help you with the visual questions—on charts, maps, cartoons, and illustrations.

A second advantage of effective multiple-choice practice is knowing when to guess and when to omit. Experience will help you develop more confidence in "educated guessing" when you are not sure of an answer, but you can eliminate two or more of the five choices. You will become more conscious of how many questions it is safe to omit and how to make that decision.

And finally, only experience can allow you to develop a sense of pacing. The best way to do this is to take full-length practice multiple-choice tests, timing yourself accurately. There are two complete tests at the end of this book. Also, every four years or so, the College Board releases a multiple-choice part of the exam. These are available from the College Board, or your teacher may use these to help you prepare.

AP EXPERT TIP

Use this book and take the practice tests about six weeks before the AP exam. Use this early practice to find weaknesses or gaps as you create your study plan.

REVIEW THE DBQS THE WEEK OF THE EXAM

Be very sure you know and can meet all six core scoring points. Review them. Refresh your memory on ways to establish bias from the documents and on ways to form groups. Look back over DBQs you have done, noting where you have been successful and also where you have made mistakes. Think about how to read and interpret the prompt and the elements of a strong introduction. Remind yourself of time limits and pacing and of issues that are frequently central to the documents, such as gender, money, religion, political power, social class, and nationalism. Review the more effective ways to cite document sources.

| **Part Two** |

DIAGNOSTIC TEST

AP EUROPEAN HISTORY DIAGNOSTIC TEST

This Diagnostic Test is a brief multiple-choice exam to help you identify your strengths and weaknesses in AP European History. The goal is to help you determine areas on which you should focus study. The questions are drawn from European history of the past 600 years and address the areas of intellectual and cultural history, political and diplomatic history, and social and economic history.

Once you have completed the exam, add up the number of questions you answered correctly and those you answered incorrectly.

If you score well, you are in terrific shape. Keep doing what you are doing. If you didn't score that high, you have some studying to do. This book should help.

Diagnostic Test Answer Grid

TO SCORE YOUR DIAGNOSTIC

Count the number of questions you got right. The approximate score range is as follows.

Test Score	Result
16–20	Excellent
12–15	Very good
10–11	Good
8–9	Fair
0–7	Poor

1. Ⓐ Ⓑ Ⓒ Ⓓ Ⓔ   11. Ⓐ Ⓑ Ⓒ Ⓓ Ⓔ

2. Ⓐ Ⓑ Ⓒ Ⓓ Ⓔ   12. Ⓐ Ⓑ Ⓒ Ⓓ Ⓔ

3. Ⓐ Ⓑ Ⓒ Ⓓ Ⓔ   13. Ⓐ Ⓑ Ⓒ Ⓓ Ⓔ

4. Ⓐ Ⓑ Ⓒ Ⓓ Ⓔ   14. Ⓐ Ⓑ Ⓒ Ⓓ Ⓔ

5. Ⓐ Ⓑ Ⓒ Ⓓ Ⓔ   15. Ⓐ Ⓑ Ⓒ Ⓓ Ⓔ

6. Ⓐ Ⓑ Ⓒ Ⓓ Ⓔ   16. Ⓐ Ⓑ Ⓒ Ⓓ Ⓔ

7. Ⓐ Ⓑ Ⓒ Ⓓ Ⓔ   17. Ⓐ Ⓑ Ⓒ Ⓓ Ⓔ

8. Ⓐ Ⓑ Ⓒ Ⓓ Ⓔ   18. Ⓐ Ⓑ Ⓒ Ⓓ Ⓔ

9. Ⓐ Ⓑ Ⓒ Ⓓ Ⓔ   19. Ⓐ Ⓑ Ⓒ Ⓓ Ⓔ

10. Ⓐ Ⓑ Ⓒ Ⓓ Ⓔ   20. Ⓐ Ⓑ Ⓒ Ⓓ Ⓔ

DIAGNOSTIC TEST

Time—16 Minutes
20 Questions

1. After World War I, the general change in attitude and outlook among Europeans was one of

   (A) optimism about the future.

   (B) slow but growing faith in economies brought about by postwar production levels.

   (C) general disillusionment and loss of faith in progress.

   (D) continued belief in the ability of military might to bring change.

   (E) strengthened desire for colonial holdings to bring economic prosperity.

2. Fresco painting during the Renaissance featured all the following EXCEPT

   (A) giant canvases filled with larger-than-life figures.

   (B) religious topics and scenes from scripture.

   (C) colors mixed into wet plaster and applied to surfaces.

   (D) nudity of the human form.

   (E) commissions from wealthy patrons, including the pope.

3. Sigmund Freud

   (A) claimed that the super ego, the conscience, controls most of human behavior.

   (B) saw dreams as keys to the unconscious.

   (C) became the focus of much anti-Semitism.

   (D) believed that the unconscious has limited influence on behavior.

   (E) wrote about the idea of a "superman" and a "master race."

4. Realism in literature

   (A) became prominent from the early 19th century onward.

   (B) was immediately embraced by readers with enthusiasm.

   (C) appealed to the emotions of readers.

   (D) saw the writings of ancient Greece and Rome as models.

   (E) included such writers as Thomas Hardy in England and Honoré Balzac in France.

5. The first European nation to venture out into the Atlantic was

   (A) Spain.

   (B) France.

   (C) Portugal.

   (D) England.

   (E) the Netherlands.

6. The Lutherans and Calvinists agreed on which of the following?

   (A) Predestination

   (B) Supremacy of religion over the state

   (C) Maintaining the office of bishop

   (D) Salvation by faith alone

   (E) Retention of four of the seven sacraments

GO ON TO THE NEXT PAGE

7. Most European governments granted women the right to vote

   (A) after the revolts of 1848.
   (B) after the unification of Italy and Germany.
   (C) around 1900.
   (D) after World War I.
   (E) after World War II.

8. The Labour Party in England

   (A) grew out of and replaced the Liberal Party.
   (B) became a major party in the early 20th century.
   (C) helped repeal the Taff Valle Act, which required labor unions to reimburse factory owners for losses during strikes.
   (D) remains one of Britain's major parties today.
   (E) did all of the above.

9. Which of the following was NOT generally advocated by the French *philosophes*, such as Voltaire?

   (A) Universal male suffrage
   (B) Freedom of the press
   (C) Religious toleration
   (D) Equal taxation
   (E) Less influence by the church

10. The early days of the Industrial Revolution in England produced

    (A) a higher standard of living for the lower classes.
    (B) sanitation and housing problems in the new factory towns.
    (C) greater demand for skilled craftsmen.
    (D) a rise in marriages and legitimate births.
    (E) all of the above.

11. Thomas Hobbes claimed that without an absolutist government to ensure law and order, human life was "nasty, brutish, and short." He based his conclusions on personal experience during the

    (A) English Civil War.
    (B) Industrial Revolution.
    (C) English Reformation.
    (D) French Revolution.
    (E) Seven Years War.

12. The huge, sweeping canvases of Eugene Delacroix and Theodore Gericault are examples of what period of art?

    (A) Neoclassicism
    (B) Romanticism
    (C) Realism
    (D) Impressionism
    (E) Cubism

13. Which of the following was TRUE of the Soviet-dominated countries of Eastern Europe in the 1950s and 1960s?

    (A) There was a widespread surge in economic productivity.
    (B) Some freedom of expression was permitted.
    (C) Labor movements such as Solidarity were organized.
    (D) Ethnic unrest sometimes erupted into violence and civil war.
    (E) Revolts in Poland and Czechoslovakia were stopped by the Soviet military.

GO ON TO THE NEXT PAGE ⟹

14. Among the food plants the Europeans brought back from the Americas, the most immediately beneficial to humans was

    (A) citrus fruit.
    (B) maize.
    (C) hot peppers.
    (D) the tomato.
    (E) the potato.

15. A behavior common to Peter the Great of Russia and Napoleon Bonaparte was

    (A) training their subjects in social manners at court.
    (B) overhauling the law code.
    (C) promotion based on merit.
    (D) fascination with ships and navies.
    (E) marriage to foreign royalty.

16. England defended herself against the power and designs of Philip II of Spain by doing all the following EXCEPT

    (A) executing Mary Stuart.
    (B) defeating the Spanish Armada.
    (C) attacking Spanish ships returning from the Americas, loaded with treasure.
    (D) marrying Mary Tudor to Philip II.
    (E) giving aid to the Dutch.

17. Maria Theresa of Austria practiced "enlightened despotism" when she

    (A) freed the serfs.
    (B) expelled the Jesuits.
    (C) reformed the law codes.
    (D) ended censorship.
    (E) fostered public education.

18. Bismarck opposed the socialists in Germany by

    (A) instituting workers' compensation and old-age pensions.
    (B) revealing his program of *Kulturkampf*.
    (C) working more closely with the Reichstag.
    (D) strengthening the army.
    (E) building railroads.

19. Which of the following was NOT a contributing factor in the revolutions of 1848?

    (A) Italian nationalism
    (B) Discontent among ethnic minorities in Eastern Europe
    (C) *The Communist Manifesto*
    (D) The heavy-handed policies of Louis Philippe of France
    (E) The liberal tendencies of the Berlin Assembly

20. A major concession that Great Britain received from the War of Spanish Succession was

    (A) possession of Canada.
    (B) ownership of sugar islands in the Caribbean.
    (C) control of Gibraltar.
    (D) dominance on the coast of South Africa.
    (E) control of all trade with Spain's American colonies.

IF YOU FINISH BEFORE TIME IS CALLED, YOU MAY CHECK YOUR WORK ON THIS SECTION ONLY. DO NOT TURN TO ANY OTHER SECTION IN THE TEST.

STOP

Diagnostic Test Answer Key

1. C
2. A
3. B
4. E
5. C
6. D
7. D
8. E
9. A
10. B

11. A
12. B
13. E
14. E
15. C
16. D
17. B
18. A
19. C
20. C

DIAGNOSTIC TEST: ASSESS YOUR STRENGTHS

The following tables show how the Diagnostic Test is broken down by time period. If you need help with the free-response questions or document-based questions, refer to Chapter 2: Strategies for Success.

Time Periods	Questions	If you missed these questions, study these chapters.
1450 to the French Revolution	2, 5, 6, 9, 11, 14, 15, 16, 17, 20	Chapter 3: The Renaissance Chapter 4: The Reformation and Religious Wars Chapter 5: Discovery, Expansion, and Commercial Revolution Chapter 6: The Age of Absolutism—Western Europe Chapter 7: The Age of Absolutism—Eastern Europe Chapter 8: Constitutionalism in England and the Dutch Republic Chapter 9: The Scientific Revolution Chapter 10: The Enlightenment Chapter 11: 18th-Century Economics and Politics Chapter 12: The French Revolution
19th Century (and very beginning of 20th century)	4, 8, 10, 12, 18, 19	Chapter 13: The Industrial Revolution Chapter 14: Conservatism (1815–1848) Chapter 15: The Rise of Liberalism (1815–1848) Chapter 16: The Rise of Nationalism (1815–1848) Chapter 17: Romanticism Chapter 18: The Age of Realpolitik (1848–1914) Chapter 19: The Rise of Socialism Chapter 20: The Age of Mass Politics (1871–1915) Chapter 21: Intellectual Movements (1850–1914) Chapter 22: The New Imperialism
20th Century (and very beginning of 21st century)	1, 3*, 7, 13	Chapter 23: World War I Chapter 24: The Russian Revolution Chapter 25: Europe Between the Wars Chapter 26: World War II Chapter 27: Immediate Postwar Issues Chapter 28: The Cold War Chapter 29: Nationalism Chapter 30: Post–World War II Society

*Although Freud began his experiments in the 19th century, he was more influential in the 20th century.

Chapters and Topics	Number of Questions	Answered Correctly
1450 to the French Revolution	10	
19th century (and very beginning of 20th century)	6	
20th century (and very beginning of 21st century)	4	

ANSWERS AND EXPLANATIONS

1. C

By the end of World War I, the Western world's optimistic faith in progress had been destroyed by the horrible deaths and mutilation of soldiers, the Bolshevik Revolution in Russia, the worldwide flu epidemic, and the economic depression that followed the war.

2. A

Fresco painting was popular in the Italian Renaissance (Michelangelo's *Sistine Chapel* and DaVinci's *Last Supper*.) Frescoes are wall or ceiling paintings done directly into wet plaster, not on canvas. The topics were usually biblical. Michelangelo used nude or nearly nude figures in some of his Sistine Chapel scenes. Most artists painted on commission, and the papacy was often a patron.

3. B

Freud concentrated on the powers of the unconscious part of the mind, which he called the id. He claimed that the id controls much of human behavior. A major key to understanding the unconscious, said Freud, was the study of dreams. He believed that in dreams, the unconscious was able to manifest itself. In (E), the terms come from Friedrich Nietzsche.

4. E

Realism in literature became prominent in the second half of the 19th century in both Europe and the United States with such writers as Hardy, Balzac, and others. Realistic authors wrote about ordinary people living mundane lives. Some, like Hardy, emphasized the element of chance as a shaper of human life. Many readers found the topics of the realists unpleasant, even disgusting. Choice (C) refers to the romantic period, which preceded realism in literature and the arts. It was writers of the Age of Reason (18th century) who looked to ancient Greece and Rome (D).

5. C

In the mid-1400s, under the leadership of Prince Henry the Navigator, the Portuguese explored the Azores and Madeiras and began to inch their way down the coast of Africa. Spain began her Atlantic voyages with Columbus in 1492. The Dutch, English, and French were considerably behind Portugal and Spain.

6. D

Choices (A) and (B) are tenets of Calvinism. The Lutherans kept bishops (C), and no Protestants kept more than two of the original seven sacraments (E).

7. D

In most European countries, women were granted the vote at the end of World War I. Suffragettes had campaigned for the vote since the late 19th century. The fact that women had been active in the war, taking men's positions in factories and serving in medical capacities, may have contributed to this change.

8. E

The Labour Party was founded around the turn of the 20th century. It gained wide support during the campaign to repeal the Taff Vale Act, which entitled factory owners to recoup from labor unions losses that resulted from strikes. By early in the 20th century, the Labour Party had replaced the Liberals. Today, Britain's two major political parties are the Labourites and Conservatives.

9. A

While Voltaire and other French *philosophes* of the 18th century advocated more individual freedom (press, assembly, religion, as well as equality before the law and in taxation), they did not trust the masses and did not advocate universal male suffrage.

10. B

In the late 1700s and early 1800s, the Industrial Revolution created greatly enlarged factory towns, such as Manchester and Liverpool. The thousands of new workers lived in extremely crowded, unsanitary conditions. Cities didn't yet have sewer or water systems, nor did they have police control or schooling in place. The factory workers were mostly unskilled labor who worked for very low wages. The displacement of families and village or rural society gave way to looser moral standards and a rise in illegitimate births.

11. A

Hobbes's *Leviathan* was the product of his unhappy experiences in the insecurity and troubled times of the English Civil War of the 1640s and its aftermath. Hobbes advocated strong central government to provide security. His idea of a "contract" between those being ruled and their ruler was that subjects turned over all authority to a central figure, the king, in exchange for protection from chaos.

12. B

Delacroix and Gericault were French artists of the early 1800s. Their huge canvases, such as *Liberty Leading the People* and *The Raft of the Medusa*, depict dramatic, emotional scenes. *Liberty* personifies Freedom as a female figure leading a cross section of French citizens, while *Medusa* portrays victims of a shipwreck beneath a storm-swept sky. Such elements reflect romantic ideas and style.

13. E

The post–World War II Soviet bloc countries of Eastern Europe were tightly controlled by Moscow and only slowly saw economic improvements. Dissent was never tolerated for long. One revolt was thwarted in Poland in 1956; Soviet tanks ended the "Prague Spring" of Czechoslovakia in 1968. Solidarity did develop in Poland but at a later date.

14. E

The potato was a welcome addition to the European diet, especially among the peasants, because it was a starch that could be stored throughout the winter. English sailors found that eating the potato skins on long sea voyages prevented scurvy. Citrus (A) did not originate in the Americas. Maize (B), hot peppers (C), and tomatoes (D) did come from the New World, but they had less of an impact at first.

15. C

Peter the Great trained his subjects in social behavior (A), forcing his court to practice more dignified behavior. He was also obsessed with ships and sailing (D). Napoleon revamped the French law code (B) and married an Austrian princess (E). Both promoted men to civil and military posts based on their abilities ("careers open to talent").

16. D

Mary Tudor, during her brief reign, attempted to return England to Catholicism. She married her cousin Philip II of Spain. After her death, Philip continued to try to press Catholicism on the English by plotting with Mary Stuart, whom Parliament and Elizabeth I eventually executed. Elizabeth also maneuvered against Spain by sending her "sea dogs" to raid Spanish ships and by aiding the Dutch in their revolt against Spain. The climax of the rivalry came with England's defeat of the Spanish Armada in 1588.

17. B

Maria Theresa made a few very cautious moves in the direction of enlightened despotism. She reduced the serfs' obligations to their landlords but did not free them (her son Joseph II would do that). Although she was personally a devout Catholic, she expelled the Jesuits from Austria to prevent their meddling in government affairs. Such a move to control the power of the Church is characteristic of enlightened despotism.

18. A

Bismarck despised the socialists and attempted to lessen their influence by initiating social reforms himself. Germany was one of the first countries to have workers' compensation and retirement pensions. His *Kulturkampf* (B) was aimed at the Church. At times he found it advantageous to work with the Reichstag (C) but generally when he wanted to oppose the conservatives.

19. C

Although Marx and Engels published *The Communist Manifesto* in 1848, it had no influence on the outbreaks of revolution. The pamphlet was produced for a small, radical party, almost unknown at the time. All the other answers here are related to actual expressions of unrest in different places in 1848–49.

20. C

The Peace of Utrecht in 1713, at the end of the War of Spanish Succession, gave England control of the Strait of Gibraltar, which she has owned ever since. England also received the *asiento*, a trading concession to Spanish America, but it was supposed to be limited to the slave trade. Britain gained Canada (A) in the Seven Years War (1763) and South Africa (B) during the Napoleonic era (early 1800s).

SAMPLE DOCUMENT-BASED QUESTION

(Suggested writing time—45 minutes)

Directions: The following question is based on the accompanying Documents 1–12.
(The documents have been edited for the purpose of this exercise.)

This question is designed to test your ability to work with and understand historical documents.
Write an essay that

- has a relevant thesis and supports that thesis with evidence from the documents.

- uses a majority of the documents.

- addresses all parts of the question.

- analyzes the documents by organizing them in as many appropriate ways as possible and
  does not simply summarize the documents individually.

- takes into account both the sources of the documents and the authors' points of view.

You may refer to relevant historical information not mentioned in the documents.

Question: Analyze attitudes toward and responses to women in the first half of the French
Revolution, 1789–1795.

Historical Background: In the early years of the French Revolution, a number of women,
especially women of the working class, the *sans-culottes,* played an active role. These women had
long-standing concerns, and at first, the Revolution seemed to invite reform. Women were primary
participants in some of the public protests. They formed political clubs and influenced legal
reforms that gave women rights to initiate divorce and to inherit and control property.

Document 1

Source: Arthur Young, English diarist and traveler in France, 1789.

Walking up a long hill to ease my mare, I was joined by a poor woman. . . . This woman, at no
great distance, might have been taken for sixty or seventy, her figure was so bent and her face so
furrowed and hardened by labor, but she said she was only twenty-eight.

Document 2

Source: Song of the Parisian fishwives, after the march to Versailles that forced the royal family
back to Paris, October 1789.

To Versailles like bragging lads
We brought with us all our guns
We had to show that though we were but women
A courage that no one can reproach us for.

Document 3

Source: Olympe de Gouge, Postscript to *Declaration of the Rights of Women*, 1791

I offer a foolproof way to elevate the soul of women; it is to join them to all the activities of men.

Document 4

Source: Etta Palm D'Aelders, Address to the National Assembly, Summer 1791

You will complete your work by giving girls a moral education equal to that of their brothers; for education is for the soul what watering is for plants; it makes it fertile, causes it to bloom.

Document 5

Source: Charles Maurice de Talleyrand, September 1791

All the lessons taught in public schools will aim particularly to train girls for the virtues of domestic life and to teach them the skills useful in raising a family.

Document 6

Source: Drawing of Women's Political Club, 1792.

Photo credit: Bridgeman-Giraudon/Art Resource, NY

Document 7

Source: Mary Wollstonecraft (English), *A Vindication of the Rights of Women*, 1791.

But, if women are to be excluded, without having a voice, from participation in the natural rights of mankind, prove first that they want reason—else this flaw in your New Constitution will ever show that man must, in some shape, act as tyrant; and tyranny, in whatever part of society it rears its brazen front, will ever undermine morality.

Document 8

Source: Paris Police Reports, September 21–22, 1793.

Malevolent people inspire women with the desire to share the political rights with men and seek to persuade them that they have as many rights as men in the government of their country, that the right to vote is a natural right that they should demand, that in a state where the law consecrates equality, women should claim all civil and military jobs.

Document 9

Source: Madame Roland, wife of the Minister of the Interior, 1793.

I am often annoyed to see women arguing over privileges that do not suit them; even the title of "author" seems ridiculous for a woman to me. However gifted they may be in these fields, they ought not to display their talents to the public.

Document 10

Source: Andre Amar, Report from the Committee of General Safety to the National Convention, November 1793.

In general, women are ill suited for elevated thoughts and serious meditations. Do you want them to be seen coming into the gallery of political assemblies as men do? They can enlighten their husbands and the man, enlightened by peaceful family discussion in the midst of his household, will bring back into society the useful ideas imparted to him by an honest woman.

We believe, therefore, that a woman should not leave her family to meddle in the affairs of state.

Article 1: Clubs and popular societies of women, whatever name they are known under, are prohibited.

Document 11

Source: Report of the Commission of Agriculture and the Arts to the National Convention, 1794.

The commission has conceived the idea of transforming the workshops into training schools in order to turn out working women able to work at home. It prevents inconveniences that might result for morals or for public tranquility from numerous gatherings of simple people who are credulous and easily led astray by perfidious suggestions of malevolence and seduction.

Document 12

Source: Jacques Louis David, *A Woman of the Revolution*, 1795.

Photo credit: Erich Lessing/Art Resource, NY

THREE SAMPLE ESSAY RESPONSES WITH EVALUATION AND ANALYSIS

SAMPLE ESSAY 1

Women were active in the early days of the French Revolution. There were various attitudes and responses to the women who participated.

Some women were reformers. One of these was Olympe de Gouge. She said that women wanted to join the activities of men. Another woman reformer was the Englishwoman Mary Wollstonecraft. She said that if women were excluded from the rights of man, then men would be tyrants.

Wollstonecraft was not the only English person who wrote about the Revolution. Arthur Young was an Englishman who traveled in France. He felt very sorry for poor French women. He said they had to work very hard, which made them look old. Etta Palm D'Aelders said that girls ought to be given education. The women in doc. 2 were proud of their participation in the Revolution.

A report to the National Convention disapproved of women in politics, so the convention shut down women's clubs. The drawing in doc. 6 shows one of the women's clubs meeting. A police report (doc. 8) also criticized women for wanting political rights, such as voting. There were various attitudes and responses to women in the French Revolution.

SCORE AND EXPLANATION

This essay would receive a score of **4**. It lacks a thesis (Rubric Point 1); it merely repeats the prompt at the beginning and at the end of the essay. There is no evidence of understanding bias or point of view. The essay does have three groups, and it uses the bare minimum of documents (in this case, three).

SAMPLE ESSAY 2

On the eve of the French Revolution economic conditions were hard for the poor, especially for women. In Paris, in particular, women became involved in revolutionary activity and pushed for reforms in women's legal rights and educational and job opportunities. Some went so far as to demand the right to vote. While many (but not all) women supported these ideas, almost all men did not.

In October 1789 the Parisian market women formed part of the mob that went to Versailles and forced the royal family back to Paris. They were proud of their participation and sang about their involvement (doc. 2). Even though the David painting, A Woman of the Revolution, dates from 1795, his portrayal showed the determination of women of the working class (doc. 12). Over the next few years, many middle-class women formed political clubs (doc. 6) and through those, pushed for reforms. One of the things they wanted was better education for girls (Etta Palm d'Aelders, doc. 4). Some reformers like Olympe de Gouge (doc. 3) insisted that women enjoy total equality with men. No doubt, d'Aelders and de Gouge spoke out for women because they were female and knew what it was to be given fewer opportunities.

Even English observers pointed out women's problems. The English traveler Arthur Young (doc. 1) wrote that poor French women lived under terrible conditions that made them look old before their time. As a foreigner, his opinion can be considered unbiased and honest. Another English writer, Mary Wollstonecraft, claimed that if the new French constitution failed to recognize women's rights, then men became tyrants, and the morality of society was undermined. Wollstonecraft was somewhat of an English version of Olympe de Gouge; they both were early outspoken advocates of women's rights.

Not everybody agreed, however. The politician Talleyrand (doc. 5) disagreed with d'Aelders about education for girls, asserting that girls needed to learn skills "useful in raising a family." Later, in 1794, a Commission advised the National Convention that the workshops for women should be converted to training schools to teach women jobs they could do at home. The report called women "simple" and "credulous" and said they would be safer not working in public. Of course, such ideas showed male prejudice against women.

Eventually, the national Convention heard a report condemning women's participation in politics. The suggestion was that women should contribute by influencing their husbands, rather than going out in public to "meddle in the affairs of government." Perhaps these male politicians felt threatened by women. As a result, the Convention prohibited women's political societies.

After this, women's influence on the Revolution declined. The early promise of a new day for French women faded away.

SCORE AND EXPLANATION

This essay would receive a score of **8**. It has all the core points and uses seven of the 12 documents. It contains four examples of bias and four groupings. The essay is especially well organized; it flows logically and clearly. It could be further strengthened by using more of the documents.

SAMPLE ESSAY 3

During the French Revolution, women began to change. Even women of the sans culottes took part in revolution activity. Of course, the women who were involved looked favorably on what they were doing because they believed in better education and economic opportunity for girls, but men generally resented and condemned women's participation in politics.

Two outspoken women who wrote in favor of equality between the sexes were the English woman Mary Wollstonecraft and her French contemporary, Olympe de Gouge. Both women felt strongly that women should enjoy all the political rights and other opportunities that men had. One would expect these writers to voice such opinions because they were women (doc. 3 & 7).

Men, however, disagreed. Talleyrand said that education for girls ought to limited to skills useful to being housewives (doc. 5). Other men agreed. Andre Amar (doc. 10) told the National Convention in 1793 that women ought not to "meddle in politics." Of course, both these speakers were male, so they probably objected to the demands of female reformers.

Not all those who disapproved were men. Mme Roland, wife of the Minister of the Interior, spoke out against women who wanted to write and get involved in public affairs. She was probably of the upper class and distrusted women from the lower ranks of society (doc. 9).

Both pieces of art show women's involvement. Doc. 6 shows a women's political club. Doc. 12 is by the famous painter of the Revolution, Jacques Louis David. David's painting shows a working-class woman who seems to approve of women in politics; she has a cynical expression, perhaps toward the politics of the day. In general, women approved of their political activity, and men condemned it.

SCORE AND EXPLANATION

This essay squeaks by as a **6**. It is well written, but it barely meets all six points of the core scoring rubric. It has a thesis in the first paragraph, it uses seven documents, and it has three groupings and three examples of bias. It does nothing beyond that, however. To score higher, this essay would need to use more documents and include more citations of groups and/or bias.

HOW TO MAKE THIS BOOK WORK FOR YOU BASED ON THE RESULTS OF YOUR DIAGNOSTIC TEST

One-half of the composite score for the AP European History exam will be based on the multiple-choice section. The three essays together are equally important. No matter what your results on this Diagnostic Test, you should review the essay exam format and expectations carefully.

How you interpret your Diagnostic score depends on your situation. How soon is the exam? If you took this test in the fall or winter, you're likely to score lower than if you took the test in the spring. Analyze the types of questions that you missed. You may have found that you are weak on particular time periods or in areas.

The questions that appeared here were drawn about equally from each of the centuries from 1450 to 2001. Missing more than one question from the same time period may indicate a weakness in knowledge of that part of the course. Look also at types of questions: Did you miss most of the art and culture questions? If so, these may be areas that warrant more study.

This review book can help. Part Three reviews the course content by chronological units. At the back of the book is a Glossary, which gives key terms and their definitions, arranged by chronological period. At the end of each unit is a 20-question multiple-choice quiz, with answers and explanations, and two essay questions with sample responses. The review chapters and quizzes can help you focus on what matters as you proceed through the course and study for tests. It can also help in April and May as you review for the national exam.

Part Four provides more testing practice: two complete exams, each with 80 multiple-choice questions, a DBQ, and a set of six FRQs. Do each complete exam in one sitting, if possible, near the end of your whole course review. Set a time and place where you can work without interruption or distraction. Such a rehearsal for the national exam will help give you a sense of pacing.

Part Three

AP EUROPEAN HISTORY REVIEW

CHAPTER 3:   THE RENAISSANCE

PRE-1450 HISTORY

The history of Europe began in the fourth century BCE with the ancient Greeks, who organized themselves into city-states and developed a polytheistic religion, written language, and forms of expression in both visual arts and literature (lyric poetry, epics, and dramas). The Greek city-states were conquered by Philip of Macedon, father of Alexander the Great, in the early 300s BCE, but this empire was as short-lived as Alexander (who died in his 30s, having trained no successor). Greek culture was preserved in "Hellenized" centers of the Middle East, especially in Alexandria in Egypt.

The Romans conquered the Greeks in 146 BCE and took over all aspects of Greek culture except the language. In the days of Julius and Augustus Caesar, the Roman Empire spread over most of Western Europe, northern Africa, and the eastern end of the Mediterranean. The advent of Christianity brought huge changes, including a shift in the center of government from Rome to Constantinople in 330 CE. The strength of Roman civilization lay in its ability to organize and govern and in its engineering talents (roads, aqueducts, public buildings). However, the Roman Empire fell apart around 500–600 CE, partly because of weak emperors and declining military prowess and partly from the pressure of invading Germanic tribes from the north and west.

During the medieval period, or Middle Ages, which followed, European life became very localized. Money disappeared. Local lords competed for control of limited areas, gathering armed, mounted men (knights) to fight for them. Most people were peasants, bound to the land, supplying the labor to produce food and everything else necessary for survival. Life for most people was short and difficult.

The one omniscient presence throughout the Middle Ages was the Christian Church. Almost everyone was Christian, with the exception of the Muslims in Spain and the small minority of Jews scattered across Europe. People saw life on earth as temporary, a preparation for eternity, and the Church possessed the keys to heaven. Most of the few literate people were the clergy; monks preserved knowledge by hand-copying texts.

The Christian Church formally split in 1054 into the **Roman Catholic Church**, centered in Italy, and the **Eastern Orthodox Church**, centered in Constantinople. The Greek and Russian Orthodox Churches would grow out of the Eastern tradition. There were differences in practices between the Eastern and Western churches, the most obvious of which was the Eastern tradition of married clergy, while the Western church promoted a celibate priesthood.

Several factors brought change in the late Middle Ages (after 1000 CE). One was the series of wars—the **Crusades**—fought in a vain attempt to wrest the Holy Land from Muslim control. The European crusaders who survived brought back with them silks, porcelains, and above all, spices, which whetted European appetites for Asian goods. They also gained knowledge of Arabic medicine, science, and navigation, which were superior to European knowledge at the time.

Another factor was the devastation of the **Bubonic Plague (Black Death)**. It is thought to have arrived in Italy from the Middle East in the middle of the 14th century, spread by a bacillus that was carried by fleas living on black rats. While the majority of historians have maintained this theory, it recently has been challenged. Specifically, some scholars think that the rate of transmission and seasonal correlations of the agent for the bubonic plague do not align with older historical accounts. Nonetheless, the plague spread throughout Europe and wiped out perhaps 30 percent of the population (exact figures are not known). After raging for two to three years, the epidemic subsided to reoccur here and there over the next several centuries. It would be a long time before people were able to investigate the cause of the dreaded disease, though the decimation of so much of the population helped end the feudal system because laborers were so much in demand.

Two major technological accomplishments completely changed the Western world. One was the development of **gunpowder**, which led to warfare conducted with muskets and cannons rather than with longbows and armored horsemen wielding swords—another factor that ended the feudal system. The other accomplishment was the invention of the printing press in the late 1300s and, along with it, the advent of paper made from wood pulp. These two inventions ended the need for expensive animal skins or parchment and meant an end to exclusive, expensive hand-copying of manuscripts.

THE ITALIAN RENAISSANCE

RISE AND DECLINE OF THE ITALIAN CITY-STATES

The history of modern Europe (indeed, of the modern world) began in the 14th century in the city-states of the northern Italian peninsula. In Genoa, Venice, Florence, and others, the merchant class became wealthy and powerful. They owned the West's latest technology in sailing ships and navigational instruments, and they engaged in a busy trade with the Arabs at the eastern end of the Mediterranean. They brought to Italy (and to Europe) extremely desirable commodities—spices (used both in medicine and to enhance the bland European diet), silks, cottons, and porcelains. Many of these products had come by sea or land from eastern Asia. Italian merchants might earn as much as a 500 percent profit in the spice trade.

Business was also based on the importation of raw wool from Northern Europe, which was woven into fine fabric in Florence and resold. The northern Italian cities had an excellent road system left over from the days of the Roman Empire, a system that enhanced the movement of goods. Agriculture also flourished; northern Italy produced grains, vegetables, and wine in surplus to trade.

Merchants used their profits to build luxurious townhomes. They enjoyed the "good life," which no longer seemed to conform to the Church's definition of life as a brief and sorrowful interval. The result was a whole new perception of human existence and of the world as very positive. The "here and now" seemed more real and more important than dreary considerations of the "hereafter."

Because the flow of money created a need for bankers, some merchants, like the **Medici** of Florence, went into banking and made even more money. The gold florin of Florence became the standard of European currency exchange.

Italian City-States

The city-states were most often ruled by **oligarchies**, committees of the wealthy and powerful. A small percentage of the population, men only, could vote. Revolts of the general population were crushed, and sometimes despots took over governments. In the center of the peninsula, the Papal States functioned like other city-states but with the pope in control. For security, the cities used hired foreign mercenaries, called **condottieri**. The states never developed political unity, which left them vulnerable to their larger, more powerful neighbors to the north, the **new monarchies** of Europe. By the early 16th century, the city-states were being overrun by invasions from France and Spain.

HUMANISM

During the Middle Ages, the Christian Church was omniscient and omnipotent, teaching that life on earth was short and sorrowful, that human beings were sinful creatures at the mercy of God's judgment, and that existence was preparation for eternity. In the Renaissance, such ideas were not exactly denied, but neither were they believed with any real conviction.

The Renaissance adopted a secular conception of life, **humanism**, and emphasized individualism. The ideal person—the **Renaissance man**—was one who used his opportunities, who demonstrated control, and who was casually expert in many areas. He could dance, fight, compose poetry, converse with ladies, or ride a horse. Those skills amounted to a quality called **virtù**. The art and literature of the period reflected this new awareness of human possibilities. The Middle Ages were rejected as "dark" and undesirable; instead, the Italians turned for models to the pre-Christian ancient Greeks and Romans.

ART, SCULPTURE, AND ARCHITECTURE

Medieval painting had used egg tempera as its medium, and it featured figures and objects in a flat, generalized, symbolic style. All trees might be round green blobs atop straight, brown trunks. The painters of the Renaissance developed **perspective**, which gave their work depth and a sense of the three-dimensional. The new medium was oil paint, and the figures and their surroundings appeared more individually lifelike. Artists like **Leonardo da Vinci** and **Michelangelo** dissected cadavers to understand the human form better, and their knowledge was reflected in their art. In Italy, art became a profession. Artists trained through apprenticeships and worked on commissions from wealthy patrons, including the powerful merchants and the papacy.

Two of the most famous creations of Renaissance art were da Vinci's *The Last Supper* and Michelangelo's Sistine Chapel paintings. These works are **frescoes**, done by mixing color into wet plaster on a wall or ceiling. It is somewhat ironic that while religion declined in the personal lives of Italians, artists of the period most often painted religious topics. A favorite was the depiction of **madonnas**, especially the Madonna and Child, as in the works of **Raphael Sanzio**.

Sculpture also underwent great changes. In the Middle Ages, sculpture was generally bas relief—that is, not free-standing but attached to its background, as in cathedral niches. In conjunction with the classical Greek concept of beauty in the human form and reflecting the study of human anatomy, sculptures were now often free-standing nudes (such as Michelangelo's *David*). One popular sculpture was the **Pietà**, featuring Mary cradling the body of the crucified Christ.

Architecture also turned to the ancients for models. In addition to their fine townhouses, the Italians built public nonreligious structures, decorated and supported by Greek columns. Perhaps the biggest innovation in Renaissance architecture was the creation of the dome, first accomplished by **Filippo Brunelleschi**.

LITERATURE

The focus of writing in the Middle Ages had been primarily theology and, after that, philosophy, law, and history. Popular stories reflected legendary figures such as King Arthur, Roland, or Robin Hood. The Italian Renaissance produced the first truly modern writers, the humanists. These men studied the writing of the ancients. Some learned Greek; many wrote in Latin. But increasingly, the modern authors wrote in the vernacular, the spoken language of their day. In the 1300s, **Dante Alighieri** wrote his *Divine Comedy* in Florentine Italian, making this dialect the primary influence on the development of modern Italian.

Another poet, **Francesco Petrarch**, also used Italian to create poetry in a new form, the sonnet. Still others, like **Giovanni Boccaccio** (*The Decameron*), went further to concentrate on secular tales. Scholars searched for classical manuscripts. A primary goal was to understand humanity, not God; everywhere, the view of human capacity was optimistic.

Two of the greatest literary creations of the Southern Renaissance were nonfiction. *The Courtier* by **Baldassare Castiglioni** described in detail proper behavior for Renaissance men and women. The other great work was *The Prince* by **Niccolo Machiavelli** (1513), who saw the great political failures of the Italian city-states. He admired the rising new monarchies of Northern Europe. *The Prince* was different in that it did not discuss morality or "God's will." Instead, Machiavelli described what effective rulers did to get what they wanted. (This book was soon seen as evil by the Church and later was condemned on Catholic lists of forbidden books.)

THE NORTHERN RENAISSANCE

The ideas of the Southern Renaissance slowly migrated north, where they were reinterpreted. While Italian ideas and art remained Christian in name, they were actually quite secular, more influenced by the ancient, pre-Christian tradition. The Northern Renaissance featured more Christian-based thinkers and writers, the **Christian humanists**, who were more spiritual in their outlook, less materialistic, and more focused on questions of morality and ethics. Like the Italians, the northern thinkers believed in the basic goodness of humanity, but they said that society had been corrupted. Goodness could be retaught, they claimed, which was an idea preparatory to the Reformation.

There also seems to have been a sort of intellectual unrest, a curiosity, a "need to know" in the north. This characteristic paved the way for the voyages of discovery and for the scientific revolution. The 1400s witnessed the founding of a number of northern **new universities**, while no new ones were established in Italy.

The north, too, developed trade and manufacturing. The **Fugger** family was to the German states what the Medici were to Florence, first as merchants and then as bankers. Mining also developed in the north, and it was in the German states where the printing press first appeared.

Northern Humanists

In the north, Latin was the language of scholarship and would remain generally so until the late 1500s. The use of Latin enabled international correspondence and the exchange of ideas. Most prominent were the Englishman **Thomas More** and the Dutch scholar Erasmus. More's *Utopia* (in Latin, "nowhere") described an ideal society set vaguely on an island in the Atlantic. Here, gold, silver, and jewels had no value. The goal for all was to develop their rational faculties. Adults engaged in lifelong learning and divided their time between manual labor and study. Thus, the word *utopia* came to mean "an ideal place."

Desiderius Erasmus of the Netherlands was a clergyman who believed in the goodness of humanity. He advocated education, which meant the study of the Bible and the classics. His idea that all should read the scriptures was indeed radical. Erasmus ignored the supernatural and laughed at theologians for believing in such ideas as original sin and the power of relics. Instead, he emphasized the life and teachings of Jesus. His *Praise of Folly* made fun of the worldliness and superstition of the Church. Despite their beliefs, neither More nor Erasmus challenged papal authority or supported the ideas coming out of Luther's rebellion in Germany.

It should be noted that humanism among the elite also brought more education to women. Daughters of the aristocracy became increasingly literate, and they were taught classical languages. One example was the French woman Christine de Pisan (early 15th century) who grew up in the court of Charles V of France and eventually wrote his biography.

Religion

Within the Northern Renaissance there developed a tendency toward religious **mysticism**. The German Thomas à Kempis said that individuals could commune with God without the Church—without ritual, sacraments, or priests and even without words. Yet Kempis did not advocate separation from the Church; he offered, instead, the possibility of a deeper personal religion.

Lay religious movements developed outside the traditional Church, perhaps because of corruption within the Church. The most prominent group was the **Brothers and Sisters of the Common Life** in the Netherlands, who practiced a faith and lifestyle called the Modern Devotion. Here, men and women lived separately and communally, but they were not monks or nuns. They took no vows, wore no special clothes, and could leave at will. They established schools and worked to relieve the poor, and their teachings emphasized humility, tolerance, reverence, love of neighbor, and duty. Erasmus, an orphan, was brought up and educated by the Brothers. This lay movement operated with the blessing of the papacy, but it created a background for the religious reforms about to emerge.

NORTHERN RENAISSANCE ART

Artistic expression flourished during the Northern Renaissance but differently than in the south. First of all, there was painting but little sculpture. Frescoes did not develop here because the climate would not allow them. In the Low Countries, towns depended on trade, as in Italy, and here also, wealthy merchants patronized the arts. (In the north, however, the Church was not an art patron, as in Italy.) Ironically, although religious faith was generally stronger in the north, the subjects of paintings tended not to be religious. The **Flemish masters** began with Van Eyck, who did portraits in oils even before Michelangelo and da Vinci. Realistic portraits were at the forefront of Northern Renaissance art (the German Holbeins (Elder and Younger) and Dürer and the Dutch artists Vermeer and Rembrandt). In another vein, the Brueghels (also Elder and Younger) created busy scenes of village life, while Bosch painted fantasy and symbolism that would influence the surrealists of the 20th century.

NEW MONARCHIES

Unlike the Italian city-states, which never united politically, large parts of Northern Europe emerged from the Middle Ages as powerful **new monarchies (Tudors, Valois, Habsburgs)**. This occurred in England, France, and Spain—each state coming under the dominance of a powerful ruling family.

The middle of the 1400s in England was marked by civil strife in the War of the Roses between two families vying for the crown. As a result of a marriage between the families, in 1485, Henry VII became the first Tudor monarch. To solidify his control over unruly nobles, Henry passed laws against "livery and maintenance" (private armies), giving the king the only military authority. In defiance of English common law, which provided for trial by jury, Henry also established the **Star Chamber**, a royal court for offending nobility, conducted without a jury.

In France, also in the 1400s, the Valois monarchy established control of most of the countryside. The French kings obtained some unique powers. First, the Valois king could tax his subjects without parliamentary consent. (In fact, the Estates General of France did not gain strength over time, as did the English Parliament; the Estates General eventually dissolved itself for 175 years prior to the French Revolution.) Another privileged custom in France was the king's prerogative to appoint bishops and abbots. (Some say this control over the Church prevented France's becoming Protestant later.)

The unification of Spain occurred somewhat differently. In 1469, with the marriage of Ferdinand and Isabella, the two largest kingdoms of the Iberian Peninsula, Castile and Aragon, were united nominally. However, there existed no common administrative, political, or judicial institutions. Nor did people think of themselves as Spanish. The common denominator of Spain was the Catholic Church. In 1492, with the conquest of Granada, the Church and government forced the Moors to convert to Christianity or emigrate, and the same policy applied to Jews. The **Inquisition**, a Church court, was vigilant to enforce religious uniformity. The powerful ruling family of Spain, the Habsburgs, also controlled the Low Countries and much of Central Europe, including Austria.

The German states did not unite. The 300-plus units ranged from large entities like Austria to independent "imperial cities" to "knights of the empire," which amounted to no more than large private estates operating as independent nations. Some of the larger states were ecclesiastical—that is, ruled by the Church—while others were "princely states" ruled by hereditary families. All of the German states were loosely bound together as the **Holy Roman Empire** under an elected emperor, who was always an Austrian Habsburg. During the 1500s, the Holy Roman Emperor, Charles V, controlled Austria, the Netherlands, Spain, and Spanish America, which gave rise to a fear of universal monarchy.

CHAPTER 4: THE REFORMATION AND RELIGIOUS WARS

During the 16th and 17th centuries, a great change swept over Western Europe. For centuries, there had been criticism of the Christian Church—for its corruption and some of its practices. The actual Reformation began in 1517 when Martin Luther posted his **95 Theses** on the church door in Wittenberg. A generation later, a second strand of Protestantism grew from the leadership of John Calvin. While both Lutheran and Calvinistic ideas seeped into England, it was a personal crisis in the life of King Henry VIII that moved the English into the Protestant camp. Over the next 100-plus years, fighting over religion erupted throughout most of Europe.

CRISES IN THE ROMAN CATHOLIC CHURCH

The Roman Catholic Church began to be recognizable by today's understanding in the late Middle Ages, with supreme authority coming from the pope, who was elected by cardinals (at the time, priests of Rome and nearby bishops). The pope declared in 1302 that **salvation** was possible only through the Church. Later in the century, the French king forced the papacy to move to France, where it remained until the early 1400s; at times there were two popes, one in France and one in Rome. Naturally, confusion over the papacy weakened the Church's image.

There were outspoken critics of the Church long before Martin Luther. In the 1300s, the English scholar **John Wycliffe** insisted on salvation by faith alone. He translated the scriptures into English and urged individual reading of them. Influenced by Wycliffe, **John Hus** in the German states condemned the worldliness of Church figures and was burned as a heretic.

At the parish level, priests were often peasants themselves, frequently ignorant, even illiterate. Many lived with common-law wives and had families. Probably, many priests were good men, though some were accused of vices such as alcoholism and gambling. As the middle class grew and became more educated, it demanded better clergy. The high positions in the Church were occupied by men from the nobility, and most such offices came with money and property. In addition, high churchmen filled high government positions (e.g., **Cardinal Wolsey** in England and Cardinal Richelieu in France).

A common practice was **absenteeism**, seldom or never residing in the area where one had a position, and **pluralism**, having more than one position and hiring a poor parish priest to do the less desirable office. In high places, a number of churchmen (including some popes) lived in luxury like princes; they were secular and corrupt. Other abuses included simony, the buying or selling of church offices, and **nepotism**, giving lucrative church jobs to one's children or other relatives.

In the 1300s, the practice of selling **indulgences** became common. It was based on the idea of a **Treasury of Merit**, which was a sort of savings bank of goodness resulting from the extra good deeds of very strong Christians. A person might make a donation to the Church in exchange for an indulgence, which would grant forgiveness for the obligation (debt) of sin or help dead souls out of **purgatory** (the Church's teaching of a place between heaven and hell, where most souls awaited entrance into paradise). These benefits, the Church said, were drawn from the Treasury of Merit. It is obvious how the sale of indulgences could be abused.

IMPACT OF THE RENAISSANCE

Both the Southern and Northern Renaissance helped create the atmosphere that fostered a religious revolt. In Italy, attention moved away from personal and inner faith to focus on a "grand show" of artistic expression. Wealth corrupted clergy, as well as laity, and even some popes kept mistresses and engaged in very worldly lifestyles. When an outspoken priest, Savonarola, criticized the Church for such abuse, he was burned as a heretic.

The very fact that religious mysticism was part of the Northern Renaissance led people to question accepted Church traditions. Some writers (Thomas á Kempis, mentioned in Chapter 3) argued that sacraments and priests were not necessary for salvation. Lay movements, such as the Brothers and Sisters of the Common Life, also urged humility and personal spirituality. Scholars sought the reading of original manuscripts, and the printing press made it possible to spread information more rapidly than in the past.

MARTIN LUTHER AND THE GERMAN STATES

A priest and professor of theology in Wittenberg in the German states, Martin Luther experienced a spiritual crisis as a young adult. He questioned his own salvation and studied the New Testament, especially the letters of Paul. Salvation, he came to believe, resulted from individual faith and faith alone.

Luther's actual revolt was a protest to a mendicant friar's selling indulgences in the German states (most sources say the profits were for the building of Saint Peter's in Rome). He registered his public protest by nailing his *95 Theses* (written in Latin) to the local church's door on the eve of All Saints Day, November 1, in 1517 according top popular lore. He immediately circulated a German translation of his *Theses* and appealed to the pope to correct the abuse of indulgences. The pope ordered Luther to stop his protest, but Luther refused and was protected by a German prince, Frederick of Saxony. Two years later, the pope ordered Luther to recant or face excommunication (being denied the sacraments—hence, in danger of hell). Luther burned the papal order.

Luther wrote prolifically in German, calling on German princes to reform the church in their states. This idea appealed to many because it meant escape from financial obligations to and authority of Rome. Luther continued to proclaim that only faith was necessary for salvation. He denied all the sacraments except baptism and communion and said that monastic life was unnatural.

In 1521, Luther was summoned before the **diet** (council) at the **Council of Worms** by Charles V, at which he was questioned repeatedly in Latin and asked to repudiate his "errors." Finally, he answered in German, "Here I stand. I can do no other." Luther was able to leave Worms safely because the diet remained divided over the issue; only a portion of the diet proclaimed him to be an outlaw.

In hiding, under the protection of Elector of Saxony, Luther worked on translating the Bible into German and spreading his ideas. More likely to convert to Luther's teaching were northern Germans; cities in the south remained predominantly Catholic. The lower clergy were more likely to convert; some began to say the Mass in German, to serve *both* bread and wine (which had not been the Catholic tradition), and even to marry. In 1525, Luther himself married a former nun.

When a large-scale **Peasant Revolt** broke out in the mid-1520s, Luther at first sympathized with the grievances. (Luther was from a peasant background himself.) But when nobles and high churchmen blamed Luther for the insurrection, he retreated and wrote a pamphlet, "Against the Murdering, Thieving Hordes of Peasants," in which he urged Catholics and reformed princes to band together to stop the fighting. More than 50,000 people died.

Originally, Luther planned only to reform abuses in the Church, but his followers gradually created a new church. When a prince turned Lutheran, his people had no choice. All Church property became Lutheran, and priests in his realm had to convert or leave. Individual religious freedom was as yet unheard of. Luther's early support came from the educated middle class, who saw Catholicism as rooted in superstition, and from a nobility eager to sever ties with Rome and confiscate Church property.

After the Peasant Revolt, Luther emphasized Christian freedom as an internal, spiritual concept; he said that in worldly matters, the good Christian owed obedience to the established authority. He reinterpreted the Catholic idea of the Mass, **transubstantiation**, the idea that in the Eucharist the bread and wine mystically became the body and blood of Christ, to **consubstantiation**, which said that the "presence" of Christ was in the Eucharist. Luther wrote powerfully and persuasively, including many hymns (e.g., "A Mighty Fortress Is Our God"). In general, he advocated a simpler, more personal religion, based on scripture and faith. The Augsburg Confession of 1530 outlined the basic doctrines of Lutheranism. The reformed religion spread across the northern German states and all of Scandinavia.

> After Luther, the Reformation shifted to Switzerland, where **Huldrych Zwingli** preached salvation by faith alone, using Erasmus's edition of the New Testament. Because he felt so strongly that all religious practice should have a basis in scripture, he and his followers smashed organs, art, and decorations in churches. He proclaimed that in the Eucharist, the symbol of Christ was present. Zwingli's reforming career was short; he was killed in battle, fighting Catholics.

CALVINISM AND ITS EXPANSION

John Calvin was French by birth and trained in the law. As a young man, he emigrated to Switzerland to escape religious persecution. After experiencing a personal religious crisis in his 20s, Calvin published *The Institutes of the Christian Religion* in Latin, the international language of scholarship. Like Luther, Calvin advocated faith, not works. He called the Eucharist the "Lord's Supper," in which the elements were symbolic only. Calvin and his followers set up their reformed church in Geneva and set out to control the city as a theocracy.

A major difference from the teachings of Luther was that Calvin taught the doctrine of **election**, or **predestination**. This was not a new concept to Christianity; indeed, it had been considered by St. Augustine but eventually rejected. The teaching was that only God could know or decide who was saved and who was damned, that humans did not have the choice to make. Those who were "chosen" were the "elect" and were said to possess "grace." These people were predestined to go to heaven.

Calvin's Geneva was a strict society with stiff regulation of daily life. Unlike Luther, Calvin thought the Church should dominate the state. The Church itself was governed by elected bodies of ministers and laymen; bishops were eliminated (thus, Calvinism with its **congregational government** was considered more democratic). Human labor was valued as pleasing to God; idleness was considered sinful. At the same time, Calvin tolerated no dissent. When Michael Servetus, a Spanish physician who had denied the Trinity, appeared in Geneva, he was seized and burned as a heretic. (Note: Denial of the Trinity—the concept of God's existing as Father, Son, and Holy Spirit—became the basis of another Protestant movement, **Unitarianism**.)

Calvinism spread to the Netherlands (Dutch Reformed Church); to Scotland, taken there by John Knox and called **Presbyterianism**; and to France, where it spread especially among the nobility, called Huguenots. In England in the 17th century, the Calvinists were called Puritans because of their desire to "purify" the Church of England, and for a brief period, they dominated England (see "English Civil War" later in this chapter). They also took their faith to the New England colonies of North America.

Protestant trends that Calvinism firmly established were a rule orientation (frivolous, loose living was suppressed), intolerance of others with differing beliefs, plain services that emphasized long sermons, and elimination of aesthetic appeal (color, images, art, incense, instrumental music). The position of women was somewhat elevated but, like Lutheranism, the monastic option was closed. Girls had to be given education to be able to read scripture. Of course, women did not play any leadership roles, but they were honored as wives, mothers, and household managers. Because the clergy married, fidelity of both spouses was expected.

THE ENGLISH REFORMATION

The shift to Protestantism in England occurred in a very different way than on the Continent, though several factors had already led the country in that direction. As early as the 1300s, following the teachings of Wycliffe (see "Northern Renaissance" in Chapter 3), a group called the Lollards had urged individual reading of scripture and personal responsibility to God. Lollards were anticlerical, speaking out against church wealth, reverence toward saints, prayers for the dead, and war. They were driven underground, but they continued to exist.

Then in the 1500s, the English reformer **William Tyndale** went to see Luther. He translated the New Testament, printed it on the Continent, and had it distributed by the Lollards. (He was also seized by Catholics and executed for heresy.)

Still, Catholicism remained alive and well in England. The English clergy tended to be better educated than those of the Continent. The big move away from Rome resulted primarily from a personal crisis in the life of Henry VIII, the second Tudor king. Because England in the 15th century was far from being a great power, Henry VII had attempted to keep the country out of war by forming alliances through marriage. He married a daughter to the King of Scotland (then a separate nation from England), and the oldest son Arthur he betrothed to Catherine of Aragon, daughter of Ferdinand and Isabella. Catherine came to England and married Arthur, and Arthur promptly died. So Henry VII petitioned the pope for a dispensation to allow his second son, the future king Henry VIII, to marry the young widow. This was granted.

Meanwhile, Lutheran ideas had crept into England, especially into the universities, Oxford and Cambridge. Henry VIII wrote a pamphlet, **"In Defense of the Seven Sacraments"** (1520), for which the pope named him **Defender of the Faith.**

Catherine was six years older than Henry. They were married 20 years and had six children, only one of whom survived—a daughter, Mary. England at this time had *never* had a queen, and the monarchy was only one generation removed from dynastic war (the War of the Roses that had brought Henry VII to power). When Catherine was in her mid-40s and unlikely to produce more children, Henry became smitten with a young woman at court, Anne Boleyn. He began to insist, around 1527, that God was punishing him for "living in sin" with his brother's widow by denying him a son. He had Cardinal Wolsey, Chancellor of England, petition the pope for an annulment of his marriage—such things had been done before. The pope, however, was controlled by Catherine's nephew, Charles V, Holy Roman Emperor, and did not grant Henry's request.

In desperation, Henry appointed Thomas Cranmer Archbishop of Canterbury, and Cranmer annulled the marriage. Henry had Catherine put away in a convent and married Anne Boleyn in 1533. Six months later, a daughter was born—Elizabeth. Within three years, Henry had Anne tried for treason and executed. In 1534, Parliament's Act of Supremacy declared the king head of the church in England. Henry's intentions were only to sever ties to Rome and to close the monasteries and confiscate church property, which he sold or gave away as rewards. However, almost immediately English clergy began to marry, conduct services in English, and stop using the confession and prayers to saints. Henry went on to marry four more times and finally had a son, Edward. Henry died when Edward was 10 years old, so Edward VI ruled with two uncles as regents. The uncles moved England further into the Protestant arena with the *Book of Common Prayer*, an order of services in English.

Edward VI died of tuberculosis six years later, and the crown went to his half-sister Mary, the very Catholic and embittered daughter of Catherine. Mary married her cousin, Philip II of Spain, and tried to return England to Catholicism. She had "heretics" burned, including Archbishop Cranmer, executing so many that she was called "Bloody Mary." After Mary's death less than five years later, Elizabeth I began a long reign (1558–1603).

Elizabeth can be labeled a **politique**, one willing to compromise for the greater good. Elizabeth restored Protestantism but not in a fanatical way. Her government required nominal membership in the Church of England and at least outward conformity to its worship, but people's private religious convictions were not questioned. Philip II continued to attempt to restore Catholicism, first through overtures of marriage to Elizabeth, and then through clandestine plots with Mary Stuart, deposed queen of Scotland and Elizabeth's cousin, who was living under house arrest in England. In 1587, Mary Stuart was executed for treason, and the next year, England defeated the Spanish Armada, thus ensuring Protestantism in England.

SUMMARY OF PROTESTANT BELIEFS

- Salvation by faith alone
- Importance of scripture, in vernacular
- Emphasis on sermons
- Two or three sacraments only
- No friars, monks, or nuns
- No saints, purgatory, or reverence for the Virgin Mary
- Symbolic Eucharist or real "presence"
- No celibacy
- "Priests" became "ministers," with no special status
- No confession, no priestly absolution

CATHOLIC COUNTER-REFORMATION

The Catholic Church responded to the spread of Protestantism in two ways. First, there was a reform movement within the Church that had begun even before Luther. Then there was the **Council of Trent**, which met off and on for nearly 20 years, 1545–1563. The result of the Council was general affirmation of almost all Catholic traditions: justification by **faith** *and* **works** (*works* defined as observance of the sacraments); confirmation of the seven sacraments and the belief in transubstantiation; the Vulgate Bible (Latin); clerical celibacy; and the retention of images, saints, pilgrimages, monasticism, indulgences, and relics—with the last two more closely regulated. Bishops were ordered to live within their dioceses and to visit religious houses. Pluralism and simony were suppressed, and new seminaries were established to train priests.

Some new orders of nuns and monks were begun, of which the most important was the **Society of Jesus**, or the **Jesuits**. Founded by the Spaniard Ignatius Loyola, the order grew rapidly and became the "militant arm" of the Church, carrying Christianity to remote Spanish colonies, operating schools, and advising monarchs.

The Church continued to use the Inquisition to punish heresy, and it published the **Papal Index of Forbidden Books**, which included all Protestant writing. The **Baroque** style in art, decoration, and music, characterized by extravagant ornamentation, became associated with the Counter-Reformation. Its goal was to impress and inspire by overwhelming the emotions. Palaces and churches were ornately decorated with gold cherubs, murals, and ceilings, and the Church remained a major patron of the arts.

The general result of Counter-Reformation efforts was to stem the tide of Protestantism. By 1560, the strongest powers in Europe—Spain, France, Austria—remained solidly Catholic, while Protestantism was confined to smaller, less important areas—distant Scandinavia or the chopped-up German states. England was the most significant Protestant nation, but in the 16th century, it was still a minor power with no overseas possessions.

SUMMARY OF CATHOLIC BELIEFS

- Salvation by faith *and* works
- Retention of all seven sacraments
- Latin Vulgate—only acceptable scripture translation
- Eucharist/Mass in Latin
- Retention of doctrine of transubstantiation
- Celibacy of clergy
- Retention of indulgences, relics, saints, pilgrimages

WARS OF RELIGION 1559–1648

The first Protestant-Catholic dispute involved conflict between Lutherans and Catholics in the German states. The fight was settled in 1555 with the **Peace of Augsburg**, which recognized the Lutheran presence where it had established itself. The agreement also said that any future German princes who turned Lutheran could not take Church property with them. There was no recognition of Calvinism.

FRENCH CIVIL WARS

The religious wars of France were political as well as religious. Protestantism developed in France, without government support, as a type of radical Calvinism. Approximately 35 to 50 percent of the nobility, especially in southwestern France, turned Protestant and were called **Huguenots**. Turning Protestant was perhaps a way for French nobility to continue their tradition of rebellion against the monarchy, and the 16th-century kings Frances I and Henry II persecuted Huguenots. In 1559, Henry II was killed in a tournament, leaving three young sons and a Medici widow determined to protect her sons' legacy. Catherine de Medici faced two strands of insurgent nobility: the extreme Catholic League, led by the **Guise** family, and the Huguenots, championed by Henry **Bourbon** of Navarre.

One by one, the **Valois** sons took the throne and, in turn, died. In an attempt to reconcile the conflict, the king's sister was married to Henry of Navarre, but the night after the wedding, several thousand Protestants were murdered in Paris and the countryside—the **St. Bartholomew's Day Massacre**—which stimulated dissension. Finally, in 1574, the last Valois son, Henry, became king, and the Catholic League was headed by Henry of Guise. The 1580s saw the **War of the Three Henrys**, in which Huguenot Henry of Navarre capitalized on the repugnant idea of Spanish intervention on the Guise side. King Henry's men assassinated Henry of Guise, and a Catholic monk, in turn, killed the king. By default then, Henry of Navarre became the first Bourbon monarch of France. However, as a Protestant, he was not allowed to enter Paris. Thus, to unify the country, Henry IV reconverted to Catholicism. He was said to have proclaimed, "Paris is worth a Mass!"

To protect the Huguenots, however, Henry granted the **Edict of Nantes**, which permitted Protestants to maintain their own fortifications and armed men and to hold services and operate schools in some towns. Protestants were allowed to worship privately anywhere. At the same time, Catholicism was recognized as the official religion of France. In 1629, at the behest of Cardinal Richelieu, the Huguenots lost their military and territorial rights. Still later, under Louis XIV, the Edict of Nantes was rescinded, and the Huguenots were persecuted once more.

DUTCH REVOLT

The Netherlands, or Low Countries, consisted of 17 provinces, each rather independent and all influenced by Calvinism by the mid-16th century. This territory fell to Philip II of Spain through inheritance. Revolt broke out in 1566 out of fear of the Inquisition; some 400 churches were attacked by fanatical Calvinists. Philip sent the arrogant **Duke of Alba** with 10,000 troops to bring the Dutch back into line. Alba's church court, the **Council of Troubles** (nicknamed the "Council of Blood"), executed prominent nobles, seized property, and applied new taxes. At one point, the Dutch flooded their countryside to drive back the Spanish. Though there was little formal central government here, the Dutch looked to the House of Orange for leadership.

Because Alba generated so much hatred, he was replaced in 1578 with the more compromising Duke of Parma, who managed to win back the ten southern provinces. The next year, the seven northern provinces declared themselves the **Union of Utrecht**. Fighting continued. Philip's plan with the Armada of 1588 was to have Spanish ships carry Spanish soldiers from the Netherlands across the Channel to attack England. But the defeat of the Armada assured Protestantism, independence, and freedom of the seas for the English and the Dutch.

The division of the Netherlands was finally settled in 1609 with the seven northern provinces an independent nation, known simply as "the Dutch." The official religion was Calvinist Protestantism, but there were many religious minorities, including Jews. Amazingly, the Dutch practiced religious toleration. The ten southern provinces remained Catholic as the Spanish

Netherlands. These provinces had been wrecked by the religious wars. The Dutch used their sea power to close the mouths of the major rivers, which prevented trade. The southern Netherlands remained a Spanish possession until 1713.

THE THIRTY YEARS WAR

Unlike the rest of Europe, the German states had no clear religious majority. Of the some 300 states, some were Catholic, some were Lutheran, and some were Calvinist, though the Calvinists were not recognized by the Peace of Augsburg. The German states were in decline before 1600; few students were in the universities, witches were burned, and the economy was suffering, in part because of the Dutch blockage of the river mouths.

One of the western German states, the **Palatinate**, became Protestant, which mattered because its ruler was one of the electors of the Holy Roman Emperor. In 1608, the Protestant German states, led by the Palatinate, formed the Protestant Union; they looked to the Dutch, the English, and Henry IV of France for support. In 1609, the Catholic states, led by Bavaria, formed the Catholic League, supported by the Spanish. Meanwhile, Austria's ambition was to strengthen the Holy Roman Empire and re-Catholicize Protestant states. Although France was a Catholic nation, she opposed the Habsburgs of Austria and wished to keep the German states disunited; thus, France often allied with Protestants.

The first "act" of the Thirty Years War came in Bohemia in 1618, when the Estates (parliament) of Bohemia threw two emissaries from the Holy Roman Emperor out a window 70 feet above the ground—the **Defenestration of Prague**. Thus began a revolt against the Habsburgs and the Church. The Estates proceeded to offer the crown of Bohemia to Frederick, Protestant ruler of the Palatinate. So Frederick began to lead a Protestant revolt. However, he got little backing from other Protestants. The Dutch could send little besides money (they were still fighting Spain). James I of England, who had succeeded Elizabeth, refused aid because he was negotiating with Spain for a marriage for his son. The Holy Roman Emperor Ferdinand and the Catholic states got support from Spain and Bavaria, the most Catholic of the German states. The Catholics won a major battle in 1620. By 1625, the first phase of the war ended with Catholic victory. Bohemia was reconquered, and land was taken from the nobility. The Jesuits set up missions and schools, and there were trials and executions. Protestantism was stamped out there, and Bohemia was **re-Catholicized**.

During 1625–1629, King Christian of Denmark took up the Protestant cause, possibly because he coveted a few German states for his son. The French, Dutch, and English sent money but few soldiers. Meanwhile, the Holy Roman Emperor Ferdinand hired a very successful mercenary general, Wallenstein, whose private army lived by pillage. In 1629, Christian of Denmark signed a peace agreement. The Catholics then declared the **Edict of Restitution**, retaking Church property taken by Protestants over the past 70 years. This was the Catholic "high point" of the war.

The Protestants then made a comeback in the 1630s under the leadership of **Gustavus Adolphus**, King of Sweden, a brilliant and accomplished man. He led a strong army, which was well equipped, uniformed, and not allowed to plunder. Gustavus Adolphus went to battle with his men and was killed in 1632. Wallenstein was assassinated, and the Holy Roman Emperor withdrew the Edict of Restitution.

The war was not over, however; the last 13 years became an international conflict, more political than religious. Fighting occurred in the Netherlands, France, and above all, in the German states. Mercenary armies on both sides committed horrible atrocities. Finally, there began to be calls for peace in the early 1640s. It took four years to work out the **Peace of Westphalia**, which was a totally secular document. Each German state was separately represented, and all maintained their independence. The treaty recognized Calvinists, and Protestants kept Church property acquired as late as 1624. Dutch independence was recognized, and the Dutch continued to control the mouths of the great European rivers. The German states sank into continued monetary inflation, class division, and general chaos. Western Europe rose from 1648, while Eastern Europe sank.

English Civil War

Because Elizabeth I was the last Tudor monarch, at her death in 1603, the crown went to the son of Mary Stuart, who became James I. The English Parliament did not like either James I or his son Charles I and refused to vote either as much money as he wished. Both insisted that they ruled by **divine right** and tried to enforce religious conformity on England in a **high-church** style, using ritual and practices closer to Catholic tradition. The Archbishop of Canterbury, Laud, tried to force high-church ritual on all English churches.

Meanwhile, a Calvinist strand of Protestants had grown in England. These dissenters, called **Puritans** because of their desire to purify the Church of England, opposed bishops and wished to eliminate the Book of Common Prayer. The House of Commons was made up of the English gentry (lesser landowners) and the prosperous merchants; an increasing number of these were now Puritans.

Charles and Parliament fought increasingly over money issues, and when Charles didn't get what he wanted, he shut down Parliament. Eventually, however, the king had to recall Parliament because he needed money to suppress rebellion in Presbyterian Scotland, which had become united with England under James I. Parliament passed the Triennial Act, requiring the King to call Parliament every three years. Bishops and the Star Chamber court were eliminated.

Finally, in 1642, open war broke out between the king and Parliament, or between the Anglicans and Puritans. The Puritans were called **roundheads** because of their close haircuts. Their military leader was **Oliver Cromwell**, who combined various Puritan forces into the New Model Army. Parliament split between Presbyterians and the more radical independents. Cromwell's army, also called the **ironsides**, defeated the king's supporters, the royalists or **cavaliers**. They eventually captured the king, whose execution was voted by a "rump" parliament of radicals after the moderates were driven out. Charles I was beheaded in 1649.

What followed was the **Interregnum** under the leadership of Cromwell, who called himself **Lord Protector**. Cromwell eventually ruled as a military dictator for almost ten years. In foreign affairs, Cromwell was forceful toward Dutch competition and toward Ireland, but in domestic affairs, he failed. The Puritans closed all the theaters and forbade popular entertainment. The English grew weary of Puritan "thou-shalt-nots." Evidence of the unsettled times was the proliferation of new religious groups: the Levellers (who advocated more equality in property ownership and in the franchise), the Diggers (extremists who desired a communal society), and the Quakers (who preached toleration and peaceful living).

Cromwell died in 1658, and his son tried to carry on. The aristocratic former members of Parliament initiated new Parliamentary elections and invited Charles's son, Charles II, to return as monarch—the **Restoration** (1660). The Church of England was restored without religious toleration of other groups. Parliament passed the Test Act, which excluded non-Anglicans from military and civilian offices.

CHAPTER 5: DISCOVERY, EXPANSION, AND COMMERCIAL REVOLUTION

NEW KNOWLEDGE AND TECHNOLOGIES

The impact of the inventions of printing and gunpowder was discussed in Chapter 3. By the mid-15th century, printing shops had spread, and literacy was growing. Printing also made censorship more difficult.

Gunpowder made the musket the new weapon of choice. Cannons transformed warfare, both on land and at sea. States depended on both mercenary soldiers and conscripts to fill their armies.

The magnetic compass had been well known to European sailors from the early 1400s, and other instruments to determine ships' positions were increasing and improving. An Arabian invention, the astrolabe, enabled sailors to determine latitude by the altitude of the sun and stars. Ships themselves became larger and narrower, better able to sail in ocean currents. The Portuguese developed the caravel, a swift three-masted sailing vessel.

PORTUGUESE EXPLORATION

The first Europeans of modern times to venture out into the Atlantic were the Portuguese in the mid-1400s under the leadership of **Prince Henry, the Navigator**. The Portuguese reached and set up colonies on the **Madieras and Azores** in the Atlantic and began inching their way down the coast of Africa. **Bartholomew Diaz** culminated these efforts by reaching the tip of Africa in 1488. Then in 1498, **Vasco da Gama** rounded the Cape of Good Hope and crossed the Indian Ocean. Thereafter, the Portuguese began to trade with Asia, fighting off Arabian competition and sometimes committing terrible atrocities against native populations. Thus, the Portuguese began cutting into the overland spice and silk trade of the eastern Mediterranean. The Italian monopoly was soon surpassed.

In 1500, **Pedro Cabral**, sailing down the coast of Africa, was blown off course and ended up landing on what is now Brazil. The papal **Treaty of Tordesillas** of 1493, which had "divided the world" between Spain and Portugal, put Brazil in the Portuguese realm; thus, Portugal claimed Brazil.

SPANISH EXPLORATION

The Genoan sailor **Christopher Columbus**, meanwhile, persuaded Ferdinand and Isabella of Spain to finance a voyage to Asia by heading west. Isabella was convinced by the assurance that Christianizing foreign peoples would be a primary goal. Columbus had seriously underestimated the circumference of the earth, but he discovered the trade winds, and his three ships reached the Caribbean in just over a month. Columbus went on to make a total of four voyages to the New World, the last in 1506. He was never able to bring back to Spain the spices, silks, or riches of which he had dreamed. He died, probably not knowing what he had discovered, but Spain would base her claims to the Americas on Columbus's voyages.

Vasco de Balboa soon followed, crossing the Isthmus of Panama in 1513. He became the first European to see the Pacific Ocean. Six years later, **Hernando Cortez** became the first of the **conquistadors**, defeating the **Aztecs** in Mexico, and shortly after that, **Francisco Pizarro** conquered the **Incas** in Peru. Partly because of the deadly effects of European diseases, such as **smallpox**, thousands of Stone Age native peoples were conquered by small bands of Spanish soldiers. Everywhere, the Spanish took missionaries and built churches, but perhaps they were more interested in acquiring pearls and gold in Mexico and silver in Peru.

In pursuit of a **Southwestern Passage** to the Pacific, **Ferdinand Magellan** took five ships down the coast of South America in 1519 and on across to the Pacific. Although Magellan himself was killed fighting natives in the Philippines, one of his ships returned to Spain in 1522. Other Spaniards, **Ponce de Leon**, Hernando de Soto, and Francisco Vásquez de Coronado, explored areas of southern North America.

COLONIZATION

Throughout the 1500s, the Spanish (and to a lesser degree, the Portuguese) established colonies in the Americas. Large plantations called *encomiendas* operated with Native American slave labor. Black slavery was less important to the Spanish colonies than it became later in the English North American colonies. Because small numbers of Spanish women emigrated to the colonies, there was soon a growing population of **mestizos** (mixed white and Indian). American-born whites were called **creoles**. Mestizos adopted the Spanish language and religion. There were soon printing presses and universities in the New World.

The French, Dutch, and English were almost a century behind the Spanish and Portuguese in attempts to colonize. English claims to North America were based on the exploration of the Italians, John and Sebastian Cabot, sailing for England as early as 1497. During the reign of Elizabeth I, the English **sea dogs John Hawkins** and **Francis Drake** became the bane of Spanish treasure ships, and Drake led the second European circumnavigation of the globe. In the 1580s, England made her first, unsuccessful attempts to start colonies on the coast of what is now North Carolina. Finally, in the early 17th century, the English began to establish lasting colonies, Jamestown in 1607 and Plymouth in 1620. A difference between Spanish colonies and those of the English was that, from the beginning, more women and more families came to the English settlements. By 1700, a string of English colonies existed along the Atlantic coast of North America, some of them peopled by persecuted religious groups—the Puritans, Quakers, and Roman Catholics.

French claims to North America stemmed from the voyages of the Italian Verrazzano and the Frenchmen **Jacques Cartier** and Champlain. French colonization began at about the same time as that of the English, but French outposts remained primarily isolated trading establishments along the St. Lawrence and Mississippi Rivers. The French who came tended to be trappers and Jesuit priests (Huguenots were forbidden to come), and their settlements remained small and scattered.

The Dutch made a brief attempt to settle and keep the colony of **New Amsterdam** along the Hudson River. However, within about 50 years, New Amsterdam was seized by the English and renamed New York. The Dutch were more successful in their trade and colonization elsewhere— at the tip of Africa and in Indonesia. The French and British competed with the Portuguese and with each other for trading influence in India. They also wrenched Caribbean sugar islands from the Spanish. The Dutch, French, and English all had **East India trading companies**.

In the 1600s, the African slave trade began in earnest, propagated primarily by the Portuguese, English, and Dutch. As cultivating labor-intensive crops (sugar, tobacco, and later cotton) grew, so did the demand for slaves. The Spanish made less successful attempts to use forced Native American labor. Everywhere, contact between Europeans and Native Americans brought decimation of native populations from European diseases.

The encounters of European and American cultures brought other changes. The Europeans brought the horse to continents where the only beast of burden had been the llama. Metal tools and weapons were also new to the Americas. The Europeans took to the Old World a number of new foods, including the white potato, the tomato, and maize and various peppers, beans, and squashes. Tobacco was also an American innovation. The Europeans soon developed tastes for tea, coffee, and chocolate from Asia, Africa, and South America.

Europe to the Americas	Americas to Africa, Asia, and Europe
Wheat	Maize
Sugarcane	Potatoes
Cotton	Beans
Horses	Tomatoes
Cattle	Pepper
Pigs	Peanuts
Sheep	Avocadoes
Goats	Pineapples
Chickens	Tobacco

PRICE REVOLUTION

The 16th century witnessed major population growth in Europe, as well as gradual inflation. More people meant a need for more food, which led to increased cost of agricultural production and rising prices. Prices also rose as a result of governments' (especially that of Spain) debasing currency. The influx of gold and silver from the Americas also added to inflation, but the wealth that flowed into Spain was never equal to her expenses in maintaining and defending her American possessions. And because Spain was involved in conflicts throughout Europe, much of the gold and silver found its way into other countries, affecting other economies.

Spain's economy further declined as a result of its expulsion of the **Moriscos**, people of Moorish descent, many of whom were excellent farmers and skilled craftsmen. Farming and textile production declined in Spain, as did the colonial market for finished goods. Also, because so much importance was placed on the Church, lay professions were seen as lesser vocations, and Spanish nobility looked with increasing disdain on industry and trade.

Elsewhere, rising prices favored commerce. To avoid the guild restrictions in towns, merchants relied on **cottage industry**, wherein spinning, weaving, and dying cloth were done as piecework in private homes. People might farm and supplement their incomes with "domestic" work. New industries, such as mining, shipbuilding, munitions, and printing, required major investment, which led to new banking practices. Although religion still often condemned usury, or the loaning of money at interest, lending and borrowing mushroomed.

MERCANTILISM

The general economic policy of European nations throughout the 16th and 17th centuries was **mercantilism**. This meant, at first, a **bullionist** economy whereby a country's wealth was measured in gold and silver. Thus, a goal was to import as little as possible and to sell more than the country purchased to create a favorable balance of trade and accumulate gold. It was important to acquire colonies to provide raw materials—again, to be as self-sufficient as possible. Colonies were thought to exist for the benefit of the mother country; they also served as markets for finished products. For example, England did not allow her sugar islands to refine sugar; raw sugar was sent to England, refined there, and resold to the island.

Another aspect of mercantilism was guarding trade secrets. Governments did not allow skilled craftsmen to emigrate, and they tried to lure workers with desirable abilities from other countries. Governments also attempted to make all citizens productive and favored enterprises that gave employment to the poor. Furthermore, governments tried to introduce new industries, such as silk production in France and finished woolen cloth in England. Internal tariffs were discouraged in favor of free trade within countries (e.g., Colbert's Five Great Farms in 17th-century France); however, on the Continent, internal tariffs were hard to abolish. To foster further national interest in exploration and trade, governments granted monopolies by backing certain merchants, as in the formation of overseas trading companies. Only merchants who were members of the favored company could trade in the designated areas. They were expected to sell the national manufactured goods and produce gold or silver to add to the national wealth.

UNIT ONE REVIEW QUESTIONS

1. A major consequence of the defeat of the Spanish Armada in 1588 was

   (A) assured independence of the Union of Utrecht.

   (B) freedom of the seas for the English and Dutch.

   (C) security of Protestantism in the Dutch republic and in England.

   (D) major expenses for Spain to rebuild her fleet.

   (E) all of the above.

2. Probably, the major attraction of Calvinism for French nobles was

   (A) a desire for religious freedom.

   (B) a form of revolt against the strongly Catholic monarchy.

   (C) the Calvinist bent toward hard work and monetary reward.

   (D) fundamental disagreements with the Catholic Church.

   (E) the fact that Calvin was French by birth.

3. Similarities between the Italian Renaissance and the Northern Renaissance included

   (A) a number of painters who portrayed the human form realistically.

   (B) intellectual curiosity that led to the founding of new universities.

   (C) a preference for fresco painting.

   (D) an interest in personal religious experience.

   (E) realistic sculpture.

4. Principles of mercantilism included all the following EXCEPT

   (A) government-backed trading monopolies.

   (B) manufacturing in colonies.

   (C) accumulation of gold and silver.

   (D) discouragement of idleness among citizens.

   (E) exporting more than importing.

5. The English Civil War immediately resulted in

   (A) an end to the Stuart monarchy.

   (B) religious toleration for Catholics.

   (C) reopening of the theaters.

   (D) more power for Parliament.

   (E) a virtual dictatorship by Oliver Cromwell.

6. The main common denominator uniting Spain in the 15th to 17th centuries was

   (A) an overseas empire.

   (B) a nationalistic desire to defeat the English.

   (C) a thriving domestic economy.

   (D) the Catholic church.

   (E) the marriage of Ferdinand and Isabella and their descendants.

7. Portugal's claim to Brazil was based on a voyage of

   (A) Pedro Cabral.

   (B) Vasco da Gama.

   (C) Ferdinand Magellan.

   (D) Bartholomew Diaz.

   (E) Prince Henry the Navigator.

8. A difference between the teachings of Martin Luther and those of John Calvin centered around

   (A) the idea of salvation by faith alone.

   (B) the doctrine of predestination.

   (C) disregard for most of the sacraments.

   (D) reliance on scripture.

   (E) services in the vernacular.

9. The Edict of Nantes

   (A) returned Church property taken by Protestants prior to the Thirty Years War.

   (B) allowed princes of German states to choose the religion for each state.

   (C) gave rights to Huguenot Protestants in France.

   (D) was rescinded by Henry IV of France.

   (E) was Luther's statement regarding the Peasant Revolt.

10. The Brothers of the Common Life in the Netherlands was

    (A) a new monastic order founded in the wake of the Council of Trent.

    (B) a monastery devoted to the preservation of ancient manuscripts.

    (C) dedicated to education and relief of the poor.

    (D) founded by the Christian humanist Erasmus.

    (E) condemned by the papacy.

11. The English colonies in North America differed from those of the Spanish and French primarily in that they

    (A) exported to the mother country.

    (B) had better relations with the native populations.

    (C) depended more on the mother country for manufactured goods.

    (D) had more women, children, and families who emigrated from England to the colonies.

    (E) relied on the mother country for security.

12. The European "price revolution," or inflation, resulted from all the following EXCEPT

    (A) the influx of gold and silver to Spain.

    (B) increased cost of food production.

    (C) usury, or the loaning of money at interest.

    (D) governments' debasing currency.

    (E) decline in population.

13. One area in which the Council of Trent insisted on closer church regulation was

    (A) the translation of scripture.

    (B) consideration of the sacraments.

    (C) the sale of indulgences.

    (D) the selection of saints.

    (E) services in the vernacular.

14. New to art in the Renaissance was

    (A) painting in oils.

    (B) the use of perspective.

    (C) freestanding sculpture.

    (D) more realistic depiction of people.

    (E) all of the above.

15. Religious reformer Zwingli and others like him destroyed church art on the grounds that it

    (A) was not mentioned in scripture.

    (B) detracted from proper prayer and meditation.

    (C) mixed mythology with religion.

    (D) used colors that were too vibrant and was thus considered "sinful."

    (E) misinterpreted figures and stories in the Bible.

16. Which of the following was NOT true of the Holy Roman Empire about 1600?

    (A) It was made up of about 300 states.

    (B) The Holy Roman Emperor exercised tight control over member states.

    (C) The Holy Roman Emperor was from the Austrian Habsburg family.

    (D) The individual states took pride in their independence.

    (E) There was a central diet (parliament) of the Empire.

17. The primary shift in thinking brought by the Italian Renaissance was

    (A) a renewed interest in art.

    (B) an outpouring of religious fervor.

    (C) ultramontanism, or great reverence for the papacy.

    (D) an interest in political unity.

    (E) appreciation for the abilities and powers of man.

18. Elizabeth I brought religious calm to England by

    (A) allowing priests to marry.

    (B) authorizing a translation of scripture into English.

    (C) acknowledging the civil rights of Catholics.

    (D) requiring only outward conformity to Anglicanism.

    (E) giving religious freedom to all groups.

19. Calvinism spread to all the following areas EXCEPT

    (A) English settlers in the northern British colonies in North America.

    (B) Scotland.

    (C) the Scandinavian states.

    (D) the northern Netherlands.

    (E) the French nobility.

20. At the end of the Thirty Years War in the formation of the Peace of Westphalia,

    (A) the Church exerted a powerful influence.

    (B) the German states kept their individual sovereignty.

    (C) the Holy Roman emperor became more powerful.

    (D) the English intervened in Continental affairs.

    (E) Spain regained its control of the Netherlands.

For the following questions, write an essay that

- has a relevant thesis;
- addresses all parts of the question;
- supports a thesis with specific evidence; and
- is well organized.

Plan your essays and write them on your own paper.

1. To what extent and in what ways did women particpate in the Renaissance?

2. Discuss the political and social consequences of the Protestant Reformation in the first half of the 16th century.

_____

_____

_____

_____

_____

_____

_____

_____

_____

_____

_____

_____

_____

ANSWERS AND EXPLANATIONS

1. E

All the choices are true. The 1588 disaster for Spain meant major military expenditures to rebuild a navy. It also ended efforts to force a return to Catholicism in England and the northern Netherlands and to end Dutch independence. After 1588, the Dutch and English moved freely onto the high seas for trade and exploration.

2. B

The French nobility had always tended to be rebellious, and opposing the Church by becoming Protestant was a way to challenge royal power. Calvin was French, (E), but this was probably not a seriously influential factor. Religious freedom, (A), was not generally expected or practiced in the 1500s. No doubt, some Huguenots felt sincere religious convictions, but it is unclear that this was widespread among the nobility (note the ease with which Henry of Navarre switched faith).

3. A

Though there were considerable differences between the subject matter and type of painting, both Renaissances produced major artists. (B) and (D) refer to the Northern Renaissance only, while (E) was restricted to Italy. The climate of Northern Europe did not permit large frescoes, (C).

4. B

Mercantilism advocated that colonies provide raw material for mother countries and serve as markets for the home country's industry. For instance, England required her Caribbean sugar islands to ship raw sugar to England. The other choices are all tenets of mercantilism.

5. E

Oliver Cromwell ruled England, mostly without Parliament, from 1649 until his death in 1658 (the Interregnum). At his death, the crown was returned to the Stuarts. The Puritans closed the theaters and forbade most public entertainment, and they were extremely anti-Catholic.

6. D

Even when Ferdinand and Isabella married, (E), joining the kingdoms of Aragon and Castile, Spain was united in name only. Each kingdom kept its own institutions of government. The interest in overseas empire, (A), and competition with the English, (B), were felt only at the highest levels of society. The economy of Spain, (C), declined rather than grew, partly because of the intense importance put on Catholicism, which included the Inquisition and forcing Christianity or emigration on peoples of Jewish or Moorish descent.

7. A

Cabral landed on the coast of South America accidentally, after a storm drove his ship off course from its intended route down the coast of Africa. Da Gama and Diaz, (B and D), went down the African coast; da Gama went on to India. Prince Henry, (E), was responsible for developing a Portuguese interest in Atlantic voyages. Although Magellan, (C), was Portuguese and traveled down the South American coast looking for a "southwestern passage," he was sailing for Spain.

8. B

Only Calvin preached the idea of the "elect" as God's chosen, destined for Heaven. All the other answers are beliefs held by both Luther and Calvin.

9. C

The Edict of Nantes was issued by Henry IV of France to protect the rights of French Protestants, whom he had formerly led. This was probably the high point of Protestantism in France. In the 1600s, first Richelieu rescinded the military rights granted by the edict, and then Louis XIV revoked the entire document.

10. C

The Brothers of the Common Life operated in the 16th century *with* papal approval, (E), but it was not a monastic order, (A and B). The Brothers modeled their lives after the teachings of Jesus, promoting charity and education. Erasmus, (D), was brought up and educated by the Brothers.

11. D

All American colonies depended on their founding country for security and for manufactured goods, (C and E). All exported raw materials to Europe, (A)—furs, gold and silver, tobacco, and later cotton. Few women or families came to either French or Spanish settlements, but from the beginning, the English colonies were more family oriented.

12. E

One of the direct causes of the "price revolution" was a rising population rather than a population decline. All the other choices are features of the inflationary trend of the 16th and 17th centuries.

13. C

Most of the stands taken by the Council of Trent amounted to affirmation of then current Church doctrine. The Latin Vulgate and Latin ritual were retained, (A and E); all seven sacraments and reverence for saints were kept, (B and D). While the beliefs in purgatory and indulgences were upheld, the Council did urge closer vigilance over the potential for abuse.

14. E

Visual art, both painting and sculpture, changed radically in the Renaissance, encompassing all the answers listed here.

15. A

Zwingli, whose brief reforming career occurred between those of Luther and Calvin, foreshadowed the Protestant tendency to base all doctrine on a strict interpretation of scripture. Because organs and stained glass were not mentioned in the Bible, they had to be destroyed. While the other answers here may have been somewhat true, the basic belief behind Zwingli's insistence on plain churches and simple services is summarized in (A).

16. B

The Holy Roman Emperor, from the Habsburg family, had very little control over the 300-plus states, which were very jealous of their individual prerogatives. There was a central diet of the Empire, but like the emperor, it had little power.

17. E

(B) and (C) are not true because the Italian Renaissance's character was distinctly secular. Political unity, (D), was a chief failing of the city-states. While answer (A) is true, the more fundamental idea behind much Renaissance expression was an awareness of the marvel of the human body and mind.

18. D

While Elizabeth I did favor a noncelibate clergy, her "middle-of-the-road" policy that calmed religious controversy was her insistence that all subjects belong to the Church of England and at least give lip service to it. Her government did not pry into individual, private religious convictions. She officially acknowledged no other religious groups, however, (C and E). Her successor, James I, authorized an official English translation of scripture.

19. C

It was Lutheranism that spread to Scandinavia. The other choices are areas affected by Calvinism in some fashion.

20. B

One significance of the peace conference of Westphalia was that its negotiations were totally secular; the Church had *no* voice, (A). The German states were represented individually and were not interested in sacrificing anything for unity, which kept the Holy Roman Empire weak.

SAMPLE FREE-RESPONSE ESSAYS

1. To what extent and in what ways did women participate in the Renaissance?

The women of the Renaissance, like those of the Middle Ages, were denied all political rights. Unlike the Renaissance man, women played a minor and narrow role in society and were rarely educated. Subjugation of women during the period was common practice. Women of all classes during this time were expected to maintain the household, by sewing, cooking, cleaning and entertaining. Peasant women worked in the field with their husbands, middle class women helped run their husbands' shops, and women of the highest class engaged in or supervised others in household tasks.

Women during the Renaissance were politically, legally and socially placed in a subservient role. During her childhood, a woman was strictly confined and often repressed by her parents, and was later turned over to a husband's control. Women who did not marry were not given their independence and could not live alone. Instead, they joined convents to become nuns or lived in the households of male relatives. They were denied independence throughout their lives, from birth until death. Men dominated them completely, making decisions, controlling the money and property. Women had little freedom, and rarely ventured far from their homes.

Women were discouraged from participating in the arts and sciences, and only a few women of the highest class were given a rare chance to distinguish themselves. Two notable exceptions were Lucrezia Borgia and Isabella d'Este. These two women were able to break the mold and achieve some measure of fame and success. Lucrezia Borgia was born into one of the most well-known families in World history, one that sought to control as much of Italy as possible. She was the daughter of Cardinal Rodrigo Borgia, who later became Pope Alexander VI. She became famous for her three politically-motivated marriages, but some critics say Lucrezia should be viewed simply as a political pawn whose numerous marriages were used for her family's political gains. Her illusion of power was created by a man, her father who controlled her life and than later her position as a mother and wife.

Isabella d'Este, who is often referred to as "The First Lady of the Renaissance" was another important woman during the 14th century. Isabella was able to break down the barriers to power and find her own independence. Born into the ruling family of the Ferra, she married Francesco Gonzaga and became the Marchioness of Mantua and after her husbands death she ruled Mantua alone. She was well educated and founded a school for young women. She promoted the arts through her home and allowed women to break away from their traditional roles.

2. Discuss the political and social consequences of the Protestant Reformation in the first half of the 16th century.

The Protestant Reformation resulted in the biggest and most fundamental change in societal norms since the fall of the Roman Empire. The Reformation was a reaction to the oppressive and domineering actions of the Roman Catholic Church and the administration through Western Europe at the time. Before the Protestant Reformation, the Pope had unrivaled power that extended not only to religious practices of the people, but to political, economic and social arenas as well. The role of the Church was all-powerful and all-encompassing, and people revolted against their lack of freedom. The events of this movement against the dominant social order represented a true revolution that shaped Western thought. This conflict divided the Christians of Western Europe into two religious groups: Protestants and Catholics.

Democracy, constitutionalism, and religious liberty were not the only social consequences of the Reformation. They were the beginning of a revolution that has implications for all aspects of life even today. An immediate and unfortunate effect of the Reformation was intolerance, which expressed itself in persecution and religious wars. Instead of generating the true spirit of Christ, the Reformation made thousands suffer on account of their religion. Another result of the Reformation was revolts and wars which caused loss of life, property and power. These included the French Civil Wars, the Thirty Years War, The Dutch Revolt and the English Civil war.

For better or worse, by annihilating the economic power of the medieval Church, the Reformation paved the way for the rise of capitalism. New ideas arose in the economic field where there were healthy changes. People were free from medieval ideas and the tyranny of the Orthodox Church. Thus, they could pursue certain economic activities such as money lending, which was criticized in the past. Owing to the Reformation, old ideas were discarded and the moneylender was given a status in society.

Though the Reformation was religious in nature, it had far-reaching effects in all fields and helped in the shaping of the modern world.

CHAPTER 6: THE AGE OF ABSOLUTISM— WESTERN EUROPE

CHARACTERISTICS AND PHILOSOPHIES OF ABSOLUTISM

In the 16th and 17th centuries, the rulers of most of the states of Europe established themselves as "absolute" monarchs, in control of taxation, the military, and religion. Such kings were the products of powerful ruling families; they provided security to subjects emerging from the chaos of religious conflict. **Absolutism** was the theory of such political writers as the English thinker **Thomas Hobbes** (*The Leviathan,* 1651). A French author, **Jacques Bossuet**, claimed that kings ruled by **divine right**, or by the will of God.

At the same time, absolute rule did not mean arbitrary power; there were reasonable and traditional limits. In Western Europe, some would-be absolute monarchs were limited to a degree by legislative bodies. The state's purpose was seen as maintenance of internal peace and the conduct of war abroad. To function effectively, absolute rulers had to keep their nobility under control.

In Eastern Europe, this was accomplished, in part, by giving the nobility almost total control over the peasantry. In Western Europe, the degree of absolute power often depended on the personal strength of the ruler and to what degree he or she could force submission to his or her nobility.

In addition, absolute rulers had the ability to collect taxes and to maintain armies (and sometimes navies) and to wage war. Strong monarchs also attempted to control religion in their realm, often by claiming authority over ecclesiastical appointments. Often, the church and state found it advantageous to work together. To create a sense of awe, great monarchs hired artists and architects to design streets, palaces, and other public buildings that would inspire admiration.

DEVELOPMENT OF FRENCH ABSOLUTISM: 1588–1643

When Henry of Navarre became Henry IV at the close of France's religious wars, his first task was to restore peace and unity to his country. To do this, he embraced Catholicism as the state religion

religion and, at the same time, preserved the rights of French Protestants via the Edict of Nantes (discussed in Chapter 5). Henry's councilors were chosen from the lower-ranking nobles, who were more loyal; his chief advisor was Sully, a Protestant. After 1593, the king never called the **Estates General**, ruling without interference from this body. To promote economic prosperity, the monarchy favored French manufacturing, especially in silk and tapestries. Henry also supported the first French colonial venture in North America.

Henry IV was assassinated in 1610, leaving behind an eight-year-old son, Louis XIII, and his Medici mother. **Marie de Medici** was never popular, but she and her son relied on the skills of **Cardinal Richelieu**. Though he was a high-ranking clergyman, Richelieu placed practical politics first (making him a *politique*). He worked to strengthen royal control through better tax collection. He divided France into 32 districts, each governed by an *intendant*, who was the king's direct representative. Richelieu revoked the portions of the Edict of Nantes that allowed the Huguenots military rights (their armies and fortresses). When the Thirty Years War began in 1618, Richelieu sided *against* the Catholic Habsburgs of Austria and Spain; he saw political advantage in siding with the Protestants. By 1643, when Louis XIII died, the way had been prepared for Louis XIV to rule as the supreme absolute monarch of the 17th century.

THE AGE OF LOUIS XIV

Because Louis XIV was only four when he became King of France in 1643, his mother, **Anne of Austria**, served as regent. She depended on an Italian cardinal, **Jules Mazarin**, to lead the government, though both she and Mazarin were criticized as outsiders. To protest rising taxes, the refractory nobility revolted against the crown in 1648, even breaking into nine-year-old Louis's bedroom. The revolt, nicknamed **the Fronde**, tried to overthrow Mazarin and give control to the nobility. It was soon put down but long remembered by the young king.

Louis XIV assumed personal rule in 1661, proclaiming, **"L'etat, c'est moi!"** ("I am the state.") First, Louis consolidated all military force under the monarchy and quadrupled the army's size to about 400,000. To avoid dependence on a single advisor, as in the reign of Louis XIII, Louis XIV surrounded himself with men of ability.

To awe and impress, Louis built the fabulous Palace of Versailles and required the nobility to reside there part of the year, where they could be watched. The Estates General was never called. The people Louis favored in government were more recently arrived to the upper levels of society, as their loyalty was more to be trusted. Tax collection in France was horribly inefficient and remained largely so mainly because the nobility paid few taxes. Louis resorted to devaluing the currency and to **selling titles and offices,** or government appointments. At the same time, Louis's government supported writers, such as the dramatists Racine (tragedies) and Molière (comedies), as well as the arts and sciences, establishing academies that fostered classical style—order, harmony, and hierarchy.

To build France's economic strength, Louis employed **Jean-Baptiste Colbert**, who advocated a vigorous mercantilism. Colbert sponsored the development of manufactures such as silk, tapestries, and other cloth by awarding tax exemptions and monopolies. He set up a large area free of internal tariffs, **Five Great Farms**, to enhance trade, while at the same time France maintained high protective external tariffs against English and Dutch products. Colbert improved transport of goods by constructing or improving roads and canals. The biggest market for French manufacturing was the expanded military.

Overseas, Colbert supported French trade in North America and initiated the French East India Company in an attempt to compete with the English and Dutch. To improve tax collection at home, he hired surveyors and map makers to assess better the country's resources.

Louis considered religious unity necessary to his absolute monarchy. Therefore, he revoked the remaining provisions of the Edict of Nantes (and some 200,000 Huguenots left France permanently). He also attempted to crack down on the **Jansenists**, a Catholic minority who pursued a doctrine of faith and divine grace similar to that of the Calvinists.

WARS OF LOUIS XIV

Under Louis XIV, France became expansionist, attempting to encroach upon the territory of its neighbors. Louis began in 1667 by invading the Spanish Netherlands, and from there, he moved against the Dutch. Here, his ambitions were blockaded by an alliance of the Dutch with other nations (**balance of power** politics, practiced by **William of Orange**). Giving up on Holland, Louis turned instead to the **Franche-Comte**, a province between eastern France and Switzerland, and took it. Louis sent financial aid to the Hungarians to fight against the Austrian Habsburgs, and he also favored the Turks in Eastern Europe for the same reason.

The **War of the League of Augsburg** broke out in 1688 between France and an alliance of Louis's Protestant and Catholic enemies. It dragged on until 1697, when it was settled by returning everything to its antebellum status.

Louis's last and greatest war was the **War of Spanish Succession**, 1702–1713, which began after the death of the Spanish Habsburg monarch **Charles II**. Charles died without an heir, willing his throne to the grandson of Louis XIV. Most of the rest of Europe feared a mega-monarchy of France and Spain and went to war to prevent this from happening. The **grand alliance** was led by William of Orange, who had become William III of England. Although William died before the end of the war, his alliance held, and French ambitions were checked.

The big winner in the **Treaty of Utrecht** of 1713 was England, which kept **Gibraltar** (seized during the war) and also received the *asiento*, the privilege to conduct slave trade with Spanish America. The British also took Newfoundland and Nova Scotia from France. Control of the former Spanish Netherlands passed to Austria, making it the **Austrian Netherlands** (Austria was far enough away not to threaten England). Louis's grandson did become King of Spain (making the Spanish royal family now Bourbon), with the stipulation that the king of Spain could not also be King of France.

Louis XIV

CHAPTER 7: THE AGE OF ABSOLUTISM— EASTERN EUROPE

DECLINE OF THE HOLY ROMAN EMPIRE, POLISH KINGDOM, AND THE OTTOMAN EMPIRE

In the 16th and 17th centuries, the declining empires of Eastern Europe, the Holy Roman Empire, the Polish kingdom, and the Ottoman Empire shared several characteristics. All were huge in territory but weak in central authority, they contained vast arrays of diverse ethnic and language groups, and all were administered inefficiently.

Voltaire said the Holy Roman Empire had never been holy, Roman, or even an empire. The whole had been split by Protestant/Catholic conflict before, during, and after the Thirty Years War. A sizeable merchant class had not developed, colonies were nonexistent, and learning was at an all time low (with one exception, the Bach family in music). The Empire did not possess a uniform calendar.

> The **Julian calendar** adopted in 46 BCE was 10 days "off" by 1580, making the equinoxes occur 10 days early. This affected the Church's calculation of Easter. Therefore, Pope Gregory removed 10 days from October in 1582 and decreed better accuracy by having years divisible by 400 not to be leap years (except millennium years). All Catholic countries immediately accepted the **Gregorian calendar**. Protestant states refused to change until 1700 and the English until 1752. Russia ignored the revision until 1918.

There were 300-plus states in the Empire, ranging from Austria to tiny entities of single cities. The emperor was chosen by the heads of nine elector states; always, an Austrian Habsburg was chosen. The multiple German states blocked the accumulation of absolute power by the Holy Roman Emperor, but individual rulers tried to acquire power within their own states. Generally, they avoided war with neighboring states; ambitious states added territory through marriage or inheritance.

East of the German states was Poland, a huge, disorganized "republic" in the sense that it elected a king. The Polish population included a variety of ethnic groups, including Germans and Jews; its official language was Latin, and the dominant religion was Catholicism. The Jews spoke **Yiddish** and lived apart under their own law. Poland's landed aristocracy was the *szlachta*, made up of some 8 percent of the population (an unusually high percentage).

Because the Polish monarch was elected, a would-be king had to make deals to be chosen. Consequently, he ended up with no power, no army, no money (the nobility paid no taxes), and no law courts. Foreigners meddled in Polish affairs, especially in monarchal elections; thus, the man elected was often not a Pole. The Polish diet could only pass measures by unanimous agreement (which was unlikely), and any member of the diet could shut it down, called **exploding the diet**, by claiming the **liberum veto**. In approximately 100 years, 48 of 55 diets were "exploded."

Historians call the Polish government of the time a "fiasco" and the country a "power vacuum." Because of its great weakness, Poland eventually disappeared from the map of Europe in the second half of the 18th century, as its neighbors, Austria, Prussia, and Russia, chopped off parts of it in three **partitions** (one in the 1770s and two more in the 1790s). Thus, Poland ceased to exist until it was re-established by Napoleon in the early 19th century as the Grand Duchy of Warsaw.

The Ottoman Empire spilled over from the Anatolian Peninsula into Eastern Europe. The Empire was a **theocracy**; Muslim religious leaders filled government positions. One Turkish practice was capturing Christian children and brainwashing them into total loyalty to the Muslim state (the **janisaries**) to serve in political and military positions. Generally, however, the Muslims treated Christians in conquered territories better than Christians treated Muslims in reverse circumstances.

By the 17th century, the military and technology of the Turkish Empire had fallen behind those of the West. Sultans became corrupt, and local authorities wielded a free hand over their subjects. But in the middle of the 1600s, the **Kiuprili family** came to power and aroused the Ottoman Empire to attempt further conquest in Eastern Europe. Thus, the Austrian Habsburgs were forced to repel Turkish advances.

CHARACTERISTICS OF ABSOLUTISM IN EASTERN EUROPE

As the old Eastern European empires declined, three states, Austria, Prussia, and Russia, gained power and prestige. Each of these was developing in unique ways, but a number of descriptors were common to all of Eastern Europe that differed from characteristics of Western Europe. Thus, the absolutism that developed in Austria, Russia, and Prussia differed from that of France.

There were fewer towns in Eastern Europe and almost no middle class; the small middle class that existed was much weaker than its growing counterpart in Western Europe. The economy of Eastern Europe was primarily agrarian, built on large estates, which formed the main social unit, and on the labor of serfs who were still bound to the land. Labor in general was less productive. The peasant class had no legal recourse; there was no court system, and landlords administered justice. Monarchs in Eastern Europe who wished to accumulate absolute authority in their realms had to work through and around the powerful traditional landed aristocracy.

ABSOLUTISM IN RUSSIA

There was always the question of whether Russia was a Western or Eastern nation; in many ways, it was both. After the Turks took Constantinople, Russia considered itself the inheritor of Eastern Christianity—hence, the term **Holy Russia**.

The incredibly cruel and violent era of Ivan the Terrible in the late 16th century was followed by even more chaos and intrigue, until Russian nobles elected a grandnephew of Ivan, **Michael Romanov**, as tsar. Thus began Russia's royal family. Russia, however, remained extremely ignorant and backward. In 1670–1671, a massive peasant rebellion led by **Stephen Razin** scared the nobility into clamping down on the peasantry and giving more authority to the tsar.

It was **Peter the Great** who, in the late 17th and early 18th centuries, developed absolutism in Russia. On visits to Western Europe as a young man, Peter was impressed with the technology and organization of the Netherlands and England, especially. His desire became to develop a state and a military equal to those of Western nations.

Peter imported military advisors and increased the Russian army to over 200,000. He recruited soldiers by villages and regions; they wore uniforms and were equipped with Western muskets and artillery. Nobility were required to serve in either the army or the civil service and were rewarded based on performance ("careers open to talent"). For most of Peter's reign, Russia fought Sweden in the **Great Northern War**, taking the Baltic coastal areas of Latvia and Estonia around 1709.

Like Louis XIV of France, Peter desired to control religion within his realm. Personally quite secular, he placed the Russian Orthodox Church under a committee of bishops, called the **Holy Synod**, and at its head he named a **Procurator**, a non-clergyperson. The more traditional and fundamentalist Christians, the **Old Believers**, rebelled but to little avail.

For many years, Peter constructed (using forced peasant labor) a new capital, St. Petersburg, his **window to the West**. Russian nobles were required to build stone houses here and reside in them for part of the year; nobles and merchants also had to pay for streets, parks, and canals.

The old representative body, the **Duma**, was never called. Peter reorganized the country into 10 territories, whose administration answered directly to the tsar. Peter taxed everything, from coffins to the right to be an Old Believer. Most manufacturing and mining operations were owned and controlled by the government; private capitalism was limited in Russia from the beginning. The nobility were required to obtain education, perhaps abroad. Peter himself simplified the **Cyrillic alphabet** and wrote a book of etiquette. He forced the nobility to practice more civilized manners, to shave their beards, and to dress in Western fashion.

One area in which Peter the Great failed was in training a successor. (His son Alexis was an alcoholic rebel, whom Peter had tortured to death.) The masses of Russian peasantry existed outside and beyond Peter's reforms, but the nobility became increasingly Europeanized. After Peter the Great, Russia played a role in European life.

ABSOLUTISM IN AUSTRIA

Apart from the Holy Roman Empire, the Austrian Habsburgs created their own empire in Austria, which was made up of Austria, Bohemia, and Hungary. The main thing holding the empire together was the Habsburg monarchy, which faced a number of unique problems. In the 17th century, most of Hungary was occupied by the Turks. Incited by Louis XIV of France, the Turks advanced even to Vienna by 1683. Several years of fighting eventually drove the Turks out of Hungary in 1697.

The Hungarian nobility, the **Magyars**, accepted the Habsburg monarchy but kept local control. They maintained their own diet and did not pay taxes to Vienna. Old local diets remained throughout all three parts of the Austrian Empire, but there was no central diet for the empire. A major problem for the Austrian Empire was the vast array of ethnic groups, each with its own language—Germans, Slovakians, Serbians, Croatians, etc. The Habsburg monarch had to work through local political institutions. As long as the provinces produced soldiers and taxes and accepted the wars and foreign policy of the Habsburg ruler, no questions were asked. Austria itself was solidly Roman Catholic, but monarchs did not try to repress the Protestants of both Bohemia and Hungary.

In 1711, **Charles VI of Austria** became the Habsburg emperor. Because he had no male heirs, Charles spent much of his reign making deals with the other nations of Europe, the **Pragmatic Sanction**, by which they agreed to accept Charles's successor, his daughter Maria Theresa, as ruler of all Austrian territory.

ABSOLUTISM IN PRUSSIA

The accumulation of absolute power in and formation of the state of Prussia hinged on the **Hohenzollern** family, which began as two separate branches in two states: **Brandenburg** in central Europe and **Prussia** in Eastern Europe. In 1618, the Prussian side of the Hohenzollerns died, and the states were united under the elector of Brandenburg (*elector* in the sense of voting for the Holy Roman Emperor). At first, Prussia and Brandenburg were not physically connected, but territory in between was slowly added through marriage and inheritance. The powerful Prussian landed aristocracy, the **Junkers**, accepted Hohenzollern authority as long as they were left alone on their own **estates**, where they had total control of their peasants.

The Thirty Years War marked the beginning of the ascension of Hohenzollern power. **Frederick William** became the Elector in 1640 (later called the "Great Elector") and used the war to ignore old rights of the landlords. Because the estates, dominated by the Junkers, did not meet regularly during the war, Frederick William gradually assumed the right to tax without their consent. He used the revenue to build a large, permanent, standing army. Then, to bring needed skills to Brandenburg-Prussia, Frederick William invited French Huguenots to immigrate.

Frederick William's son **Frederick** used the War of Spanish Succession (1701–1713) to gain still more authority. In exchange for supplying troops to the Holy Roman Emperor, Frederick received the right to call himself **King *in* Prussia**—soon he was known as **King *of* Prussia**. A large and powerful military continued to dominate Prussian life. The Junkers had unquestioned power over their peasants and were not greatly taxed. Laws forbade the sale of "noble land" to nonnobility. The nobility served as officers in the army, and the peasants supplied the foot soldiers. Military needs dominated the economy; most of the civilian population remained poor. The middle class was small, submissive, and never powerful. Prussian life emphasized duty, obedience, and service.

Strangest of the early Hohenzollern monarchs was **Frederick William I** (1713–1740), whom historians describe as "earthy" and "crude." Only the military mattered; Frederick William doubled the army to 80,000, making it the 4th-largest army in Europe, while Prussia was only the 12th-largest country. Frederick William I centralized government power to manage the military; soldiers collected taxes, did public works, and served as police. The king recruited tall, handsome young men from all over his kingdom into an elite force, but he almost never used any of his army to fight. Frederick William I despised anything that hinted of "culture," which caused major friction with his son, the future Frederick II ("the Great"), who played the flute and composed music.

CHAPTER 8: CONSTITUTIONALISM IN ENGLAND AND THE DUTCH REPUBLIC

ENGLAND

THE RESTORATION

The Stuart monarchy returned with **Charles II** in 1660 after the Cromwell interlude. Charles was not a strong king, but he was popular because the English sought an end to chaos. The monarchy's income switched from old feudal dues to direct tax revenues controlled by Parliament. Unlike the Continental aristocracy, the English upper classes paid taxes and participated in the government.

Charles II had spent years at the court of Louis XIV and maintained Catholic sympathies. His court expressed a revulsion against the recent Puritan past in its extreme Baroque style, the **rococo**. Charles made a secret agreement with Louis XIV, promising to declare himself Catholic in time in exchange for money. Parliament, meanwhile, enforced the **Test Act**, which excluded non-Anglicans from military and civil office. Supporters of the king were known as Tories, and his opponents were Whigs.

Because Charles II died (1685) without legitimate heirs, the throne went to his brother **James II**, who was openly Catholic. James ignored the Test Act, dismissed Protestant ministers, and declared freedom of worship. In 1688, James's (much younger) second wife gave birth to a son, who was baptized Catholic. At that point, Parliamentary leaders, both Whig and Tory, combined to invite James's Protestant daughter Mary (from his first marriage) and her husband William of Orange of the Netherlands to "invade" England. William had grown up during the Dutch struggle against Spain and had spent his energies maintaining European alliances against Louis XIV of France—that is, **balance-of-power** politics. No one within or without England came to James's aid, so **William and Mary** came unchallenged across the Channel and became William and Mary of England.

THE GLORIOUS REVOLUTION

John Locke labeled the events of 1688 the **Glorious Revolution**, because it amounted to a bloodless regime change in England. More recent historians have seen these events as a movement of the landed aristocracy for their own interests. William and Mary signed the **English Bill of Rights** in 1689, which reaffirmed the Test Act but allowed **dissenters** to worship and maintain their own schools. However, Anglicanism remained the established Church of England. The Bill of Rights assured the rights of Parliament, in particular, in financial control. The Glorious Revolution also meant that the English gentry (moderate to large landowners) controlled the government through the House of Commons. Parliamentary legislation provided for Protestant inheritance of the monarchy; following William and Mary, who were childless, the crown went to Mary's sister Anne. James II and his descendants lived in France and were known as **pretenders** to the English throne.

One of William's accomplishments was the establishment of the Bank of England. The English government carried a national debt, but it always repaid, so wealthy private citizens readily invested in it, which provided the government with a boundless line of credit.

THE STUART MONARCHY

James I, 1603–1625

Charles I, 1625–1649

(Interregnum, 1649–1660)

Charles II, 1660–1685

James II, 1685–1688

William III and Mary II, 1689–1702/1694

Anne, 1702–1714

THE DUTCH REPUBLIC

DOMINANCE OF THE MIDDLE CLASS

The Dutch Republic has been called "an island of plenty in a sea of want." As in the Italian city-states of the Renaissance, power gathered in the hands of the merchant class, whose trade, banking, and storage facilities surpassed those in the rest of Europe. The Dutch gold **florin** became the international unit of monetary exchange, and Amsterdam was the center of world banking. Double-entry bookkeeping further inspired fiscal confidence, both domestically and internationally, and Dutch credit was good.

In 1600, the Dutch owned some 10,000 ships, sailed every sea, and controlled most of the shipping of Northern Europe. They launched their sea power as fishers and proved themselves successful in building canals for still better transport of goods and windmills for power.

By reclaiming land, the Dutch had a prosperous agriculture, specializing in dairy products and tulips. Single families built townhouses and enjoyed a diet of home-produced meat, fish, and dairy products, plus imports such as tea, coffee, cocoa, and other goods from around the globe. Paintings of the time suggest pleasantly furnished homes that included furniture, tapestries, servants, and pets. In the 1600s, the Dutch may have had the highest standard of living in the world.

GOLDEN AGE OF THE NETHERLANDS (C. 1600–1650)

The wealthy Dutch merchant class provided patronage for the arts. Artists were "craftspeople" who learned their profession through apprenticeships. The **Dutch Reformed Church** (Calvinist) spurned art, so few artists painted biblical topics. Aside from portraits, artists commonly did landscapes, seascapes, and still lifes.

Another area of skilled development was **lens grinding**. **Antoni Leeuwenhoek** developed the first microscope, and **Christian Huygens** improved the Dutch telescope, with which he viewed the rings of Saturn. Huygens also developed **pendulum clocks**, and clock making became another Dutch skill.

In general, the Dutch lived comfortably but not ostentatiously. Excess was considered sinful and identified with the "loose-living" French. Above all, the Dutch maintained a sense of duty and hard work. Despite their Calvinistic faith, the Dutch kept a rather secular lifestyle, including a relatively free press. The English and French sometimes published in Amsterdam to avoid censorship.

In 1602, the Dutch East India Company began a trade monopoly with the Far East—India, Ceylon, and Indonesia. The Dutch named the tip of South America **Cape Horn** and began settling on the coast of South Africa by the mid-17th century. In 1612, they established the colony of **New Amsterdam** in North America, and they established Jakarta in Indonesia in 1619. In 1641, the Dutch were the only Europeans not excluded from Japan when that nation shut itself off from the outside world.

POLITICAL STRUCTURE

The Dutch Republic was made up of seven provinces, each of which maintained a stubborn independence. Each selected a chief executive, a *stadholder*, but there was no national *stadholder*. There was an estates general, but the representatives (called "High Mightinesses") could act only in accordance with the individual provincial estates. However, the provinces usually chose the same person as *stadholder*, the head of the **House of Orange**.

When there was a military threat, the *stadholder* could claim more power, but in peacetime, allegiances shifted back to the burghers, who concentrated on trade and manufacturing. After William of Orange was chosen *stadholder* by six of the seven provinces in 1673, he tried to consolidate power like European monarchs, but the Dutch provinces would not allow this to happen and continued to exist in a decentralized republic until 1795. Power remained in the hands of wealthy merchants and bankers, and provincial courts protected the rights of citizens.

RELIGIOUS TOLERATION

Early in the 17th century, Dutch Calvinism was challenged by the teaching of Joseph Arminius, who modified the doctrine of predestination. After initial controversy, the Dutch granted the **Arminians** protection from persecution. Other religious groups soon sought toleration there. Catholics and Jews were welcomed (though Jews were excluded from the guilds). **Baruch Spinoza**, from a refugee Portuguese Jewish family, worked as a lens grinder but wrote philosophy discussing the nature of reality and human conduct. Christian minorities escaped persecution at home by fleeing to the Dutch republic—Quakers, Puritans, Huguenots, Mennonites, and others. While no group had as many rights as the Calvinists, life was better in the Netherlands for the refugees than in their home countries. The overall result for the Dutch was enrichment of both the economy and the culture of the country.

ANGLO-DUTCH WARS

Inevitably, the successful trade and shipping interests of the Dutch came into conflict with those of the British. In 1651, during the Cromwell era, England passed the first of its **Navigation Acts**, requiring goods coming into the country to arrive in ships from the exporting country or in British vessels. The Navigation Acts led to three indecisive wars between the British and the Dutch, 1652–1674. During these **Anglo-Dutch Wars**, England annexed the Dutch colony of New Amsterdam, renaming it New York.

These conflicts, as well as Dutch defense against the designs of Louis XIV, who coveted his wealthy northern neighbor, were draining to the republic. Although the Dutch continued to trade worldwide, they did not develop a colonial empire, partly because few citizens were enthusiastic about emigrating to distant colonies.

However, the balance-of-power politics of William of Orange held together. European alliances checked the ambitions of Louis XIV, and the Dutch republic persevered. In 1689, William became King of England, which ended the conflict between the Dutch and the English and solidified opposition to the aggression of France. Nevertheless, by the 18th century, the vitality of the Dutch republic declined as the strength of England grew.

CHAPTER 9: THE SCIENTIFIC REVOLUTION

Certain epochs in the history of humankind may be termed cataclysmic—that is, world changing. The period we call the **scientific revolution** is one of those periods.

The innovative thinkers and experimenters of the 17th and 18th centuries changed people's view of the universe from a primarily religious view to a predominately secular one. Science came to be recognized as important work, and the scientific method of inquiry was defined. Instead of scattered individuals working in isolation, scientific societies and communities formed, and scientific ideas influenced practical human activity and social institutions. The term *modern* became tied to ideas of science, and the awareness and application of these ideas led to the Age of Enlightenment.

ASTRONOMY

Before the scientific revolution, the human concept of the universe drew from the Greeks (Aristotle in the fourth century BCE and **Ptolemy** in the second century CE). It was **geocentric**: The earth was seen as fixed and motionless. Around the earth, it was believed, were invisible moving **crystal spheres**, to which were attached the sun, moon, stars, and the five known planets.

Beyond the spheres was heaven. The spheres were considered pure, light, and good. Things made from the earth, such as soil and rocks, were called "dross" and were considered heavy, coarse, and bad. Such things tended to move *down*, while the purer things of the heavens seemed to be *up*.

In the 14th century, scholars at both Oxford and Paris had begun to question Ptolemaic theory. Interest in mathematics had also begun around that time. By the early 16th century, the Polish scholar **Nicholas Copernicus** (Latinized version of his name), who had studied in Italy, considered an old Greek idea—that the sun, not the earth, might be the center of the universe. The Ptolemaic system didn't fit Copernicus's observations (with the naked eye—he had no telescope).

Copernicus's work was ultimately published near his death in 1543. (Ironically, he dedicated it to the pope.) This new theory, called *On the Revolutions of the Heavenly Spheres*, was **heliocentric**, putting the sun—not the earth—at the center of the universe. It was the earth that moved, Copernicus claimed, not the stars, and the universe was much bigger than anyone had imagined.

Both Calvin and Luther immediately condemned Copernicus. The work was little known at first, however, and even when it was, it was regarded as mere theory, not fact. Therefore, the Roman Catholic Church, less inclined to literal interpretation of scripture, ignored Copernicus.

In the 1570s, two new phenomena appeared in the skies—a bright new star and a new comet— proving that the heavens and crystal spheres were not unchanging. One observer of these events was the Danish astronomer **Tycho Brahe**. Brahe knew little math and rejected Copernican theory. He believed that the planets revolved around the sun and the sun/planet system then revolved around the earth and its moon (thus, a geocentric concept). Brahe was supported by the King of Denmark and had an observatory but no telescope.

For 20 years, Brahe observed the night sky daily and kept meticulous records of what he saw. When his patron king died, he moved to Prague, where a young **Johannes Kepler** worked for him during what proved to be the last year of Brahe's life.

Upon Brahe's death, Kepler inherited his extensive data and, along with his own knowledge of math, developed his own theories. Influenced by an English publication in 1600 on magnetism, Kepler could prove mathematically by 1609 that the paths of planets were ellipses, not circles, and he knew that the speed of planets varied within their **elliptical orbits**. Ten years later, he established mathematical laws to show that the length of time of a planet's orbit varies proportionally with its distance from the sun; he had established a formulaic relationship between space and time.

Contemporary with Kepler was the Italian **Galileo Galilei**, a mathematics professor at the University of Padua. Galileo did experiments to study motion and acceleration by constructing an incline of grooved wood, rolling metal balls of various sizes down the groove, and measuring the time they took to reach the bottom. The result was the development of laws of uniform acceleration. Further experiments led to laws of motion.

Galileo read about the Dutch invention of the telescope and built himself one. With it, he saw four moons of Jupiter and Saturn's rings. He studied the moon, saw its mountains, and concluded that its surface was not smooth and perfect but uneven, like the earth's surface. He announced that the Milky Way was made up of clusters of stars.

Soon, Galileo was consulting in practical affairs with the makers of cannons, pumps, and navigation instruments, such as astrolabes and quadrants. He corresponded with Kepler and invited him to Padua, where he said they would laugh together at the theology professor who refused to look through the telescope. Galileo proceeded to criticize in print the ideas of Aristotle and Ptolemy and found himself on trial by the Church. He was forced to recant his statements in support of Copernican theory and was condemned to house arrest for the last four years of his life.

SCIENTIFIC METHOD

Galileo can be credited with advancing the scientific method of gaining new knowledge through experimentation. However, others before him had already begun to to think in those terms. The 16th-century French essayist **Michel de Montaigne** posed the question, "What do I know?" and answered, "Nothing."

Later, **Francis Bacon** in England and **René Descartes** in France (early 17th century) went beyond merely doubting information from the past; they taught ways to obtain knowledge reliably. By practicing these methods, humans could gain new and useful knowledge that could be applied to control nature, create useful inventions, and improve the standard of living.

In 1620, Bacon published Volume 1 of *Novum Organum* (he only got to a second volume before his death in 1626), in which he called for a new thinking based on observation. (Bacon's own experiments were limited, because he did not know math.)

According to Bacon, the path to knowledge was to do a great many hands-on investigations, and from the details of many examples, one might be able to draw conclusions. This **inductive reasoning**, or **empirical method**, proceeded from the concrete to the abstract. Bacon insisted that this method would produce more knowledge and that the knowledge would have more practical application. Thus, said Bacon, scientists should organize, cooperate, and specialize to "overcome necessities and miseries of humanity." What emerged was the idea of the possibility of progress.

Following Bacon, Descartes published *Discourse on Method* (1637), a work on the philosophy of thinking. Bacon had advised "washing the mind clear of opinions." Descartes, who had read Bacon, said one should start with a blank slate, doubting everything. He began with the knowledge of his own existence: *Cogito, ergo sum* ("I think; therefore, I am."). The idea was to break everything into as many parts as possible, then to begin with the simplest idea and move slowly to more difficult levels. Descartes divided everything into matter (the physical world) and mind (the spiritual world). Matter could be discovered and described mathematically— for instance, through laws of motion—and enable humans to understand and control their environment.

Still later, Kepler, Galileo, and Newton applied the thinking of Bacon and Descartes to their work. Each used the accumulation of mathematical data and details from numerous investigations to come to new understandings and establish various laws governing the universe. As Bacon had predicted, that knowledge proved reliable in practical applications.

NEWTON

Isaac Newton was born in England in the year that Galileo died. It was Newton who synthesized, or put together, Kepler's laws of motion for heavenly bodies and Galileo's laws of motion for things on earth. The result was the law of universal gravitation, the forces of attraction and repulsion between objects. Newton saw in Kepler's laws the concept that planets were pulled toward the sun by a force inversely proportional to their distance from it. The moon is bound to the earth in the same way; tides are proof.

Thus, Newton took the work of Descartes, Kepler, and Galileo and developed a synthesis of the laws of motion. After a period of intense study of physics, Newton published ***Principia Mathematica*** (1687)—*Mathematical Principles of Natural Philosophy*—a work on the laws of dynamics, motion, mechanics, and how things move in relation to each other. Newton's work proved that all motion, anywhere, could be timed and measured.

SUMMARY OF CONTRIBUTIONS TO ASTRONOMY

Nicholas Copernicus (Polish): Heliocentric theory

Tycho Brahe (Danish): 20 years of observation data

Johannes Kepler (Bohemian): Elliptical orbits of planets

Galileo Galilei (Italian): Laws of earthly motion; moons of Jupiter and Saturn, rings of Saturn; moon's surface

Isaac Newton (English): Synthesis of earlier work into universal laws of motion and gravity

MEDICINE

As in astronomy, knowledge of the human body until the 16th century was based on the work of **Galen**, a second-century contemporary of Ptolemy. Galen discussed four bodily "humors" (blood, phlegm, yellow bile, and black bile) and two types of blood ("bright" blood in arteries and "dark" blood in veins). For centuries, when people dissected a human cadaver (a practice condemned by the Church) and found things that didn't agree with Galen, they assumed themselves to be wrong.

In the 1500s, **Vesalius** (Flemish) became the founder of biological science. Vesalius dissected and studied cadavers and was the first to assemble a human skeleton. He published *On the Fabric of the Human Body* in 1543, the same year Copernicus published his book.

The Englishman **William Harvey**, after years of work in the laboratory using animal vivisection, published *On the Movement of the Heart and Blood* (1628), in which he accurately explained blood circulation. The invention of the microscope advanced knowledge almost immediately. With it, the Italian **Marcello Malpighi** confirmed Harvey's study and went on to discover blood corpuscles, spermatozoa, and bacteria, and he published drawings. A Dutchman, **Regnier de Graaf**, first described ovaries, again disproving Galen.

Despite the above discoveries, care of the sick remained primitive into the 18th century. Medical care was practiced not only by surgeons and physicians but also by apothecaries and faith healers. There was still widespread belief in demons and evil spirits. The sale of drugs was unregulated. Surgeons could amputate and cauterize, but without anesthesia, agony and shock often killed. There was no knowledge of germs or bacteria, so a simple wound could lead to infection and death. Physicians came mainly from the upper classes and tended to limit their treatment to people of means. Bleeding was still practiced throughout the 1700s at the onset of any illness. Hospitals for both the physically and mentally ill were places of horror.

The biggest medical advancement of the 1700s was the development of the smallpox inoculation by **Edward Jenner**, an English country doctor. Smallpox could be deadly; survivors were often left disfigured with scars.

In the early 1700s, the Turks had learned how to place under the skin of healthy people a tiny amount of matter from the sore of an infected person. The inoculated person would then develop a mild case of the disease, though about 1 in 50 died. By the late 1700s, Jenner made a related observation: For some reason, milkmaids did not get smallpox, though they often got the milder cowpox, which produced sores on their hands from sores on the cows' udders. Jenner concluded that it must be the cowpox sores that somehow protected the milkmaids. After 18 years of study and inoculating people with cowpox matter, Jenner published his findings in 1798. His results were soon replicated in Austria, and smallpox became the first disease conquered by inoculation.

SUMMARY OF ADVANCES IN MEDICINE

Vesalius (Flemish): Structure of the human body

Harvey (English): Blood circulation

Malpighi (Italian): Corpuscles, spermatozoa, bacteria

de Graaf (Dutch): Ovaries

Jenner (English): Smallpox inoculation

IMPACT OF THE SCIENTIFIC REVOLUTION ON EUROPEAN SOCIETY

It was in Newton's day that the first scientific societies came to be: the **Royal Society** in England (1662) and the **Royal Academy of Science** in France (1666). The Royal Society began with 100 men and doubled its membership within eight years. These organizations were granted recognition by the government and allowed exchanges of new ideas. They met, did research, and published their findings, which included more than mathematics and natural sciences. Generally, women were excluded (in accordance with the belief that they were less capable than men—though some female scientists worked on their own).

Bacon's prediction about the practical application of science came true. In navigation, Europeans could finally determine longitude and predict tides; the demand for better instruments was huge, and the world was better mapped than ever before. There was also a big market for Dutch optics in telescopes, binoculars, and microscopes. Governments seeking commercial and military advantage were interested in everything connected to weaponry and trajectories, which advanced with the application of calculus (developed by Newton). Improved firearms gave Europeans advantages worldwide. By the beginning of the 18th century, Europeans were on the path to developing the steam engine, which would revolutionize manufacturing and transportation.

Where did religion fit in the new world of scientific thought? Most scientific thinkers did not see a contradiction between religion and science, but there did develop a current of skepticism. **Edmund Halley**, a friend of Newton, said that the comet of 1682 was the same one that had been observed at regular intervals in the past, and he accurately predicted its return in 1757. A French Huguenot, **Pierre Bayle**, wrote about speculations on the comet, saying that there was no basis for much of human opinion. Bayle advised open-minded toleration, as did the Englishman **John Locke** in his *Letter on Toleration*.

The English justice system was influenced by the new emphasis on factual information. After 1650, hearsay evidence was disallowed, and no longer did more atrocious crimes require less evidence. After 1696, persons charged with felonies were entitled to legal counsel. The new sense of evidence also led to a decline in the belief in witchcraft.

Other sciences developed. One was paleography, the deciphering, reading, dating, and authentication of manuscripts. Some went so far as to apply the new knowledge of textual criticism to scripture, a practice that was condemned by the Church and by Louis XIV's government.

In 1690, John Locke's *Essay Concerning Human Understanding* offered the concept of the human mind as a **tabula rasa**, or blank slate. Locke rejected the idea of heredity, as well as the Church's teaching of original sin. He claimed that humans were influenced by what they were taught, by sensory influences. Therefore, it was possible, through education, to create a better society. Hence, European thought began to have a sense of social progress.

Another product of scientific reasoning was the concept of natural law, that there were inherent rights and wrongs that were not confined to any one people or belief system. Such ideas were universal, not made up by a person or group out of selfish motive. Such natural laws could be discovered through the application of reason, which led to the 18th-century conception of the human mind as rational, and the period was known as the Age of Reason.

UNIT TWO REVIEW QUESTIONS

1. One reason for the lack of religious art in the Netherlands was

    (A) the presence of many diverse groups, which made it difficult to please without offending.

    (B) that Dutch artists tended to be secular in their outlook.

    (C) that the Dutch Reformed Church was not an art patron and did not permit art in its churches.

    (D) that Dutch nobility commissioned only portraits.

    (E) that the Dutch merchant class was religious but did not patronize the arts.

2. Edward Jenner developed the smallpox inoculation

    (A) after observing Turkish results using "matter" from a sore of the disease.

    (B) after studying English milkmaids.

    (C) by using a Dutch microscope to isolate the bacteria.

    (D) after reading Bacon's discourse on scientific method.

    (E) after doing all the above.

3. All the following are policies pursued by Cardinal Richelieu in France EXCEPT

    (A) siding with the Catholic Habsburgs in the Thirty Years War.

    (B) revoking the Protestant military privileges of the Edict of Nantes.

    (C) putting political obligation above his duties to the Church.

    (D) advising Marie de Medici while her son Louis XIII was a minor.

    (E) dividing France into districts and governing through *intendants*.

4. Above all, Peter the Great of Russia desired

    (A) a strong heir to follow in his footsteps.

    (B) a progressive, educated nobility.

    (C) a moderate church with an educated clergy.

    (D) the development of capitalistic enterprise, especially in mining and textile manufacturing.

    (E) a state and military equal to those of the West.

5. At the end of the War of Spanish Succession, the Spanish Netherlands

    (A) became an independent nation.

    (B) remained the possession of Spain.

    (C) passed to Austria.

    (D) became a French property.

    (E) was joined to the Dutch republic.

6. John Locke believed that

    (A) heredity and environment shaped human development.

    (B) heredity alone determined people's outcome.

    (C) environment and experience molded humans.

    (D) it was not possible to make humanity better.

    (E) education played only a minor role in human growth.

7. The Dutch were successful in agriculture, primarily in the production of

    (A) grains.

    (B) sheep for wool and flax.

    (C) flowers for perfume production.

    (D) butter and cheese.

    (E) fresh fruits and vegetables.

8. The Hohenzollerns of the early 17th and 18th century Brandenburg-Prussia expanded holdings through

    (A) the Thirty Years War.
    (B) marriage and inheritance.
    (C) fighting the Habsburgs.
    (D) confiscating Church property.
    (E) all of the above.

9. One difficulty the Habsburgs of Austria had to face that Western Europe did not have to address was

    (A) a multitude of ethnic minorities.
    (B) seizure of the capital, Vienna, by the Turks.
    (C) strong influence of the Catholic Church.
    (D) a growing, demanding middle class.
    (E) the threat of France as a powerful neighbor.

10. Absolute rule included all these aspects EXCEPT

    (A) control of religion.
    (B) control of the military.
    (C) control of taxes and other forms of revenue.
    (D) domination of artistic expression.
    (E) unlimited and arbitrary control over subjects.

11. The major difference between Tycho Brahe and Johannes Kepler was that

    (A) Kepler corresponded with Galileo.
    (B) Kepler used a telescope, while Brahe did not.
    (C) Kepler used mathematics, while Brahe did not.
    (D) Kepler accepted Copernican theory, while Brahe did not.
    (E) Kepler did all the above, while Brahe did not.

12. A result of the general religious toleration in the Netherlands was

    (A) much public disagreement over religious issues.
    (B) a diverse population that enriched the culture.
    (C) total equality for Jews.
    (D) exclusion of Jews and gypsies.
    (E) censorship of the press.

13. A similarity between Louis XIV of France and Peter the Great of Russia was that both

    (A) placed laymen at the head of the Church to control religion better.
    (B) appointed men to civil and military positions based on ability.
    (C) were fascinated with ships and sailing.
    (D) created a new seat of government and required the nobility to be present.
    (E) spent almost their entire reigns in one long war.

14. Poland fell apart for all these reasons EXCEPT

    (A) a long line of Polish kings wasted the nation's resources.
    (B) the king had no power to act.
    (C) the Poles couldn't agree on a Polish monarch, so foreigners often ruled, the result of meddling and intrigue.
    (D) any member of the Polish diet could get the body dismissed.
    (E) the king had no army.

15. The Roman Catholic Church was interested in having an accurate calendar in order to

    (A) celebrate the birth of Christ accurately.
    (B) calculate the age of the world.
    (C) establish the date for Easter.
    (D) have the solstices fall on the correct days.
    (E) know when the Christian year began.

16. Which of the following statements is TRUE of Europe before the scientific revolution?

    (A) Surgeons could amputate limbs and cauterize blood vessels.

    (B) Educated people generally did not believe in witchcraft.

    (C) The Church encouraged dissection of cadavers to obtain more knowledge of the human body.

    (D) Comets were understood in a secular manner.

    (E) The sun was considered the center of the universe.

17. Galileo got into trouble with the Roman Catholic Church because he

    (A) promoted Copernican theory.

    (B) used a telescope.

    (C) talked about the speeds of falling objects.

    (D) said the moon's surface was similar to the earth's.

    (E) argued points of scripture with a Church cardinal.

18. A result of William and Mary's acceptance of the English monarchy was

    (A) toleration of Catholics in England.

    (B) England's taking the colony of New Amsterdam.

    (C) England's opposing the Grand Alliance against Louis XIV.

    (D) restoration of the monarchy as superior to Parliament.

    (E) an easing of tensions between the English and the Dutch.

19. A Hohenzollern assumed the title of King of Prussia as a result of

    (A) the death of the last family heir in Prussia.

    (B) governing without the Estates during the Thirty Years War.

    (C) supplying troops to the Holy Roman Empire during the War of Spanish Succession.

    (D) an agreement with Austria over Poland.

    (E) a hope to keep Russia from expanding westward.

20. Eastern Europe differed from Western Europe in the 1600s in that

    (A) Eastern Europe had few towns of any size.

    (B) most of the population of Eastern Europe were serfs, bound to the large estates.

    (C) the landed aristocracy of the East were very powerful.

    (D) there was little to no middle class in the East.

    (E) all the social conditions above were true.

For the following questions, write an essay that

- has a relevant thesis;

- addresses all parts of the question;

- supports a thesis with specific evidence; and

- is well organized.

Plan your essays and write them on your own paper.

1. Describe some of the factors that stood in the way of Peter the Great's modernizing Russia at the turn of the 18th century.

2. Discuss ways that the 17th-century Dutch Republic differed from its neighbors, telling how these differences contributed to the country's success.

_____

_____

_____

_____

_____

_____

_____

_____

_____

_____

_____

_____

_____

_____

_____

ANSWERS AND EXPLANATIONS

1. C

In the Netherlands, the arts were supported primarily by the wealthy burghers (merchants), who commissioned work for their homes and businesses. Nobility existed but tended to be uninterested in art. The majority religion was the Dutch Reformed Church, which followed the Calvinistic trend of eliminating art from its churches.

2. B

Smallpox is caused by a virus, which Jenner could not have seen under a microscope. He must have known about the Turkish experiments, but he did not go to Turkey to see them. He did, however, study English milkmaids for nearly 20 years, who contracted the mild disease cowpox, and he realized that they were not susceptible to smallpox.

3. A

Even though Richelieu was a cardinal, he put his clerical duties in second place, behind politics, (C). As part of his attempts to centralize government and increase the monarchy's power, he did (B), (D), and (E). However, on the international scene, his policy was always to oppose the powerful Habsburgs of Austria. During the Thirty Years War, he allied France with Protestant states.

4. E

In his attempt to modernize Russia, Peter the Great did (A), (B), (C), and (D). However, his overall purpose was (E): He wanted to strengthen Russia to the point that it could compete with the more advanced nations of the West. His travels abroad had shown Peter how backward his nation was.

5. C

Spain lost the Southern Netherlands in 1713. Although France had tried to take and to keep it during the war, it was now given to Austria. This pleased the British because the Austrians were too far away to build strength there. England has always preferred neutral or friendly powers to be across the Channel.

6. C

Disregarding any influence from heredity, (A and B), Locke claimed that each person was born with a "blank slate" (his tabula rasa), which would be written upon by experience and environment. Thus, it was crucial to educate people to make them better; answers (D) and (E) are then false.

7. D

In agriculture, the Dutch excelled in the production of flower bulbs, especially tulips (not a choice here), and dairy products, such as butter and cheese, which could be transported to increasingly distant markets.

8. B

Although the early Hohenzollern kings took great pride in building up their military, they avoided risking their soldiers in war, (A and C). Their holdings were acquired mainly through inheritance (as when the Prussian side of the family died out and the Elector of Brandenburg inherited Prussia). Gradually, the Hohenzollerns filled in the gaps between the two states.

9. A

Austria always had the problem of dealing with a diverse population, which contained such minorities as Serbs, Croatians, and Slovaks, each with its own language and culture. Answer (B) is not acceptable because the Turks never actually captured Vienna, though they did threaten it. The middle class, (D), was neither large nor pushy. Austrian government was pressured by the Catholic Church, but so was France's, (C), and *all* nations surrounding

France found themselves threatened by French ambitions, (E).

10. E

Absolute monarchs attempted to control all the areas mentioned in (A), (B), (C), and (D). However, absolute rule could not be arbitrary—that is, rulers could not do anything they wished, solely because they wished it. Rulers had to bow to tradition, customs, and expectations. In some countries absolute power was also checked by legislative institutions (parliaments, estates, diets, etc.) and/or a court system.

11. E

Brahe did not believe in Copernican theory, use a telescope, or rely on math; his successor Kepler did. Kepler also was a contemporary of Galileo, and the two corresponded. Thus, all the answers are true.

12. B

Dutch culture (and the economy as well) was bolstered by immigrants, who were generally accepted and even welcomed. Jews did not have total equality, (C)—for example, they were not allowed to join guilds. However, they had most other rights; only gypsies were excluded, (D). The Dutch practiced the least amount of censorship in Europe, (E), and people from other countries often published in the Netherlands.

13. D

Louis XIV demanded that French nobility reside at Versailles for part of the year (where he could watch them), and Peter the Great required Russian nobility to build stone houses in St. Petersburg and live there part-time, for the same reason. Answers (A), (B), (C), and (E) are true of Peter only. Louis fought a number of wars, but they were different wars, separated by brief intervals of peace, (E); Russia

fought Sweden in the Great Northern War for most of Peter's reign.

14. A

The Polish king's position was one of great weakness. He possessed no resources to waste and no power or military through which he could act, (B and E). Any member of the diet could have it dismissed by using his veto power, (D), and foreign meddling meant that the person chosen to rule was frequently not a Pole, (C).

15. C

Easter is a "moveable feast." It falls on the first Sunday after the date of the first full moon that occurs on or after March 21, spring equinox. To calculate it correctly, the Church needed March 21 to be accurate, and it wasn't before the Gregorian calendar was established in 1582.

16. A

Before the scientific revolution, almost everyone, including Luther and Calvin, believed in witchcraft, (B), and comets were considered signs from God, (D). Before Copernicus's ideas were accepted, a stationary earth was thought to be the center of the universe, (E). The Church condemned dissections of cadavers, (C), for centuries. Surgeons did amputate and cauterize but without anesthesia and with no knowledge of sanitation—thus, patients often died.

17. A

Galileo was charged with advocating Copernican theory, which the Church had condemned. Though he recanted, he was still punished with house arrest. Although the Church disapproved of telescopes, (B), and Galileo's ideas about the moon, (D), these behaviors were not chargeable offenses.

18. E

The ascension of William and Mary to the English throne assured a Protestant monarchy and improved relations between the British and Dutch, following conflict over the Navigation Acts. The new monarchs had to sign the Bill of Rights, which formally recognized Parliament's superiority over the monarchy, (D). England had taken New Amsterdam, (B), earlier, during the fighting over the Navigation Acts. William's becoming King of England cemented England's place among nations of the Grand Alliance against Louis XIV, (C).

19. C

The title "King *in* Prussia" was granted to the Hohenzollern Frederick III by the Holy Roman Emperor in 1701 in exchange for Prussian troops. It was then an easy transition to "King *of* Prussia." Frederick's predecessor, Frederick William (the Great Elector), had begun to build Hohenzollern power by operating without the Estates during the Thirty Years War, (B).

20. E

All choices here are true. Eastern Europe was still somewhat feudal in the 1600s—a wealthy aristocracy owned the land, and peasants were still bound to the soil as serfs. There were few towns, and the middle class was small and insignificant.

SAMPLE FREE-RESPONSE ESSAYS

1. Describe some of the factors that stood in the way of Peter the Great's modernizing Russia at the turn of the 18th century.

Peter the Great became tsar of Russia with the intention of making it a more modern nation that could compete with the nations of Western Europe. Peter had made two trips to Western Europe, so he was painfully aware of how far behind the West his nation was. Making Russia "modern" was not an easy task because of the size of the country, its social and economic structure, and its isolation.

Russia was a giant country that spanned two continents. Its population varied greatly from region to region, and most lived rurally, with little contact beyond their estate or village. The majority of the people were serfs, bound to the land and illiterate. They could be bought and sold, and they lived at the mercy of the landlords, who had total control over their peasants. There was no court system to hear grievances. Transportation remained a huge problem, and Russia had no year-round seaports. The middle class was so tiny that it exerted little influence. Cities were few in number, small, and isolated, and even centers of population had few public or private institutions similar to those of the West—hospitals, workshops, offices, or manufacturing facilities.

Peter faced possible revolt from two sources—the peasants and the "streltsi," a sort of noble "old guard" of Moscow. Peter left the peasants under the control of their landlords, but he tried to eliminate the "streltsi." He totally reorganized the army, training soldiers with foreign officers and supplying with them with Western weapons and Western-style uniforms. Those who performed well in the army or civil service were advanced in rank without regard to social background. (Actually, Peter strengthened serfdom by permitting the sale of serfs without land to mines or manufacturing facilities in the towns.)

Part of Peter's reorganization for better control included a firmer handle on the Orthodox Church. He placed at the head of its governing body, the Holy Synod, a lay person whom he appointed, the Procurator. Thus, Peter kept firm control on the Church. One religious element in Russia was the Old Believers, fundamentalists who had rebelled against earlier Church reform. Peter had no patience with Old Believers and taxed them for the privilege of belonging to the sect. He also ordered them and the rest of his court to cut their beards, which he considered signs of backwardness.

To combat ignorance, Peter ordered the upper class to educate their sons, even abroad. He simplified the alphabet and forced the court to learn and practice polite manners similar to those of the West. He overhauled the organization of the government by dividing the country into 10 districts to be administered by agents of the tsar.

Peter certainly opened the door to the West and made Russia more involved in European affairs. He also fought an uphill battle at home because of the vast ignorance and turbulence of the Russian people. Peter brought changes to the lives and outlooks of the nobility, but the peasants' lives remained much the same.

2. Discuss ways that the 17th-century Dutch Republic differed from its neighbors, telling how these differences contributed to the country's success.

Although the Dutch Republic was quite small among European nations (made up of only seven small provinces), it was one of the most successful of the 17th century. Some have estimated that it possessed the highest standard living in the world at that time.

The Dutch took the Protestant work ethic to heart. They were ambitious and hardworking; they lived comfortably but not extravagantly; their Calvinist faith forbade luxury. Because they were a seafaring nation, they had access to many imports, including foodstuffs not common elsewhere. The Dutch had begun their sailing by fishing. By the 1600s, they owned thousands of ships and sailed globally, with colonies in North America, South Africa, and the East Indies. With their ships and trade, the Dutch made money and maintained an outstanding system of banking and finance. Credit was available, and the Dutch gold coin, the florin, was widely trusted as a unit of international exchange.

At home, the Dutch had developed agriculture, specializing in dairy farming. They made butter and cheese, which could be exported, and they also became experts in tulip cultivation. Another specialty of the Dutch was lens grinding, which led to the manufacture of eye glasses, telescopes, and microscopes, which contributed to the scientific revolution of the 17th century.

The Dutch were remarkable in two other major ways. One was their lack of centralized government. There was a national legislature of sorts, an estates general, but not a central governing figure. Each province chose a leader called a <u>stadholder</u>, and provinces sometimes elected the same person. The real power in the country, however, was the prosperous merchant class.

The second major difference between the Dutch and the rest of Europe was their policy of religious toleration, which no other country practiced at that time. Because of it, all manner of refugees, from French Huguenots to English Catholics to Portuguese Jews, came here. The Dutch even offered incentives to some groups. The immigrants contributed to both the economic and cultural life of the county. Because of the diversity, there was little censorship. Writers from other nations sometimes sought publication in the Netherlands because of the lack of censorship.

By the end of the 17th century, the strength and uniqueness of the Dutch Republic began to decline for a variety of reasons. However, for almost a century, it must have been the ideal place to live and work in Europe.

CHAPTER 10: **THE ENLIGHTENMENT**

IMPACT OF THE SCIENTIFIC REVOLUTION

Above all, the scientific revolution emphasized a belief in reason, observation, and analysis. Because mathematical laws had been discovered and those laws controlled so much of the universe, thinkers concluded that there must be **natural law** that applied to everything—something inherent in the universe that was true for all people in all places and times. How did one discover such truth? The answer was through reason.

Such faith in reason led to a belief in progress, an idea that life for humanity could improve with each generation. Education was a key part of such a belief. If, as John Locke argued, the human was born with a "blank slate" to be written upon, how a person developed depended upon his surroundings and experiences in the world. It was, therefore, possible to create "better" human beings. It followed, then, that people must be free to think and that there must be freedom of expression and of the press.

Faith in reason also tended to shun religion as superstition. God was seen as existing but not in a very close or personal way. This became the age of **deism**, a religious view that explained God as the mastermind and creator of the universe (sometimes called the "watchmaker"). The theory was that God set the universe in motion to operate by natural laws but was thereafter not personally involved in human affairs.

ENLIGHTENMENT PHILOSOPHY

The Age of Reason, or the Enlightenment, was defined by a belief in progress based on education and tolerance, ideas that have remained beliefs in the modern world. People felt that conditions would improve with each generation and that these changes for the better would affect everyone. Thinkers and writers popularized the ideas of leading figures of the previous century: Bacon, Descartes, Bayle, Spinoza, and especially Locke and Newton. Voltaire, for example, made Newton known to the French; his close friend, Madame du Chatulet, translated Newton's work into French.

Enlightenment thinkers believed that principles of morality—ideas of what is right or wrong—were not limited to one religion. Diderot (French) talked about the people of Tahiti, who had established a national social order, untouched by Christianity. Deist writers, like Voltaire, demanded freedom of religion and an end to the extreme degree of power that the French Church held over government.

The reading public had greatly expanded. Newspapers, magazines, **coffee houses**, and reading rooms were popular. New readers demanded and appreciated wit; they wanted writing that was interesting and clear. The middle class was growing in number and was more educated.

All countries practiced censorship (though to a minor degree in England and the Netherlands). In France, the censorship process was complicated by pressures from the Church, the Parlement of Paris, the royal government, and the printers' guilds. To get around laws against criticizing the Church or the state, French writers could publish in England or the Dutch Republic, or they could write in doublespeak. They wrote, for instance, about the Polynesians, when everyone knew the topic was the French. Style became very important for an increasingly sophisticated reading public.

Another way that ideas spread was through the **salons**. These were regularly scheduled social gatherings in the homes of women of the upper middle class or nobility (such as Madame de Geoffrin), where guests conversed with artists, writers, scientists, and sometimes political figures. In addition to the salons as a medium for the spread of ideas, there was the organization of the **Freemasons**, which began in England and spread to the Continent. The Masonic lodges were supposed to be secret organizations (an idea that opposed enlightened thought). They drew people from all social classes and promoted a faith in progress and toleration.

Enlightenment thought focused on reason, education, progress, individual freedom, toleration, and reform. Such ideas led eventually to the two great revolutions of the 18th century in the British North American colonies and in France.

EXCEPTIONS TO ENLIGHTENMENT THOUGHT

Faith in reason tended to reject religion, as evidenced by the deists. Certainly, not everyone in the 18th century was a deist; in fact, many expressed religious enthusiasm. In music, there were the hymns of the Englishman Isaac Watts (e.g., "Joy to the World" and "O God, Our Help in Ages Past"), Handel's *Messiah*, and the religious compositions of Johann Sebastian Bach.

In the German states, a branch of evangelical Lutheranism called **pietism** developed. It emphasized the inner experience of ordinary people, seeking something they called an "inner light."

Such experience affected the emotions, rather than reason. Groups met outside traditional Lutheran services for Bible reading and discussion. After a brief period of popularity, however, the movement faded, and Lutheranism remained the state religion of the northern German states.

In England, a number of Protestant groups existed outside the established Church of England (Quakers, Presbyterians, Unitarians, etc.). All English dissenters, including Catholics, faced discrimination. They were barred from attending the universities and from holding high public office. A new movement developed in the 1700s around the person of **John Wesley**, an Anglican priest. After a conversion experience, Wesley spread the word of joy and salvation to the poor. He sought out coal miners and prisoners and preached in the open fields. With his brother Charles (who wrote hymns), Wesley came to the American colonies, where he carried out a revivalist movement. He stressed public confession of sins (which offended some of the more educated classes), work, and self-discipline; he also condemned dancing, drinking, and gambling. Wesley never left the Anglican Communion, but his followers went on to found the Methodists.

Another English evangelist of the same period was George Whitfield, who also came to the colonies and preached in the open air. There were also American counterparts to the evangelical movement such as Jonathan Edwards in New England. This movement, in England and the colonies in North America, was called the **Great Awakening**. It lasted about 20 years and was at its height around 1740. The established churches—Lutheran, Catholic, Anglican—frowned upon these revivalist movements as competition.

THE *PHILOSOPHES*

The word *philosophe* is French for philosopher, but except for a few of the most important thinkers/writers of the 18th century, most *philosophes* were not philosophers. In general, they were reformers, not revolutionaries; they were popularizers of the ideas of the scientific revolution.

Some historians call the greatest achievement of the Enlightenment the multivolume French *Encyclopedia*. (Its full name was *Encyclopedia; the Rational Dictionary of the Sciences, the Arts, and the Crafts*.) Produced by **Denis Diderot** and **Jean d'Alembert**, the volumes were published over a 20-year period in the middle of the 18th century. The complete work contained hundreds of thousands of articles by a tremendous variety of writers, as well as thousands of illustrations and pieces of art. The ambition was to classify all knowledge from around the world and to make it available to everyone. The authors ranged from the great names, such as Voltaire, to simple craftsmen writing about their tools. Some articles spoke out against monarchy and repressive government (writing by Rousseau, for instance).

Publishing the *Encyclopedia* presented many challenges. Censorship was a constant problem; publishers sometimes altered articles to keep the authorities happy. After the first volume, the French government temporarily banned it, and the pope placed it on the Index of Forbidden

Books. At one point, an attempted assassination of Louis XV was blamed on the *Encyclopedia*; for a while, the publication of Volume 7 was halted, and Diderot was put in jail. The 17 volumes were completed in 1772 and sold across the Continent and even in North America.

Not all *philosophes* were French, but three Frenchmen ranked as the greatest and most influential:

1. **Baron de Montesquieu** came from the landed aristocracy. A member of the parlement of Bordeaux, Montesquieu was in favor of a resurgence of the nobility. He believed in the importance of the upper class and its ability to share ruling power. Montesquieu's ***The Spirit of Laws*** (1748) was a comparative study of republics, monarchies, and despotic societies. Montesquieu said that different types of governments were suited to different climates, history, geography, and customs. In France, he admired the parlements, the 13 district courts that claimed the right to rule on the constitutionality of laws; Montesquieu saw this institution as a defense against the powers of the king and royal absolutism. Especially, he admired the English balance of power among the king, Parliament, and an independent court system.

> Framers of the U.S. Constitution would be influenced by Montesquieu's balance of power ideas.

2. **Voltaire** was the pen name of **Francois Marie Arouet**, who was from the middle class. As a young man, Voltaire went to prison for criticizing the government, and he fled later to exile in England after insulting a nobleman. All his life, Voltaire worked for individual liberty and equality before the law. He admired English religious liberty and freedom of the press. Voltaire differed from Montesquieu in regard to the parlements, seeing them as operating in the narrow, selfish interests of the nobility. Instead, he saw hope in enlightened rulers who worked for the interests of the people (against the selfish interests of the nobility). He greatly admired Frederick the Great and, for a while, lived at his court.

   Generally, Voltaire's opinion of the institution of the Church was negative. He despised its bigotry, intolerance, superstition, and power. (His famous expression was "Ecrasez l'infame!" or "Crush the infamous thing!") However, Voltaire saw religion in general as something good because it gave people hope and inspired better behavior. Although he believed strongly in freedom of thought and religion, he was not a democratic thinker; he had a low opinion of the masses. Voltaire admired enlightened rulers who practiced religious toleration and encouraged the arts and sciences.

3. **Jean Jacques Rousseau** was born a Swiss peasant. Rousseau came to France as a teenager, supporting himself by working odd jobs. He was not recognized as a writer until age 40. A strange and paranoid man, Rousseau is described by some historians as arrogant and

self-righteous. He began to achieve fame after winning an essay contest that debated the question of whether science had strengthened or weakened morality. Rousseau's argument was that modern society was corrupt and artificial and that primitive or "natural" man was the ideal, essentially good human beings. In particular, he admired Native Americans (though, of course, he had never seen one).

Rousseau was perhaps more a harbinger of the romantic age to come in the early 19th century; he attacked reason as a delusion. The finest human traits, he argued, were such things as kindness and honesty, and he advocated sympathy, intuition, and conscience. Regarding politics, he spoke vaguely about republican government of small states (like his native Geneva), but he didn't totally trust democracy. Though he was personally religious, he condemned organized religion, both Catholic and Protestant.

Rousseau's *Social Contract* (1762) saw government as an agreement among people. He defined a "general will" as the combination of individual wills. Rousseau was less concerned about the actual mechanisms of government, so long as they honored the general will of the people. Kings or elected officials were merely delegates of that sovereign, sacred general will. Rousseau's ideal state was one in which all people felt a sense of membership (possibly because he always felt himself an outsider).

Not many people read *Social Contract* during Rousseau's lifetime, however. His best sellers were two novels, *Emile* and *Nouvelle Heloise*. *Emile* was about the one-on-one education of Emile by his tutor, Jean Jacques. Everything was taught through hands-on experience, such as learning about plants by growing, handling, and dissecting them. Emile grew up to marry Sophie, who had been given a more intellectual education than was commonly thought appropriate for women at that time.

Voltaire made fun of Rousseau's pursuit of the primitive, but Rousseau's thinking had a big influence. His stirring words, "Men are born free, yet everywhere they are in chains," became a proverb of the French Revolution a few years later. His idea of government as a contract recalled the earlier ideas of Locke and Hobbes, but the difference was Rousseau's idea of an agreement among people.

Others, outside of France, espoused ideas similar to those of the French writers. Frederick II of Prussia and Catherine of Russia were writers (Catherine studied law, and Frederick composed music), and both hosted literary and scientific men. Maria Theresa of Austria was too religious to be classified as a *philosophe*, but her son Joseph was the ultimate *philosophe*. In Scotland, the philosopher David Hume wrote from a point of view similar to that of the French thinkers, and the economist Adam Smith applied enlightenment ideas to manufacturing and trade. The English writer **Edward Gibbon**, in his ***Decline and Fall of the Roman Empire***, went so far as to blame the Christians for the collapse of Rome, saying that they diverted public attention to the hereafter, rather than to the problems of the day. In Italy, the Marquis di Beccaria wrote about legal reform. (These people and others are discussed in the next two sections.)

IMPACT OF THE ENLIGHTENMENT ON EUROPEAN SOCIETY

In France, the search to discover the laws of nature led to questions about laws to govern the economy. The result was a group of thinkers known as the **physiocrats**—called economists by their critics. Among the physiocrats were men in high government positions, such as Quesnay, who was physician to Louis XV, and Turgot, minister to Louis XVI.

The physiocrats opposed guild regulations and price controls, advocating instead a policy of laissez-faire. **Laissez-faire** meant letting the economy move freely in its own way, without tariffs or other regulatory controls. They also pushed for much-needed fiscal and tax reform in France. The physiocrats favored strong government that could overcome existing trade obstructions and help new industry get started. In Germany, the **cameralists** pushed for economic changes similar to those advocated by the physiocrats.

In England, **Adam Smith**, a philosophy professor at the University of Glasgow, published *Wealth of Nations* (1776). Like the physiocrats, Smith said that national wealth could be increased by the removal of barriers. He opposed mercantilism, which insisted on colonies being for the benefit of the mother country. Smith suggested that England could lose her American colonies without losing trade. The purpose of government, according to Smith, was to guarantee peace, security, and justice so that economic activities could flourish. Smith wanted the government uninvolved in manufacturing and trade; these activities were best left to supply and demand and private initiative. Both Smith and the physiocrats measured a nation's wealth by its production of goods, not in its stocks of bullion (a mercantilist principle). However, the physiocrats pointed to the land/soil as the source of wealth, which made their view more agrarian, while Smith claimed a nation's wealth was measured by the labor of its people.

Much of the Enlightenment stemmed from France, and French was the international language, but the French brought English ideas to the Continent. One example was the rapid translation and spread of Smith's *Wealth of Nations*.

In the area of legal reform, the Italian nobleman **Marquis di Becarria** read the French *philosophes*, and in 1764, he published ***On Crimes and Punishments***. Becarria believed the state had to protect its citizens, including those accused of crimes. He argued for standard laws controlling the punishment of crimes, based on equality before the law (which did not exist at the time). Becarria's position that a person was innocent until proven guilty later became a basic concept of Western law. Becarria said "sin" should not be related to crime and that opposition to religion was not a crime. A crime's seriousness, he said, should be based on its degree of damage to society.

Condemning capital punishment, except for crimes that threatened the state, Becarria was appalled by crowds at executions, and he spoke out against the use of torture. His ideas influenced some of his contemporaries, who banned torture and even execution.

ENLIGHTENED DESPOTISM: AUSTRIA, PRUSSIA, AND RUSSIA

Enlightened despotism might be called enlightened absolutism because it grew out of earlier forms of absolutism. Though it manifested itself in different ways with different rulers, there were certain trends. One was that enlightened despotism came from a secular basis. No enlightened despot claimed to rule by divine right, and the tendency was toward religious toleration. Some monarchs restricted the Church in various ways, such as expelling the Jesuits or closing convents and monasteries.

Enlightened despots claimed their power for the good of their people. They sponsored reforms in the direction of the modern—that is, codification of laws, innovations in agriculture, broadening of education, and efficiency in government. Such rulers wanted rapid results and tended to move arbitrarily, ignoring customary restraints of the past, much of which they disregarded as feudal or old-fashioned.

Ironically, in the seat of enlightenment thought, France, enlightened despotism had the least success. Louis XV had a long rule, 1715–1774, but he was not a strong monarch, too fearful of controversy to push issues. The French government's biggest problem was its lack of money. The tax system was extremely uneven and corrupt; only the peasants paid significant taxes. Louis's unsuccessful attempts at reform are discussed in Chapter 12; his failures became major causes for the French Revolution.

Enlightened despotism was also not practiced in 18th-century England. When William III died in 1702 (Mary had died in 1694), the throne passed to the last Protestant Stuart, Mary's sister Anne, who ruled until 1714. At Anne's death, the crown went to the nearest Protestant royal relative, the German George I of **Hanover**. Both George I and his son George II were more German than English, and their lack of identity or involvement with English government allowed Parliament to grow in power and control over English affairs. George III was the first Hanover to be truly English, but by his ascendancy in 1760, Parliament was firmly in control of the government of Britain.

In three European nations, however, enlightened despotism controlled royal policy for a number of years. In the Austrian Empire, **Maria Theresa** became queen in 1740 and immediately had to fight for her kingdom in the War of Austrian Succession (Chapter 11). The war revealed the weakness of this hodgepodge kingdom, but Maria Theresa used it to consolidate her people and centralize royal power from Vienna. She employed able advisors, especially Kaunitz, who helped her impose royal authority over Austria and Bohemia. The fractious Magyars of Hungary were left alone, but Bohemia lost its constitutional charter, and local diets could now only consent to taxes imposed by the central government.

Local authority was removed from the nobility and given to professional salaried employees of the state. Despite her personal religious faith, Maria Theresa expelled the Jesuits. She established a trade union and limited the power of guild monopolies, and the economy prospered, particularly in Bohemia. As for the institution of serfdom, Maria Theresa reduced the number of days that serfs were obligated to work for landlords and passed laws to protect them from abuse (though it is questionable to what degree these new regulations were enforced).

During the last 15 years of her reign, Maria Theresa shared power with her son **Joseph II**, who grew increasingly impatient with what he considered his mother's slow, cautious ways. After her death in 1780, Joseph ruled alone for 10 years as the epitome of enlightened despotism, passing over 10,000 laws. Joseph acted quickly and arbitrarily. He totally abolished serfdom and installed equal taxes and equal justice. Landlords could no longer administer justice to their serfs. Punishments for crime were made less severe, and capital punishment was abolished.

Toleration was granted to all religions, including the Jews, who were given total civil rights (very unusual at the time). Joseph encouraged what he saw as good in Catholicism and did away with what he viewed as wasteful. Though he established many churches, he also reduced the number of religious holidays and closed one-third of the convents and monasteries, keeping the ones who educated youth or performed charity. With money from confiscated church property, Joseph supported hospitals, which began Vienna's reputation as a center of medicine. To improve education, the government provided teachers and texts for about one-quarter of Austria's children, a high percentage for the time.

While Maria Theresa had tiptoed around the contentious Magyars of Hungary, Joseph tried to force his programs on everyone. He insisted that all government business be conducted in German, which minority groups resented. The peasants disapproved of what they perceived as a lack of reverence for religion. Joseph tried unsuccessfully to establish an overseas trading company, similar to his grandfather's failed Ostend company. Joseph died in 1790 at age 49, disillusioned and disappointed, appreciated by neither nobility nor peasants. He had not been able to delegate and had trained no successor. The Austrian middle class was small and not ambitious. Many of Joseph's reforms were repealed immediately, but some lasted.

Joseph's successor was his brother **Leopold**, who had ruled in Tuscany (Italy) and done well there. (Leopold had studied the constitutions of Virginia and the United States.) He ignored the pleas of his sister Marie Antoinette in France in the early days of the Revolution. Austrian nobility did not get back all its power in the diets, which Joseph had taken away, and the peasants kept the right to move, marry, and choose an occupation. Leopold died after only two years as King of Austria, and his son Francis II was not as wise as his father; Austria was soon at war with revolutionary France.

SUMMARY OF ENLIGHTENED DESPOTISM IN AUSTRIA

Maria Theresa	Joseph
Consolidation of central authority	Fast, arbitrary action
Trade union	Abolition of serfdom
Salaried government employees	Equal justice and taxes
Limitations on guilds	Elimination of capital punishment
Reduction in obligations of serfs	Religious toleration
Expulsion of Jesuits	Reduction in number of religious houses
	Civil rights for Jews
	Government-sponsored schools

Frederick II (later called "the Great") became King of Prussia at the same time that Maria Theresa inherited Austria (1740). His first move was to violate the Pragmatic Sanction and take Silesia from Austria (discussed in Chapter 11). Frederick ruled another 23 years after the Seven Years War. He was an enlightened despot primarily because of his personal study and intellect. Having corresponded with Voltaire before becoming king, Frederick had Voltaire reside at his court at Potsdam for two years. Even though an argument terminated the relationship, Voltaire still admired Frederick as the ideal ruler. He read, loved the arts, played the flute, and wrote music.

Calling himself "first servant of the state," Frederick also applied a number of enlightenment practices to government. He established religious toleration for all except Jews. He built a large Catholic church in Berlin, though Prussia was predominantly Lutheran. Frederick improved education and simplified the laws, eliminating torture and creating appellate courts. He improved agriculture by giving peasants tools, stock, and seeds after the Seven Years War. The government drained swamps and introduced new crops, such as clover (a nitrogen-fixing plant) and potatoes. Frederick attempted to foster modern technological improvements, such as the iron plow.

Frederick's government encouraged manufacturing, especially in textiles and metals (to benefit the army). Trying to force the country to be self-sufficient, he heavily taxed imports, such as coffee, and tried unsuccessfully to make Prussia grow its own tobacco. Although Frederick abolished serfdom on his own estates, he didn't tamper with the social system at large. He wanted to keep the landed aristocrats, the Junkers, as officers and the peasants as soldiers; thus, education for peasants was limited to basic reading and writing. These policies, of course, were not enlightened. Frederick also preferred that his Junker officers not marry; he disliked paying widows' pensions. Like Joseph of Austria, Frederick trained no successors. Twenty years after Frederick's death, Napoleon's army easily conquered the country.

SUMMARY OF ENLIGHTENED DESPOTISM IN PRUSSIA

Frederick II

Personal habits and action—music; freedom for own serfs

Religious toleration (except for Jews)

Improved education

Friendship with Voltaire

Elimination of torture

Appellate courts

Scientific improvements to agriculture

Russia, meanwhile, played *no* role in the enlightenment; no Russian thinker was known in the West. Following Peter the Great (who died in 1725), there was a period of resurgence of the nobility and a series of several rulers, the most significant of whom was Peter's daughter, **Elizabeth of Russia**, who ruled 1741–1762.

Elizabeth's successor was her nephew, **Peter III**, who married a minor German princess, **Catherine**. Catherine despised Peter. She became friends with military men, who deposed and killed Peter. Catherine became czarina, but as a foreigner, she was, in some ways, an usurper who depended on the nobility for her support.

One of Catherine's first moves (and an enlightened one) was to call a meeting of delegates from every class except serfs to consider a codification of Russian law. To prepare, Catherine read Montesquieu and Becarria. Delegates met for about 18 months, accomplishing some codification but certainly not all. Perhaps the most important result was the knowledge Catherine gained of her adopted country.

Catherine instituted some reforms, including some degree of religious toleration and restriction of the use of torture. She increased the number of provinces from 20 to 50. It seems that Catherine had ambitions to reduce or reform serfdom, but any tendency in this direction was thwarted by Pugachev's Rebellion, 1773–74. Reminiscent of the peasant revolt of Stephen Razin in the 1600s, **Pugachev** led thousands of rebellious serfs up the Volga River, pillaging, killing, burning, and proclaiming an end to serfdom, taxes, and military conscription. Pugachev was eventually captured and executed, but the rebellion stopped any plans to reform serfdom. The landlords got more complete authority than ever over the rural masses.

Like Frederick, Catherine was personally enlightened. She read, studied, wrote, and corresponded with the French *philosophes*. She had Diderot visit Russia. Catherine established a school for daughters of the nobility and authorized the first private printing presses in Russia. In foreign affairs, Catherine was expansionist, seeking to take territory from Poland and from the Ottoman Turks. She participated in all three **divisions of Poland**. As she aged, Catherine groomed her favorite grandson, Alexander, to be her successor.

SUMMARY OF ENLIGHTENED DESPOTISM IN RUSSIA

Catherine

Personal habits—reading, writing, study

Correspondence with French *philosophes*

Attempt at codification of law

Some religious toleration

Some restriction of torture

School for daughters of nobility

First private printing presses

CHAPTER 11: 18TH-CENTURY ECONOMICS AND POLITICS

AGRICULTURAL REVOLUTION

By the end of the 1700s, England was the first European nation to launch the Industrial Revolution. Preparation for this change in society and economics had begun almost 100 years earlier with innovations to agriculture. One practice that changed was the medieval custom of leaving one-third of the arable land fallow each year to allow it to "rest" and rebuild nutrients. In the 1700s in England, farmers began planting all the land every year but rotating with nitrogen-fixing crops (e.g., **clover**) and root crops (e.g., **turnips**) that withstood colder temperatures.

Another important new crop was the **potato**, brought from North America. Potatoes were a godsend in that they gave the poor a stable starch that could be stored through the winter. The soil was also renewed through the use of fertilizers, mostly animal manure. In addition, English farmers engaged in better animal breeding practices that produced larger sheep and fatter cattle.

From the Middle Ages, in England and on the Continent, every community had **common land** on which landless peasants could graze a cow or from which they might pick berries or gather firewood. First in England, and later on the Continent, these common lands were enclosed (by Parliamentary decree in England) by the major landowners. The results of this **enclosure** were twofold: First, more land came under cultivation by the ablest producers, and second, landless peasants now had either to work as day laborers on the large farms, work at home in **cottage industry** (discussed in the next section), or move to the cities to seek jobs. Thus developed the mobile workforce necessary for the factory jobs of the Industrial Revolution.

The English gentry tended to be more actively engaged in the everyday workings of their estates than landowners on the Continent. The English farmer was more apt to plan and operate actively the planting and growing of crops, the harvesting, and the breeding of animals, rather than merely collect rents from peasants. English farmers were very successful, producing an estimated two and one-half times the yields of Continental farmers. Another consequence was that England enjoyed a greater food supply produced by a smaller percentage of the population. It also meant surplus money that would be available for investment in manufacturing and/or trade.

The changes that revolutionized agriculture in England slowly came to the Continent, but they were less effective there because most farming tended to be at the subsistence level. The peasants on the Continent were often limited to primitive tools and had no draft animals or livestock for meat or milk. That also meant little manure for fertilizer. The further east one went, the more likely it was that the peasants were serfs, who were less inclined of their own accord to change traditional practices. Farmers who owned their own land were more likely to embrace innovations to improve productivity.

COTTAGE INDUSTRY

The majority of Europeans in the 1700s were rural, but not everybody engaged in agriculture. A number of men, women, and children worked at home in cottage industry (also called the **domestic** or **putting-out system**). This arrangement was attractive because merchants were not bound by guild arrangements outside the towns. England had much less in the way of a guild system, and it had no internal tariffs, which further aided the transport of goods.

The majority of cottage workers were engaged in some aspect of the production of woolen cloth—carding, spinning, weaving, and dying might take place in a series of locations. A merchant transported the goods among locations, paying employees low wages for their labor. Smaller numbers of people were engaged in silk and linen production. (By the time cotton cloth became big business, textile manufacturing had become more mechanized and had shifted from private homes to mills.) Other types of production that used the domestic system included copper, tin, and iron manufacturing, as well as the making of leather goods. Many families farmed and engaged in some type of cottage industry to supplement their incomes.

MID-CENTURY WARS

The 18th century began with the War of Spanish Succession. After it ended in 1713, there was peace until the late 1730s, when conflict over trade with colonies erupted between England and Spain. In 1739, an English ship captain named Jenkins appeared before the House of Commons and displayed his "pickled" ear, which he said he had lost to the Spaniards. An outraged Parliament declared war on Spain, and a brief conflict known as the **War of Jenkins's Ear** ensued. Within a year, a more widespread conflict began on the Continent.

In the 1700s, professional armies waged war; civilian populations were generally unaffected. Armies and navies were made up of men considered "economically useless," often forcibly enlisted. Governments kept productive citizens at home, working. Nations also hired foreign mercenaries. Soldiers were well trained, enrolled for long terms, dressed in brightly colored uniforms, and armed with smoothbore muskets with bayonets. Except in England, little patriotic feeling existed.

Frederick II became King of Prussia in 1740, the same year that Maria Theresa became Queen of Austria. Maria Theresa's father had spent most of his reign negotiating the **Pragmatic Sanction**, by which other nations agreed to acknowledge Maria Theresa and accept the Austrian Empire intact. Despite all of this, Frederick invaded **Silesia**, the most prosperous part of Maria Theresa's empire.

Frederick's background had been full of conflict with his overbearing, militaristic father. Young Frederick had favored music and poetry, but his father forced him to serve in the army and government. The government in Prussia was heavily involved in the economy; it built canals, sponsored industry, and managed agriculture, stocking grain in good harvest years. Frederick kept his Junker military officers under his personal control; he tolerated no appeals or arguments from anyone.

Silesia was attractive to Prussia because it was a manufacturing region with natural resources, and its addition doubled Prussia's population. Other European countries also disregarded the Pragmatic Sanction and joined in the war against Austria. Only the Dutch and English supported Austria, and because neither had a large standing army, their help consisted more of money than manpower. France used the war as an excuse to take the Southern Netherlands from Austria. In India, where the British and French competed for trading outposts along the coast, the French took control of Madras from the English. Bohemia rebelled against Austria, offering its territory to another German state, Bavaria. Maria Theresa successfully sought support from the Hungarian **Magyars**, who helped her recover Bohemia. After the horribly bloody battle of Fontenoy in 1745, in which the French beat the English and Dutch, Maria Theresa offered Frederick Silesia in exchange for peace. The Southern Netherlands was returned to Austria. The **Treaty of Aix-la-Chapelle** (1748) returned everything to prewar conditions, except for Silesia, which Frederick kept.

The resulting peace was an uneasy time. Maria Theresa and her very able advisor, **Count Kaunitz**, as well as other nations, worried about Prussia's power. Also Austria wanted Silesia back. Eight years later, in 1756, a second war began, this time much more widespread—the first actual global conflict. All nations switched sides; England and the Dutch supported Prussia, while other nations joined Austria. In addition to fighting in Europe, the British and French fought in India, North America, and the Caribbean.

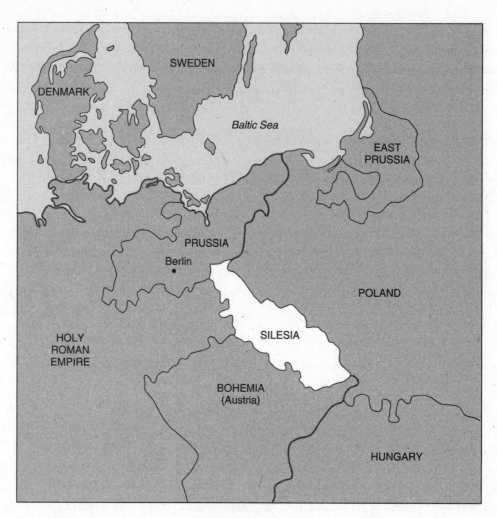

Map of Silesia 1740

The English and Dutch could not aid Frederick any better than they had aided Maria Theresa in the first war. Frederick resorted to desperate means, including stealing and recruiting soldiers everywhere (his men surrounded churches during services and impressed—forcibly enlisted— the men as they exited) and melting down all metal to make coins. Fortunately for Frederick, his enemies did not get along well with each other. Austria wouldn't promise her Netherlands to France, and France and Austria did not have a history of friendship. Czarina Elizabeth died during the war, and her successor, Peter III, liked Frederick and made peace.

Much of the fighting took place outside of Europe between France and England. The American phase, the **French and Indian War**, had begun in 1754 over competition for territory in the Ohio River valley, which the French claimed. A combined force of British colonists (George Washington among them) and the British army captured the French **Fort Duquesne**, renaming it Fort Pitt for the brilliant William Pitt at the head of the British government. The British navy seized the

French sugar islands in the Caribbean. The decisive battle in North America occurred near Quebec in 1759, when the British under General Wolfe scaled the cliffs of the St. Lawrence River and defeated the French on the **Plains of Abraham**. This battle ended the conflict in North America with the British as the victors.

> The British national debt doubled because of the war in America and led to attempts by Parliament to tax the American colonists. The war also burdened the already frail French treasury.

Again in the **Seven Years War**, there was fighting between the British and French over outposts in India. The most publicized event was the **Black Hole of Calcutta**, when a local Muslim ruler, with French backing, locked 146 Englishmen in a tiny cell, where most suffocated. In the end, French troops were defeated, and the British navy kept French ships away. The war paved the way for British ascendancy in India.

Two treaties ended the Seven Years War in 1763, the **Treaty of Hubertusburg** between Austria and Prussia and the **Treaty of Paris** between England and France. Prussia kept Silesia, and Austria kept the Southern Netherlands. Canada went to England, as did all of North America east of the Mississippi River. Territory west of the Mississippi went to Spain (who would lose it to Napoleon about 40 years later, later to be sold to the United States). Because France had skillful negotiators at the peace talks and Pitt no longer led England, France got back her sugar islands. Despite that, England's sea power had proved a great boon, and British world trade mushroomed in the second half of the 18th century, despite a second war in North America.

THE IMPACT OF THE AMERICAN REVOLUTION

The American colonists seemed to make little effort to defend themselves in the French and Indian War. Afterward, they were still vulnerable to Native American attacks (**Pontiac's Rebellion**, for instance) and continued to depend on the British military for defense. Parliament tried to make the colonists pay more of these expenses by invoking various taxes in the late 1760s and early 1770s. Though such measures as the Stamp Act were common taxes in Europe, they were new and objectionable to the Americans, who claimed that Parliament had no right to tax citizens who were not represented in Parliament. The British government pointed out that many citizens of England did not have direct representation in Parliament; the Americans retorted that they should have!

Much of the Revolutionary rhetoric reflected the enlightenment. Thomas Paine's *Common Sense* drew on Rousseau's idea of a "social contract" and John Locke's argument that governments received power through the consent of the governed. Jefferson's argument in the Declaration of Independence came directly from **John Locke**: the idea that all men were entitled to life and liberty and that the purpose of government was to protect the rights of the governed. Locke and Jefferson said that when a government failed in that task, it was the right, even the obligation, of the citizens to change that government.

When England recognized the independence of her former colonies in 1783, the news spread swiftly across Europe. For many, this victory proved that the ideas of the Enlightenment could be made reality. The United States of America was born, and then when it did not fall apart, the proof continued. The constitutions of the 13 states, as well as the national Constitution, all sought to guarantee personal rights and to ensure separation of powers (the idea of Montesquieu).

The American victory also made the English fearful of losing still more colonies. Therefore, Parliament repealed the Test Act for Canada and gave the Catholic Church there the status of an "established church." (The colonial citizens of Canada at the time were mainly descendants of French settlers and were Catholic.) In 1791, England instituted a more centralized administration of Canada and stronger control of its colonies elsewhere.

An even greater consequence of the American Revolution outside North America was in France. After the American victory at the **Battle of Saratoga** in 1777, the French were persuaded to aid the American cause. Without the French money, troops, and arms, there was a real possibility that the American patriots would lose their fight for independence. However, the results for France were grave. The French treasury, already teetering on bankruptcy, was wrecked by the strain of the American Revolution. The financial crisis created by the war soon led to the French Revolution. At the same time, a number of Europeans, especially the French, were in the British colonies during the war; these men carried home firsthand experience of the politics and lifestyle of the Americans. In addition, the French were impressed by the American ambassadors during and immediately after the Revolution: Benjamin Franklin, Thomas Jefferson, and John Adams.

CHAPTER 12: THE FRENCH REVOLUTION

LONG-TERM CAUSES

In the 18th century, French society was still legally divided into **three estates**. The clergy, the first estate, included about 100,000 people. The Church owned 10 to 15 percent of the land but paid no taxes. Instead, the Church presented an annual **volunteer gift** to the state, considerably less than what taxes would have been. The Church performed certain important roles, which included operating schools, keeping vital statistics (births, marriages, deaths), and providing relief to the poor. The Church collected a **tithe** (actually less than 10 percent) from all landowners. Men of noble backgrounds held all the top Church positions and lived well, while parish priests at the bottom of Church hierarchy were poor and hardworking. Naturally, such disparity led to resentment.

The second estate, the nobility, perhaps 400,000 people or about 2 percent of the population, owned 20 to 25 percent of the land. Serfdom no longer existed, but the nobility retained certain privileges, such as exemption from most taxes and exclusive rights to hunt and fish. The nobility also possessed privileges that produced income, such as eminent property rights, which allowed them to collect fees on legal documents such as deeds and wills, and banalities, which were fees the lord charged peasants to use the village wine press, grist mill, and ovens. Most noble landowners, including the Church, were not engaged directly in agriculture but divided their land and leased it to peasants. France did not practice "big agriculture" as did England, Eastern Europe, or Southern plantations in North America.

The third estate made up the bulk of the population, everyone from wealthy merchants and well-educated professionals down to the lowest peasants. Among the educated middle class, there was much discontent over the privileges of the nobility. Peasants owned about 40 percent of the land and leased the rest. Farming methods were primitive, and peasants and laborers had no reserves if crops failed or if there was no work. Between 1730 and 1780, prices rose 65 percent, while wages increased only 22 percent.

The big pitfall of French politics had always been money. Louis XV made only half-hearted attempts at tax reform. Then the government borrowed money to fight the American Revolution, and the deficit soared. Of course, the state could have repudiated the debt, but this would have been disastrous to the citizens who had lent it. Furthermore, there was no paper currency that could be devalued.

Louis XVI became king in 1774, in his early 20s, and proved to be an incredibly weak monarch, more interested in hunting and tinkering on clocks than the affairs of government. Louis's wife, **Marie Antoinette**, was much despised as a frivolous foreigner, popularly referred to as the "Austrian whore."

Further problems for the peasants included a shortage of farmable land—much lay fallow. Laws governing the movement of grain promoted speculating and hoarding, and because most of the peasants' diet was bread, grain shortages brought fear of starvation. In addition, the tax burden on the poor was enormous—the *taille*, a land-use tax; a poll tax; the *gabelle*, a salt tax; plus the tithe to the Church. Peasants wanted more land and tax relief.

Amazingly, France had half the war debt of England, with far more people. France was a wealthy country, but the wealth was mostly untaxed. The closest Louis XV came to tax reform was his appointment of **Maupeou** as chancellor. Until this time, tax reform had been impossible because the parlements, or district courts, declared any move to tax the nobility unconstitutional. Maupeou shut down the traditional parlements and created new ones, whose judges were salaried employees of the state and whose positions came without property. The Maupeou parlements had no right to judge the constitutionality of government actions or to reject laws. Naturally, there was a loud outcry from the nobility.

Before the new parlements could really function, Louis XV died (1774), and his grandson was too young and too weak to stand up to the nobility. He was persuaded to dismiss Maupeou and reinstate the old parlements. Between 1774 and 1789, Louis XVI went through a series of able ministers who, each in turn, tried to reverse France's downward slide into financial chaos. **Turgot**, a physiocrat, resigned because of lack of support for his program to improve the distribution of grain. Then **Necker**, who was Swiss, was replaced by **Calonne**, followed by **Brienne**. Proposals for change included a more direct land tax, the abolition of internal tariffs, and the seizure of some Church property. Nothing changed. Finally, in the fall of 1788, in financial desperation, Louis XVI agreed to call an **Estates General**, something that had not occurred in France for 175 years.

1789–1791

THE NATIONAL ASSEMBLY

In the months before the meeting of the Estates General, a debate raged over how the estates would vote. The Parlement of Paris ruled that, as in 1614 (when the body had last met), voting would take place by order. This meant that little reform was likely to occur because the clergy and nobility would cancel the wishes of the third estate. The government decreed that the third estate could have as many delegates as the other two estates combined but that voting would still be done by order.

In January 1789, Abbé **Joseph Sieyès** wrote a pamphlet, *What Is the Third Estate?* He argued that the nation could lose the first two social classes and suffer little loss, but the third estate was the nation itself.

In preparation for the meeting, all regions of the country were invited to submit, by estates, grievance lists, called *cahiers*. In general, these petitions showed a desire for a constitutional monarchy with taxes and laws coming from an Estates General. People wanted legally guaranteed liberties, better economic conditions for parish priests, and abolition of internal trade barriers.

When the meeting began in **May 1789**, the third estate refused to act until the king ordered the other two estates to meet with it. A standoff ensued for six weeks, during which some priests joined the third estate. When the third estate declared itself the **National Assembly** (a revolutionary act because it had no legal precedent), it was locked out of its meeting room. Thus, on June 20, 1789, the Assembly moved to an indoor tennis court, swearing to continue to meet until France had a new constitution (the **Oath of the Tennis Court**). The king, indecisive as always, sided with the nobility and dismissed Brienne, his last liberal finance minister, who had been urging fiscal reform.

Meanwhile, bread prices rose rapidly because of a bad harvest the previous year, and perhaps 20 percent of the population was out of work. Rumors flew about, emotions ran high, and there was much unrest. Responding to fears of a military threat, a Parisian mob attacked the **Bastille** on July 14, hoping to seize weapons and gunpowder. (The Bastille was an old armory now used as a jail.)

The National Assembly went back to work on a new constitution while the countryside experienced a general breakdown of law and order. In some places, peasants broke into manor houses and burned feudal documents that recorded their obligations, reoccupied recently enclosed common lands, took over forests, and quit paying taxes. No doubt, some simply sought food and grain. Some noble landlords panicked and fled the country, to be known as the **émigrés**; the king's brother, the **Count of Artois**, became their spokesperson.

The king accepted a citizens' committee as the new government of Paris, and a national guard was appointed to keep order. At its head was Lafayette, who adopted the **tricolor flag** (red and blue for Paris and white for the monarchy). The Assembly could restore order only by granting the peasants' demands: hunting rights and an end to banalities and to all things feudal.

By August 1789, the Assembly had produced the **Declaration of the Rights of Man and Citizen**. It listed as basic human rights liberty, property, security, resistance to oppression, freedom of religion, due process of law, and taxes by common consent. Although only men could vote and hold office, women were also active in the early years of the revolution. **Olympe de Gouges** wrote *Rights of Women* (1791), declaring women's rights to education, to control property within marriage, and to initiate divorce. She spoke of a "social contract" between men and women and hinted that men were not free unless women also had rights. The Assembly defined marriage as a civil contract and legalized divorce in 1792. Women also received the right of equal inheritance of family property. However, only one revolutionary leader, Condorcet, argued for sexual equality; others saw the political arena as strictly for men. The Assembly first restricted women's right to petition and to gather in political meetings, and by 1793, it closed all women's political clubs.

In October 1789, a large mob (perhaps 100,000 people, mostly women) went on the **march to Versailles** from Paris, demanding bread and that the royal family return to Paris. The king then submitted to the Assembly's decree, giving him "suspending power" over legislation, by which he could delay its becoming law (not a veto power). The Assembly also replaced the hodgepodge of weights and measures with a national metric system. Monopolies and guilds were outlawed, and the **Chapelier Law** forbade unions and strikes. The Assembly abolished slavery in France but not in the colonies, which provoked an uprising against plantation owners in Hispaniola (Haiti), led by **Toussaint L'Ouverture**, and which eventually led to an end of all French slavery.

Because tax collections had ceased, the government had no money. The state then seized Church property and issued paper money, *assignats*, using the property as collateral. The land was then sold, but *assignats* were not recalled, which led to disastrous inflation. The state also began to sell abandoned property of the émigrés.

With its property taken and the tithe gone, the Church could no longer support itself. Not wishing to separate Church and state, the Assembly passed the **Civil Constitution of the Clergy** in September 1790. Voters now elected clergy at all levels, there were no longer archbishops, and papal authority had to come through the National Assembly. Dioceses were drawn to correspond to the now 83 departments, which had replaced the old 130 French provinces. The clergy was now paid by the state, monasteries were closed, and new taking of religious vows was forbidden. Clergy were required to take an oath of loyalty to the new government. Those who did, the **swearing** or constitutional clergy, saw themselves as patriots and defenders of the rights of man, but this meant defying the pope. The **refractory**, or nonswearing, clergy saw themselves as the true Church and accused the swearing clergy of selling out to keep their jobs. People tended to prefer the refractory clergy, and the Assembly was ambivalent in its enforcement of the oath.

Supporters of the revolution organized into clubs (e.g., the **Jacobin Club**) or caucuses. The most influential club was nicknamed the "Jacobins" because it met in an old Jacobin monastery. The Jacobins were a powerful political force that determined much of what happened in the Assembly. In June 1791, the royal family tried unsuccessfully to flee the country. Many outspoken critics, such as **Georges-Jacques Danton** and the radical journalist **Jean-Paul Marat**, began to advocate a republic.

THE LEGISLATIVE ASSEMBLY

The new constitution went into effect in September 1791. No former member of the Assembly could sit in the new Legislative Assembly, which would last only 10 months. The government was now a constitutional monarchy with a unicameral Legislative Assembly. A radical branch of Jacobins from the coastal department of Girond became the dominant element for a while.

The rest of Europe watched France, some in admiration, some in horror. After Louis and Marie Antoinette's attempt to flee, the King of Austria, **Leopold**, brother of Marie Antoinette, met the King of Prussia in August 1791 and issued a statement called the **Declaration of Pillnitz**. Leopold said in it that he would use military force to "restore order" in France, if other nations joined him. Leopold, who was plagued by expatriate émigrés, hoped the Declaration would have a sobering effect on France. However, the opposite happened. Leopold died suddenly, and his less cautious son **Francis II** succeeded. A paranoid France declared war on Austria, and soon France was fighting Prussia as well.

1792–1799

THE NATIONAL CONVENTION

Though the war abroad did not go well for France at first, a wave of patriotism swept the country. The patriotic **"La Marseillaise"** became the national anthem. It began with these stirring words:

> Arise, Sons of Liberty!
>
> The day of glory has arrived!
>
> Against us is tyranny!
>
> The bloody flag is raised!

By the spring of 1792, the royal family was under house arrest. When the Prussian army invaded France, rumors flew, and prisoners were summarily executed (**the September massacres**). The draft of a republican constitution began, and September 1792 was declared **Year I** of the republic. A new revolutionary calendar renamed the days and months by the seasons (for example, July, a hot month, became "Thermidor"). People were addressed as "citizens," and churches were converted to **temples of reason**. Religious celebrations and holidays were made secular.

Meanwhile, the revolutionary armies defeated Austria and took the Austrian Netherlands, abolishing everything feudal in the occupied territory. French occupation of the Southern Netherlands brought England and the Dutch Republic into the coalition against France.

The Assembly, now called the National Convention, was split between the **Girondins**, who said the revolution had gone far enough, and the Jacobins, who said that anyone opposed to their agenda was antirevolutionary. Outside the Convention, major pressure came from the **sans-culottes**, or working class (so-called because they did not wear the knee britches of the middle and upper classes), who pressed for even more extreme measures. The Girondins ignored the sans-culottes, but a still more radical wing of the Convention, **the Mountain** (so named because its members sat in the upper tiers of the Convention hall), listened to them.

The king was found to be secretly corresponding with Austria and was executed for treason in January 1793. The sans-culottes demanded price and currency controls, rationing, and requisitioning to keep goods flowing. They found their spokesperson in the Convention in the leader of the Mountain, **Maximilien Robespierre**.

THE COMMITTEE OF PUBLIC SAFETY

The Convention appointed a committee of 12, the Committee of Public Safety, to run the government. Robespierre was a powerful member of the group. The Convention's aims were to win the war against France's enemies, to keep order, and to suppress opposition to the government. Laws soon took away all rights of accused prisoners. This was also when women's political gatherings were banned. What followed was **the Terror**, 1793–94, a period of slightly less than a year, in which the Convention sought to eliminate all enemies of the Jacobins, especially the Girondins. Victims included the former queen, Marie Antoinette; **Olympe de Gouges** (*Rights of Women*); and the French scientist Lavoisier, "father of modern chemistry." Estimates of the total number of executions range from 18,000 to 40,000. Ironically, the Convention adopted a feminine symbol of the revolution, **Marianne**.

Meanwhile, the war continued abroad. The Committee issued a "levée en masse" to recruit all able-bodied men into the army. Economic controls included confiscation of coins and foreign money, no exporting of gold, laws against hoarding, and wage and price controls. People were told what and how much to produce.

A second constitution was completed in 1793 but never used. The Committee issued pamphlets to teach better farming, opened military schools for all boys, and abolished slavery in the colonies. Religion by now had become extremely deistic (a process called **dechristianization**), with services to a "Supreme Being" and "Reason" impersonated by an actress. Some churches were turned into army barracks. As the Terror continued, Robespierre turned on his former supporter Danton. People came to connect fear, insecurity, and death with the idea of revolution and republicanism.

By July 1794, conservatives and radicals in the Convention turned against Robespierre and had him executed by **guillotine** (the **Thermidorean Reaction**). By the fall of 1794, the Committee of Public Safety was done away with and economic restraints were removed. Inflation soared and bread riots erupted, which were squelched by the army. The poor felt betrayed and dropped out of the revolution. Some people had become wealthy during the revolution, and these now joined former aristocrats. There was a return to expensive tastes in clothing, which had been unpopular prior to 1795, and a demand to reopen the churches.

THE DIRECTORY

The Thermidorians wrote a third constitution (actually, the second one that was used), which went into effect in 1795. Most males could vote for "electors," who then chose members of the new national legislature, made up of two houses, a dominant lower house called **the 500** and **the Elders**. The Assembly then chose the executive branch, a committee of five, called the **Directory**, which lasted until 1799. The constitution of Year III (1795) included France and Belgium, although Austria had not surrendered Belgium nor had England agreed. Initial unrest in Paris to the new government was put down by a young general, Napoleon Bonaparte—who achieved his first public notice. Some focused attention on the dead king's brother, Louis XVIII, who now lived in Italy. Many did not like the new government but also did not want to return to the old. They did not want manorial lords and dues back, and they wanted to keep former church lands.

In 1796, Napoleon married a widow, **Josephine de Beauharnais**, who had close ties with the Directory and helped him get a military commission to northern Italy. Here, Napoleon drove out the Austrians and set up a new government, the **Cisalpine Republic**, modeled after France. The Directory was willing to return some territory to Austria in exchange for recognition of the French presence in Belgium, but Napoleon argued for keeping both northern Italy and Belgium.

France was to have republican elections in 1797, but the candidates all leaned toward the royalists (who favored a return of Louis XVIII), and many were promising peace with England and Austria. The Directory appealed to Napoleon, who sent a general and military protection. The resulting coup d'etat of Fructidor (September 1797) reduced the Directory to three members and abandoned elections. France signed the **Treaty of Campo Formio** with Austria, keeping both Belgium and northern Italy. Then the Directory repudiated the *assignats* and the government debt, creating still more financial chaos, violence, and instability.

Napoleon returned from Italy and was assigned an army training to invade England. To upset the British, Napoleon slipped through the British navy in the Mediterranean and invaded Egypt. He took with him archeologists and scholars, and here a French soldier happened upon the **Rosetta Stone**, the key to translation of Egyptian hieroglyphs. The British navy cut off Napoleon in Egypt, and the Russian army wrecked the Cisalpine Republic in northern Italy. In 1799, however, Napoleon was able to return to France (again sneaking through the British naval barricade), and with the help of Sieyès in the coup d'etat de Brumaire (November 1799), Napoleon seized control of the country.

IMPACT OF THE REVOLUTION

Where did France stand in 1799? What was the result of 10 years of revolution? Much had changed. The monarchy was abolished. All remnants of feudalism were gone, as were titles and privileges of the nobility, guilds, and manors. Local government and military jobs were now salaried positions. The Church had lost much of its power; its future position was yet to be determined.

For 10 years, the French had endured violence and insecurity; everyone longed for peace and security. Many were left with distaste for republicanism, which they connected to the Terror, unchecked inflation, and economic ruin.

People outside France also had mixed views of the revolution. Certainly, monarchs trembled at the results of the revolt in France, but persons of the middle and lower classes were inspired to dream of escape from feudal customs and from control by the Church and the nobility. In places like Italy and the German states, which lacked political organization, the French model was impressive.

NAPOLEONIC FRANCE

EARLY YEARS

As a result of the coup d'etat de Brumaire (November 1799), Napoleon became First Consul of France, part of a triumvirate. Although the new **consulate** government appeared to have democratic institutions, Napoleon was actually a dictator. A **plebiscite** immediately approved the new constitution. Indirect elections chose a Senate, which chose a Tribunate from a list of 6,000 notables. The Legislative Body had very little power over proposing or approving laws.

The welcome gift Napoleon offered was peace. Russia withdrew from Italy, and Napoleon defeated Austria a second time, reconfirming Campo Formio. In 1802, he settled with England. At home, he enforced law and order, which the French coveted after years of chaotic violence. Napoleon offered a general amnesty to émigrés and refugees who had fled; the only condition was acceptance of the new order. To prevent opposition, Napoleon installed a secret police and suppressed the media. The number of French newspapers shrank from 73 to 13; survivors became instruments of propaganda.

Napoleon made peace with the Church through the **Concordat** with the papacy. Catholicism was acknowledged as the major religion in France, not a state religion. People kept church property acquired during the revolution. The government nominated bishops and paid clergy (it paid Protestant clergy, as well). The revolutionary calendar of 1793 was abandoned; Sundays and religious holidays were restored.

Napoleon added the **Organic Articles** to the Concordat. The Articles said that papal decrees, called "bulls," and other Church orders were subject to government approval. The clergy were also required to read government pronouncements from the pulpit. A new catechism (program of religious education), which was quite secular and politically oriented, was put into place.

Napoleon kept a number of revolutionary changes: the metric system, the end of all things feudal, and a salaried bureaucracy to run the government. He rewarded people in both the military and the government according to their abilities (**careers open to talent**). There were no titles (at least, in 1800) and no tax exemptions. The Thermidorian military academies were closed and replaced with a limited number of **lycées**, also military schools for boys, whose purpose was patriotic indoctrination. Elementary education was ignored.

One of Napoleon's greatest accomplishments was a complete overhaul of the French legal system into the **Napoleonic Code**, divided into a criminal code and a civil code. Citizens were declared equal before the law, and freedom of religion was guaranteed. The Chapellier Law (forbidding labor unions and strikes) was reaffirmed, and women lost the legal gains they had made in the revolution. Men (fathers and husbands) controlled all property once more, and a woman had no rights to her own earnings. In cases of adultery, women were punished much more severely than men.

Generally, one's status in early Napoleonic France was defined by wealth, including ownership of property and service to the state. Moving upward required education, ability, and money, but it was quite possible. The army and bureaucracy were the means of advancement.

Napoleon balanced the budget of France at first and was very popular until his wars began to take their toll. In 1802, he had the legislative body name him "consul for life," with power to designate his successor and to amend the constitution at will. In 1804, he took the title of emperor in a big **coronation** ceremony, at which he placed the crown on his own head.

The great French artist of both the revolution and the Napoleonic era was **Jacques Louis David**. David captured the spirit of the revolution in such paintings as *The Oath of the Tennis Court, Oath of the Horatii,* and *Death of Marat.* He greatly admired Napoleon and painted Napoleon crowning Josephine at the coronation. In *Napoleon Crossing the Alps*, David depicted the emperor on a great, charging steed; actually, Napoleon rode a mule across the mountains.

WARS

Even before Napoleon turned to conquest in Europe, he had to address a revolt in Haiti, the result of his reinstating slavery in French colonies. He had gotten **Louisiana**, which was all the territory in North America west of the Mississippi River, back from Spain in 1800 and had dreams of an American empire. However, the strains of fighting a distant war under tropical conditions forced Napoleon to sell Louisiana to the United States.

Napoleon despised England and first attempted to defeat its navy. This failed in the Battle of **Trafalgar** of 1805 off the coast of Spain. He was more successful in a land battle against Austria and Russia at **Austerlitz** in December 1805. In the German states, Napoleon dissolved the old Holy Roman Empire and consolidated territory into a much smaller number of states, and these states were loosely organized into the **Confederation of the Rhine**. At first, the Germans welcomed the more efficient government and unity that Napoleon brought. Alexander, nephew of Catherine the Great, took his armies home, leaving Prussia alone to face Napoleon and certain defeat. Napoleon re-created Poland as the **Grand Duchy of Warsaw**, and in 1807, he signed the **Treaty of Tilsit**, a sort of nonaggression pact with Alexander of Russia.

Then, Napoleon's attention returned westward. Without a navy (destroyed by the British at Trafalgar), he could not invade England, so instead, he issued the **Berlin Decrees**, establishing the **Continental system**, which required all French allies to boycott British goods. His aim was to destroy the British economy.

In Spain, Napoleon forced the Bourbon monarch to abdicate and put his brother Joseph on the throne, backing him with a large French army. (Napoleon put members of his large family in ruling positions in many of his conquered territories.) What resulted in Spain was the **Peninsular War**, a long, bloody guerilla conflict. The French abolished the inquisition and closed monasteries and convents, all of which was offensive to the Church and the Spanish people, who viewed the French as godless infidels. The war dragged on for five years and was a drain on France.

The peak of Napoleon's career occurred from 1809–1811. Napoleon divorced Josephine because she hadn't produced an heir. He then arranged a marriage with the daughter of the Austrian emperor, Francis II, negotiated by the new chief minister of Austria, **Clement Metternich**. A big royal marriage took place in 1810, and in 1811, the 19-year-old **Marie Louise** produced a son for 40-year-old Napoleon.

Everywhere Napoleon conquered, he took the "blessings" of France—the metric system, abolition of the manorial system, restriction of religious authority, religious toleration, an end of the guild system and internal tariffs, and more efficient taxation. However, as time passed, France was increasingly resented, especially in the German states, as nationalism grew there. Alexander of Russia objected to the Grand Duchy of Warsaw; Napoleon had originally hinted that Alexander might expand westward. Therefore, Alexander withdrew Russia from the Continental system in 1810 and signed a treaty with England.

Furious, Napoleon assembled a grand army of some 700,000 soldiers and marched to Russia. Unable to confront Russian forces in Poland, as he had hoped, Napoleon entered Russia in the summer of 1812. The Russians kept retreating, leaving nothing in their wake to help the French (scorched-earth policy), which forced Napoleon to employ long supply lines. By the fall, Napoleon's army fought the indecisive battle of **Borodino** near Moscow; the city itself was deserted and burnt. Too late, Napoleon's army attempted to retreat westward and was caught in the throes of a deadly northern winter. A small fraction of Napoleon's huge army survived the ordeal. Napoleon himself left his army and rushed back to France to form yet another army. The Prussians and Russians signed a new alliance in February 1813, and the British supported the effort financially. Napoleon's army was soundly defeated in October at the Battle of Leipzig. In March 1814, Russia, Prussia, Austria, and England signed the **Quadruple Alliance**. Napoleon's **abdication** occurred in April, and after a failed suicide attempt, he was exiled to **Elba** in the Mediterranean, keeping his title and income.

Louis XVIII, brother of Louis XVI, was installed as a constitutional monarch. The leaders of the Alliance, plus **Maurice Talleyrand**, representing France, met in Vienna to work out the many questions facing Europe after the Napoleonic era (details discussed in Chapter 14). Before the Congress of Vienna ended in the spring of 1815, Napoleon escaped from Elba, returned to France, raised a new army, and fought for another three months, the **100 days**. After a final defeat at **Waterloo** in Belgium, Napoleon was sent to the British island of **Saint Helena** in the South Atlantic, where he died in 1821.

UNIT THREE REVIEW QUESTIONS

1. Voltaire and Montesquieu had a similar outlook in their opinions about

   (A) who should rule.
   (B) the parlements.
   (C) separation of power.
   (D) England.
   (E) a social contract.

2. Financial consequences of the French and Indian War in North America included all the following EXCEPT

   (A) a heavily indebted French government.
   (B) acceptance of financial responsibility by English settlers for their defense.
   (C) doubling the British national debt.
   (D) more taxes on British colonists in North America.
   (E) a "war of words" by the Americans against Parliament.

3. A result of the enclosure of common lands was

   (A) the creation of a mobile workforce.
   (B) the purchase of more land by peasants.
   (C) a switch to production of chickens, which could be housed.
   (D) better use of land, such as growing clover.
   (E) bankruptcy of English farmers.

4. Catherine the Great was somewhat limited in the Enlightenment reforms she could initiate mainly because

   (A) she was female.
   (B) she was fearful after the violence of Pugachev's Rebellion.
   (C) Russia was a large, backward country.
   (D) she was more interested in conquest.
   (E) Russian law was cumbersome and difficult.

5. The following activities could have been part of a cottage industry activity EXCEPT

   (A) dying of cloth.
   (B) tanning leather.
   (C) carding wool (straightening fibers, preparatory to spinning).
   (D) weaving.
   (E) making steam engines.

6. A result of Napoleon's invasion of Egypt in 1798 was

   (A) the deciphering of hieroglyphics.
   (B) Russia's overrunning northern Italy.
   (C) surprise that his forces slipped past the British navy in the Mediterranean.
   (D) that the Directory saw him as useful in the change it was planning.
   (E) all the above.

7. Part of Napoleon's settlement with the Catholic Church

   (A) acknowledged it as the established church.
   (B) gave back some of the confiscated Church land.
   (C) restored the tithe.
   (D) had the government pay clergy salaries.
   (E) retained the secular revolutionary calendar.

8. The Great Awakening was

   (A) a deist group that studied science.
   (B) an evangelical religious movement.
   (C) a committee of the Royal Society in France.
   (D) an article for the *Encyclopedia*.
   (E) a popular novel by Rousseau.

9. The general purpose behind the Terror was to

   (A) make France a republic by eliminating Marie Antoinette.

   (B) make a statement to France's enemies.

   (C) eliminate any opposition to the revolution.

   (D) clear out the overcrowded prisons.

   (E) punish the clergy who refused to sign an oath of loyalty to the revolution.

10. Sieyès's *What Is the Third Estate*? argued that

    (A) the clergy and the nobility contributed little to the life of the country.

    (B) the estates should vote by estates.

    (C) the third estate should have the right to vote.

    (D) taxes on the poor should be reduced.

    (E) all citizens should be equal before the law.

11. Choosing "Marianne" as a symbol of the revolution was ironic in that

    (A) "Marianne" was pictured as a chaste, noble goddess.

    (B) liberty trees and hats earlier had symbolized the revolution.

    (C) the Convention had denied women any role in the revolution.

    (D) the constitution had not granted property rights to women.

    (E) women had marched to Versailles in the fall of 1789.

12. A fact that was true of both Frederick the Great of Prussia and Joseph II of Austria was that

    (A) both decreed total religious toleration.

    (B) both closed monasteries dedicated to prayer and meditation.

    (C) both freed all serfs.

    (D) neither improved education.

    (E) neither trained a successor.

13. Thomas Jefferson advocated which of the following ideas, which had its origins in the writing of John Locke, in the American Declaration of Independence?

    (A) People have the right to own property.

    (B) The purpose of government is to protect individual rights.

    (C) The king was responsible for abuses of power.

    (D) Governments may curtail certain freedoms in time of crisis.

    (E) People are entitled to pursue happiness.

14. The main purpose of the *Encyclopedia* was to

    (A) blast what the *philosophes* saw as superstition in religion.

    (B) spread the ideas and technology of the Enlightenment and scientific revolution.

    (C) collect articles from writers around the world.

    (D) present information without offending French censors.

    (E) do all of the above.

15. As allies in the War of Austrian Succession and the Seven Years War, the English and Dutch were somewhat limited in that they

    (A) were not wealthy enough to contribute large sums of money.

    (B) were too far away to be useful.

    (C) were not terribly interested in the politics of Continental Europe.

    (D) were primarily naval powers, so they could offer only limited army support.

    (E) changed sides between wars, so their loyalties were somewhat confused.

16. Maupoeu wished to do away with the old parlements of France because

    (A) they interfered with the king's efforts to raise an army.

    (B) the judges were frequently corrupt.

    (C) they blocked tax reform by declaring new measures unconstitutional.

    (D) they had close ties to the Church.

    (E) they were carryovers from the Middle Ages and, therefore, hopelessly out of touch with modern politics.

17. Early in the French Revolution, the National Assembly agreed to peasant demand for an end to all things feudal in order to

    (A) restore law and order.

    (B) get the support of the sans-culottes.

    (C) carry out Rousseau's ideas from his *Social Contract*.

    (D) punish the nobility for not supporting the third estate.

    (E) carry out the principles of the new constitution

18. The main purpose of the French salons was to

    (A) honor men like Voltaire and Rousseau.

    (B) provide a forum where men of letters could exchange ideas.

    (C) give aristocratic women an important societal role.

    (D) give foreigners like Franklin and Jefferson opportunities to meet the French.

    (E) avoid censorship in France.

19. Napoleon was welcomed in northern Italy and in the German states mainly because he

    (A) brought the metric system to replace a multitude of outdated weights and measures.

    (B) eliminated old feudal obligations.

    (C) had the backing of the Church.

    (D) redistributed land to the peasants.

    (E) brought unity and stronger government.

20. The scientists, thinkers, and writers of the scientific revolution gave 18th-century Europe a belief in

    (A) progress.

    (B) natural law.

    (C) hope for the future.

    (D) education.

    (E) all of the above.

For the following questions, write an essay that

- has a relevant thesis;
- addresses all parts of the question;
- supports a thesis with specific evidence; and
- is well organized.

Plan your essays and write them on your own paper.

1. Evaluate the degree to which Napoleon practiced enlightened despotism.

2. Describe the life of a European peasant in the 18th century in the areas of diet, work, health care, entertainment, and beliefs.

_____

_____

_____

_____

_____

_____

_____

_____

_____

_____

_____

_____

_____

_____

_____

_____

ANSWERS AND EXPLANATIONS

1. D

Both Montesquieu and Voltaire admired England, though for different reasons. Montesquieu liked the separation of power, (C), while Voltaire praised the freedom of expression and lack of censorship. Montesquieu favored the parlements, (B); he belonged to one. Montesquieu thought the nobility should share in the government, while Voltaire felt the best ruler was an enlightened despot. The reference to a "social contract," (E), is to Rousseau.

2. B

In defending the Americans from the Indians, the British spent great sums, (C), which they tried to recoup in taxes later, (D), to which the Americans strongly objected, (E). The French also increased their national debt, (A). What did not happen after the French and Indian War was an assumption by the Americans of fiscal responsibility for their defense.

3. A

Enclosing common lands forced some marginal farmers to give up agriculture and seek jobs in town, creating a population that would go where jobs were. The enclosed land was generally purchased by the wealthy, (B). None of the other answers is logical. More farmers did grow clover, (D), but this was not related to enclosure.

4. B

Although the other answers are true, none of them were especially limiting to Catherine's ambition to reform. But the violence of Pugachev's rebellion was so intense that Catherine feared the Russian peasants and left their regulation totally in the hands of their masters, without state interference.

5. E

All aspects of cloth making were first done as part of cottage industry—(A, C, and D). Leather working, (B), could also occur as domestic industry. When an efficient steam engine was developed, however, its manufacture became part of a factory operation.

6. E

Napoleon got into military trouble in Egypt, suffering defeats by the British. But his ability to sneak his army through the British navy into Egypt and then to reappear in France was impressive. Leaving the Cisalpine Republic he had set up in northern Italy opened the way for Russia to wreck it temporarily. Napoleon soon returned and retook the Cisalpine. The French discovery of the Rosetta Stone in Egypt led to translation of hieroglyphics.

7. D

Napoleon's Concordat said that the Catholic Church was the major religion of France but not a state religion, (A). No former Church land was returned, (B), nor was the tithe reinstated, (C). The revolutionary calendar was abandoned, (E), in favor of the traditional, prerevolutionary calendar.

8. B

The Great Awakening featured nontraditional Christian ministers, such as John Wesley and George Whitfield, who held revivalist meetings in the fields and preached public confession of sins and salvation by faith.

9. C

While (A) and (B) are somewhat true, as was (E) at times, the major, overall purpose of the Terror was to eliminate anyone who opposed the revolution. The victims came from all social classes and included both men and women.

10. A

What Is the Third Estate? insisted that the third estate was the heart of the country. Sieyès said that if the clergy and nobility disappeared, that France would not have lost a lot. This argument was presented as part of the debate over whether delegates to the Estates General should vote by head or by estate; Sieyès said by head, (B). While Sieyès might have favored (C), (D), and (E), he did not write of these things in his pamphlet.

11. C

Shortly before creating the symbolic "Marianne," the Convention had closed women's political clubs and denied women the right to speak in public meetings. (A) and (E) are true but not ironic. (B) is also true but irrelevant here. (D) is simply not true; the constitution had recognized women's property rights.

12. E

Both Frederick and Joseph proclaimed religious toleration, but Frederick excluded Jews, while Joseph gave Jews total civil rights, (A). Only Joseph did, (B) and (C). Both leaders improved education, (D). Neither delegated well or trained a successor, and consequently, many of the reforms of each faded after the kings died.

13. B

Locke listed property ownership, (A), as a basic right, along with life and liberty, but Jefferson substituted "pursuit of happiness" for property, (E). Neither writer mentioned choice, (D). In the Declaration, Jefferson listed multiple abuses of British power, all of which he blamed on George III, (C); perhaps that was more effective than blaming Parliament, but this didn't come from Locke. Both writers argued that men instituted government to protect basic rights and if these rights were violated, people had the right, even the obligation, to change the government.

14. B

While Diderot and d'Alembert tried to override superstition, (A), even more their purpose was to inform readers by spreading information about technology, science, and modern philosophy. They did draw on a wide range of contributing writers, but they were mainly French, (C). Censorship was a big problem throughout the publishing process, (D), but avoiding censorship was not seen as a central goal.

15. D

It is true that England and the Dutch Republic switched loyalties from Austria in the first war to Prussia in the second, (E), but all other states switched loyalties as well, moving from Prussian support to Austrian support, the opposite of England and the Netherlands. (A) and (C) are simply false; the British and Dutch were quite wealthy and interested. Distance, (B), was not an insurmountable problem; the English also fought in North America (Seven Years War) and India (both wars). However, neither country had a large standing army; they did contribute some soldiers, but mainly they sent money.

16. C

Maupeou was Louis XV's last, desperate effort to reform the tax system, under which the clergy and nobility paid few taxes. Each time the government tried to change the tax laws, the parlements declared the measures unconstitutional and refused to enforce them. Choice (A) is untrue. (B), (D), and (E) are somewhat accurate but are minor factors compared to (C).

17. A

In the summer of 1789, law and order broke down across the countryside. Peasants quit paying taxes and tithes; some occupied enclosed common land or broke into manor houses. Abolishing feudal dues and banalities seemed the only way to stop the violence. The sans-culottes, (B), were the urban poor, who were more influential in 1792–94. The first new constitution was not finished until 1791 (E), and (C) and (D) were not issues.

18. B

Certainly, the French salons seemed, to some degree, to fulfill the purposes named in (A), (C), (D), and (E). Their main reason for existence, however, was to provide an exchange of ideas among the interested and educated. Topics and speakers represented art, music, science, and politics. The salons were important as centers of thought and helped spread ideas of the Enlightenment.

19. E

Though Napoleon's armies took the blessings of the French Revolution, including uniform weights and measures and an end to feudal obligations (A and B), the main benefit he brought was unity and better government. He drove Austria out of northern Italy and organized it as the Cisalpine Republic, a vast improvement in government for the people. In the German states, he combined many smaller states into larger, more efficient ones and administered a loose organization of all the German states (formerly the Holy Roman Empire), now called the North German Confederation. Choice (C) is irrelevant, and (D) didn't happen.

20. E

Thinkers of the 18th century believed in all of these things. Discovery of mathematical laws governing the universe convinced thinkers that natural law existed for all things and that it might be discovered through reason. Its discovery and implementation would bring increasing human progress. Writers like John Locke advocated that people could be taught in ways that would improve their lives. It was a period of great optimism.

SAMPLE FREE-RESPONSE ESSAYS

1. Evaluate the degree to which Napoleon practiced enlightened despotism.

Many of Napoleon's actions, especially in the early years of his control of France, maintained the reforms of the revolution and reflected the practices of enlightened despotism. He showed enlightenment toward religion, the law (with some exceptions), and his idea of "careers open to talent," to name a few. On the other hand, where he felt his power threatened, his actions were more despotic than rational.

Napoleon kept a number of the changes the revolution had brought. All the feudal customs and privileges of the nobility stayed gone; there were no nobility, no titles, no hereditary offices, and no sale of jobs or titles. Government positions were salaried, and in both the military and government, employees were rewarded according to performance, not birth status.

Like enlightened despots of the past, Napoleon himself was not particularly religious, and he wished to keep religious influence under control. This he accomplished through the Concordat with the pope, which recognized the Catholic Church as the "major" religion but not as a state church. The government reserved the right to approve all papal communications, but it also restored the traditional Christian calendar. Religious toleration was the standard.

A major aspect of enlightened government had been legal reform, and in one sense, Napoleon was the greatest ruler in this respect. He totally reorganized the French law code, which had influence even beyond the borders of France. His Code made all citizens equal before the law.

Napoleon's regime brought peace and security, at least in its early years. He offered a general amnesty to émigrés who would accept the new order. There were no more tax exemptions, and at first, the budget was balanced and the currency was secure. Napoleon kept the metric system.

In education, Napoleon established lycées, military schools for boys, but there were not great numbers of these. There were, however, scholarships for poorer boys. In elementary education, Napoleon did almost nothing, which was not enlightened. Another unenlightened policy was removing the gains women had accomplished in the revolution by taking away their rights to property and money and making divorce more difficult. In the colonies, Napoleon restored slavery, which led to a second revolt in Haiti and resulted in the sale of Louisiana to the United States.

Napoleon didn't trust his people. He established a huge spy network whose head reported directly to the emperor. He also drastically reduced the number of newspapers and used the remaining ones as avenues of propaganda. He kept the Chapelier Law that forbade unions and strikes, also unenlightened policy.

After Napoleon crowned himself emperor, and, especially, after he married into the Habsburg royal family, he became more pompous, greedy, and expansionist. His desires for empire and his wars went against enlightenment thought, even though he claimed that he was bringing the benefits of the French revolution to distant places.

2. Describe the life of a European peasant in the 18th century in the areas of diet, work, health care, entertainment, and beliefs.

Most European peasants of the 1700s lived in the country and farmed, either on small plots that they owned (in Western Europe), as day laborers (also in Western Europe), or as serfs (in Eastern Europe) on large estates. In Western Europe, there might still be available common land, which meant that the peasant might graze a small number of livestock there, or he might have access to woods for fuel. The rural peasant might earn a bit more by doing "cottage" labor. He and his family could do contracted textile work, such as carding, spinning, weaving, or dying woolen fabric. Less common was work with the other textiles, linen or silk. A rural peasant's home was a hut, usually without glass windows. Furniture was limited. People slept on mats on the floor and sat on benches.

In the towns, the urban poor might work as servants or, in England in the late 1700s, in the new mills, where hours were long, the work was irregular, and the wages were low. In towns and cities, the workers lived in dark, crowded conditions, and burning coal for steam in the mills polluted the air. There were no sewer systems or city water supplies yet.

The main element in the peasant diet was bread, estimated at one pound to two and one-half pounds per person per day. Before 1750, this was mostly dark bread, made from rye, barley, or oats. Later in the century, more white bread was available (also more sugar—both unhealthy). Peasants ate little meat or fish, unless they happened to live near a large body of water. The poor ate from wooden bowls. Some beans and cabbage were available, and the potato from North America entered the diet. Potatoes were a godsend because they could be stored for months.

People of all classes were subjected to the same diseases and many of the same health hazards. The poor turned mostly to faith healers and apothecaries for remedies. Midwives delivered babies, and women of all classes frequently died in childbirth. Doctors could amputate and cauterize, but there was no anesthesia and no knowledge of sanitation. Bleeding was standard treatment for illness. The one dangerous disease that became preventable at the end of the 18th century was smallpox (the result of the work of Edward Jenner).

In rural communities, rich and poor attended the same church, though there could be class differences in areas where more than one religious domination existed. Many poor lived outside the religious community, and there were some missionary efforts toward them. The uneducated still believed strongly in witches, ghosts, and miracles. Those who were literate read almanacs, which contained weather predictions, astrology, and proverbs. There were also "how-to" books and popular stories from oral traditions, such as those about Robin Hood, Charlemagne, and King Arthur. Entertainment consisted of local celebrations, such as carnivals, and local fairs. Drinking at a tavern, storytelling, and sports like wrestling also provided diversion.

The average life span was longer than it had been in the Middle Ages, and perhaps the lives of the poor were not quite as harsh. However, great gulfs between the lifestyles of the poor and the wealthy, or even between the poor and the middle class, still existed.

CHAPTER 13: THE INDUSTRIAL REVOLUTION

WHY ENGLAND WAS THE FIRST TO INDUSTRIALIZE

The Industrial Revolution—the shift from production by human and animal power to production by machine—was like the scientific revolution in that it changed the world. The process began in England around 1780 for a variety of reasons. Through private ownership, industrialization grew out of capital accumulated from trade and agriculture. In Western Europe, the concept of private property had been important since the Middle Ages; it was basic to personal and political liberties.

Before the Industrial Revolution had come the agricultural revolution, during which the enclosure of common lands, crop rotation, new crops, and more use of fertilizer made farming a profitable "big business." English agriculture provided more than twice the yields of Continental farming. Because there was less land available to rent, rents rose and common lands began to disappear. These conditions created a mobile workforce—people who either worked for wages on the big farms or moved to the towns for jobs in the newly established mills, especially in northern England. At the same time, the owners of production accumulated profits that they could use for investment.

Another advantage the English possessed was the largest merchant marine in the world with access to markets everywhere. The old staple of English manufacturing had been woolen cloth. Merchants could sell all that could be made. Cotton seemed to offer even more possibilities if it were possible to get past the slow methods of hand production. (Raw cotton, of course, had to be imported, while wool came from English sheep.) Men of wealth from agriculture and business were willing to invest in new ideas for better, quicker production in hopes of still higher profits. Thus, the first moves toward mechanization came in textiles.

In the 1730s, **John Kay** developed the **fly shuttle**, which allowed one person instead of two to operate a loom. More efficient weaving increased the existing gap between spinning and weaving; there was never enough yarn. Thirty years later, **James Hargreaves** created the **spinning jenny**. Its multiple spindles enabled spinning to keep up with weaving for the first time.

The next innovation came in 1769, when **Richard Arkwright** applied waterpower to the spinning process. Arkwright set up mills with his invention in the hill country of northern England, where waterpower was available; he made a fortune.

Cottage industry continued to thrive throughout the 18th century, mainly because the new machinery was still more expensive than hand labor. It required more space and greater investment. However, the number of factories steadily grew. The biggest boon to cotton manufacturing was the cotton gin, invented by Eli Whitney in the United States; the gin mechanically removed the seeds from cotton and revolutionized cotton production. By the 1790s, manufacturers were applying the steam engine to cotton mills.

HALLMARKS: STEAM ENGINE, IRON, AND RAILROADS

Wood was required to make charcoal for use in the process of smelting iron ore, but by 1700, there was a shortage of it. Foundries were forced to switch to **coke** (carbonized coal). A greater demand for coal meant deeper mine shafts, which tended to fill with water. In 1702, **Thomas Newcomen** developed a steam engine that could pump water out of mines, but the device was inefficient, burning so much coal that it was useful *only* in coal mines.

In 1763, **James Watt** of the University of Glasgow began to improve the Newcomen engine with the financial backing of **Matthew Boulton**, a manufacturer of various items from toys to buttons. By the 1780s, the two men were making steam engines for England and for export. Shortly after 1800, steam engines were used to propel riverboats. (**Robert Fulton** was credited with this innovation when he sailed his steamship, the *Full Moon,* on the Hudson River in the United States.)

In the 1820s, the steam engine was applied to land travel. The first successful steam locomotive, **George Stephenson**'s *Rocket,* traveled the new rail line from Liverpool to Manchester at the roaring speed of 16 miles per hour! The age of the railroad had begun, and land transport was revolutionized.

SOCIAL IMPACT

In the 100 years between 1750 and 1850, the population of England and Ireland tripled, mushrooming especially in the new industrial cities such as Manchester and Liverpool. Rapid urbanization created enormous housing problems. Before the days of public transportation, workers had to live within walking distance of the mills. Dwellings were drab and crowded, and neither sewers nor public water supplies existed. Steam power in the factories came from burning coal, which polluted the atmosphere of urban areas.

The new factory towns demanded unskilled labor, and skilled craftsmen often found themselves out of work, unable to compete with the more cheaply made mill products. Wages remained very low, too low for a man to support a family, so women and children also worked (though they were paid less than the men). The head of a household might negotiate a deal to have his whole family employed together. There was work only as long as the factory had orders to fill; unemployment was common, and laborers weren't paid when they didn't work. Factory hours were long, around 14 hours per day. On the farms, people had worked long hours as well, but that work was usually outside, offering far more variety than the tedious, boring repetition of factory labor. Workers were not organized in any way.

Factory owners, called **cotton lords**, were often self-made, hard-working men; a number were dissenters. They looked at the landed aristocracy as idlers and saw the poor as lazy. Believing that they were providing a social service by giving jobs to the poor, the cotton lords generally opposed government interference. But in 1802, **Robert Peel**, a cotton lord, pushed the first Factory Act through Parliament. The law attempted to regulate conditions under which pauper children worked in factories, though it accomplished little because there was no agency to inspect and enforce it. Another problem was frequent breakdown of the traditional family; because young people left the customary constraints of their village or rural communities for work in the cities, family life suffered, and the number of illegitimate births rose dramatically.

Studying the problems created by the new industrial communities was a new breed of scholars, the economists. The **Manchester School** of classical economists advocated the **laissez-faire capitalism** principles defined by Adam Smith's *Wealth of Nations*. The feeling was that a natural law applied to the world of manufacturing and trade and that the natural law was based on Smith's principle of supply and demand. Smith contended that the job of government was to provide security, which would create an atmosphere conducive to production, but government should leave production itself to private interests along with all other aspects of human endeavor. Trade should be absolutely free with no tariffs; the economists believed it would regulate itself.

One member of the Manchester School was **Thomas Malthus**, an English clergyman who was disturbed by the population increase. In his ***Essay on the Principle of Population***, Malthus compared humans to lemmings, the tiny rodents whose populations exploded until they outstripped the food supplies, at which point they committed mass suicide. Malthus's friend **David Ricardo** expressed an equally pessimistic theory in his **iron law of wages**. Ricardo claimed that, if workers were paid more, they would produce more children, who would consume the increase. Therefore, he said, the working class would forever exist at subsistence levels.

REFORMS

The first half of the 19th century brought some changes and reforms to English trade and manufacturing, many of them initiated by the Tories in Parliament. (The Whigs worked more for electoral reform.) Prime Minister Robert Peel, son of the cotton lord, was sensitive to the needs of business and to the ideas of free trade. The restrictions of the old Navigation Acts, as well as tariffs, were reduced. British colonies were freed to trade with anyone. The laws barring non-Anglicans from civil and military positions were rescinded, and Catholics received equal civil rights. Parliament reduced the number of crimes punishable by death and established professional police forces (nicknamed "**bobbies**" for Robert Peel).

In 1833, England abolished slavery, and that same year, Parliament passed the **Factory Act**, which limited the number of hours children under age nine could work. Perhaps more important, the Factory Act provided for paid inspectors and procedures for enforcement. Then in 1842, women and girls and boys younger than 10 were forbidden to work in the mines. Prior to the **Mines Act**, children and young women worked in the mines as **hurriers**, pulling carts and loads of coal on rails to the surface. (Their small bodies also meant they could crawl through the air shafts of mines.) The most far-reaching factory reform was the **Ten Hours Act** of 1847, which limited women and children to 10-hour shifts. This translated into 10-hour days for everyone because all employees needed to work the same shifts. In addition, governments tried to put all citizens to work with **Poor Laws**, which made relief more unpleasant than work. English communities established **workhouses** or **poorhouses** for the indigent. These miserable places were described vividly in the novels of Charles Dickens.

INDUSTRIALISM ON THE CONTINENT

As Belgium became independent in 1831 (see Chapter 16), it also became the scene of the greatest industrialization on the Continent. It too emerged from a cottage industry of textile workers, and because it was densely populated, there were both the desired labor force and a market for products. Trade through Belgium's ports, such as Antwerp, also opened markets and provided profits for investors. In addition, Belgium had coal to fuel the age of steam, so the advent of railroads spurred even more rapid development.

Though France was a prosperous country and much larger than its neighbors, it industrialized more slowly than they did. It had coal deposits, but because they were not close to deposits of iron ore, the iron industry didn't immediately thrive. It had agriculture, but it was not a nation in which farming was big business, as in England. It had investment, but French investors were more cautious, and banks were not set up as investment institutions. The building of railroads would slowly improve opportunities in France, but the Chapelier Law forbidding unions and strikes remained in place until 1864, while strikes became legal in England 40 years prior to that.

The German states at the beginning of the 19th century were primarily agricultural and, of course, disunited. But slowly, centers of industry began to emerge, especially in the **Ruhr Basin**, which was rich in both coal and iron ore. Another advantage in the German states was the **Zollverein**, the tariff union developed by Friedrich List; it included 80 percent of the German states. A major developer in the Ruhr region was **Alfred Krupp**, who put together a thriving steel works by the middle of the 19th century.

In Eastern and Southern Europe (Spain, southern Italy, and Russia), there was little development. (The exception was in northern Italy in Piedmont and Lombardy, where a prosperous textile industry developed.) These areas lacked capital and a middle class of any size, and governments were uninterested in encouraging manufacturing and trade. Spain lacked navigable rivers and did not build railroads until the second half of the 19th century. Russia also lacked transportation and entrepreneurs.

CHAPTER 14: CONSERVATISM (1815–1848)

CONCERT OF EUROPE: 1815–1823

The Congress of Vienna began meeting in the fall of 1814, after Napoleon's first abdication, for the purpose of settling questions of territory and politics in the wake of Napoleon. Representatives of all countries came, but only those of the major nations mattered: Talleyrand of France, Castlereagh of England, Metternich of Austria, and Alexander of Russia. From the beginning, Russia refused to discuss Turkey and the Balkans, and Britain refused to address freedom of the seas or questions of colonies and overseas empire. The British kept the Cape of Good Hope and Ceylon, which they had taken from the Dutch. Some borders had to be redrawn in Europe; some old rulers were restored, and some territories were assigned to other powers.

One aim of the peace talks was to create a system of strong states around France. The Austrian Netherlands was transferred to the Dutch, which pleased Britain, and the Dutch Republic became the **Kingdom the Netherlands**, ruled by the House of Orange. Austria got most of northern Italy outright and maintained influence over the rest. (Metternich kept garrisons and secret police throughout Italy.) There was no attempt to restore the Holy Roman Empire, and nobody paid attention to the German nationalists.

A new kingdom of Poland was created out of land Austria and Prussia had taken in the 1700s, and the new entity was known as **Congress Poland**. The king was Alexander, which meant that Russia actually controlled Poland. Prussia got part of Saxony, which had cooperated with Napoleon during his conquests.

France was getting good terms at the Congress of Vienna (partly because Talleyrand was a skillful negotiator) when Napoleon escaped from Elba and did his 100 days. Afterwards, France was obligated to pay an indemnity of **700 million francs**. **Louis XVIII** was returned as a constitutional monarch. (He had been installed after Napoleon's first abdication but had fled Paris during the

100 days.) The treaty framers now included a clause forbidding any Bonaparte from ruling France in the future.

Alexander was very religious personally, and he insisted on a document known as the **Holy Alliance**. Its content referred to rulers of European nations as "delegates of Providence" and claimed that their actions were based on "sublime truths" of religion. Austria and Prussia signed, but England refused—**Viscount Castlereagh** called the Holy Alliance "sublime mysticism and nonsense." In the immediate future, the Holy Alliance became an excuse for the suppression of revolutionary, or even liberal, activity.

The big powers agreed they would continue to meet to address future issues of international concern; some call these countries the **Concert of Europe**, because they were all "singing the same song." After Vienna, the first gathering was at the **Congress of Aix-la-Chapelle** in 1818. There, the great powers agreed to withdraw postwar occupation troops from France, and they accepted the idea of allowing private bankers to manage the reparations payments. Britain drifted slowly out of unison with the other Congress powers. Other problems the meeting considered included the slave trade and the Barbary pirates off the coast of Africa, but because Britain refused to discuss either issue, nothing happened.

In 1812, while French troops occupied Spain, the **Cortes** (the parliament) of Spain had approved a very liberal constitution, which made ministers responsible to the Cortes. The constitution guaranteed property rights, freedom of the press, and freedom from arbitrary arrest. In 1814, however, the Bourbon monarchy was restored, and **King Ferdinand VII** refused to recognize the constitution. Rebellion broke out in 1820, and Alexander and Louis XVIII wanted to intervene, but England would not agree to this proposal. Naples and Sicily also were scenes of revolt against post-Vienna restored rulers. The **carbonari**, a nationalist group, led the Italian opposition.

In the fall of 1819, Metternich and Alexander met once more at Troppau in the state of Galicia. Alexander, who had once seemed to champion liberalism, had now been won over to the conservatives. The two leaders composed the **Protocol of Troppau**, which called for collective international action in the interest of general peace and stability. Castlereagh and England refused to participate, but Prussia joined Alexander and Metternich. The three powers authorized Metternich to send an Austrian army into Naples, which restored order there and reinstated an incompetent, brutal king.

Meanwhile in 1821, Greece revolted against its masters, the Ottoman Turks. This situation put the Congress powers in a dilemma. They looked down on the Turks as godless infidels, but at the same time, the Ottoman Empire was the old, established order, and the traditional stand of the Congresses had been to suppress rebellion against the established order. **Alexander Ypsilanti**, a Greek who had fought in the Russian army, led a band of followers from Russia into Romania, also part of the Ottoman Empire. He expected Greeks to rise up and join the cause and to get Russian support. Metternich feared that if part of the Ottoman Empire converted to a Greek empire, it would be under Russian domination.

A last meeting occurred at the **Congress of Verona** (Italy) the next year (1822). Here, Alexander agreed not to support Ypsilanti; Greek independence would come a few years later (discussed in Chapter 16). The Turks then put down the revolt in Greece. The British did not attend the Verona meeting. With British objections gone, France asked for authorization to send an army to Spain to quell revolutionaries and troublemakers there. Russia, Prussia, and Austria approved, and the French army entered Spain in 1823, welcomed by the masses, who did not trust the liberal "heretics." Church and king were restored, and the revolutionaries were punished.

The revolt against Spain in South America, led by **Simón Bolívar** and **José de San Martin**, occurred at this time. Alexander suggested at the Congress of Verona that Europe do something about the situation, but the British totally opposed any move in that direction. Because the British controlled the seas, nothing could happen, and the result was that little of South America remained under European control by the end of the 1820s. (The United States, meanwhile, issued its Monroe Doctrine, declaring any "meddling" by European powers in the Western Hemisphere a hostile act. The United States depended on the British navy, at first, to enforce the Monroe Doctrine.)

There were no more Congress meetings. As an international force, it had failed. When Austria stopped revolution in Naples and France did likewise in Spain, each was acting in its own selfish interest. After 1818, the British no longer cooperated with Continental powers.

RUSSIA

Alexander I died suddenly in 1825. In his later years, he had become increasingly conservative, employing censorship and secret police. As a result, many liberal thinkers (younger Russian nobles who had been educated in Western Europe and influenced by the Enlightenment, as well as Russian army officers who had occupied France after 1815) hoped to see Alexander's brother **Constantine** become the next tsar. They dreamed of a more Westernized government with a constitution and even freedom of the serfs, and they formed secret societies to work toward those goals.

Constantine, however, had already given up his right to the throne in favor of his brother **Nicholas I**. The ensuing uprising, called the **Decembrist Revolt**, was soon put down, and Nicholas proved himself to be extremely conservative and repressive.

FRANCE: 1815–1830

At the time of Napoleon's first abdication, Talleyrand suggested a return of the Bourbon monarchy in the person of Louis XVIII. (Louis XVII, son of the executed king, had died in prison during the revolution.) Louis was now old and in poor health—not very exciting after Napoleon—but he was safe and peaceful. He was unlikely to try to recapture recent conquests, and he was a legitimate monarch in the eyes of Europe.

Louis signed a **Charter**, promising a national legislature elected by a limited franchise. Principles from the revolution and the Napoleonic period remained in place: equality before the law, religious freedom with Catholicism as a state religion, the Napoleonic Code, organization of the country by departments, and property rights from the revolutionary and Napoleonic periods. Only large property owners could vote; they elected a two-house Assembly. France was returned to its 1792 borders.

Despite Louis XVIII's willingness to cooperate, in early 1815, a **white terror** swept over France, in which returning émigrés tried to punish former revolutionaries and Bonapartists. When Napoleon escaped Elba to launch his 100 days, Louis fled, returning to Paris after Napoleon's final defeat. Reaction continued, including Catholic attacks on Protestants. In 1820, the assassination of the king's nephew led to still more repression. When Louis died in 1824, his successor was the Count of Artois, **Charles X**, who had been the spokesperson for the conservative aristocracy since the early days of the revolution. Another conservative move was the government's plan to reduce the interest on the public debt, which hurt the French middle class who had loaned money to the state.

Opposition to the government built in the late 1820s, fueled by rumors that the king planned to rescind constitutional restraints on his authority. In 1829, Charles appointed as his chief minister one of only two men who had refused an oath of loyalty to Louis XVIII's Charter. The opposition was fueled by romantic writers like Victor Hugo and, by 1830, the Chamber of Deputies (lower house of the Assembly), which opposed the king. The result was the July Revolution of 1830, which is discussed in the next chapter.

GERMAN STATES: 1815–1830

During the Napoleonic period, writers and thinkers in the German states began to express nationalism for the first time (see Chapter 16). Especially, ideas of German nationalism dominated the universities, where students formed clubs, collectively called the **Burschenschaft**. Metternich of Austria eyed this phenomenon with distrust, seeing it as a dangerous youth movement and possible threat to the status quo. Actually, Metternich had no authority in the German states beyond the fact that Austria was a member of the **German Confederation**, a continuation of the loose organization Napoleon had dubbed the Confederation of the Rhine.

Austria in these years was the leading German state, and Metternich had no desire for German unity for fear that it might detract from Austria's central power and authority. The Burschenschaft, in its advocacy of German nationalism, also supported the idea of a united Germany, but its actual deeds were limited. Occasionally, there was a public demonstration or a march; for the most part, Burschenschaft supporters confined their activities to writing.

In 1819, however, a member of the Burschenschaft murdered an extremely conservative public figure. Metternich then persuaded Prussia to join Austria in the passage of the **Carlsbad Decrees**, which were then submitted to the diet of the Confederation for approval. An ultraconservative document, the Carlsbad Decrees outlawed the Burschenschaft and applied censorship throughout the German states. University students and professors would be watched. Teachers who offended were blacklisted, making it impossible for them to be hired anywhere. Metternich was now firmly in control and would remain so until 1848.

ENGLAND: 1815–1832

In England, the term *corn* meant wheat, oats, or barley—any grain. (The British use the word *maize* for what Americans call corn.) For a long time, England had maintained tariffs or import limits on foreign grain, the **Corn Laws**, to protect English farmers. These restrictions hurt consumers because bread prices were kept high, and they hurt manufacturers because they had to pay their workers higher wages.

The Napoleonic wars created a shortage of grain imports, so more grains had to be raised at home, and prices remained steadily high. After 1815, it was again possible to import grain, but the landed aristocracy wished to prevent imports, which would cause grain prices to fall. New legislation forbade the import of grain unless prices skyrocketed.

The grain controversy occurred during bad economic times for English laborers. There was much unemployment at the time and much unrest. In 1819, a large demonstration of some 80,000 took place outside Manchester at a place called St. Peter's Fields. The crowd was peaceable, demanding universal male suffrage, annual elections for the House of Commons, and the repeal of the Corn Laws. The local authorities panicked and fired on the crowd, killing 11 and wounding about 400 more. The British government thanked the soldiers for upholding social order and passed new restrictions limiting public meetings. The incident was labeled the **Peterloo Massacre** by the press.

In Parliament, there was no pretense of numerical representation; there had been no changes in electoral districts since before the Industrial Revolution. New industrial cities like Manchester, Birmingham, and Liverpool had no representation at all. The old argument was the same that had been given to the American patriots in the 1770s—that all English citizens were "virtually represented" in Parliament. There were places with representation in Parliament that now had few or no residents; these were called **rotten boroughs**. **Pocket boroughs** were districts said to be "in the pocket" of some wealthy landowner who was routinely re-elected without opposition. Only 1 out of every 15 males could vote. The result was the Parliamentary debate that led to the Reform Bill of 1832 (discussed in Chapter 15).

AUSTRIAN EMPIRE

Metternich controlled Austria and heavily influenced the rest of the German states until 1848. Except for Russia, the Austrian Empire was the most populous European state, made up of Austria, Bohemia, and Hungary, each with its own majority language. The Austrians spoke predominantly German, the Bohemians Czech, and the Hungarians Magyar, but there was also a multitude of minority languages: Serbian, Croatian, Slovenian, Slovakian, and others. Austria also controlled two major parts of northern Italy, Venetia and Lombardy. Vienna, capital of the empire, was second only to Paris. The most influential member of the German Confederation, Austria also had considerable say over all of Italy. The only independent Italian state was Piedmont Sardinia (formerly Savoy). Metternich disparagingly referred to Italy as a mere "geographical expression."

For 30 years, Metternich stayed successfully in control by ignoring all expressions of nationalism. His idea of government was that of a benevolent ruling house, the Habsburgs who had no special connection to the peoples they ruled. Such ideas were about to be a half century out of date; nationalism and liberalism could not be dismissed indefinitely.

CHAPTER 15: THE RISE OF LIBERALISM (1815–1848)

CHARACTERISTICS

Liberalism was the product of the Enlightenment. Generally, liberal-minded people were the educated members of the upper middle class, often professionals. Liberals believed in constitutions and representative government that protected such human rights as freedom of expression and of religion and equality before the law. English liberals favored constitutional monarchy, and on the Continent, they advocated written constitutions.

Such thinkers, however, were not democrats; they did not trust the masses and did not, at first, favor universal male suffrage. They were strongly opposed to revolution. Almost none, with the exception of John Stuart Mill, promoted voting rights for women. In economic affairs, liberals preferred laissez-faire policies and disapproved of old guild regulations, tariffs, and modern attempts of laborers to organize into unions. They shared the ideas of Adam Smith—that governments should stay out of business except to protect private property and maintain an atmosphere conducive to manufacturing and trade.

Liberals were quite secular and civilian in their points of view. They rejected Church teachings that humans were basically evil and had to be kept in line by religious and governmental restraints. Established churches were undesirable in their eyes. They were equally distrustful of the military and everything connected to it. Change might be appealing, but the liberals preferred that it come through legislation. Following Enlightenment thought, the liberals believed in human improvement and progress. They trusted science and education and that which was modern and enlightened.

ENGLAND

The elections of 1830 weakened the conservative majority in the House of Commons to allow passage of a bill to reduce pocket and rotten boroughs. The House of Lords refused to cooperate until **King William IV** threatened to create more peers (lords) if they didn't agree. The result was the **Reform Bill of 1832**, which approximately doubled the number of men in England who could vote. The bill did not give numerical balance to electoral districts, but it did eliminate some of the smaller boroughs, whose seats were reallocated to the new industrial centers.

There were two other major liberal movements in England before 1848. One was the formation in 1838 of the **Anti–Corn Law League**. Defenders of the Corn Laws worried about the country's balance between agriculture and industry, while opponents argued that the grain tariffs kept grain prices unnaturally high, which hurt wage earners.

In 1845, blight struck the potato crop of Ireland, which spelled disaster for Irish peasants in the form of starvation and disease. The next year, the Tory Prime Minister **Robert Peel** joined the Whigs to repeal the Corn Laws. The **Irish potato famine** convinced Peel that, without reform, there would be a major uprising. Peel's action did get the Corn Laws repealed, but his courage caused him to fall from power. The Irish peasants, dominated by absentee British landlords, did not benefit greatly from the repeal. Repeated crop failures in 1848 and 1851 resulted in mass Irish migration, mostly to the United States. The repeal did prove the ability of the British government to compromise. The reform also committed England to an international economic system, depending on foreign trade.

A second British phenomenon was the **Chartist Movement**, which was tied into the Anti–Corn Law movement. It was based on the idea of a great charter, or a national petition with thousands of signatures, that would be presented to Parliament. The Chartists composed a working-class movement whose main issue was universal male suffrage. The group spoke out for Parliamentary reform in more equally drawn districts, secret ballots, and salaries for members of Parliament. At first, the movement grew slowly, but difficult economic times gave it more attention. The Chartists got over 3 million signatures on their petition, which was rejected by Parliament. The movement gradually died, but its influence helped pass the Mines Act of 1842 and the Ten Hours Act of 1847. Slowly, most of its ideas would become reality, and in 1867, there was a second voting reform bill. All the Chartists' desires eventually were passed, except for annual elections to Parliament, which ceased to be an issue.

FRANCE: REVOLUTIONS OF 1830 AND 1848

When the Chamber of Deputies continued to oppose **King Charles X**, he dissolved it and called new elections, which liberals won. In consequence, Charles X issued four **July Ordinances**.

The first dissolved the newly elected Chamber before it met, the second censored the press, the third greatly reduced the franchise to exclude the upper middle class, and the fourth called for new elections based on the revised franchise.

The immediate reaction came from the working class, students, and intellectuals, who became mobs in the streets, putting up barricades and flying the tricolor flag of the revolution. The king's soldiers became targets of the mob and refused to support Charles. In desperation, the king abdicated and fled to England.

On the recommendation of the elderly **Marquis de Lafayette**, France replaced Charles with his cousin, **Louis Philippe**, Duke of Orléans. Louis Philippe was careful to downplay the royal image. He dressed in the equivalent of today's business suit and carried an umbrella. Some historians have suggested that Louis Philippe deliberately misled Lafayette into thinking he was more liberal than he actually was. His reign lasted for 18 years, until 1848; it was called the July Monarchy, and the king was labeled the **Orléanist**. The flag was the tricolor of the revolution.

Louis Philippe was quite conservative, even though the government maintained an appearance of liberalism. He wanted the support of the upper bourgeoisie, and he catered to them. Reformers and democrats were disappointed. In 1840, France was involved in an incident in Egypt, when the French supported a local ruler who rebelled against the Turks. Other states, led by England, opposed France, fearing that a breakup of the Ottoman Empire would invite disaster, possibly opening the Middle East to Russian influence. France was forced to back down, which looked bad on the international scene and invited criticism. At home, French workers demanded the vote.

In February 1848, the workers planned a big rally in support of electoral reform. **François Guizot**, Louis Philippe's much despised, excessively conservative premier, forbade the rally. Crowds gathered despite Guizot, and the army refused to make the people disperse. The king dismissed Guizot, but the same day, the army fired on the crowd, killing about 40 people. News of the killings spread rapidly as the mob carried bodies through the streets. Barricades went up, as in 1830, and street fighting resulted. Louis Philippe abdicated, hoping the Chamber of Deputies would give the crown to his grandson. The French, however, were disillusioned with monarchy. Instead, the Chamber of Deputies appointed a committee as a **provisional government**, made up of republicans and one socialist, **Louis Blanc**.

The provisional government proclaimed universal male suffrage, an end of slavery in the colonies (again), and abolition of the death penalty. People planted "liberty trees" again, a practice from the revolution. The French were divided about what direction to take. The **Orléanists** favored leadership from one of Louis Philippe's sons, while the **legitimists** wanted the return of a Bourbon descendent. Then there was Louis Napoleon Bonaparte, nephew of the original Napoleon. The republicans were also divided. There were various socialists (see Chapter 19); followers of **Louis Blanc** demanded government help to provide jobs, especially because unemployment in Paris was at crisis level.

The provisional government opened **national workshops** at the insistence of Louis Blanc, but the men were given little meaningful work. Mostly, they did digging projects on the roads. Nevertheless, there were far more applicants than jobs, a sign of the desperate times. The provisional government agreed to a 10-hour day. Women began to organize and make demands, which frightened the upper class.

Elections to the National Assembly were held in April, and conservatives were the big winners, mainly because of the predominantly rural peasant vote, which was antiliberal, antiworkshops, and antitaxes. The election results produced riots in Paris. The violence escalated when the provisional government closed the workshops because it no longer had the money to support them. **General Cavaignac** stopped the violence with violence. Estimates of the casualties ranged from 1,500 to 10,000, and many were deported to Algeria. This unsettled time was called the **Bloody June Days**.

Meanwhile, the provisional government was drafting a constitution. Because of the violence in June, the decision was to create a strong executive power, and presidential elections were scheduled even before the constitution was finished. Four candidates ran, but Louis Napoleon Bonaparte was the winner by a huge majority. The election and its aftermath are discussed in Chapter 18.

CHAPTER 16: THE RISE OF NATIONALISM (1815–1848)

GREECE AND BELGIUM: INDEPENDENCE

After the failure of Ypsilanti in 1821 to arouse support for Greek independence, Western writers took up the Greek cause. Most notable were the English poets **Percy Shelley** and **Lord Byron**, who were living in Italy in the early 1820s. Shelley drowned in 1822, but Byron went to Greece and continued to plead the Greek cause until his death (from a fever, not a battle wound).

The Turks continued to alienate the West. First there was the incident of a massacre of Greek residents on an island. The French romantic painter Delacroix publicized this event in a large, emotional canvas. Then, the Turks executed the Christian leader of Constantinople.

Eventually, England took a stand for an independent Greece and persuaded France and Russia to join her side. In 1827, the three nations signed the **Treaty of London**, which threatened Turkey with military action if it did not grant Greece its freedom. The Turks rejected the proposal, so the allies sent a naval force that destroyed the Turkish fleet. Russia tried to take advantage of Turkish weakness by moving into Moldavia and Wallachia in Eastern Europe (both part of the Ottoman Empire). Both France and England voiced disapproval and forced Russia to back down; Russia settled for claiming the two states as protectorates. The Greeks got their independence from Turkey in 1832.

The Congress of Vienna united what had been the Austrian Netherlands and the Dutch Republic, creating the Kingdom of the Netherlands. The government was a constitutional monarchy, ruled by the House of Orange. Economically, the union was very successful. Belgium was an industrial nation, which complemented Dutch agriculture and trade. Politically, however, the union was not popular. The Dutch king tried to be an absolutist who wanted strong central control, while the Belgians were used to virtual independence. Austria had always been too far away to be deeply involved in Belgian life. The Belgians were Catholic, while the Dutch were Calvinists. The Belgians spoke French or Flemish; they resented being forced to use Dutch as the official language.

About a month after the July Revolution in France (1830), Belgian leaders asked for self-government. The initial Dutch response was militant. About three days of fighting ensued, until the Dutch withdrew. Belgium then proclaimed its independence and began to draft a constitution.

Nicholas I of Russia strongly objected to this turn of events in Western Europe and voiced a desire for intervention to restore the situation in Belgium to what it had been. But in January 1831, the Polish diet declared Poland independent of Russia, and Nicholas was forced to turn his policing remedies to problems closer to home. The Russian army invaded Poland and quashed the revolt there, while Belgium proceeded to establish its statehood.

The Belgians chose the **son of Louis Philippe** as king, but England strongly objected to this plan. (This was 1831; Louis Philippe had just become King of France.) Louis Philippe then refused to let his son accept the Belgian crown. The choice then shifted to a German prince who had married into the English royal family. France and England conferred and agreed to set up Belgium as a perpetually neutral country. The understanding was that if Belgium were invaded, France and England would defend her. Thus, Belgium became a constitutional monarchy with a two-house parliament elected by about 1 out of every 30 Belgian males.

As for Poland, Nicholas sent in a large fighting force to bring the country back into line. Many Poles hoped for aid from France or England, but none came. Poland lost its somewhat independent status again and was merged into the Russian Empire.

GERMANY: PHILOSOPHIES OF NATIONALISM AND THE REVOLUTIONS OF 1848

Before 1800, the Germans had been the least nationally minded people of Europe. Divided into multiple small states, they prided themselves on having an international, cosmopolitan outlook. In 1784, a Protestant clergyman, **J. G. Herder**, published *Ideas of the Philosophy of the History of Mankind.* Herder said that imitation of foreign ways was shallow and artificial, that German ways were different from those of others. He spoke of a ***volkgeist***, or spirit of the people, which he said came from the common folk. Herder did not say that the German *volkgeist* was better than that of other people or that it was in conflict with them, but that the German *volkgeist* was simply different. This idea was the opposite of the thoughts of Enlightenment thinkers like Voltaire, who said that certain truths were operative for all people of all places and times.

Volkgeist was a romantic idea because it emphasized genius and intuition over reason. It stressed the differences, rather than the similarities, among people. German thinkers resisted the concept of classical rules that applied to everyone. Such thinking provoked a reaction against Napoleon and French influence. During the French occupation of the German states, **J. G. Fichte**, a professor of philosophy, took the *volkgeist* idea still further. He declared that the German spirit, which could be seen in the customs, folklore, and institutions of the people, was not only different from that of other cultures but also superior and nobler. Therefore, it must be kept pure from outside influence.

Other German writers urged unity based on language, history, and folk traditions. A pair of linguists, the **Grimm brothers**, traveled the German states studying dialects. They learned folklore in their travels, which they turned into *Grimm's Fairy Tales*, an expression of *volkgeist* (and for which the brothers would be remembered).

At about the same time, **G. W. F. Hegel** further contributed to dismantling the Enlightenment concept of everything as fixed and unchanging. Hegel said reality itself was a process of endless change; all history, he claimed, resulted from a series of change, a process he labeled the **dialectic**. This was evidenced in the tendency of the human mind to proceed through the reaction of opposites. A given state of affairs Hegel called thesis. This thesis produced the concept of an opposite state, the antithesis. Eventually, there would be some kind of reconciliation or fusion of the conflicting ideas—this was the synthesis. (Karl Marx soon incorporated this theory into his philosophy.)

Following Hegel were two more influential writers, historian **Leopold von Ranke** and economist **Friedrich List**. Ranke claimed in 1830 that the Germans had a mission to create a purely German state. He seemed to feel that the same processes, such as a parliamentary government and constitutionalism, that had developed in Western Europe did not necessarily apply to Germany. Friedrich List viewed economics also from a very nationalistic stance. He said the principle of laissez-faire benefited England, keeping it the world's industrial center while using other countries to supply raw materials. For a nation to develop its own culture, said List, it must have cities, factories, and capital of its own. A developing country needed tariffs, at least at first, to protect its burgeoning economic system.

When France revolted against Louis Philippe in February 1848, the news rapidly spread across Europe. By March, there were riots in Berlin, which frightened the King of Prussia, **Frederick William IV**, into promising a constitution. Meanwhile, delegates from all the German states assembled in Frankfurt, meeting 1848–49. The **Frankfurt Assembly** debated the question of a unified Germany. There had been 39 states since the Congress of Vienna, and in a few of those, violence in March of 1848 had caused a collapse of the governments.

What stood in the way of German unity? First of all, each small state and its ruler were very jealous of their independence and had no desire to sacrifice individual power and privilege. There were two large German states, Austria and Prussia, and neither wanted the other to dominate the minor states. The social group most opposed to unification was the landed aristocracy of East Prussia, the **Junkers**, who took great pride in being Prussian and felt contempt for the rest of Germany. However, those who lived in the central or western states viewed the easterners as backward.

In reality, Prussia was not backward. It had a popularly elected parliament responsible to public will. Also, the Zollverein, or free tax union (the creation of List), encouraged a productive economy. After the March riot, Friedrich William allowed an elected Prussian assembly to meet in Berlin. This **Berlin Assembly** was a Prussian affair only, different from the all-German Frankfurt Assembly that convened at about the same time. Surprisingly, the Berlin meeting turned out to be very liberal and very anti-Junker. The Assembly voted support for Polish refugees (from Russia). It went so far as to promise self-government of two eastern regions of Prussia. The Germans living in these two areas refused to accept this decree, and the Prussian army stationed there supported the local Germans. After some time passed, Frederick William changed his mind about a constitutional assembly and shut down the Berlin meeting.

The Frankfurt Assembly, like the French National Assembly of 1789, did not exist through any legal precedent. The Frankfurt meeting was different, though, in that there was no aspect of national unity already in place. The members of the Assembly were professional people: lawyers, government officials, Catholic clergy, and businessmen—people who had no desire for revolution. The Assembly also had no connection with the masses. When riots broke out in Frankfurt in September 1848, the Assembly had to ask the Prussian army to restore peace because the Assembly possessed no authority in its own right.

A second incident that highlighted the Assembly's weakness involved Schleswig and Holstein, the two German states at the base of Denmark. In 1848, Denmark attempted to annex Schleswig. The Frankfurt Assembly wished to defend the Germans in Schleswig, but with no resources or army, it could only ask Prussia to help once more. (England and Russia objected to Prussian intervention, so nothing happened.)

A central question facing the Frankfurt Assembly was how to define Germany. Would a united Germany include Prussia? Austria? Bohemia? (Historians call this debate the question of "big Germany" or "little Germany.") Austria made no secret of its disdain for the whole idea. By the spring of 1849, the Assembly produced two important documents. The first was the **Declaration of the Rights of the German People**, which emphasized individual rights (freedom of religion, press, and assembly). While this document resembled the American Declaration of Independence and the French Declaration of the Rights of Man and Citizen, there was a major difference. The American and French declarations talked about rights of man, of all human beings, while the German statement emphasized German rights.

The second document was a constitution for a united Germany that excluded Austria. The Assembly offered leadership of a united state to Frederick William of Prussia, who scornfully refused the crown. Frederick William had no intention of submitting to a constitutional monarchy, nor did he wish to fight Austria, fighting that might be required to keep such a position. The old Prussian Junkers, Frederick William's main support, preferred to stay "Prussian" rather than to submerge themselves in an all-German state. Thus, the Frankfurt Assembly failed, and German unity had to come 20 years later in a very different way.

ITALY: REVOLUTIONS OF 1830 AND 1848

Following the Napoleonic era, nationalism continued to be an issue in areas like the German states, Poland, and Italy, where political unity did not exist. Italian nationalism was referred to as *resorgimento*, or resurgence of an Italian spirit or identity. During the Napoleonic era, a secret society of Italian nationalists had originated in Naples, calling itself the **Carbonari**. The spokesperson for Italian nationalism was **Joseph Mazzini**, who started out as part of the Carbonari. In 1831, Mazzini organized his own group, called **Young Italy**.

In northern and central Italy in 1831, there were outbreaks of violence but with no unity, and within a few weeks, insurgent groups surrendered either to the Austrian army or to papal forces. Young Italy circulated much literature and tried several times to initiate a movement toward Italian unity. All these attempts failed, and Mazzini was forced to live in exile, but he continued to influence Italian politics. In 1834–36 and in 1844, Mazzini attempted Italian revolts, all of which ended in futility. However, Mazzini never gave up; he and his followers would try once more in 1849.

In 1829 in Paris, the Italian composer Rossini presented his opera *William Tell*, which glorified the Swiss hero who had refused to submit to Austrian rule several centuries earlier. The work could be seen as a metaphor for Italian patriotism against domination by Austria.

In 1848 and 1849, there were two outbursts of Italian nationalism. When upheaval occurred in Austria in March 1848, the independent northern Italian kingdom of Piedmont-Sardinia tried to take advantage of Austria's current vulnerability by invading Lombardy and Venetia, territories in northern Italy occupied by Austria. Piedmont's ambition was to enlarge its holdings in northern Italy, and for a while, Italian patriots from all over the peninsula joined the cause. The uprising continued for about three months. Its leaders tended to be idealists—writers, professors, students, and intellectuals—rather than men with economic or social interests. The peasants (the bulk of the population) had little sense of nationality.

The second round of revolt occurred in Rome, following the assassination of a high church official, minister to the pope. The pope fled Rome, and radicals declared a new government with Mazzini as one of three rulers. The King of **Piedmont** was inspired to invade Lombardy again. But the uprisings were short-lived. The Austrians soon defeated the army of Piedmont once more. In Rome, Mazzini and his supporters were driven out and the pope restored by a French army that had been sent to re-establish order.

AUSTRIA: MULTIETHNIC EMPIRE AND THE REVOLUTION OF 1848

When news of the **February Revolution** in France spread across the Continent, the first reaction in the Austrian Empire came in Hungary, where the fiery speaker **Louis Kossuth** made a speech about liberty. Kossuth's speech was printed in German and spread to Vienna, where workers and students revolted, putting up barricades, fighting, and invading the royal palace. A terrified Metternich resigned and fled to England. Revolution spread throughout the empire. The Hungarian diet declared independence from Austria, while still recognizing the Habsburg monarchy, and Austria granted Bohemia the same status.

The representatives of the German states meeting in Frankfurt invited Bohemia to participate, but the Czech majority in Bohemia wasn't interested in a united Germany, where Czechs would form a small minority. Instead, the Czechs called for an **All-Slav Conference** in Prague in June 1848. Representatives from various Slavic groups within the Austrian Empire attended. The tone of the meeting turned out to be more anti-German than anti-Austrian. The group demanded equal recognition with other nationalities. The Germans in Bohemia, meanwhile, favored the Frankfurt Assembly. The Austrian Emperor Ferdinand refused to acknowledge any group. When fighting broke out in Prague, the Austrian army restored order and shut down the Slav congress.

In Hungary, Kossuth's Magyar party moved the capital to Budapest, in the center of the state, and changed the official language to Magyar. Though Magyars made up slightly less than half the population of Hungary, they attempted to "Magyarize" the country. Other groups—Serbs, Croats, Slovaks, etc.—strongly resisted. The Croatians revolted under the leadership of a general, **Jellachich**, and other minority groups joined the Croats. Seeing this as an opportunity to oppose the Magyars, Emperor Ferdinand gave Jellachich Austrian support.

In Vienna, revolutionaries feared the power of Jellachich's army and rose in violence. Ferdinand fled the country. After the Austrian army put down the uprising, the old order of Church, military, and landed aristocracy decided to install a new emperor, Francis Joseph, 18-year-old nephew of Ferdinand. The leadership believed that if Ferdinand were gone, the government would not have to keep promises he had made. The Magyars continued to fight in Hungary, so Francis Joseph invited Tsar Nicholas of Russia to send 100,000 Russian soldiers, who defeated the Magyars in August 1849.

SUMMARY OF THE REVOLUTIONS OF 1848

General Desires

    Constitutions

    Independence and unification of nationalist groups

    End of serfdom and manorial dues in Eastern Europe

France

    February Revolution

    Conflict between reformers and king's minister Guizot

    Barricades in streets

    Abdication of Louis Philippe

    Provisional government

    Bloody June Days

    National Workshops

    Elections—Louis Napoleon Bonaparte

Austrian Empire

    Violence in Vienna—Metternich's flight

    Italian rebellion

    Magyar revolt—led by Kossuth

    Pan-Slav meeting in Prague

    Jellachich and Serb-Croatian army against Magyars

    Abdication of Ferdinand—Francis Joseph

    Russian army to restore order in Hungary

Italy

    Revolt of northern provinces against Austria—defeat

    Rebellion around Rome—Mazzini—French army

    Mazzini driven into exile

German States

    Frankfort Assembly—debate over "big Germany" or "little Germany"

    Berlin Assembly—shut down

    Declaration of the Rights of the German People

    Constitution for a united Germany—rejection by Frederick William IV

    End of attempt at unification

CHAPTER 17: ROMANTICISM

CHARACTERISTICS, CONTRASTS WITH THE ENLIGHTENMENT, AND NATIONAL REVOLUTION

The 18th century was the age of reason, characterized by a belief in natural law, science, and the power of the human mind. For models, the rationalist thinkers turned to the patterns of ancient Greece and Rome; hence, they were called neoclassicists. In the late 18th century, a rebellion began against these ideas. Rousseau began to talk about "natural man," which he pictured as a glorified peasant or as the "noble savage" of the Americas. By the turn of the century, the movement was well underway in England among writers and artists.

In Germany, romanticism emerged in part as a rebellion against the French occupation. The movement here was called **Sturm und Drang** (Storm and Stress). An early example was Goethe's *The Sorrows of Young Werther.* The major emphasis was on nature, the emotions, and the individual. Nature was a source of inspiration and knowledge. The romantics gave importance to the subconscious mind and to things mysterious.

While the classicists of the previous age wanted answers to everything, the romantics gloried in the unexplainable. They looked to the Middle Ages for inspiration. **The Grimm brothers** (discussed in Chapter 16) concentrated on folklore, which related to the idea of the *volkgeist*, or spirit of the common people. Another German, **Friedrich von Schiller**, spoke of the passions of the senses and of the soul, as manifested in the person of a hero. **Wolfgang von Goethe** took his hero, **Faust**, from medieval legends and depicted him struggling against the supernatural and against society. While the thinkers of the Enlightenment prescribed a universal system applicable to all people in all places and times, the romantics subscribed to a very individualistic point of view, emphasizing creative genius that was immune to universal rules. Such originality could come from one writer or artist or from a whole people. Thus, romanticism grew hand in hand with nationalism in such places as the German states, where philosophers praised the unique character of their culture.

ROMANTIC LITERATURE

The official beginning of romanticism in literature was the publication in 1798 of the *Lyrical Ballads* by **Samuel Taylor Coleridge** and **William Wordsworth** in England. Wordsworth turned to nature for guidance. In "The Tables Turned," he wrote this:

> One impulse from a vernal wood
> May teach you more of man,
> Of moral evil and of good,
> Than all the sages can.

Coleridge's biggest contribution to *Lyrical Ballads* was his mysterious tale in poetry "The Rime of the Ancient Mariner," which also emphasized the sacredness of nature and contained hints of the supernatural. Even before Wordsworth, the English mystical poet **William Blake** spoke out for the poor, especially children. Both Wordsworth and Blake saw industry as evil and ugly, polluting the natural landscape and dehumanizing.

Another precursor to the 19th-century romantics, who, like Blake, was little known during his lifetime, was the Scotsman **Robert Burns**. During his short, colorful life, Burns drew on Scottish folklore and wrote poetry in Scottish dialect. His subjects were the common people. **Sir Walter Scott**, also from Scotland, wrote historical novels and long narrative poems that retold events of the past in terms of heroic action that glorified the individual.

A generation after Wordsworth came a second group of English romantic poets, the most prominent of whom were **Percy Shelley, Lord Byron**, and **John Keats**. These writers were often loners who wrote about rejection by society and about not being understood. Like their predecessors, they glorified nature as a source of inspiration. As noted in Chapter 16, Shelley and Byron championed the Greek fight for independence from the Ottoman Turks.

In their reverence for the Middle Ages, some romantic writers turned to **gothic** tales, which featured the mysterious, the supernatural, and death with settings in large, spooky old houses surrounded by violent weather. Two English examples of gothic literature were *Frankenstein* by **Mary Shelley** and *Wuthering Heights* by **Emily Brontë**.

On the Continent, the French novelist **Victor Hugo** wrote inspiring tales of heroic action, *The Hunchback of Notre Dame* and *Les Misérables*. Both novels featured the poor and outcast of society. In Russia, the poet and novelist **Alexander Pushkin** reflected the romantic spirit, as did a number of early 19th-century writers in the United States (**Ralph Waldo Emerson, Henry David Thoreau, Edgar Allan Poe, Nathaniel Hawthorne**, and **Herman Melville**). Romanticism would rule the international literary world until the second half of the century.

ROMANTIC ART AND MUSIC

Even before the romantic period officially began, a one-man revolt took place in the art of the Englishman William Blake. From early childhood, Blake claimed to see visions that inspired his painting. Trained as an engraver, Blake deviated from the artistic standards of his day, the oil portrait of people in classical stances, and painted in watercolor, often including images of God and angels in his art. Blake illustrated the pages of his poetry with his original watercolors. More recognized on the English romantic scene were **John Constable** and **J. M. W. Turner**, both of whom turned to nature for subjects. Constable portrayed tranquil, idealized rural scenes with cottages, farm animals, trees, streams, and hillsides. Turner's landscapes were more mystical, rendering nature's power and terror in pictures of fires, smoke, and fog.

French artists also portrayed the political spirit of the times. In *Liberty Leading the People,* **Eugene Delacroix** idealized the July Revolution of 1830. His painting showed people of all classes, determinedly following a goddesslike Liberty, carrying the tricolor flag. Another of his huge canvases of heroic action scenes was *Massacre at Chios,* portraying Greek refugees from the Turks, struggling for survival. *Raft of the Medusa,* painted by **Théodore Géricault**, pictured stormy seas and skies, illustrating the fate of survivors of a shipwreck attributed to an incompetent commander who had achieved his post through political favoritism. Unlike its neoclassical predecessor, characterized by frozen poses and horizontal and vertical lines, romantic art was full of action and emotion; the lines of paintings tended to be diagonal.

In music, there was not as radical a change from the classical to the romantic. **Ludwig von Beethoven** was something of a bridge between the two periods. Incorporating new structures and harmonies, Beethoven was one of the first composers to achieve wealth and fame in his lifetime. He composed string quartets, symphonies, and sonatas for the new instrument, the **piano**, which superseded its predecessor, the harpsichord, in that its volume could be controlled. The orchestra, which had been small and compact, was now greatly expanded with new instruments and modifications of older ones. The conductor now stood in front of the orchestra and no longer played an instrument with the group.

The Austrian composer **Franz Shubert** drew on romantic lyric poetry and folk songs, especially Hungarian gypsy tunes, for his operas, Masses, symphonies, piano sonatas, and quartets. **Franz Liszt** became a pioneer in composing primarily for the piano, and the Italian **Niccolò Paganini** accomplished something similar for the violin. Concerts were a popular form of entertainment, drawing the middle class as well as the wealthy. Music was also a part of family life; people played instruments, and children had music lessons. Even middle-class homes often had pianos.

UNIT FOUR REVIEW QUESTIONS

1. The Factory Act of 1802 was the first attempt to regulate English industry. It failed to bring change because

    (A) the poor insisted on working long hours for the money.

    (B) labor unions were opposed to the legislation.

    (C) there was no way to enforce the regulations.

    (D) the followers of Adam Smith insisted that government avoid meddling in industry.

    (E) compared to workers on the Continent, English laborers had good conditions.

2. All the following are true of romantic literature EXCEPT

    (A) it came after neoclassicism and spanned the 19th century.

    (B) it looked to the Middle Ages for inspiration.

    (C) its poetry glorified nature.

    (D) some novels contained elements of the supernatural.

    (E) it featured the lives of the poor and outcast.

3. In 1830 in France,

    (A) Louis Philippe abdicated during the February Revolution.

    (B) a provisional government planned for the future.

    (C) the government opened national workshops.

    (D) Charles X tried to apply his July Ordinances.

    (E) Louis XVIII died.

4. The German philosopher J. G. Fichte expanded on the idea of *volkgeist* by saying that

    (A) it applied to other nationalities as well as to Germans.

    (B) the common people possessed truer qualities than the nobility.

    (C) the German *volkgeist* was superior to that of other cultures.

    (D) the Germans had never been able to express their unique characteristics.

    (E) German unification was necessary.

5. The Belgians and Dutch did not get along well as a united nation primarily because

    (A) the Dutch were agricultural and the Belgians were industrial.

    (B) the Belgians resented Dutch attempts at absolutist authority.

    (C) there was controversy over selecting a king.

    (D) the British and French would not guarantee their security.

    (E) the Dutch refused to extend their religious toleration to Belgium.

6. Other minorities in Hungary became alarmed by Louis Kossuth and his pro-Magyar movement when

    (A) Magyar became the official language of Hungary.

    (B) the Magyars moved the capital to Budapest.

    (C) Kossuth made fiery, nationalistic speeches in the Hungarian diet.

    (D) the Austrian emperor abdicated and fled.

    (E) the Russian army invaded Hungary.

7. The Congress powers used the Holy Alliance as an excuse for

   (A) opposition to the Ottoman Turks, who were Muslim.

   (B) religious intolerance within the member states.

   (C) Church control of education.

   (D) political intervention in Naples and Spain to suspend nationalist and liberal activity.

   (E) restoring the pope after outbreaks of violence in Rome in 1848.

8. In 1848–49, the King of Piedmont-Sardinia twice invaded Lombardy in hopes of

   (A) unifying Italy under Piedmont-Sardinia.

   (B) driving the Austrians out of northern Italy.

   (C) joining forces with Young Italy, which had attacked Rome.

   (D) restoring the pope, who had fled Rome.

   (E) establishing law and order in Italy after outbreaks of violence.

9. Frederick William IV rejected the constitution written by the Frankfurt Assembly for a unified Germany because

   (A) he looked with disdain on submitting to constitutional monarchy.

   (B) he feared opposition from Austria.

   (C) his Junker support was not interested in German unity.

   (D) there was nothing legal or binding about the actions of the Frankfurt Assembly.

   (E) of all of the above.

10. Wolfgang von Goethe's *Faust* was a piece of romantic literature in that it

    (A) was a heroic adventure story.

    (B) condemned the evils of the Industrial Revolution.

    (C) drew on a medieval legend involving a deal with Satan.

    (D) was based on a classical story from Greek mythology.

    (E) glorified the beauties of the natural world.

11. The political leadership of Austria in 1848 did not allow Ferdinand, the emperor who had fled, to return to his position mainly because

    (A) it was attracted to the youthful energy of his nephew Francis Joseph.

    (B) the old emperor had antagonized Bohemia and Hungary.

    (C) of pressure from the rebellious minorities.

    (D) of pressure from Nicholas I of Russia.

    (E) with Ferdinand gone, the government would not have to honor promises he had made.

12. Delacroix's painting *Liberty Leading the People* symbolically portrayed events of

    (A) the July Revolution of 1830.

    (B) the February Revolution of 1848.

    (C) the French Revolution.

    (D) the Bloody June Days of 1848.

    (E) all of the above.

13. The Chartist movement in England advocated all the following EXCEPT

    (A) universal male suffrage.

    (B) salaries for members of Parliament.

    (C) minimum wage.

    (D) more equality among voting districts.

    (E) voting by secret ballot.

14. Metternich distrusted the Burschenschaft mainly because

    (A) he was suspicious of liberal university professors and students.

    (B) the organization promoted German unity and nationalism.

    (C) it had Marxist connections.

    (D) it was openly opposed to established authority.

    (E) its activities were secret.

15. Tsar Nicholas I of Russia demonstrated his strong conservatism in all the following incidents EXCEPT

    (A) brutally defeating an attempted uprising in Poland in 1830.

    (B) desiring to intervene in Belgium in 1830.

    (C) sending troops to restore order in Hungary in 1848.

    (D) overrunning the Cisalpine Republic in northern Italy in Napoleon's absence.

    (E) causing many Poles to flee to Paris and other Western cities.

16. Arrange the work of the following men, all related to steam power, in correct chronological order, from earliest to latest: (1) Robert Fulton, (2) George Stephenson, (3) James Watt, (4) Thomas Newcomen.

    (A) 4, 3, 2, 1

    (B) 3, 4, 1, 2

    (C) 1, 2, 4, 3

    (D) 4, 3, 1, 2

    (E) 2, 1, 4, 3

17. All the following are true of music concerts in the 19th century EXCEPT

    (A) only the upper class attended concerts.

    (B) orchestras were larger than in the past.

    (C) the conductor no longer played an instrument.

    (D) the piano was a new instrument.

    (E) a number of new or improved instruments appeared.

18. The Declaration of Rights of the German People differed from the French Declaration of the Rights of Man and Citizen in that the German document

    (A) denied freedom of religion to Jews.

    (B) addressed only the German people.

    (C) declared freedom of speech but not of assembly.

    (D) ignored feudal obligations.

    (E) avoided the issue of private property.

19. David Ricardo had a pessimistic outlook toward the English factory workers. He believed

    (A) overpopulation was about to doom the working class.

    (B) laissez-faire policies were necessary to expand trade.

    (C) paying workers more would only encourage larger families, who would consume the excess.

    (D) education wasn't necessary for the poor.

    (E) all of the above.

20. Hegel was a German philosopher who

    (A) said that a given state of affairs, a thesis, would produce an opposite state, the antithesis.

    (B) developed the idea of *volkgeist*, or spirit of the people.

    (C) said that each culture had unique characteristics.

    (D) had no influence on future thinking or theories.

    (E) glorified all things German as superior to other cultures.

For the following questions, write an essay that

- has a relevant thesis;
- addresses all parts of the question;
- supports a thesis with specific evidence; and
- is well organized.

Plan your essays and write them on your own paper.

1. Unlike the revolutions of 1848, those that occurred around 1830 brought some measure of success. Evaluate the improvements that 1830 brought to some parts of Europe, as well as the failures that occurred in other places.

2. Describe the lives of mill workers in one of the industrial centers in England in the late 18th or early 19th century.

_____

_____

_____

_____

_____

_____

_____

_____

_____

_____

_____

_____

_____

_____

_____

ANSWERS AND EXPLANATIONS

1. C

Though the Factory Act of 1802 attempted to reduce hours and improve working conditions of English mill workers, there was no agency in place to inspect factories or enforce the law. (A) and (D) are factual, but these issues were ignored by Parliament. There were no labor unions yet, (B), and at the time, the industrial age had not reached the Continent, (E).

2. A

What makes choice (A) untrue is its second half: The romantic period ended about the middle of the 19th century, to be followed by the Age of Realism. All of the other answer choices are true.

3. D

The revolt in response to Charles X's July Ordinances led to his abdication. (A), (B), and (C) all occurred in the revolutions of 1848. The death of Louis XVIII, (E), was in 1824.

4. C

J. G. Herder, who originated the idea of *volkgeist*, defined it as a unique cultural personality, a spirit of the people most discernable in the lives of the common people. Herder did not say that one culture was better than another, only different. (A) and (B) are aspects of Herder's original ideas. During the Napoleonic period, Fichte advocated the German *volkgeist* as superior to that of other cultures. (D) and (E) would be developed by German nationalists later in the 19th century.

5. B

Until its unification with the Dutch Republic in 1815, Belgium had been under the control of Austria, but Austria had not exercised very strict control. The new Dutch monarch attempted to practice absolutism, despite the constitution, and the Belgians were resentful. (A) is true and should have been a positive force for unity, but negative factors surpassed this advantage. The controversy in (C) relates to later in 1830, after Belgium declared its independence. (D) and (E) are simply not true.

6. A

The Hungarian revolt of 1848 began with Kossuth's emotional speeches in the Hungarian diet, (C). The Magyars declared their independence and moved their capital to Budapest, (B). What alarmed other minorities was the diet's decision to make Magyar the official language, (A); Magyar is a very difficult non-Indo-European language, and less than 50 percent of the Hungarian population was Magyar. (D) and (E) occurred also, but they weren't factors behind the arousal of other minorities in the Austrian empires.

7. D

The Holy Alliance was the idea of Alexander I and the Congress of Vienna; it was agreed to by the other powers except for England. It was then used as an excuse for maintaining the status quo, especially in Naples, where Austria restored order, and Spain, which France invaded. (A) is true but did not come up frequently; (B) and (C) are irrelevant. (E), in 1848, came after the Holy Alliance had ceased to exist.

8. B

Piedmont-Sardinia was the only independent state in Italy. It wanted to extend its influence over the rest of northern Italy but wasn't interested in unifying the whole peninsula, (A). Accomplishing this goal required driving out Austria, which controlled Venetia and Lombardy. Piedmont-Sardinia first took advantage of unrest and violence occurring in Vienna and then of outbreaks of violence in Rome. Piedmont-Sardinia had no specific connection to Mazzini and Young Italy, (C), however, nor any interest in choices (D) and (E).

9. E

The first outbreaks of violence in Berlin in 1848 caused a reaction of panic in Frederick William IV, and although he promised Prussia a constitution, he soon recovered his nerve and shut down the Berlin Assembly gathered to write Prussia a constitution. He let the Frankfurt Assembly proceed, though it had no legal precedent, and he totally disregarded its actions for all the reasons in (A) through (D).

10. C

(A), (B), and (E) are characteristics of romantic literature but are not prominent in the Faust story. Goethe was one of several authors who produced a version of the medieval legend. (Christopher Marlowe, contemporary of Shakespeare, was another.) The fact that a 19th-century author drew on a medieval legend makes it romantic.

11. E

Both Nicholas and the ethnic minorities applied pressure to the government in Vienna, but in different ways, and neither affected the decision to choose new leadership (C and D). (A) and (B) are somewhat true but irrelevant.

12. A

Like Hugo's *Les Misérables*, *Liberty Leading the People* was based on the July Revolution of 1830. Liberty was symbolized as a fearless goddess, carrying the revolutionary flag and leading a cross section of French people across the bodies of those who had died for the cause of freedom.

13. C

The Chartist movement addressed issues related to voting and Parliament. The only answer choice here not related to those topics is minimum wage, which was not under consideration by anyone in the middle of the 19th century.

14. B

During his entire time in power, Metternich feared and avoided the joint concerns of German nationalism and unification. The center of such activity was the German universities—at least, the ideas were discussed there. Choice (A) is accurate, but it doesn't go far enough, making (B) the better choice. Marxism, (C), wasn't known beyond a tiny handful of Europeans. The Burschenschaft had actually challenged almost no one, making (D) untrue, and its clubs did not pretend to be secret organizations, (E).

15. D

Though Russia did "meddle" in northern Italy at one point, this was in 1797, many years before Nicholas became tsar in 1825. Nicholas did do all the other things, including (E); when Russian troops quashed the Polish revolt in 1831–1832, thousands fled to the West.

16. D

Thomas Newcomen developed the first (inefficient) steam engine (4). James Watt refined it (3). Robert Fulton developed the steamboat (1). George Stephenson invented the steam locomotive (2).

17. A

All the statements are true except (A). In the 19th century, the middle class attended concerts, often owned pianos (a newly developed instrument), and provided their children with musical instruction.

18. B

The French Declaration of the Rights of Man and Citizen and the American Declaration of Independence addressed human beings in general, but the Declaration of Rights of the German People addressed Germans only. It did guarantee civil rights to all, including Jews.

19. C

David Ricardo formulated the iron law of wages, which said that workers would only have more babies if they were paid more. (A) is related to the theories of Thomas Malthus, and (B) applies to the classical economists in general. Ricardo might have agreed with choice (D), but it was not part of his theory.

20. A

Hegel was famous for his development of the dialectic, which focused on a thesis, antithesis, and resolution. (B), (C), and (E) are related to other German philosophers, and choice (D) is not true because Karl Marx would be influenced by Hegel's dialectic.

SAMPLE FREE-RESPONSE ESSAYS

1. Unlike the revolutions of 1848, those that occurred around 1830 brought some measure of success. Evaluate the improvements that 1830 brought to some parts of Europe, as well as the failures that occurred in other places.

A major goal of the great powers as they left the Congress of Vienna was to keep everything in Europe the way it was. They had witnessed the violence and suffering that had resulted from the French revolution and the Napoleonic wars, and they wanted to prevent anything similar in the future. So their aim was to quash any hints of nationalism or liberalism, anything that might bring change. This proved not to be entirely possible over time, however. Pressures built in various places throughout the Continent, and around 1830, and again around 1848, there were outbreaks of revolution. In 1848 and 1849, after some initial success, all these attempts ended in failure. But this was not the case in 1830–1832. Although some of the revolts ended disastrously, there were several successes.

Italy was one of the scenes where revolution failed in the early 1830s. The problem that Italian patriots saw was lack of unity and foreign and papal domination. Except for the independent kingdom of Piedmont-Sardinia in northwestern Italy, the rest of northern Italy was directly under the control of Austria, and Austria also kept a strong influence over the rest of the peninsula, which was divided into a series of small states. The ones in the center of Italy, around Rome, were under papal authority, and in the far south was the Kingdom of Naples. In both northern and central Italy in 1831, there were attempted revolts against Austrian domination, but in both places, the rebels were soon conquered by Austrian might. This was the time when Joseph Mazzini began to be influential in the movement toward Italian unity, through his organization Young Italy, but he was forced into exile, from which he would continue to spread propaganda.

There was more success in Greece. The Greeks had been struggling for a decade to escape from the Ottoman Empire. An earlier attempt to gain independence in the early 1820s, led by the patriot Ypsilanti, had ended in defeat when the great powers refused to help the Greeks. But the Greek cause was then taken up by Western writers, especially British romantic poets, and by the late 1820s, both England and France were willing to back the Greeks. When the Turks refused the demands to release Greece, England and France destroyed the Turkish fleet, and Greece gained her independence in 1832.

Although England was not the scene of an actual revolution around 1830, certainly there was discontent and demand for reform. One of the problems was the inequity by which members of Parliament were elected. The voting districts had

had no revision for a great many years and had no relation to population. Especially, the new industrial centers such as Liverpool and Manchester had no representation at all, while there were other boroughs which sent men to Parliament but where few, or perhaps no, people lived. The other complaint was that only a very limited number of males could vote, namely men of wealth and property. After much debate and pressure from the monarchy, the House of Commons passed the Reform Bill of 1832. The new measure still did not give numerical representation to voting districts, but it did remove some of the "rotten boroughs" (the districts where few people lived) and reassigned those seats to the new industrial towns. The Bill approximately doubled the franchise, but still only men of considerably means qualified.

A third area where revolutionary change occurred was in Belgium. Until 1815, Belgium had always been under foreign domination, first by Spain and, after 1713, by Austria. The Congress of Vienna had joined Belgium to the Dutch republic and created the Kingdom of the Netherlands with the ruler from the Dutch house of Orange. This looked like a good "match" because, economically, the two complemented each other. The Dutch offered a strong agricultural base and a merchant marine for world trade, while the Belgians were industrialized. But there were differences. The Belgians spoke French or Flemish and disliked having the business of government in Dutch; also, the Belgians were Catholic and the Dutch were Protestant. These might have been endured, had it not been for the absolutist ambitions of the Dutch monarch. The Belgians were used to virtual independence from the Austrians and strongly resented the authoritarian nature of the new regime. When the leaders of Belgium declared their independence, the Dutch at first resisted but soon backed down. With the agreement of France and England, then, Belgium became an independent state.

When the Belgians first began their revolt, Nicholas I of distant Russia urged the great powers to intervene to restore order. But before he could do anything more than protest, he had problems closer home when the Poles revolted. So instead of sending a Russian army to Western Europe, the tsar was forced to use his military to stop revolution in Poland, which he did brutally. The Poles' attempt to achieve independence was soon defeated, and Poland stayed under the thumb of Russia.

2. Describe the lives of mill workers in one of the industrial centers in England in the late 18th or early 19th century.

The new mill towns in England grew suddenly and haphazardly, with a great many negative consequences. Thousands of people left their previous homes in the countryside and moved to the cities to find work. It is questionable whether their lives were better here than in the country; certainly, they remained miserably poor. The problems they encountered in town were different from those on the farms.

Housing was perhaps the biggest problem. Because there was as yet no public or mass transportation, workers were forced to live within walking distance of their jobs. And because so many people descended on the towns so quickly, housing was very inadequate. There was tremendous overcrowding; sometimes whole families, or even multiple families, lived in single rooms. Such things as running water and flush toilets did not exist. In fact, the towns had no public water supplies yet and no sewer systems. Living in such crowded, unsanitary conditions also made the spread of disease quite rapid.

There were problems of what to do with the children. If they didn't work in the mills with their parents, they tended to roam the streets, getting into trouble, because the towns had no school systems yet. There was also little security because urban police forces were a thing of the future. Most of the new industrial towns sprang up in the north of England, where the climate is often gray, and this was coupled with pollution from coal smoke because the factories burned coal to produce steam to run the machines.

The millwork itself meant very long days, generally of between 10 and 14 hours. The labor in demand was unskilled, so wages remained very low. Oftentimes, because of their smaller bodies, women and children were more desirable than men, but they were always paid less. Jobs were very uncertain; one had work only so long as the mill had a contract to fill, and no work meant no pay. Orphans living in public or private facilities were often put to work in the mills. In the beginning, the head of a household might negotiate labor for his whole family in the same place. Later, this practice was less common. Another place where children and young women worked was coal mines, again putting in long hours in unpleasant conditions. The pay for mine work was generally higher than factory wages. Both the factories and the mines could be dust-filled places, which took their toll on human lungs.

In the early days of industrialization, there was no organization among the workers. But the fact that so many of them were crowded together would help generate solidarity that eventually would translate into labor unions. The Christian churches sometimes offered modest help to the poor urban workers and miners; the early Methodists modeled missionary work of this type. Some denominations eventually set up "Sunday schools," designed to teach literacy and religion to children who worked the other days of the week.

Public awareness slowly developed in regard to the problems and needs of the urban poor. The first attempt to legislate improvements was the Factory Act of 1802, which tried to reduce working hours and improve working conditions.

But because the bill included no methods of enforcement, it brought virtually no change. However, the Factory Act of 1833 and the Ten Hours Act a few years later were more effective because they did legislate agencies of enforcement. The number of working hours gradually was reduced, and the age at which children could be employed rose. Later in the century, with the advent of labor unions and, eventually, with the expanded franchise, more legal reforms helped improve wages and working conditions. By the end of the 19th century, living standards for factory workers rose considerably from the levels at the turn on the 18th century.

CHAPTER 18: THE AGE OF REALPOLITIK (1848–1871)

AFTERMATH OF THE REVOLUTIONS OF 1848

The revolutions of 1848 failed for several reasons. The people behind the movements tended to be idealists, such as students, professors, philosophers, or professional people. They were primarily from the educated middle class. Nowhere were the masses engaged for long, nor did the revolutionaries have widespread military support.

In most places, the middle class was small and not well developed. The ruling regimes in various countries were shaken but not toppled permanently. There were only a few truly liberal changes: In France, universal male suffrage came about, and in Eastern Europe, serfdom and old manorial privileges finally disappeared.

In Prussia, Frederick William issued his own Prussian constitution in 1850, after rejecting the all-German proposal of the Frankfurt Assembly the year before. Under the new constitution, Junkers maintained their power, and men from lower economic levels could not vote. The provisional government of France led to the second French empire under Louis Napoleon Bonaparte, discussed below. Austria got a new young emperor, Francis Joseph, who would rule until the First World War. Austria also regained control of Bohemia and Hungary and kept its hold over a large portion of Italy.

Idealism and romanticism disappeared as utopian dreams not to be trusted. In their place, people turned to materialism and what was termed *realism*. Attention turned to science, to observable facts. In the German states, the term was **realpolitik**, or the politics of reality, which emphasized law and order and hard work. People became more skeptical toward religion, but religion was still important to preserve order. Being tough-minded was desirable. Such attitudes drifted into literature and art as well, perhaps because of the invention of photography. Writers claimed no longer to romanticize life but to report it as it actually happened (see Chapter 21). This direction of thinking shaped politics and society of the Western world in the second half of the 19th century.

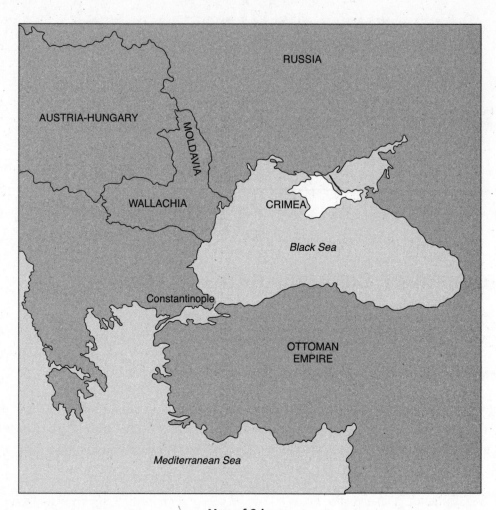

RUSSIA

AUSTRIA-HUNGARY

MOLDAVIA

WALLACHIA

CRIMEA

Black Sea

Constantinople

OTTOMAN
EMPIRE

Mediterranean Sea

Map of Crimea

CRIMEAN WAR

The Crimean War (1853–1856) was a rather minor war, but it brought significant consequences. Most importantly, it helped make possible the unification of Italy because it weakened Russia and Austria, the main countries trying to maintain the status quo. It was the first war covered by correspondents and the first war in which female nurses cared for wounded soldiers.

In 1853, Nicholas I of Russia moved troops into **Wallachia and Moldavia (Romania)** with the excuse of protecting Christians in the Ottoman Empire. Western Europe, especially France, was distressed by the Russian presence here and urged the Turks to resist. In late 1853, war broke out between the Ottoman Empire and Russia. The British and French soon joined the Turks. Piedmont-Sardinia also joined the fight in hopes of having a voice at the peace talks for the purpose of advancing Italian unification. The Austrian Empire did not join either side but sent troops into Wallachia and Moldavia, forcing Russia to retreat.

All the fighting took place on the Crimean Peninsula (see map on page 190). The British navy blockaded Russia in both the Black Sea and the Baltic. In 1855, Nicholas I died, and his successor, Alexander II, asked for peace. At the treaty talks, Russia gave up her claims of protecting Christians beyond her borders. Moldavia and Wallachia were united and recognized as self-governing. Russia was also forbidden to put ships on the Black Sea.

During the war, the English woman **Florence Nightingale** organized and trained a group of female nurses who went to the **Crimea**. They found terrible conditions of filth and malnutrition, and they revolutionized field hospitals, dramatically dropping the mortality rate among the wounded.

THE SECOND FRENCH EMPIRE UNDER LOUIS NAPOLEON

After the Bloody June Days of 1848, the French Assembly limited freedom of the press and of assembly. It closed political clubs and forbade women to meet. The provisional government was in the process of writing a constitution with a strong executive power, a president, but the violence frightened the government into a decision to hold elections even before the constitution was complete.

There were four candidates: **General Cavaignac**, who had used the army to restore order in May when the provisional government had shut down the national workshops; **Alexandre Ledru-Rollin**, a socialist; **Alphonse Lamartine**, a poet and political moderate; and **Louis Napoleon Bonaparte**, nephew of the first Napoleon. Both Ledru-Rollin and Lamartine had connections to the provisional government, which had recently established an unpopular tax. They and Cavaignac received a tiny percentage of the vote, which was by universal male suffrage. Louis Napoleon won by a huge majority, probably because of name recognition.

Louis Napoleon was practically unknown in France, having only returned from exile in 1848 and been elected to the constituent assembly. His father, Louis Bonaparte, had been the most liberal of the clan, serving as King of Holland during the heyday of his famous brother. Louis Napoleon had a mixed career in various countries; in Italy and the German states, he had been a radical, but in England, he had opposed the Chartists. Karl Marx said that Louis Napoleon could be everything to everybody because he was virtually unknown. Prior to the election, he had written and circulated two pamphlets, "Napoleonic Ideas" and "**The Elimination of Poverty**." These and the name convinced the majority of the voters that he would do *something* to improve the sagging economy. Many people were unemployed. In 1848, Louis Napoleon was elected to a four-year term, sharing power with a conservative Assembly.

By the spring of 1849, Louis Napoleon and the legislature used a brief insurrection as an excuse to suppress public meetings, expel socialist members of the Assembly, impose censorship, and take the vote away from the poorest third of the population. In 1850, the **Falloux Law** returned control of all schools to the Church. When violence erupted in Rome, Louis Napoleon sent French troops to oust the republican government Mazzini and his followers had established and to restore the pope, who had fled. French troops would remain in Rome for the next 20 years.

Then, posing as a friend of the people, Louis Napoleon returned universal male suffrage, but at the same time, he shut down the Assembly. There was protest, but Louis Napoleon used the army to quell it. He then called for a popular vote and was elected for a 10-year term as president. The next year, he proclaimed himself Emperor Napoleon III (the original Napoleon's son had died almost 20 years earlier).

Napoleon III was not a great general as his uncle had been, but he knew how to appeal politically to the public. He insisted that the forms of a country's government were of much less consequence than its economic and social realities. He carefully controlled the national legislature, leaving it generally powerless. Like his famous uncle, Napoleon III married a princess (Spanish) and maintained a brilliant, showy court life.

Domestically, Louis Napoleon renovated and modernized. He hired a city planner, **Baron Haussman**, to revamp Paris into a city of wide boulevards, parks, monuments, railroad stations, and public buildings. He modernized the water supply and sewers. All these projects provided many jobs, and the newly widened streets created convenient access for the military. France had never had a banking system equal to that of England; Louis Napoleon brought into being two new institutions: the **Credit Mobilier**, specifically to loan money to the public, and the **Credit Foncier**, to loan money to landowners to improve agriculture.

In transportation, the government built railroads, replaced wooden sailing vessels with steamships, and backed **Ferdinand de Lesseps** and his company in the construction of the **Suez Canal** in Egypt (1859–1869). The French economy prospered, and large corporations developed. To help the poor, Napoleon built hospitals and asylums and distributed free medicine. In 1864, labor unions and strikes became legal. Despite objections, Louis Napoleon leaned toward free trade.

In foreign affairs, Louis Napoleon was less successful; wars ruined the Second Empire. Briefly, in 1858–1859, Louis Napoleon joined forces with Piedmont-Sardinia in northern Italy in an attempt to push the Austrians out of Italy (discussed next). After the French-Piedmontese armies won two battles, Napoleon III suddenly backed out, partly because of Catholic opposition in France and partly because of threats from Prussia. France made a sudden, hasty peace with Austria, leaving Piedmont on its own once more.

A few years later, Louis Napoleon got involved in Mexico. While the United States was occupied with its own Civil War, England, Spain, and France sent a military force to collect debt by seizing the customs houses in Mexican ports. England and Spain withdrew, however, once they realized that Louis Napoleon had a larger, more unilateral plan—to set up a French state in Mexico with an Austrian archduke, **Maximilian**, as its puppet ruler. By the close of the American Civil War, the United States demanded that France withdraw. French troops were recalled, and Maximilian was executed. The whole fiasco made bad press for Louis Napoleon at home.

Thus, in 1870, when it appeared that the French had been insulted by Prussia, and vice versa, by the Ems Dispatch (see below), a "little war" seemed to be the solution to restoring patriotic loyalty at home. The war was short and disastrous for France, even after calling home the French troops that had been stationed in Rome for two decades. Napoleon was captured on his way to England (fleeing the country), and France became a republic once again.

UNIFICATION OF ITALY

In the middle of the 19th century, the Italian peninsula was still divided into about a dozen small states, plus some very tiny ones. The growing discontent of the Italian people led to revolts in 1848–1849, none of which succeeded. These events proved that it would be difficult to dislodge the Austrian presence in northern Italy. And because the pope had been threatened, certainly he would offer no support to the cause of nationalism.

Both the Habsburg influence in the north and papal power in central Italy were obstacles to unification. Another problem was the economic difference between the prosperous north, which had industry, waterpower, and markets, and the much poorer agricultural south. The only independent Italian state was Piedmont-Sardinia, where **Victor Emmanuel** became king in 1848, under a liberal constitution. Described by historians as poorly educated and uncouth, the extraordinary thing Victor Emmanuel did was to appoint **Camillo di Cavour** prime minister in 1852.

Cavour came from a liberal, aristocratic background. Because he was not the eldest son in his family, he had turned first to the military, where he was too radical to fit in. Returning to civilian life, he had been successful in farming, employing the latest agricultural knowledge and equipment; still later, he had also excelled in business and banking. He had traveled to France and England and been impressed with the prosperity and efficiency of those countries.

Under the new constitution of 1848, Cavour was elected to parliament, then chosen as minister of commerce and agriculture and, finally, as prime minister. He worked to improve the economy with more credit, lower tariffs (to attract foreign investors), more railroads, and an improved army. He sought to control the Church by taxing its property, limiting the income of bishops, and holding the clergy answerable to civil law. Cavour's goal was to expand the borders of Piedmont over most of northern Italy; he was not interested in the Papal States in central Italy or the poor states in the south.

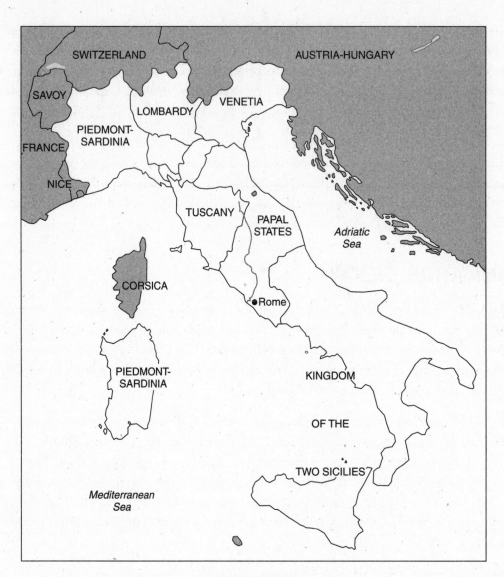

Unification of Italy

The other possible catalyst for unification came from the remnants of the revolutions of 1848, whose spokesperson was still Mazzini and his Young Italy organization. Mazzini advocated the right to vote and work, and he preached unity and democracy, not only for Italy but also for the downtrodden everywhere—Poles, Hungarians, and the various Slavic groups. All of Mazzini's efforts in the past had failed, which had brought some discredit to the movement. In 1853, Mazzini's followers tried to start yet another revolt in Lombardy. When Cavour heard of it, he informed Austria, which quashed the attempt. Cavour coveted all of northern Italy for Piedmont-Sardinia, but he needed help to drive Austria out of **Venetia and Lombardy**.

First, Cavour negotiated trade agreements with England and France; then Piedmont-Sardinia participated in the Crimean War. In the late 1850s, Cavour was able to work out an agreement with France by promising her **Savoy and Nice** on France's eastern border (see map). France kept Russia from getting involved by hinting at a possible revision of the Treaty of Paris (settling the Crimean War), which forbade Russian ships on the Black Sea. France sent troops to Piedmont-Sardinia after Cavour was able to provoke Austria into being the aggressor.

Together, the French and Piedmontese troops won two battles, but then Louis Napoleon got cold feet. He feared reprisals from the German states (Prussia was threatening), and he worried that Piedmont-Sardinia could become more powerful than France might wish on its eastern border. Without consulting Piedmont, France made peace with Austria in the **Treaty of Villafranca**, giving Piedmont Lombardy but not Venetia. Other parts of northern Italy clamored to join Piedmont-Sardinia, so the **Treaty of Turin** (1860) granted to Piedmont-Sardinia Italian territory down to the Papal States (except for Venetia). France got Nice and Savoy and continued to bolster the pope's power in central Italy.

Meanwhile, the inheritor of Mazzini's spirit was **Giuseppe Garibaldi**, who had fought in Lombardy in 1848 and in Rome in 1849. Forced into exile, he had lived as a guerilla fighter in South America since then. Personally, Cavour distrusted the methods and spirit of Mazzini and Garibaldi, but he now saw Garibaldi as useful. Thus, Cavour financed Garibaldi's volunteer army of **red shirts** as it entered the southern tip of Italy and began to march north. Garibaldi's movement was extremely popular and gained members and momentum as it traveled northward; he claimed to take Sicily in the name of Victor Emmanuel of Piedmont-Sardinia.

Cavour feared that Garibaldi might provoke war with the French stationed around Rome, or if the army threatened Venetia in the north, it might invite conflict with Austria. So Cavour sent the Piedmontese army south to "join" Garibaldi. Cavour's real purpose was to keep Garibaldi away from Rome and to prevent any independent exploits. To prevent Garibaldi from seizing power and to prevent troubles with France, Cavour conducted a plebiscite to verify Italian support for unification with Piedmont-Sardinia. Victor Emmanuel met Garibaldi in central Italy and symbolically united the north and south.

Not included in the unification were Venetia in the north (still controlled by Austria) and Rome in the center. Victor Emmanuel assumed the title of King of Italy in 1861, and Garibaldi retired to a small island. Camillo di Cavour died unexpectedly the same year.

The remaining unification took place in 1866 and 1870. Italy received Venetia in 1866 as a reward for siding with Prussia in the conflict between Prussia and Austria over Schleswig and Holstein. Then, the Franco-Prussian War (described next) in 1870 forced France finally to withdraw troops from Rome. At that time, Italian troops entered Rome and made it the capital. The city voted to join Italy, and papal control was reduced to the Vatican.

A number of problems remained. The government of Italy was not very democratic; the franchise remained quite restrictive. Another problem was the economic disparity between the north, which was industrialized, cultured, and progressive, and the poor, agricultural south. Italy was also lacking in natural resources. Some Italian patriots were concerned about what they termed the *irridentia*, or unredeemed—neighboring areas that they felt should be part of the new Italy. The papacy continued to disapprove of the new government, making it impossible for Italians to be good Catholics and good patriots at the same time.

Recognition of the Vatican as a state did not occur until the 1920s, with Mussolini.

SUMMARY OF THE UNIFICATION OF ITALY

1848:   Rebellion against Austria in Northern Italy

1849:   Rebellion in Rome

Both rebellions failed: Austria defeated revolt in north; France restored order in Rome.

1856:   Prime Minister Cavour entered Piedmont into Crimean War.

1858:   France joined Piedmont against Austria, briefly.

Lombardy ceded to Piedmont; Austria kept Venetia.

Northern Italy voted to join Piedmont.

1860:   Garibaldi's Thousand (red shirts) moved north.

Piedmontese army moved south.

All of Italy united except for Rome and Venetia.

Victor Emmanuel became king.

1866:   Italy gained Venetia as reward for opposing Austria in Austro-Prussian war.

1870:   French troops withdrew from Rome; Rome became capital.

UNIFICATION OF GERMANY

As in Italy, there were obstacles to unification in Germany. The upper classes were fearful of change, especially in the wake of the revolutions of 1848–1849. The repressions that followed those outbreaks caused many liberals and democrats to flee (many to the United States), so unification would not come from them.

Another question remaining from the earlier attempt at unification was which of the two larger German states—Prussia or Austria—would lead or whether either or both would be included in a united Germany.

Prussia had an advantage that Austria lacked—a homogenous population, mostly German. Its government had a strong administration supported by the powerful Junkers. Many Germans had developed the idea that German life was different from that in the West; they had rejected the individualistic point of view of the romantics in favor of a group mentality.

The Frankfurt Assembly failed to unify Germany in 1848–49 because it had no power and because the German people were fundamentally not revolutionary but sober, law-abiding, and respectable. The tariff union, the **Zollverein**, which included all the German states except Austria and Bohemia, had been very successful. Austria suffered economically from her exclusion and tried in vain to influence other German states away from the Zollverein. Industry was growing, especially coal and iron production.

In 1861, Prussia received a new king, **William I**, who accepted the constitutional restraints of 1850. More liberal men were elected to the Prussian parliament, men who had earned money from industry and who saw advantages to unification. Such people watched Italian unification with interest. William wanted military reform, but his plan required money, subject to parliamentary approval. The Prussian military was no larger than it had been in 1815, even though the general population had grown tremendously. The wealthy middle class who now dominated parliament refused to grant money to the military. William I dismissed parliament, held new elections, and still failed to get approval for new military spending.

In 1862, William appointed **Otto von Bismarck** as his chief minister. Bismarck, who had been a diplomat to Russia, England, and France, was a conservative Junker at heart. However, he was totally Machiavellian, willing to do whatever was necessary to get what he wanted. He adopted a calculating policy (called realpolitik) to run the state based on pragmatic and material goals, rather than theoretical or idealistic ones. Historians have described Bismarck as practical, opportunistic, and doggedly determined. Bismarck ignored the parliament, moving ahead with enlarging and reforming the army. He built railroads around plans for transporting troops—an army general planned the railroads.

Bismarck developed a policy of friendliness toward Russia at the expense of Austria. When Austria called a meeting of the German states to discuss reform of the German Confederation, Bismarck talked William into not attending. He continued efforts to keep Austria out of the Zollverein, while at the same time, he allowed Russia to pursue fleeing Poles into eastern Prussia. (Russia was already annoyed with Austria because of her enmity in the Crimean War; Prussia, on the other hand, had not participated.)

Attention then shifted to the states of **Schleswig** and **Holstein**, just south of Denmark (see map). Both states had been ruled by Denmark, but Holstein, the more southern of the two, had been a member of the German Confederation. A 17th-century decree ruled that the two states could not be separated. Holstein's population was predominately German; Schleswig's was more mixed. After violent resistance to Denmark in both states in 1848, in 1852, an international agreement put both under Danish authority without allowing Denmark to incorporate them outright. When Denmark tried again to take over Schleswig totally in 1863, Austria and Prussia agreed to prevent that by going to war against Denmark. Denmark lost the short war.

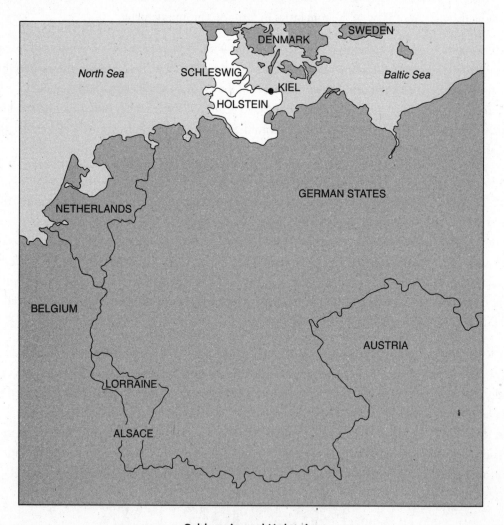

Schleswig and Holstein

Afterward, Prussia occupied Schleswig (the more northern state), and Austria occupied Holstein. Arguments soon ensued because Prussia had to travel through Holstein to get to Schleswig. Bismarck pretended to work on the situation, when he actually desired war with Austria in hopes of getting both territories and the port city of Kiel for Prussia. Bismarck promised Venetia to Italy in exchange for support against Austria. Austria, meanwhile, tried to take the question before the German federation diet, but Bismarck argued that it had no authority in the matter. He accused Austria of aggression and ordered the Prussian army into Holstein. The **Seven Weeks War** was actually over in three weeks. Prussia had the advantage of better-trained soldiers, the new **needle gun** (forerunner of the machine gun), and superior railroads (planned for military maneuvering). Then Bismarck quickly made peace with everyone before there could be further action.

Bismarck then dissolved the former German Confederation and created a new union of 22 states, the **North German Confederation**. A few south German states were not included because they were still under Austria's influence. The new confederation had a constitution and bicameral parliament. William I was president, and Bismarck was the chancellor; the chancellor answered directly to the president, not to the parliament, as in other Western governments. The new organization was no longer a loose grouping of individual states but truly a united nation-state. The lower house of the parliament, the Reichstag, was elected by universal male suffrage.

Next, Bismarck reversed an earlier disdain for parliament and "courted" its members, even getting them to approve earlier (and illegal) military spending between 1862 and 1866. Bismarck influenced some of the outstanding states with economic temptations related to the Zollverein. He then decided that a war with France would scare the others away from allegiance to Austria.

Meanwhile, Louis Napoleon in France was in decline. His attempt earlier in the decade to establish an empire in Mexico with Maximilian had ended in disaster and brought criticism. Louis Napoleon, therefore, needed glory. At the time, the throne of Spain was vacant, and the Spanish had offered the crown to a Hohenzollern, a cousin of William I. France was very opposed to the idea, fearing a German presence on both sides, and he put pressure on William I not to allow this to happen. William complied and rejected this offer, though it was extended three times.

First, Bismarck assured himself of his position internationally. Austria still blamed France for the loss of Lombardy. Italy was resentful about the loss of Savoy and Nice, and if the French went to war, they would finally have to withdraw their occupation troops from Rome. To keep the British out, Bismarck made them aware of documents that revealed Louis Napoleon's scheme to seize Belgium and Luxemburg, which England would never tolerate. The British were also disgruntled about France's meddling in Mexico.

Working behind the scenes, Bismarck got Spain to extend the Hohenzollern invitation yet again. An angry France, having thought the affair was settled, sent its ambassador, **Vincent Benedetti**, to see William I, who was at a resort called Ems. William readily agreed to Benedetti's demand that

Prussia not allow the Hohenzollern prince to become King of Spain, but Benedetti also demanded that Prussia add a guarantee of "at no time in the future." This, William politely refused. William then reported the incident via telegram to Bismarck, who carefully condensed the message into a press release designed to seem as if Germany had been insulted. The telegram became known was the **Ems dispatch**.

The result was the brief **Franco-Prussian War** of 1870. As Bismarck had hoped, the south German states supported Prussia, while France had no allies and was easily defeated. The Prussians captured Louis Napoleon as he attempted to flee the country. France declared itself a republic, but Paris wouldn't surrender until after a four-month siege, during which residents resorted to eating sewer rats and the zoo animals.

In January 1871, William I became the ruler of the German Empire, which included all the German states except Austria. The new nation kept the constitution of the North German Confederation, which made its ministers responsible to the emperor rather than to the Reichstag. France received harsh terms in the peace settlement, including an indemnity of 5 billion gold francs and the forfeiture to Germany of **Alsace and Lorraine** on its eastern border.

SUMMARY OF THE UNIFICATION OF GERMANY

1848:	Frankfurt Assembly failed to unite German states.
1864:	Prussian/Austrian War waged against Denmark over Schleswig and Holstein.
1866:	Seven Weeks War waged between Prussia and Austria; Prussia won, giving Venetia to Italy.
1867:	North German Confederation was formed; south German states still unattached.
1870:	Franco-Prussian War began, provoked over Ems dispatch.
	Siege of Paris
	France was defeated and ceded Alsace and Lorraine to Germany.
	The German Empire was born with William I as ruler.

AUSTRO-HUNGARIAN EMPIRE

Austria was left out of the German Empire, but the Austrian Empire survived until 1918. After 1849, most of its citizens did not want separation from Austria. Francis Joseph proved to be very conservative, very Catholic, and very narrow-minded. Yet the emperor himself and the traditional loyalty to the monarchy helped hold the empire together. At the same time, Francis Joseph also remained very dependent on the military for stability. Under Alexander Bach, minister of the interior, the **Bach system** of internal efficiency and material progress was designed to make people forget about liberty.

Another unifying factor was the support of the German upper middle class—the manufacturers and bankers. The **Ringstrasse**, the grand boulevard built in Vienna, was but one example of Austrian prosperity; it held the prosperous city center, public buildings, and expensive housing. Vienna became a great cultural center for music, medicine, and science.

Other major cities were also German speaking. If a person wanted to advance, he needed to speak German. The government enjoyed the support of the nobility from all ethnic groups, not only the Germans. This class enjoyed its privileges and wished to keep things the way they were.

Unlike the new German Empire, which was Protestant in the north and Catholic in the south, Austria had religious unity. The government worked with the Church to keep people under control. There was little tolerance anywhere for liberal or nationalistic activity that the government perceived as a threat. The Church had some judicial power—it could try clergy, and it had authority in cases involving marriage. The state eliminated civil marriage, and the Church once more controlled education. Protestants could not teach in Catholic schools, and Jews had limited property rights.

At the same time, the economy was liberalized. Trade and railroads expanded, and the tax system was uniform. To solve the disgruntlement among the Magyars, Austria created the **Dual Monarchy**, or the *Ausgleich,* an agreement between the Germans of Austria and Bohemia and the Magyars of Hungary (note that the Slavs were not included). Each country, Austria and Hungary, had its own constitution, parliament, and ministers responsible to the parliament. The official language was German in Austria, Magyar in Hungary. The two countries shared a king and common ministers of finance, foreign policy, and war. Both Austrians and Hungarians were appointed to those posts.

Under this plan, minorities had no place, and in Hungary, they made up slightly more than half the population. While Austria practiced universal male suffrage, only one-fourth could vote in Hungary. There, the landed aristocracy still dominated government, while minority groups tended to be poor and uneducated.

CHAPTER 19: THE RISE OF SOCIALISM

UTOPIAN SOCIALISTS

In the early 19th century, republicanism sometimes turned into one of the varieties of socialism. There were a number of different types of socialists, but they held some beliefs in common. In general, socialists disapproved of current economic systems. They thought it wrong for owners of production to possess so much power and wealth; they questioned both private enterprise and private ownership of the means of production. They wished for a fairer distribution of income among the working class. Competition and the concept of laissez-faire met disapproval among the socialists.

One of the early socialists was the English cotton lord **Robert Owen**, who tried to improve the lives of his employees. He paid them higher wages and reduced the number of working hours. He built schools, housing, and stores for his workers and tried to control drunkenness and other vices.

Most of the early **utopian socialism** occurred in France. The nobleman **Saint-Simon** had fought in the American Revolution. He and his followers talked about a planned society in which the public owned both capital and industrial equipment. Big public projects, they argued, would make the best use of resources and labor. Saint-Simon wrote about a fantasy situation in which all French nobility and clergy died, leaving only the workers. France would continue to function much as before, but if the same thing happened to the productive citizens, the laborers, the country would sink into disaster.

Perhaps the strangest of the early utopian socialists was another Frenchman, **Charles Fourier**, who, like Saint-Simon, also advocated a planned society. Fourier called his imagined utopian communities **phalanxes**. Each phalanx would consist of exactly 1,620 individuals who represented all the skills necessary to make a society function. Claiming that marriage was limiting and confining, Fourier advocated total sexual freedom among men and women, which invited much criticism of his ideas as immoral. However, Fourier was never able to establish a phalanx because he never had the money to finance one.

Women were represented among the socialists in the person of **Flora Tristan**. Tristan suffered discrimination when the French government refused to recognize her parents' Spanish marriage, declared her illegitimate, and took her inheritance. Tristan's husband was abusive, and separation gave him custody of their children. Tristan, therefore, fought for equality for women in marriage and in the workplace, demanding more equitable wages for female workers.

Early in the 19th century, there were several attempts to form planned utopian communities, often in the United States. The most famous of these was **Brook Farm** in Massachusetts, which included some major writers such as Nathaniel Hawthorne. Brook Farm lasted about five years. Another such community was **New Harmony** in Indiana, founded partly as a project of the British industrialist and reformer Robert Owen. It, too, only lasted about five years.

Another French utopian was **Etienne Cabet**, who wrote a novel describing an ideal city with economic harmony and education. Craftsmen, especially, were attracted to Cabet's vision, some going so far as to establish various utopian settlements in the New World, all of them short-lived.

After 1815, the working class of Paris felt left out. They found a spokesperson in **Louis Blanc**, who proposed **national workshops**, state-supported manufacturing centers set up to provide jobs for the unemployed. Blanc was part of the provisional government in France following the abdication of Louis Philippe (1848) and was able to put his plan into action. The workshops were swamped with applications (an indication of the desperation of the times), and the workers were given little meaningful work. After a brief trial, the government closed the workshops and sent the men to the army.

MARXIAN SOCIALISM

The principles of Marxian socialism were the result of collaboration between two Germans: **Karl Marx** and **Friedrich Engels**. Marx was of Jewish background (his grandfather was a rabbi), but his deistic father had converted to Christianity for the sake of convenience. Marx grew up with Enlightenment ideas. During his university days, he was influenced by the philosophy of Hegel's dialectic (see Chapter 16). When he couldn't get a job after his university days, he became a radical journalist. Writing from an atheistic point of view got him in trouble with Prussian censors and the government to the point that he was exiled. Marx went to France, where he was influenced by the French socialist writers and thinkers.

In Paris, Marx met Friedrich Engels, a well-to-do German industrialist who was running a family-owned manufacturing operation in England. In 1844, about the time that the two met, Engels published *The Condition of the Working Classes in England*. Engels knew some of the more radical Chartists, but he saw no promise in their ideas. Engels and Marx agreed that labor received a gravely disproportionate share of the national income. The owners of production seized most of it. Government and religion, they concluded, were both controlled by the wealthy and powerful.

In their view, no one dealt with the problems of the poor, while family life disintegrated among the urban working class.

Meanwhile, a tiny, secret, radical group of revolutionaries living in Western Europe called itself the Communist League. Its members were mostly German; the word *communist* had only a vague meaning at the time. This group asked Marx and Engels to write a program for the League. The result was the ***Communist Manifesto***, a 50-page pamphlet published in 1848. Written in German, the work was printed in England to avoid censorship.

This booklet played *no* role in the revolutions of 1848—in fact, almost no one knew about it. Engels went back to his factory in Manchester, and Marx also settled in England, where he studied, wrote, and produced Volume 1 of ***Capital*** in 1867. Engels edited and published two more volumes after Marx's death.

The principles of Marxism were drawn from several sources. From the concepts of the German philosopher Hegel came one of Marx's basic ideas, which he called **dialectical materialism**. This theory said that all history was logical and predetermined and that all was in the process of change. In the French Revolution, which was a major milestone, the middle class had won. This class, the **bourgeois**, now controlled the means of production; they were the capitalists, and capitalism was the thesis of the Hegelian dialectic.

The next step involved the emergence of the **proletariat**, the workers, who would form the dialectical antithesis and lead to the end of capitalism, the Hegelian resolution. Private ownership would disappear, followed by communism. Marx and Engels talked about the "alienation of labor"—the claim that workers were estranged from the products of their work because they received little benefit from them. Women and children, especially, were exploited by the current system. The workers, the proletariat, had no country; their loyalties should belong to each other, regardless of national boundaries. The *Manifesto* ended with these words:

> **The proletarians have nothing to lose but their chains. They have the world to win. Workingmen of all countries—Unite!**

In *Capital*, Marx discussed the subsistence theory of wages, which somewhat resembled Ricardo's iron law of wages, an idea being dismissed at that time because wages and standards of living were, in fact, rising. Marx said that the workers had no chance of rising above a minimum economic level because the present system didn't allow them to improve their lot.

Another of Marx's ideas was the **labor theory of value**, which insisted that the worth of a human-made object was determined by the amount of labor that went into its creation. Others abandoned this idea as an inadequate explanation of the value of products.

A third aspect of Marxian theory was the idea of **surplus value**, which Marx defined as the difference between an object's cost of production and its selling price. Workers were being robbed because they received only a tiny portion of the value of the products they made; the greater portion went to the bourgeois capitalists, the private owners. But with competition, the bourgeois would destroy or absorb each other until few remained. Then, the proletariat would rise up and destroy the remaining bourgeois. The triumph of the working class would lead to a classless society.

For the present, Marx said, a class war existed; the classes opposed each other and the weak were exploited. Therefore, the workers could not "get soft" or "give in," especially to minor concessions such as a slight increase in wages or a social benefit. Employers were the enemy. Institutions of society—government, churches, law, and morality—all were products of the bourgeois designed to keep the proletariat in line. Marx claimed that his brand of socialism was superior to that of other thinkers, that it was scientific. He argued that his ideas were based on scientific analysis and that they *had* to happen. Other socialists, he felt, were utopian dreamers. He believed that people would see the logic of such ideas at once.

Of course, nothing of the sort happened. People were not battle-minded nor exclusively class-oriented. Most people were genuinely religious, and many felt patriotism toward their states. Only the economic and political disasters of the early 20th century, coupled with the force of Lenin, enabled Marxian theory to be put into practice later.

IMPACT OF SOCIALISM ON EUROPEAN POLITICS 1815–1871

Even after the Napoleonic period, French urban workers remembered the early days of the Revolution when their voices had been heard. The conservative reaction of the years following 1815 was, to them, an interruption in the pursuit of better conditions for the working class. The words of the French utopian socialists gave hope in the face of legal discrimination, being forced to carry identification papers, and having no political voice in the 1820s and 1830s. Skilled laborers were opposed to laissez-faire laws. They wanted the right to organize and favored government involvement in the economy.

In 1839, Louis Blanc published *Organization of Work*, proclaiming the socialist message of state-supported workshops. By 1848, a number of radical republicans had been influenced by the utopian socialists and the realities of poverty among the urban lower class. Thus, as a member of the provisional government, Louis Blanc campaigned for permanent workshops operated by the government. Blanc believed that the workshops would be the beginning of a move away from capitalism toward a more cooperative, noncompetitive order.

Others in the provisional government were willing only to sponsor temporary workshops. Thousands of unemployed men flocked to join the workshops, which were assigned mostly manual labor on the roads. However, both the upper classes and the peasants of France feared the socialists and the workshops. Blanc was soon expelled from the provisional government. The workers rose in revolt in May, to be put down by the army. Then in late June, the Parisian workshops were closed, and the men could either join the army or go to workshops in rural areas. This action brought an outbreak of violence known as the Bloody June Days, again put down by the military after much death and injury. The working class was left bitter and disillusioned.

The Chapelier Law forbidding unions and strikes (originated during the Revolution) remained in place in France for a few more years. However, the building and renovation projects of the second empire provided jobs and income. The government built hospitals and asylums and distributed free medicines. Despite their illegality, labor unions formed, and in 1864, they became legal in France, as did the right to strike.

The earliest English trade unions developed after 1824 and were, at first, primarily organizations of skilled workers (because unskilled workers could not afford the dues). Skilled workers, in combination with middle-class radicals, held public demonstrations that helped get passed the Reform Bill of 1832 (see Chapter 15).

The Chartist movement of the 1830s and 1840s aimed for more voice in government for the working class. Delegates from labor unions and other grassroots representatives met in London in 1839. The movement tried repeatedly (and in vain) to pressure the House of Commons into acknowledgment of its petition with over 3 million signatures. However, the passage of the Mines Act of 1842 and the Ten Hours Act of 1847 was due in part to the publicity of working-class grievances. Generally, by 1850, the British working class turned to labor unions, rather than to the government, to pressure employers to improve their lot.

Marxism did not find supporters in mid-19th-century Europe. Wages rose slowly, and the working class formed unions and gained the franchise by 1870. Then with the formation of labor parties, the working class was able to function through the political system, so there was no longer a desire to destroy the government. Marx, of course, disapproved of this direction, calling it "opportunism." But by 1870, laborers as a class were finding a voice through unions and their own political parties.

CHAPTER 20: THE AGE OF MASS POLITICS (1871–1915)

CHARACTERISTICS

The period of the late 19th century up until the beginning of the First World War was an optimistic period. Everywhere, there was confidence in progress. Developments in science and technology seemed to open endless positive possibilities.

At the same time, other people were more aware than ever of the shortcomings of the modern world. The working class was becoming more vocal through unions and political parties. Increasingly, governments moved toward social legislation. Universal male suffrage was common. Feminism was demanding economic and political rights for women.

Nationalism became a more powerful force than ever before. In Western states, especially England and France, patriotism grew and became increasingly antiliberal, exhibiting itself in the international competition of imperialism and in rising tariffs to protect national economies. In Eastern Europe, nationalism could be a more internally divisive factor among the multiple cultural and ethnic entities. In some places, anti-Semitism increased. Fear of trade unions and socialists led many formerly liberal thinkers to become increasingly conservative.

By the turn of the century, nations felt the need to build armies and navies and to form alliances with other nations. Such behavior helped pave the way to World War I.

THE THIRD FRENCH REPUBLIC

The Franco-Prussian War ended with the siege of Paris, which lasted for four months before the city surrendered to Prussia. Bismarck insisted that only a properly formed government could negotiate a peace settlement. Finally, after the siege ended in January 1871, France had elections by universal male suffrage for a National Assembly. Generally, people feared republicanism, associating it with violence, turbulence, and destruction of religion. Only about one-third of the 600 deputies elected were republicans.

However, it was Parisian republicans who had held out against Prussia during the siege. Now, they refused to accept the authority of the new National Assembly sitting at Versailles, and they set up, instead, a revolutionary municipal council called the Commune. The **Paris Commune** was, in a sense, a revival of ideas from the Revolution, opposing the wealthy and the clergy and demanding government controls on various aspects of the economy (wages, prices, etc.). The result was a great outbreak of violence between March and May of 1871. The Communards went so far as to burn public buildings and execute the bishop of Paris. The National Assembly won and punished the Commune participants with imprisonment, deportation, and execution in an effort to wipe out revolutionary activity. Thus, the **Third Republic** began in an atmosphere of violence and terror.

The majority of the Assembly favored monarchy, but there was disagreement over whether to choose a Bourbon or an Orléanist. Finally, by a vote of one, the Assembly voted to form a republic with a president, a two-chamber parliament, and a council of ministers, headed by a premier. The legislature was composed of a Senate, elected indirectly, and a **Chamber of Deputies** chosen by universal male suffrage. The new government went into effect in 1875.

Two years later, President **Marshall MacMahon** tried to oust a premier he disliked but who had the support of the Chamber of Deputies. MacMahon dissolved the Chamber and called for new elections. When he got the same results a second time, he eventually resigned. Consequently, the position of president declined, and the premier and his ministers did the actual governing.

One serious, persistent political problem in France was the existence of multiple parties (unlike England, which was able to maintain a two-party system). To govern, a group had to make deals and form coalitions to get a majority vote; sometimes this was difficult.

By 1879, republicans won both houses of the Assembly. The Third Republic became a sort of center government between the Church and monarchists on the right and the socialists on the left. It maintained freedom of the press and of assembly. The government made primary education free and required, and it built village schools.

Several events of the late 19th century tested the Third Republic. The first potential threat came from the **Panama Canal** scandal of 1881. In the 1860s, Ferdinand de Lesseps had successfully headed the French company that constructed the Suez Canal. Now, a group attempted to repeat the feat in Central America. However, Panama was a very different landscape than Egypt. The mountainous terrain required the construction of locks, and the tropical climate meant heat, humidity, malaria, and yellow fever, all of which made the project much more difficult and much more expensive.

Company officials bribed government employees and journalists, hoping to get public support for a massive government loan and trying, at the same time, to solicit investment through the sale of shares. The undertaking never materialized. The company went bankrupt, and a lot of people lost large sums of money. Right-wing newspapers published details of the scandal. Some of the bankers involved were Jewish, which sparked a campaign of anti-Semitic publicity despite a legal acquittal of almost all involved. The entire event negatively affected people's opinion of the government.

A few years later, another incident involved **General Georges Boulanger**, a popular minister of war who had risen quickly through the ranks. Boulanger won the support of the working class by making clever speeches in which he talked about recapturing Alsace and Lorraine. The monarchists seemed to have the idea of using Boulanger by getting him elected to the Chamber of Deputies and then urging him to overthrow the Republic. After a couple of elections, Boulanger was finally chosen as a Deputy from Paris, but he was threatened with charges of treason and fled the country. He committed suicide in Belgium.

Then in 1894, a Jewish army officer, **Alfred Dreyfus**, was accused of selling French military secrets to Germany. Supposedly, Dreyfus's handwriting made him appear to be a traitor; he was secretly court-martialed, found guilty, and imprisoned on Devil's Island off the coast of South America. The Dreyfus family was denied access to the evidence against the young officer.

Two years later, a new chief of army intelligence, **Georges Picquart**, became convinced that it was not Dreyfus but a **Major Esterhazy** who was guilty. Picquart turned over his findings to the government. Not wanting negative publicity, the army transferred Picquart to Tunisia. It tried Esterhazy and declared him innocent, despite a mountain of evidence against him.

At this point, the French novelist Emile Zola wrote a newspaper article "J'Accuse," condemning the army and government for its cover-up. The political right and the Church spoke out against Dreyfus, some demanding that Jews lose their citizenship. Others, including socialist groups, demanded a new trial for Dreyfus. Meanwhile, the Dreyfus file was discovered to have new documents, badly forged. When this news became public, the forger, a Colonel Henry, committed suicide.

Finally, in 1899, there was a new trial, but Dreyfus was pronounced guilty a second time and returned to Devil's Island. The president then pardoned and released him, but his rank was not restored until 1906, 12 years after the original trial. The entire affair made the Church look bad and shifted French politics away from the far right. France officially established separation of church and state in 1906.

Over the years, the Third Republic gradually won the loyalty of the mass of the French people by proving that democratic republicanism was compatible with law and order and economic prosperity. Industrial workers were not as well off as those in England or Germany, but there were fewer of them in France. Late 19th-century French life was generally pleasant and secure. Farmers, bankers, businesspeople, artists, writers, scientists—most lived comfortably. France remained less industrially developed than Britain or Germany, partly because French investors were less eager to take risks. The presence of multiple political parties remained a stumbling block to government, and discontentment continued among industrial workers.

THE GERMAN EMPIRE

The Empire that emerged from the unification process was made up of 25 states, each of which maintained considerable autonomy. The national parliament, the Reichstag, had limited power. The chancellor was not responsible to it, nor could it propose legislation. Both foreign and military affairs were controlled by the emperor and chancellor. Unlike in England, the upper chamber had more clout than the lower. The Prussian aristocracy (the Junkers) continued to control the army and civil service. The German middle class tended to be compliant and loyal. Politically, Germany developed several socialist parties and a Catholic Center Party, all despised by Bismarck.

Bismarck remained chancellor until 1890. He preferred to have parliamentary support, but it was not necessary, in his opinion. He proceeded in whatever direction that seemed useful at the time. For example, Bismarck was certainly never a liberal, but when he had opposition from the Junkers, he sided with the liberals.

In 1864, the pope published his *Syllabus of Errors*, which was a general condemnation of all things modern and progressive. To Bismarck, the document seemed antinationalistic. Then in 1870, the Church issued the doctrine of **papal infallibility**, which claimed that when the pope spoke from his religious position, he spoke for God and, therefore, was beyond error. Alarmed by all of this, Bismarck developed an anti-Church campaign he called *kulturkampf*, or battle for civilization. German liberals supported this plan. The Jesuits were expelled from the country. Some priests were arrested and some emigrated, and Catholic worship was restricted. The government recognized only civil marriage, and Catholics were excluded from high civil service positions. In all of this, Bismarck was not very successful. Eventually, the Church appeared to be less threatening, and Bismarck turned his wrath to the socialists.

Bismarck hated and feared socialism, equating it with anarchy. The **German Social Democratic Party** formed in 1875. When there were two assassination attempts against William I, Bismarck (unjustly) blamed the socialists and persuaded the Reichstag to pass legislation restricting their meetings and writings. For a while, the party was outlawed; it simply went underground. Bismarck was not able to destroy socialism.

To outdo the socialists, Bismarck began to sponsor social legislation. The government created a form of social security—sickness and accident insurance, old-age pensions, and retirement benefits. These programs were financed through compulsory contributions by wage earners and their employers. This was the first such program (50 years before the United States passed similar legislation).

William I died in 1880, and shortly thereafter, so did his son. Thus, the 29-year-old grandson of William I became **William II**. The new emperor soon quarreled with the elderly Bismarck and forced him to retire for "health reasons." Bismarck left in bitterness and died within two years.

William II did not defeat the socialists any more than Bismarck had. More and more were elected to office, and by 1912, German socialists claimed a majority in the Reichstag, which alarmed the conservative middle class and the aristocracy. However, German socialists were **revisionists**—that is, they worked with existing authority, not against it, even though they were still excluded from the highest positions in government.

After the Franco-Prussian War, Bismarck had kept Germany at peace with all neighboring countries, which was something that William II was unable or unwilling to do. William II took his country in an increasingly militaristic direction. He enlarged the army, reviewed troops, and christened ships. The conservative middle class became increasingly nationalistic and anti-Semitic. These tendencies helped pave the way for the events that led to World War I (see Chapter 23).

GREAT BRITAIN

Victoria became Queen of England in 1837 and ruled for over 60 years, until 1901. Victoria herself was the personification of respectability, and the **Victorian Age** demonstrated a British contentment, self-confidence, and faith in self-reliance and progress. Victoria's husband, Prince Albert, was partly responsible for the Great Exposition of 1851, a world's fair in London. Its primary structure was the remarkable **Crystal Palace**, which housed some 13,000 exhibits, half of them British. The Exposition celebrated industry and was an opportunity for England to show off her accomplishments.

By 1850, the Tory party had become the **Conservatives**, led by **Benjamin Disraeli**. Disraeli's family background was Jewish; his father had converted to Christianity. Professionally, Disraeli was a novelist, but he was also a skilled politician and speaker. He flattered Victoria, and she adored him.

The Whigs became the **Liberals** and were led by **William Gladstone**. Gladstone was a very religious man; he had considered becoming a clergyman. Some historians say that Gladstone made an issue of his religion. His first high office was Chancellor of the Exchequer (treasury), where he sought to reduce government spending and waste. Gladstone generally disapproved of colonialism, arguing that it was too costly. He wished to make the Liberals the party of reform, including further reduction of the power of the monarchy—the queen disliked him intensely.

There was more and more pressure in England to expand the franchise. Seeing that Louis Napoleon in France used universal male suffrage to achieve goals, Gladstone supported expanding the vote. At first, the Conservatives opposed the idea. Disraeli eventually sensed that voting reform was inevitable and that it might benefit the Conservative party. Thus, Parliament passed the **Reform Bill of 1867**, which extended the vote to male heads of households. Suffrage was extended again in 1884, but female suffrage was postponed until after World War I.

Throughout the last 30 years of the 19th century, the Conservative and Liberal parties alternated in power; both brought reform. In the 1870s, the Liberals voted in the secret ballot for competitive exams for civil service jobs, an end to the sale of army commissions, admission of non-Anglicans to Oxford and Cambridge, and required school attendance for children under 13.

The Conservatives then improved public sanitation, conditions in mines and factories, and housing for the poor. In these measures, they were influenced by the writing of a public health reformer, **Edwin Chadwick**, and his *On the Sanitary Conditions of the Laboring Population of Great Britain*. The Liberals added workers' compensation and shorter workdays.

Just after the turn of the 20th century, the **Labour Party** formed and competed with the Liberals, eventually replacing them. The Labourites influenced the Liberal government to work for still more social welfare. Between 1906 and the First World War, the Liberals adopted unemployment insurance and a minimum wage. To pay for such reforms, Parliament established a progressive income tax.

THE "IRISH QUESTION"

From the 1660s and before, the Irish had bitter grievances against the British, who looked down upon them as inferior. The Irish had remained backward peasants on land owned by British landlords, against whom they were defenseless. The Irish were required to pay tithes to the Church of England, though they themselves had remained solidly Catholic. Gladstone was able to "disestablish" the Anglican Church in Ireland, but the Irish demanded **home rule**. Gladstone agreed and split the Liberal party in an attempt to provide it.

As part of the Irish strategy, Irish tenants and laborers organized to avoid landowners who rescinded leases when tenants were unable to pay rents. Much of this strategy was aimed at one agent of the landowners, a man named Boycott—hence, the word in modern English.

Irish home rule remained a divisive issue. Around the turn of the century, numerous organizations and activities expressed Irish nationalism. One such group was the Gaelic League, which praised the Gaelic language and encouraged its expression, especially in music. A number of writers were involved in the cause: poet **William Butler Yeats**, novelist **James Joyce**, and playwrights **John**

Millington Synge and **Sean O'Casey**. The Abbey Theater in Dublin became the center of Irish cultural expression.

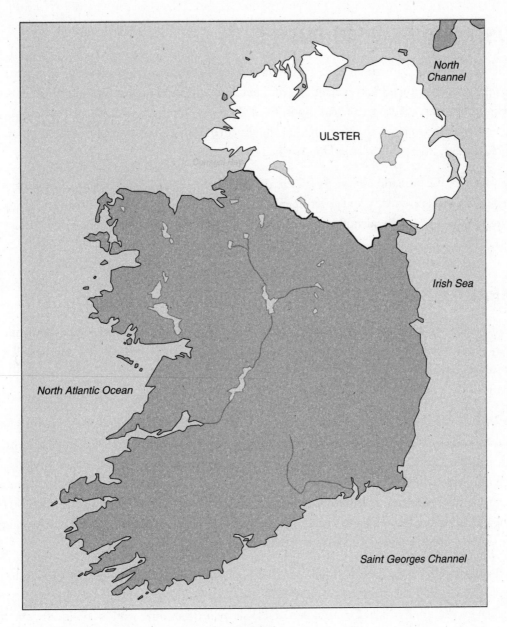

Ireland

The one exception to Irish nationalism was in the northeast corner of Ireland, the area of **Ulster**. Here, a large portion of the population was Protestant, and two-thirds opposed home rule. The Ulstermen formed militia units and militantly opposed the idea. In 1914, on the eve of World War I, the British Parliament voted for home rule for all of Ireland except for Ulster, which became

Northern Ireland, part of the United Kingdom. However, home rule did not go into effect until after the war.

AUSTRO-HUNGARIAN EMPIRE

Under the Ausgleich, Austria and Hungary were partners in the Dual Monarchy, but Hungary was the "junior" partner. In actuality, Emperor Francis Joseph and his advisors controlled finance, foreign policy, and war. To try to get support from all ethnic groups, Austria adopted universal male suffrage. In Hungary, the Magyars were too fearful of losing control to allow expansion of the franchise; thus, most minorities in Hungary had no voice.

The year after the formation of the Ausgleich, the Nationality Law (1868) recognized minority languages in schools, church, and government but without giving political identity to any group. Slavic peoples increasingly identified with Russia. This kind of discontent became a major cause of World War I.

IMPACT OF SOCIALISM

Traditionally, the working class tended to be anti–free trade and anticapitalism. Once they gained the franchise, they used their political power toward goals of social democracy. Besides the ballot as a means for change, workers had two choices: to abolish the capitalists (advocated by socialism) or to bargain with them (through the unions.)

Intellectuals—the more educated middle class who took up the cause of the workers—tended more toward the ideals of socialism. Actual workers, however, preferred unionism to accomplish more immediate and more concrete goals, such as higher wages or other benefits. Trade/labor unions, originally illegal across the Continent, became accepted by the late 19th century. By 1900, union membership included approximately 2 million in England, 850,000 in Germany, and 250,000 in France. Because British workers were more successful with bargaining through their unions, they were slower to form a political party than were workers on the Continent.

The British Labour Party formed around 1900 through the efforts of trade union officials and middle-class intellectuals. In 1901, the **Taff Vale Act** made unions responsible for employers' financial losses during strikes. Opposition to Taff Vale helped galvanize workers politically, and by 1906, the Labour Party elected 29 members of Parliament, which then repealed the law.

In 1864, the First International Working Men's Association, the **First International**, met in London. Its leadership was taken over by Marx, who expelled the more moderate socialists, such as Mazzinians and **Lasallians**. (Lasalle had been a moderate, or revisionist, German socialist, willing to compromise with existing government.) Marx had no patience with socialists who cooperated with the state; he preached destruction of governments. Marx also drove away the Russian anarchist Michael Bakunin, who blamed the state as the source of many ills. Above all, said Marx, the state was the product of the economic system, so the economic system itself should be the main target. When the Paris Commune formed its revolt in 1871, the First International thought that the long-awaited class war was beginning. Marx's praising it scared off possible followers.

Afterward, the First International faded. In 1875 in Germany, the Marxian and Lasallian socialists joined to form the German Social Democratic Party. In France, there were various socialist and Marxian groups, but they did not unify into a socialist party until 1905. In 1881, two Russian exiles living in Switzerland, **Georgi Plekhanov** and **Paul Alexrod**, formed the **Russian Social Democratic Party**. Socialist parties formed the Second International in 1889 and continued to meet every three years until 1914.

Marx died in 1883. His politics were less successful in Italy and Spain, where the population was more illiterate and most people could not vote. Radicals here were more likely to be anarchists, advocating overthrow of the existing government. In England, there was almost no Marxism. In the late 19th century, middle-class intellectuals formed the **Fabian Society**, named for a Roman general. The Fabians included some well-known public figures, such as George Bernard Shaw and H. G. Wells. The Fabians did not see a need for class conflict. They contented themselves with small gains and eventually joined the labor unions to form the Labour Party.

Generally, workers concentrated on concerns within their own countries. They worked for such things as factory legislation, minimum wages, and social insurance. Between 1870 and 1900, real wages rose about 50 percent. The revisionists took the view that class conflict did not necessarily have to occur because workers could be heard through voting, trade unions, and labor parties. They disagreed with Marxists over the necessity of class war and dictatorship of the proletariat.

In France, the term *syndicalism* applied to trade unions. A retired engineer, **Georges Sorel**, advocated violence against capitalists in preparation for a great general strike. He believed that such a total walkout would destroy both capitalism and the state and establish trade unions as the supreme power in France. Such ideas, of course, never materialized. They had more appeal in Spain and Italy, where unions were weaker and needed sensational appeal.

Meanwhile, "orthodox" Marxists condemned socialists who participated in government. The Russian Social Democratic Party held its party congress in London in 1903 (most Marxists were in exile). Here, Lenin (see Chapter 24) demanded an end to revisionism. His ideas carried, and those who supported Lenin called themselves **Bolsheviks** ("majority," though actually they were fewer in number than their opponents). Those willing to work with the bourgeois liberals or democrats were the **Mensheviks** ("minority"). However, in 1903, Russian Marxists were of virtually no significance either in Russia or in the world at large. Generally, wages for the working class continued to rise, and workers had the vote, unions, and their own political parties.

REALISM IN LITERATURE

About the middle of the 19th century, romanticism in literature and art gave way to **realism**. Authors no longer wrote adventure tales of superheroes or fantasies implying connection to the supernatural. Writers ceased to glorify nature as being in accord with the human spirit, and the emotional optimism of the romantics was gone. Instead, writers concentrated on ordinary characters and the problems of daily existence. Many topics were not especially pleasant—sex, violence, alcoholism, slums, factories, and slaughterhouses.

Some writers, first in France and then elsewhere, took realism a step further into the school of **naturalism**. These writers viewed the universe as neutral, at best—maybe even as hostile. Human beings became victims of chance and the environment. The French author **Emile Zola** claimed to be as objective as a scientist, reporting his observations of human behavior. In the poetry, novels, and plays of the naturalists, humans were like pawns on a chessboard, devoid of individual freedom and victims of chance, subject to manipulation by heredity and the environment. Other naturalistic French writers included **Honoré de Balzac** and **Gustav Flaubert** (*Madame Bovary*).

Realism spread to England in the novels of **George Eliot** (Mary Ann Evans): *Silas Marner* and *Middlemarch.* **Thomas Hardy** moved toward naturalism with his emphasis on chance, fate, and luck in such novels as *Return of the Native* and *Tess of the D'Urbervilles.* Hardy expressed a similar philosophy in his poetry. The poetry of **Matthew Arnold** regarded the human condition with dismay and referred to degenerate beings as philistines.

In drama, the Norwegian playwright **Henrik Ibsen** produced a series of "problem plays" that focused on realistic social issues, many of them controversial. Early presentations of *A Doll's House* caused riots when the main character Nora walked away from her husband and children to find herself, while *Ghosts* explored questions related to venereal disease. Writing and producing in the last years of the 19th century, Ibsen became known as the father of modern drama; his plays are still performed.

Another literary direction became science fiction. Writers like **Jules Verne** incorporated geography, science, astronomy, physics, and new transportation into such works as *Around the World in Eighty Days* and *Twenty Thousand Leagues under the Sea.* The taste for realistic fiction and a fascination for science fiction have continued to the present day.

SOCIAL AND POLITICAL REFORMS

The social reforms that Bismarck brought to the German Empire have been discussed earlier in this chapter. To compete politically with the German socialists, Bismarck instigated laws to insure workers against accidents and disability and to give them some degree of old age pension. By 1900, many German workers received small payments during illness or recovery from injury and a decent burial. The number insured grew steadily until World War I.

In Britain, the Poor Law of 1834 still forced the indigent into disgraceful workhouses. This law remained in effect well into the 20th century. However, other reforms were forthcoming. The Factory Act of 1875 reduced factory hours to 56 per week. The Artisans Dwelling Act of the same year provided for state inspection of housing facilities to hold them to a minimum standard. In 1897, the Workingmen's Compensation Law assigned employers responsibility for accidents among workers.

The first pensions in Britain came with the Old Age Pension Act of 1908. Unlike the German system, which was mandatory, the English National Insurance Bill allowed voluntary wage deductions toward a social insurance program. In Britain, workers were less ready to help unemployed fellow workers. After 1891 in England, elementary school became free. Still another reform came in 1911 when Prime Minister Asquith, with the help of King George V, forced through the Parliamentary Act of 1911, in which the House of Lords gave up its right to veto financial bills.

France produced less social reform than did England or Germany. Around the turn of the century, the Chamber of Deputies removed the requirement that workers carry identity papers. They also created an arbitration system for strikes and employer liability for accidents. Women and children were limited to a 10-hour workday beginning in 1904. The government began to monitor safety and sanitation in the workplace. In the 1890s, politicians became alarmed at the declining birth rate in France, and the government began to offer assistance to unmarried mothers.

An area that received much publicity but little action in the late 19th and early 20th centuries was women's rights. Women were excluded from universities and could not vote or control their own money. Such prominent people as Queen Victoria and the biologist T. H. Huxley opposed equality for women. In England, women did receive the right to vote in local elections. Organizations in England, France, and Germany demanded more education, more jobs, and equal wages for women. Some English feminist groups became violent, bombing the home of politician David Lloyd George and engaging in hunger strikes when they were arrested. The British leader of the movement was **Emmeline Pankhurst**. However, there was little national progress toward women's rights until after World War I.

CHAPTER 21: INTELLECTUAL MOVEMENTS (1850–1914)

SCIENCE

SCIENTIFIC BREAKTHROUGHS

Throughout the 19th century, the steam engine was improved, and it dominated power machinery until World War I. But other forms of power also emerged in the latter part of the 19th century that eventually revolutionized human life. **Michael Faraday** (English) began the process by creating the first primitive generator. In 1867, the German **Werner von Siemens** developed the first **dynamo**, and after 1870, commercially practical generators were possible. In 1881, England had its first electric power station, and shortly after the turn of the century, countries were building hydroelectric power stations and coal-fired, steam-generated electric plants.

After the American Thomas Edison invented the light bulb, the Englishman Joseph Swan planned electrically lit homes and towns. In addition to lighting, electricity began to be applied to transportation. Berlin had the first electric railroad in 1879, and by the next year, electric streetcars and subways began to replace horse-drawn buses. By 1900, electricity began to be applied to home appliances, such as sewing machines. The advent of electric power changed factories totally. Now, countries without coal could industrialize because power no longer depended on steam. Within the factories, electricity revolutionized production by making possible conveyor belts, cranes, and machine tools.

Other amazing innovations revolutionized transportation. In 1885, **Karl Benz** invented the **internal combustion engine**, which became the key to the automobile. By 1897, **Rudolf Diesel** produced the **diesel engine**, which burnt a combination of kerosene and oil and could move bigger loads than the gasoline engine. Ships converted from coal to oil, and in 1900, **Graf von Zeppelin** produced the first airship, a **dirigible**. Three years later, the American Wright brothers flew a craft powered by a gasoline engine. On the ground, automobiles caught on immediately, and the number of cars tripled between 1906 and 1912.

A number of breakthroughs occurred in medicine, as well. In France, **Louis Pasteur** became convinced of the **germ theory of disease**, which he proved in several ways during his career. He showed French winemakers that the process, which became known as *pasteurization*, or heating to a certain temperature, would kill microbes that caused spoilage. The same process was later applied to milk. Pasteur used his ideas in other ways and produced a vaccine for rabies in 1885. Within a very few years, the principle of vaccination was extended to a number of other diseases— diphtheria, typhoid, cholera, and plague.

Joseph Lister used Pasteur's ideas in hospital settings in the treatment of wounds and the care of surgery patients. He proved that the use of carbolic acid as a disinfectant greatly reduced the number of infections. Other medical innovations before the turn of the 20th century included the invention of X-rays and the conquest of yellow fever.

In 1856, the Englishman **Henry Bessemer** forged steel from pig iron by forcing air through molten metal to reduce the carbon content. Eventually, this process cut the cost of making steel by two-thirds. After 1870, most iron production switched to steel for the construction of lighter, smaller, and faster machines and engines. Most affected were railroads, ships, armaments, and heavy machinery. By 1910, German steel production was twice that of Great Britain.

Other innovations took place in the chemical industry. First of all, in the 1860s, the Russian scientist **Demitri Mendeleyev** classified the chemical elements. Later in the century, a change in the method of making soda enabled the French and Germans to take the lead in the production of alkalis used in the textile, soap, and paper industries. By the turn of the century, Germany produced 90 percent of artificial dyes, as well as photographic plates and film. (Germany's superior chemical industry soon became a major asset in World War I.) Other areas of new chemical developments involved the manufacture of fertilizers, which revolutionized agriculture, and the first man-made fabric, rayon. The Swedish chemist **Alfred Nobel** first produced dynamite in 1867, which enabled engineers to construct tunnels and large canals; it also benefited industry.

A major area of new developments in the latter 19th century was communication. The telegraph and telephone were American inventions that quickly spread to Europe, as did Edison's phonograph a few years later. In 1901, **Guglielmo Marconi** made the first trans-Atlantic radio transmission. After 1900, the manufacture of radios mushroomed. The first silent films were made in the 1890s, including footage of the coronation of Nicholas II of Russia. By 1908, France already had over 1,000 movie theaters.

In factories, precision tooling made possible the use of interchangeable parts, which enhanced production of almost all commodities. By 1900, there was an especially large consumer demand for such things as sewing machines, clocks, bicycles, electric lights, and typewriters.

The "new physics" of the 20th century began just before the end of the 19th century with the discovery of radioactivity in 1896 by the Frenchman Henri Becquerel. Then, the Polish born physicist **Marie Curie** and her husband **Pierre Curie** (French) continued the study of radiation, and Madame Curie isolated radium as a radioactive element in 1910. However, she was denied admission to the French Academy of Sciences because of her gender. An English contemporary, **Ernest Rutherford**, discovered alpha and beta rays, and from this idea, he suggested the design of atomic structure, consisting of a nucleus with a positive charge and negatively charged electrons circling it. These new concepts led to an even more complex understanding of the universe and of matter, developed by the 20th-century physicists Max Planck and Albert Einstein, discussed below.

DARWINISM

Charles Darwin challenged the idea of a regular, orderly, harmonious universe that had been believed since the Enlightenment. In the 1830s, when he was in his early 20s, Darwin went on a five-year expedition on the HMS *Beagle* to Latin America, the South Pacific, and the **Galapagos Islands**. Darwin witnessed animals on the islands, untouched by outside influence, and compared them to those on the continents. He also collected specimens, studied fossils, and concluded that the earth and life on it were *very* ancient. Slowly, he decided that all life had gradually evolved from a common ancestral origin and that this evolution was shaped by the struggle for survival. In 1859, he published ***On the Origin of Species by the Means of Natural Selection***.

Darwin was not the first to voice such ideas. As early as 1809, the Frenchman **Jean-Baptiste Lamarck** had suggested that plants and animals evolved based on their responses to their environments, but his opinions had been ignored. Geologists also had been considering evidence of vast changes in the earth over time.

Darwin held that all life, plant and animal, was in a constant state of change that resulted from chance. For instance, in a species of yellow birds, if by chance some of the yellow offspring were occasionally born with brown spots, and if the brown spots allowed those birds to hide better from predators, then the birds with spots would be more likely to survive, reproduce, and pass on their characteristics to succeeding generations. In time, the entire species would change from being all yellow to brown spotted. This was what Darwin termed **survival of the fittest**. He also used the term *natural selection*, by which he meant that this process simply occurred; that is, the fittest—those individuals within a species who happened to possess the most useful characteristics—were the ones who survived because they adapted better to their environment.

After Darwin's book, the Austrian monk **Gregor Mendel** experimented with garden peas and showed how traits were inherited, but his findings were not known until 1908. Immediately, Darwin's book became a best seller (to his surprise), because it created controversy. Many were offended because Darwin's ideas seemed to contradict traditional Christianity. Others, like biologist **T. H. Huxley**, vehemently defended Darwin. Darwin's ideas were not out of line with secular science of the day; no other scientists incorporated religion into science. What was disturbing was that Darwin's theory made humans feel less in control; the universe became neutral, or even hostile, in its relationship to humanity. Nothing was fixed or unchanging. Things happened by chance; where, then, were morality, religion, and norms of right and wrong?

Darwin's first book did not address human beings, but a second work in 1871, *The Descent of Man*, applied his ideas to humans. Despite the popular notions that circulated, Darwin did not say that humans came from monkeys. What he did propose was that all primates, including humans, had evolved from common ancestors.

One result of Darwin's ideas was the philosophy of the **social Darwinists**, who applied the concept of survival of the fittest to human behavior and to nations. Competition was a good thing, they said. Westerners justified their cultures and economies as superior to those of other parts of the globe—specifically, to those of Africa and Asia. These ideas became arguments for imperialism. The British scientist Herbert Spencer said that nations, like species, struggled to survive and the winners were the fittest, while the inferior were eliminated. Such attitudes led to smug convictions among some Europeans of cultural superiority, looking down in disdain at the peoples of Africa and Asia. For some, it became an excuse for anti-Semitism or even for war, which they saw as a sort of proving ground.

At home, some social Darwinists also applied ideas of the fit and unfit. The **Eugenicists** advocated selective breeding and sterilization of humans who, in their estimation, carried inferior traits. In many places, legislative bodies passed laws against interracial marriage, and there was much talk about racial purity.

At the same time, anthropologists were studying physical and cultural characteristics of the history of humankind. They concluded that no culture or society was better than any other. All societies, they said, were adaptations to their environments and produced their own customs, or mores, accordingly. **Sir James Frazer**, in his *The Golden Bough*, showed that many Christian traditions, such as the customs that accompanied the celebrations of Christmas and Easter, had their origins in pagan rites. His ideas reinforced the findings of anthropologists and, along with Darwinism, seemed to weaken traditional Christian concepts.

FREUD

Another blow to the idea that humans were rational beings in charge of their lives came from the work of **Sigmund Freud**, a Viennese medical doctor. Freud wished to treat nervous disorders. He wrote later that he found only two possible treatments available. The first, electrotherapy, he declared useless.

Freud did find possibilities with the second option, hypnosis. As he studied the positive results he got from that treatment, he became convinced of the power of the unconscious. In 1900, he published *The Interpretation of Dreams*, in which he discussed his ideas of **psychoanalysis**. Dreams were important as keys to the unconscious mind. Freud believed that much of human behavior was controlled by the unconscious, by drives and past experiences totally unknown to the conscious mind. It was human nature, said Freud, to forget, or repress, ideas and memories that were uncomfortable, but these things still affected behavior by influencing from the hidden but powerful unconscious side of the brain.

Freud divided the human mind into three parts: id, ego, and super ego. He called the basal, instinctive, unconscious part of human existence the **id**. This was the source of animal drives and physical appetites, the lust for pleasure and avoidance of pain. Of course, a normal person in civilized society could not allow the id to dominate. This was where the **ego**, the conscious mind or reason, took over and prevented the primitive side of nature from controlling everything. The conscience was the **super ego**, the accumulation of learned morals, customs, and inhibitions that allowed the ego to keep the id under control. Together, the ego and super ego repressed the id, preventing the consciousness from being aware of a lot of the id's animalistic urgings.

All of life, said Freud, was a battle among the three parts of being, with the primitive drives of the id always trying to break out and control. The most powerful of all drives was sexual; he claimed that the sex drive was basic to much of human behavior. The efforts of the ego and super ego to restrain such urgings led to strong feelings of guilt and other negative reactions. In psychoanalysis, which included the study of dreams, the therapist helped the patient understand the unconscious side of his or her mind, which helped resolve internal conflict and psychoses. Many people found Freud's ideas disturbing because they seemed to prove that humans were not rational beings and that much of what had been comforting in the sense of man's power over his own behavior was essentially untrue. Like the theories of Marx and Darwin, the ideas of Freud would greatly influence 20th-century thought.

PLANCK AND EINSTEIN

The work of examining the behavior of particles in the subatomic world built on the findings of the Curies (see page 223) and developed into a new physics. Around 1900, the German physicist **Max Planck** began to say that the energy of atomic particles was emitted or absorbed in specific units he called quanta. Their emission or absorption, however, was highly irregular. Planck's **quantum theory**, which wasn't finalized until 1925, seemed to oppose the concept of energy that had been in place since Newton's time. The idea that energy was emitted irregularly and unpredictably seemed to contribute a note of irrationality and change humanity's basic understanding of the universe. Planck's theories also suggested that this energy was indistinguishable from matter, another new idea.

In the early 20th century, **Albert Einstein** was a German working in a patent office in Switzerland. In 1905, he published a paper, "The Electro-dynamics of Moving Bodies," and in it lay his famous formula $e = mc^2$, or energy equals mass times the square of the speed of light. In Newtonian physics, space and time were absolute quantities, and gravity was the result of objects' interaction with each other. Einstein said that every object produced a field to which other objects responded. Space and time were not absolute, Einstein insisted, but relative to the observer; neither existed outside human experience. If all matter disappeared, so would space and time.

The theory explained the energies within the atom that eventually would be applied to releasing energy beyond anything previously imagined. The old Newtonian laws simply did not apply to the subatomic world, but Einstein's ideas were not readily understood or accepted among scientists. As time passed, Einstein refined his theory into a joint explanation of gravitation, electromagnetism, and subatomic behavior. Einstein's ideas would be keys to the atomic age to come.

ARTISTIC MOVEMENTS

REALISM

Realism formed a core movement in art in the middle of the 19th century, perhaps in part from the influence of photography, which had come into existence in the 1840s. Artistic realism may also have reflected the literary and political direction of the times. One important group of realistic artists became known as the **Barbizon school** painters, because their center was the village of Barbizon outside of Paris. These artists focused on rural peasant life, painting scenes of planting, harvesting, animals, and peasants. Such paintings as *The Gleaners* and *The Angelus* by **Jean Francois Millet** dignified the lives of French peasants.

Another French painter who tried to portray ordinary people realistically was **Gustave Courbet**, who saw romanticism as an escape from reality. Courbet's realism was often disturbing to viewers, and his work was sometimes denounced as vulgar. His *The Bather* (1853) showed a plumpish, rather ordinary woman stepping out of a pool. French critics were not shocked by the nudity, which was an accepted artistic element, but by the unattractiveness of the female figure, standing awkwardly in what should have been a classical pose. It almost seemed as if Courbet were mocking the classics. Louis Napoleon struck the painting when he saw it (and Courbet then painted an unflattering portrait of Napoleon III).

Courbet's *Studio of a Painter* was somewhat similar to Velasquez's *Maids of Honor*, but Courbet moved the artist to the center of the painting. The numerous figures on the canvas were realistically rendered. Of the great crowd, Courbet had only two, a small boy and a nude model, actually looking at the artist at work.

In England, there was a movement toward realism in art, but it lacked the powerful personality of a Courbet. Most famous was **Ford Maddox Brown's** *The Last of England*, which featured English emigrants setting out to sea. Brown's realistic detailed style was later passed on to **Dante Gabriel Rossetti**, who founded a still different school of art, the pre-Raphaelites.

IMPRESSIONISM

The label *impressionism* ironically resulted from negative criticism of **Claude Monet's** *Impression Sunrise* in 1874. But Monet's new direction was preceded by the work of **Eduard Manet**, whose painting did not begin to exhibit the shimmering immediacy of impressionism until late in his life. Manet's earlier work was more in tune with realism of Courbet. His controversial *Luncheon on the Grass* depicted two fully clothed, well-dressed men in company with a totally nude woman. Perhaps Manet intended the piece as a statement of independence, proving that the artist could include whatever he wished to create an effect. His primary attention was on the use of light and color. The flesh tones of the nude stand out in sharp contrast to her neutral and dark companions and their background.

By the time of his last major canvas, *A Bar at the Folies-Bergeres* (1870), Manet's style seemed to have changed radically, while still concentrating on color and light. Manet painted a serving girl at a bar, standing in front of a mirror that reflected the girl's back (solidly black) and the chandelier and crowded room. The busy background was a change from the neutral, almost blank, background he had used in *The Fifer* years earlier. While the painting showed the seemingly rapid, jabbing brushstrokes soon to be adopted by Monet and **Auguste Renoir** (in contrast to Manet's earlier, deliberately smooth style), Manet seemed to retain an independence of expression in *Bar*. The barmaid's reflection is unrealistically off center, and the reflection of her male customer seems less a reflection than an image of direct reality.

Claude Monet took Manet's ideas of bright color and light and applied these to the out-of-doors. His work often featured water (river, boat, and bridge scenes) and snow, all of which seemed to flicker with dabs of color. Monet painted trains, and another impressionist, **Camillo Pissaro**, did city street scenes, both always striving to capture a first impression. What made these painters different was that they strove to produce the vibrancy and immediacy of the outdoor atmosphere, especially in the interplay of light and shadow created by quick, bold brushstrokes. Monet had a portable boat studio constructed from which he could paint scenes of the Seine, which flowed through his village of Argenteuil, a few miles from Paris. Here, his life intertwined with Renoir's. Manet lived here for a time, as well, and Manet, Monet, and Renoir all did renderings of Monet's wife and child. Renoir often painted social scenes—cafés, concerts, dancehalls—as in *Le Moulin de la Gallette* (1876), where the dabbling of sunlight and shadow play across the faces of the crowd.

An unusual impressionist was the female artist **Berthe Morisot**, sister-in-law of Manet, who developed her own impressionist style. Often, Morisot used pastels, and her paintings featured women, children, and domestic scenes. However, she exhibited the brushstroke style and emphasis on freshness and light that characterized other impressionists.

Like Manet and Monet, **Edgar Degas** also painted café scenes (*The Glass of Absinthe*) but with an entirely different attitude. His figures in the painting exude isolation rather than light-hearted happiness. The paintings that made Degas famous were his pastels of ballet dancers and other entertainers. Oftentimes, he portrayed the stage from odd angles.

With the exception of the American woman Mary Cassatt, the impressionist artists were almost exclusively French. Their great works were done in the last decades of the 19th century. However, even before the century's end, some artists were going in still different directions.

POST-IMPRESSIONISTS

Beginning as contemporaries of the impressionists, the **post-impressionist** successors kept their emphasis on light and color, but at the same time, they emphasized structure and form. Foremost among the post-impressionists was **Paul Cézanne**. Cézanne said that all forms in nature were based on the cone, the cylinder, and the sphere. He deliberately distorted perspective by simplifying forms and employing dark outlines of figures. His subjects included portraits, still lifes, and landscapes.

Another contemporary who went in an entirely different direction was **Georges Seurat**. During his short career (he died at age 32), Seurat's few paintings moved toward a style called **pointillism**. Instead of casual, quick strokes recording a quick impression, Seurat's very deliberate style placed tiny dots of color side by side, with the idea that they would merge and blend in the beholder's eye. Actually, they did not totally blur. The viewer could still see the tiny dots, which, in a sense, kept the shimmering, vibrant aspect of the impressionists.

It could be said that Cézanne and Seurat were turning impressionism into a more disciplined, more traditional style, but the next artist, **Vincent Van Gogh**, went in an opposite direction. The first significant Dutch painter since the 17th century, Van Gogh's art career was shorter even than Seurat's. He believed that art should be an expression of its creator's feelings. Swirling skies and dynamic colors characterized such works as *Starry Night* and *Wheat Field and Cypress Trees*.

Still another post-impressionist was **Paul Gauguin**, who began his adult life as a stockbroker. After deciding to paint full-time, Gauguin first went to live among the peasants of Brittany in western France. He developed a style there, inspired by folk art and medieval stained glass, forfeiting perspective for flatter, simplified figures outlined in black. Gauguin soon traveled to the South Pacific and spent the rest of his life painting the natives of Tahiti. His interest in the "primitive" could be traced to the romantic fascination with the "noble savage," but the earlier romantic thinkers and writers had certainly never put their ideas on canvas as Gauguin did.

Influenced by other impressionists and post-impressionists, such as Degas and Gauguin, **Henri de Toulouse-Lautrec**, a small, deformed man, painted scenes of Parisian nightlife but from a very different perspective than that of the impressionists. Toulouse-Lautrec's judgment of his figures was incisive and merciless. He bypassed the light happiness of the impressionists. Unlike Renoir's rendition of the *Moulin de la Galette*, Toulouse-Lautrec's *At the Moulin-Rouge* was a much darker scene, one devoid of joy and enjoyment. The flatness of the figures showed the influence of Gauguin.

A final post-impressionist of significance was a Norwegian artist who went to Paris to work—**Edvard Munch**. There, Munch was influenced by Toulouse-Lautrec, Van Gogh, and Gauguin. His most famous work was *The Scream* (1893), which demonstrated qualities from the three French painters in both its style and subject matter.

LES FAUVES

The term *les fauves* literally meant "wild beasts," a nickname given to a few early 20th-century French artists. During the few years that the movement existed, its members were united not so much by a common theme or style but by an independent spirit of experimentation. Many of the fauvists shocked their viewers with their use of distortion and boldness of color and line. A founder and leading artist of the fauves was **Henri Matisse**. Unlike some of the post-impressionists, who saw and painted a dark side of human existence, Matisse's goal was simply to transmit a supreme joy of expression. He simplified his forms and colors to a radically small number of basics. In *The Red Studio*, a bright, solid red canvas contains scattered, simplified images of pictures and other furnishings. The sense of the three-dimensional is barely maintained by a thin line to distinguish between wall and floor.

In Germany, the Russian **Wassily Kandinsky** encompassed the fauves and went a step further. Around 1910, he began to abandon any effort toward representation of people or objects. His art became completely abstract in form, but it incorporated the myriad bright colors and brushstrokes of the fauves. The titles of Kandinsky works were equally indefinite—such as *Sketch I for "Composition VII."* The fauves and those influenced by them paved the way toward cubism and other abstract art of the early 20th century.

CUBISM

The pioneering work of **Pablo Picasso** and **Georges Braque** established an alternative to fauvism—**cubism**. This school of art was also called synthetic cubism because it "put things back together" and collage cubism because the work often contained pasted-on images. Especially, Picasso and Braque used the cut-and-paste method to create still lifes. The glued-on items were often drawn upon or painted over, but they also kept something of their original identity. They became part of an overall expression of an image, while at the same time maintaining some of their individual definition. Picasso's *Still Life with Chair Caning* and Braque's *Newspaper, Bottle, Packet of Tobacco* are examples of collage cubism.

Before synthetic cubism became established, the term *cubism* was invented by critics to describe other work by Picasso and Braque that seemed to be dominated by angles, lines, and planes in strange geometric distortions. One of the earliest examples is Picasso's *Les Demoiselles d'Avignon* (1907), a composition of five female nudes and a still life. The women's bodies are depicted as simplified geometric patterns of almost unvarying color. Another example is Braque's *Composition with the Ace of Clubs*, in which the artist overlaid multiple patterns of lines and planes. Even more complex and more abstract geometric planes defined the work of Frenchman **Marcel Duchamp**. In his *The Bride* (1912), the planes begin to resemble machinery, an idea that would soon characterize the futurist painters.

Picasso used the World War I years and the decade immediately following to further experiment in both types of cubism, eventually abandoning connections to the original shapes. Picasso's greatest work may be *Guernica* (1937), his huge creation in response to fascist saturation bombing of a town during the Spanish Civil War (1936–39, discussed in Chapter 25). The symbolism, the cut-and-paste figures, and the overlaying of geometric shapes and lines combine to tell the world the horrors of the event. *Guernica* drew on methods from several styles of the early 20th century.

EXPRESSIONISM

During and immediately after World War I, artists first in New York and Switzerland and, later, in Germany and France, created a movement they called **dada**. In French the word meant "hobby horse," but that definition had no relationship to the movement except that its lack of relevance implied nothingness and nonsense. Disillusionment with the war experience led some to join dada, cubism, and **futurism** into a bitter, satiric, nihilistic style. Their work was called **expressionism**. The paintings showed various distorted interpretations of suffering and the war experience. An example was Max Ernst's (German) *Europe after the Rain* (1933), which appeared to be a strange imitation of an aerial relief map of the Continent. Constructed of oil and plaster, Europe looked mutilated in the painting. Still later, another German, George Grosz, painted *The Survivor* (1945), which showed the horrors of war in the distorted image of a terrorized, lone figure crawling through filth and debris.

The general trend of art in the early 20th century was toward greater and greater abstraction. The ordinary viewer was often left puzzled or disenchanted by the strangeness and subjectivity of artistic expression.

SUMMARY OF LATE 19TH- AND EARLY 20TH-CENTURY ART

Realism

Perhaps influenced by photography; akin to political and literary movements of the time

Subjects: Ordinary people presented in realistic detail

Artists: Millet (French), Courbet (French), Brown (English)

Impressionism

Important interplay of light and shadow created "shimmering" effect

Used bright colors; quick, dabbing brushstrokes

Artists: Manet, Monet, Renoir, Pissaro, Morisot, Degas, Cassatt (all French except Cassatt, an American)

Post-Impressionism

Some artists kept color and light of impressionists but added structure and form.

Artists: Cézanne (French): cone, cylinder, and sphere; Seurat (French): pointillism—tiny adjacent dots of color; van Gogh (Dutch): swirling, dynamic colors; Gauguin (French): flattened, simplified figures; Toulouse-Lautrec (French): darker, sadder figures; Munch (Norwegian): moving color, traumatic emotion

Les Fauves

Used bright colors; simplified images

Artists: Matisse (French): simplified forms and colors;
Kandinsky (Russian/German/French): totally abstract imagery

Cubism

Used geometric planes, abstract images, collage

Artists: Braque (French), Picasso (Spanish), Duchamp (French)

Expressionism

Dada—nonsense, disillusionment, satire

Artists: Ernst (German), Grosz (German)

CHAPTER 22: THE NEW IMPERIALISM

CHARACTERISTICS OF THE NEW IMPERIALISM

The first period of colonization had followed the age of overseas discoveries, but by 1800 or shortly thereafter, most of these colonies had gotten their independence. In 1815 at the fall of Napoleon, only one empire remained—the British. There were no more colonial rivalries for about 60 years. Then suddenly after 1870, the acquisition of colonies became national goals once more. Within 20 years, the industrial nations of the West divided the world. A world map in 1900 showed only nine or ten colors; the earth was controlled by nine or ten nations.

The new colonialism, or **new imperialism**, was different from that of the past, mainly in size. One to three centuries earlier, Europeans had simply bought things, raw materials such as agricultural products: tea, coffee, or coconut. This new version of imperialism operated on a much larger and more complex scale. Europeans built factories and warehouses, established mines and plantations, and built railroads. Before long, they had huge overseas financial investments, and to secure those investments, Europeans meddled in local politics. They took over foreign territory and ruled it as **protectorates**; they might govern indirectly, acting through native authority; or in some places, the Westerners merely maintained a **sphere of influence**.

In the earlier form of colonialism, European powers had treated foreign rulers with respect, even in distant places. By the late 19th century, however, the world had drastically changed. The Industrial Revolution, science, technology, and money had made the nations of Europe into great powerhouses who considered themselves vastly superior to underdeveloped nations. At the same time, the major non-European empires were in decline, which made European takeover relatively easy. Thereafter, it took only a small number of European troops to control an area or a country. If the local people resisted, the foreigners had the power to punish severely. The only non-European nation strong enough to resist European domination was Japan (which would eventually practice its own version of imperialism).

A technological advancement that contributed to military superiority was the machine gun, developed by the British. At the time, no other weapon compared to it. The British also invented a bullet that exploded on impact. Steamships and the international telegraph permitted faster travel and quicker communication between distant points, and the Suez Canal greatly reduced the distance to the Far East. An earlier determent to activity in the tropics had been the debilitating disease malaria, which was caused by tiny parasites in the blood stream and spread by mosquito bites. By the late 19th century, the Europeans had quinine to control and prevent malaria.

Motivations for the new imperialism were many. Some cited missionary zeal—the desire to spread Christianity and the blessings of civilization (education, medicine, etc.) to the backward of the earth. Other Europeans traveled for the purpose of botanical of zoological exploration or mineral discovery. Some simply went to see the sights or to hunt; these people often expected to enjoy the conveniences and security of their home countries.

Commercial interests fueled much imperialism. Europeans demanded certain goods that had to be imported: tea, coffee, rubber, oil, coconut and coconut oil (used in soap and candles and, soon, in margarine), and **jute** (a fiber used in burlap, twine, carpets, sacks, and rope and grown only in India). After 1873, Europe experienced an economic depression in which prices of manufactured goods fell, heightening the desire for new markets to maintain profits. Competition ran high. Imperialists argued that a nation had to have a colonial empire to supply raw materials and to serve as a market for finished goods. High tariffs kept the products of other nations out of one's own system, which became a sort of neo-mercantilism.

Investors believed great profit was available from investment in less developed areas. This created a shift from the exportation of capital primarily to developed nations, as when British money had built railroads in the United States. Great Britain invested more heavily in foreign areas than did any other European nation, with 25 percent of its total wealth invested abroad in 1914. Not everyone agreed with this philosophy. The Englishman **J. A. Hobson** argued in 1903 that if workers were better paid, they could more readily afford to buy the products of industry and foreign markets would be less necessary. **Lenin** also condemned imperialism as the highest and final stage of capitalism.

A feebler argument for acquiring colonies was to give surplus population a place to go and still be part of their home countries. This idea was unrealistic; most people who emigrated went to the Americas, not to colonies.

What did happen on the international scene was the development of an intense competition for colonies. Each nation seemed to fear that if it didn't grab a certain territory, a rival nation would. Owning colonies became a sign of status and prestige. **Social Darwinism** played a role in the psychology of the times; many Europeans saw themselves as the "fitter" race, meant to rule and care for the less fortunate. The greed for economic gain and power was accompanied by humanitarian interests, but often, even these motivations carried the stigma of racism. **Rudyard Kipling** expressed that idea in "**White Man's Burden**":

Take up the White Man's burden—
The savage wars of peace—
Fill full the mouth of Famine
And bid the sickness cease;

And when your goal is nearest
The end for others sought
Watch sloth and heathen folly
Bring all your hopes to naught.

> The United States was also a major imperialist nation in its high-handed relations with Mexico, its annexation of Hawaii, and the Spanish-American War (1898–1899), from which the United States took Puerto Rico and the Philippines and set up Cuba as independent.

IMPERIALISM IN AFRICA

The first African nation to become involved with Europe in the 19th century was Egypt, which became economically important as a cotton producer in the 1860s, during the American Civil War. Egypt was still a part of the Ottoman Empire, but it had established its own hereditary rule. It enjoyed a busy trade with Europe through the port city of Alexandria on the Mediterranean. To modernize its agriculture to meet European demands, Egyptians borrowed money, irrigated, and developed landlordism. In the 1860s, the French built the Suez Canal. Some Egyptians became wealthy, educating their sons in Europe and making Cairo into a "European city." The country sank so deeply into debt that, eventually, it couldn't pay even the interest on the enormous loans. At that point (1875), Egypt sold its canal shares to the British.

Egypt still couldn't meet payments. The British and French then forced Egypt to appoint Europeans to supervise government finances, which gave Europe financial control of the country. The Egyptians responded with riots, which the British quelled with military force. England said the occupation was temporary, but the British would stay until the middle of the 20th century, not giving up the canal until 1969. Egyptians remained in government positions, but they were mere puppets controlled by England. In the late 1880s, **Evelyn Baring** served as a very able British administrator. He reformed the economy to improve the lot of the peasants, while at the same time maintaining the production that the British demanded.

The French protested the British presence in Egypt, but France proceeded to build a protectorate over Tunisia and to advance into Morocco. This was an expansion of the hold France already had on Algeria. European involvement in North Africa created incidents that helped set the stage for World War I (see Chapter 23).

Europeans dubbed Africa the *dark continent* because they knew so little about it below the Sahara. In 1841, the Scottish medical missionary **David Livingstone** became one of the first white men to explore the African interior. Without a political or economic agenda, Livingstone explored the Zambesi River and saw Victoria Falls. When no one heard from Dr. Livingstone for years, the West decided he was "lost." The *New York Herald* sent **H. M. Stanley** to find him. Stanley did so in 1871; Livingstone died soon thereafter and was buried in Africa.

Stanley, meanwhile, was awed by what he saw in Africa and tried to tell the world. He caught the interest of **Leopold, King of Belgium**, who involved himself as a private citizen. In 1879, Leopold organized the Congo Association to explore and develop central Africa, sending Stanley to make treaties with local leaders. He also sent agents to secure rubber and ivory; the Europeans considered all the interior of Africa to be "free land." Explorers began to arrive from other nations—France, Germany, and Portugal. At first, European governments were hesitant about African involvement, but they were pushed by small but powerful, organized minorities. The fear grew among European nations that if one didn't claim a certain territory, a neighbor would, and soon there would be nothing left. Having colonies became a symbol of international clout.

In 1885, **Otto von Bismarck** of Germany hosted the international **1885 Berlin Conference** to set up rules for how to acquire African territory. The decision was that a country with holdings on the coast had first rights to claim the interior. Occupation must be physical, with administration and troops, and a nation was obligated to inform other countries of its claim.

Also, the 1885 conference set up the Congo Association as an international state, making it the **Congo Free State**. At a second conference in Brussels in 1889, Leopold promised to stop the slave trade and to reduce traffic in firearms and liquor. However, little happened because there was no way to enforce these measures. Although Leopold became rich personally, he could not make the organization profitable and borrowed from the Belgian government. By the early 20th century, the Belgian government took over the enterprise, making it the **Belgian Congo** and curbing some of the worst abuses, such as forced labor.

Between 1885 and 1900, there was a mad dash to claim African territory. Every bit of Africa was taken over, except for Liberia and Ethiopia. Everywhere, a similar process occurred. A few white men appeared and approached a local chief with documents to buy land or set up mining concessions. Then the Europeans operated through the chief. A big problem was labor; Africans had no concept of the European idea of continued or tedious labor for wages. The Europeans resorted to forced labor, or they established taxes or took so much land that native people had to work for the Europeans. Sometimes, a whole tribe might be moved to a reservation, and men had to live in compounds far from their families to work for the Europeans.

Slowly, conditions improved somewhat in the 20th century. Europeans tried to curb tribal warfare, slavery, superstition, disease, and illiteracy. A class of educated, westernized Africans eventually emerged. Some went to universities in Europe or the United States, and they resented European exploitation and paternalism.

It was inevitable that the scramble for African territory created friction and rivalries among European nations. Italy claimed **Somaliland** and **Eritrea**, barren coastal areas near the Red Sea. In 1896, Italy attempted to take Ethiopia and failed; for the first time, Africans were successful against European invasion. The major powers—England, France, and Germany—preferred to have minor powers like Italy or Portugal holding territory bordering their own claims because they were less of a threat.

Germany entered the imperialistic race rather late, partly because Bismarck was not enthusiastic about acquiring colonies. Germany ended up taking territory on the east and west coasts, Cameroon and southwest Africa in the west and German East Africa on the other side. Germany eyed the Congo in the center, dreaming of an east-west band.

France owned all of northwest Africa, while the British possessed a north-south belt on the eastern side of the continent. The English spoke of a "Cape to Cairo" band of territory. A big promoter was **Cecil Rhodes**, for whom Rhodesia was named. The British and French came into conflict over the Sudan in the **Fashoda Crisis** of the 1890s.

In the 1880s, the British expanded south from Egypt, but they encountered a native revolt at **Khartoum**. The Muslim rebellion was led by the **Mahdi** and defeated an Egyptian army. The British sent an expedition up the Nile, led by General Charles "Chinese" Gordon, hero of the Taiping Rebellion in China (see next section). Gordon's forces ended up besieged by the Mahdists and defeated. Gordon was killed, and Gladstone's Liberal government was blamed for not responding more quickly.

In 1895, Britain officially claimed the Sudan, just as the French were becoming more involved in the region. The British announced to France that any future French activity in the Sudan would be regarded as an unfriendly act. In 1898, the English commander Lord Kitchener retook Khartoum, killing 11,000 Mahdists. Occupied at home with the Dreyfus scandal (see Chapter 20), the French bowed out of the Sudan.

Another place where Britain faced crisis was in South Africa. The first Europeans to settle in South Africa were the Dutch, who came in the early 1600s and established a colony. When the British took South Africa 200 years later, the descendants of the original Dutch, now called **Afrikaners**, retreated inland and set up new claims in the Transvaal and Orange Free State. The British remained along the coast in Natal and Cape Colony. The English and Afrikaners did not get along very well.

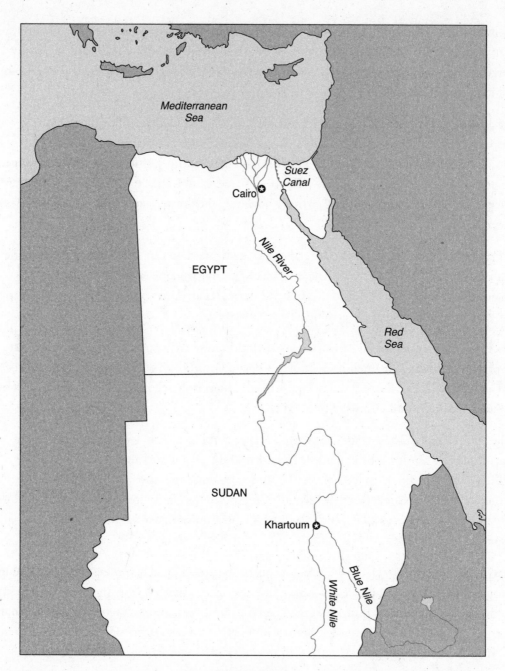

The Nile River

Each group lived independently of the other until near the end of the 19th century, when gold and diamonds were discovered in the 1890s in the **Transvaal**. People rushed in, and **Johannesburg** became a boomtown almost overnight. The Afrikaner **Boers** ("farmers" in Afrikaans, the dialect that had developed from the original Dutch language) hated the influx of foreigners and were hostile to them. To restore order in 1895, Cecil Rhodes, the multimillionaire in charge of British operations, sent a military force into the Transvaal under the leadership of a man named Jameson (the **Jameson Raid**). The Boers fought fiercely and defeated the British. William II of Germany sent a congratulatory telegram (the **Kruger Telegram**) to Paul Kruger, the Afrikaner governor of the Transvaal.

Finally, there was a war between the British and the Afrikaners. The **Boer War** lasted three years, 1899–1902, and the British won. The Afrikaners had to take an oath of loyalty to England, but the Transvaal and Orange Free State received self-government. However, in 1910, the two states voted the join the Union of South Africa.

After the Boer War, there was little territorial change in Africa. Italy took **Libya (Tripoli)** from the Turks in 1911. Colonial rivalries embittered international relations and helped create World War I. After the war, Germany lost all her colonies, and still later in 1935, Italy finally took Ethiopia.

IMPERIALISM IN ASIA

European involvement in Asia included India, Southern Asia, China, and various islands. The most "ideal" colonies were British India and the **Dutch East Indies**. Both had internal business and exported more than they imported. They had rich and varied natural resources that did not compete with those of Europe. Both colonies were divided by languages and religion, which made them easy to govern through a civil service under a European. Neither was threatened by any other European power.

At first, the Dutch controlled only the island of Java. However, in the second half of the 19th century, other European countries began moving into Southeast Asia. Fearing competition, the Dutch expanded control throughout the island chain that is now called Indonesia. Here, they practiced a type of forced labor that required farmers to deliver stated amounts of certain crops, such as sugar cane or coffee. On the positive side, the Dutch allowed native peoples to keep their languages, Malay and Javanese, which helped preserve their culture. This practice also slowed down the assimilation of Western ideas like democracy.

India was first administered through the **British East India Company**. That changed in 1857 after the **Sepoy Rebellion**. The British army in India at the time was made up mostly of native soldiers, or sepoys. India was a great mixture of peoples, languages, and dialects, and there was much dislike of the British for displacing local landowners and rulers and suppressing some customs, such as widow burning. The Hindus feared rumors that the British would abolish the caste system. Then there spread another rumor that the British greased rifle cartridges with animal fat, which offended both Muslims and Hindus. The result was the Sepoy revolt, which killed about 200 English women and children.

The British government punished the natives with hangings and by burning villages. Then the English eliminated the East India Company and ruled the southern part of India directly. The northern third of India was left as native states under Indian rule but with British "guidance."

The English did bring change to India: irrigation, railroads, cottage industry, police, and a justice system. Indians were encouraged to produce things useful to Britain: rice, opium, jute, indigo, and tea. Not allowed were products that competed with those of England, such as finished cotton cloth or salt. Unlike the Dutch in the Indies, the British demanded that schools, government, and business conduct affairs in English. A number of bright young Indian men went off to Oxford and Cambridge and then served in the government.

Increasingly, these men demanded a larger role in Indian political life. In 1885, the Hindus formed the National Congress Party, and in 1906, the Muslims formed the India Muslim League. Both groups pressured the British for more self-rule, which the British granted slowly. Complete independence did not come until after World War II.

France became involved in Southeast Asia in the late 1850s in what became known as **French Indochina**. The islands of the South Seas were claimed by various European countries: Tahiti—France; Fiji—Germany; the Marshals and Samoa—Germany. Meanwhile, Russia pushed southward, especially east of the Caspian Sea. Russia, of course, always felt a need for warm water ports. In Persia (modern Iran), Russian interests came into conflict with those of Great Britain. The British had built a telegraph line through Persia to India. After 1900, oil deposits here became increasingly important. The British made loans to Persia, and so did the Russians. Finally in 1907, England and Russia divided Persia into spheres of influence.

The British expanded into Burma in the 1820s and then into Malaya. In China, the British tried to trade for silks, tea, and other Chinese luxury items. However, there was almost nothing from the West that interested China. British merchants found that the Chinese would buy opium, which they could get from India. The Chinese government was in the hands of the declining Manchu dynasty, which tried at first to control trade carefully. Foreign merchants had to live in Canton and trade through local monopolies; the sale of opium was forbidden. When the British tried to smuggle opium into China, the result was conflict in the form of several **opium wars**. Eventually, British and French troops occupied Peking (Beijing) and burned the summer palace. Then they forced treaties on the Chinese, which gave foreigners privilege and protection and favorable trading terms. Hong Kong, Canton, and Shanghai were established as treaty ports, and Europeans demanded that they not be held accountable to Chinese law (extraterritoriality).

The Manchu dynasty was so weak that the Chinese themselves revolted against it in what was called the **Taiping Rebellion**, a 14-year civil war in the middle of the 19th century. The rebels were fighting their own government, not the Europeans, protesting poverty, exorbitant rents, and other financial issues. The British eventually stepped in to restore law and order (under "Chinese" Gordon). The result was a treaty system that gave foreigners even more privileges.

Meanwhile, Japan had remained shut off from foreigners from the early 1600s until the middle of the 19th century, when the Americans sailed into Tokyo harbor and demanded that Japan open her doors. Afterwards, Japan modernized very rapidly, adopting a Western economy, industry, and military. And like the West, Japan adopted imperialism. Japan first came into conflict with China over activity in Korea. In a brief war in 1894, Japan easily won and forced China to cede her Formosa (modern Taiwan) and the **Liaotung Peninsula** (see map, Port Arthur).

In 1891, Russia had begun its **Trans-Siberian Railroad** to **Vladivostok** on the Pacific and was eyeing Manchurian territory as a possible shortcut to the coast. Thus, Russia was wary of Japanese influence in China; the Germans and French felt likewise. Russia, France, and Germany pressured Japan into giving up claims to the Liaotung Peninsula. Russia then leased the Liaotung from China and obtained the right to build railroads in Manchuria. The French and British proceeded to make minor claims as well.

In fear that China was about to be divided up, the United States had announced an **open-door policy** in China in 1878. Chinese territory would remain intact and independent, trading with all nations. The Chinese themselves felt betrayed and victimized. One result was the **Boxer Rebellion** (so named from a Western misunderstanding of the name of a Chinese society). The Boxers aimed their hatred at foreigners and Chinese Christians. European powers, along with the United States and Japan, restored order. China was charged an indemnity of $330 million. The Manchu government lasted until 1912. Its collapse brought civil war, which opened the way for the development of Chinese communism.

Japan and Russia continued to compete for influence in Manchuria. Japan sought raw materials and mainland markets; she also wanted recognition as a great power. Russia, meanwhile, had troubles at home. Nicholas II had been tsar since 1894. He needed an overseas crisis and expansion to weaken criticism at home. In 1904, Japan attacked Russia at **Port Arthur**, and the result was the brief **Russo-Japanese War**. Both countries sent armies to Manchuria (and Western observers went to watch). Russia sent her Baltic fleet all the way around, to have it destroyed by the Japanese. The Japanese were also victorious in Manchuria. The shocked West saw a nonwhite nation defeat a European one.

U.S. President Teddy Roosevelt brokered the peace settlement, the **Treaty of Portsmouth** of 1905. Japan got the Liaotung, Port Arthur, a preferred position in Manchuria (still part of China), a protectorate over Korea (which Japan annexed outright in 1910), and the southern half of the formerly Russian island of Sakhalin. As a result of the war, Russia turned attention westward again to the Balkans, where a series of crises would lead to World War I. The war with Japan made plain

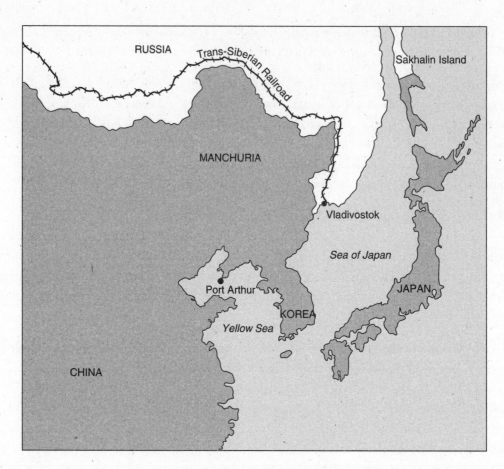

Trans-Siberian Railroad

Russian weaknesses, which led to a brief revolution in 1905. The Japanese victory also gave hope to other non-European countries, in addition to producing a desire for Western technology. At the same time, these countries developed stronger motivation and commitment to their national character and culture. The Japanese victory was a step toward World War I, the Russian Revolution, and an eventual revolt in Asia against European domination.

UNIT FIVE REVIEW QUESTIONS

1. Revisionist socialists

   (A) preached class war and international revolution.

   (B) were followers of Karl Marx.

   (C) refused compromise with existing governments.

   (D) were characterized by the Lasallian socialists of Germany.

   (E) advocated overthrow of church and state.

2. A major difference between northern and southern Italy was that the

   (A) north was more economically progressive.

   (B) north had natural resources.

   (C) south had better farming.

   (D) south had oil.

   (E) All of the above are true.

3. Cavour sent Piedmontese troops to meet Garibaldi for all these reasons EXCEPT that he

   (A) feared an encounter between the red shirts and French troops in Rome.

   (B) did not wish for Garibaldi to become the people's hero with too much power.

   (C) was anxious for Piedmont-Sardinia to encompass southern Italy, as well as the north.

   (D) felt disdain for the Mazzini-style revolution but also found it useful.

   (E) wanted to avoid upsetting Austria in the north.

4. In 1866, Prussia conducted the Seven Weeks War against Austria in order to

   (A) take Holstein, as well as Schleswig.

   (B) get the Austrians out of Italy.

   (C) teach a lesson to the southern, Catholic German states.

   (D) create a show of force against the French.

   (E) keep Austria out of the Zollverein.

5. Naturalism in literature

   (A) said that the world is good and is overseen by a benevolent God.

   (B) contended that man is at the mercy of chance in a neutral universe.

   (C) said evil is ever present and perhaps overpowering.

   (D) argued that nature is good and will in time defeat the forces of evil.

   (E) became a major trend early in the 19th century.

6. Sigmund Freud

   (A) claimed that the super ego, the conscience, controls most of human behavior.

   (B) saw dreams as keys to the unconscious.

   (C) became the focus of much anti-Semitism.

   (D) believed that the unconscious has limited influence on behavior.

   (E) made humans feel more in control of their lives.

7. Artists who demonstrated cubism included

   (A) Monet and Renoir.

   (B) Degas and Pissarro.

   (C) Seurat and Gauguin.

   (D) Kandinsky and Munch.

   (E) Picasso and Braque.

8. The scientific theories of Ernest Rutherford, Max Planck, and Albert Einstein

  (A) challenged Newtonian physics.

  (B) further explained Newtonian physics.

  (C) were readily understood and accepted by the masses.

  (D) were closely connected with the ideas of Charles Darwin.

  (E) said that the subatomic world behaved similarly to the visible world.

9. The Boxers of China favored the

  (A) creation of a democratic government.

  (B) overthrow of the Manchu dynasty.

  (C) expulsion of foreigners.

  (D) opening of all Chinese ports to foreign trade.

  (E) end of the smuggling of opium.

10. The Kruger Telegram was evidence of

  (A) international rivalries in Africa.

  (B) competition between England and France in the Sudan.

  (C) German support of British involvement in Africa.

  (D) concern over the disappearance of David Livingstone.

  (E) international bias against the British.

11. The Fabian Society was a(n)

  (A) group of English literary people, authors of literature in the school of realism.

  (B) group of English socialists.

  (C) Italian party advocating imperialism.

  (D) French trade union.

  (E) secret Marxist group in Germany.

12. In South Africa around the turn of the 20th century, descendants of Dutch settlers

  (A) got rich from the discovery of gold and diamonds in the Transvaal.

  (B) retreated inland to escape the British.

  (C) fought the British in the Boer War.

  (D) assimilated themselves into British colonialism.

  (E) refused to join the Union of South Africa.

13. The Mahdi rebellion in the Sudan succeeded for a while because the

  (A) Mahdists were aided by the French against the British.

  (B) Mahdists had surprisingly modern weaponry.

  (C) British had no military leaders in Egypt to send to the Sudan.

  (D) Liberal government in London was reluctant to support conquest in the Sudan.

  (E) All of the above are true.

14. The doctrine of Papal Infallibility implied that the

  (A) pope was divine.

  (B) pope spoke for God and was, therefore, above error.

  (C) papacy opposed the Italian government.

  (D) papacy favored modernity and progress.

  (E) pope favored democracy in Italy.

15. Which of the following is NOT true of Louis Napoleon?

    (A) He modernized Paris with wide streets and parks.

    (B) He married a Spanish princess and maintained a brilliant court life.

    (C) He established national banks in France.

    (D) He built hospitals and asylums.

    (E) He conducted brilliant foreign policy.

16. In England, the work of Edwin Chadwick resulted in

    (A) free elementary education.

    (B) the founding of the Fabians.

    (C) the beginnings of the Labour Party.

    (D) paid sanitation inspectors for rooming houses.

    (E) the Reform Bill of 1867, which expanded the franchise.

17. The Dual Monarchy for Austria and Hungary was least satisfactory to

    (A) Germanic peoples in Austria.

    (B) Slavic peoples in both countries.

    (C) Magyars in Hungary.

    (D) Catholics in both countries.

    (E) the Bohemian aristocracy.

18. Italy did NOT get control of Rome until

    (A) Garibaldi took it as his red shirts marched north.

    (B) the Franco-Prussian War in 1870 forced recall of the French troops.

    (C) the Austrians forced the French to withdraw.

    (D) the combined forces of Victor Emmanuel and Garibaldi pressured the French to leave.

    (E) the pope no longer felt dependent on the French.

19. The impressionist artists

    (A) concentrated on the effects of light and often painted out-of-doors.

    (B) painted street scenes and railroad stations.

    (C) gathered around Monet at Argenteuil, a suburb of Paris.

    (D) frequently featured sunlight on water.

    (E) did all the above.

20. Late 19th- and early 20th-century Italian politics were hindered by all the following EXCEPT

    (A) meddling by the church.

    (B) lack of a two-party system.

    (C) corruption.

    (D) continued economic division between north and south.

    (E) lack of democratic institutions.

For the following questions, write an essay that

- has a relevant thesis;
- addresses all parts of the question;
- supports a thesis with specific evidence; and
- is well organized.

Plan your essays and write them on your own paper.

1. Through specific examples from more than one country, discuss ways in which the Catholic Church stood as (or was perceived as) a force opposing representative government and progress in the late 19th century.

2. Analyze three arguments that people and nations of the late 19th century used to justify imperialism.

_____

_____

_____

_____

_____

_____

_____

_____

_____

_____

_____

_____

_____

_____

_____

_____

ANSWERS AND EXPLANATIONS

1. D

The revisionists were non-Marxists. They were willing to compromise with governments through political parties and labor unions. They advocated no radical changes. Marx had no patience with the revisionists.

2. A

Northern Italy was much more progressive and more economically developed than the south. People were more literate; there were manufacturing, trade, and modern farming. No part of Italy had natural resources, (B).

3. C

Cavour found the principles and mode of operation of Mazzini and Garibaldi distasteful and did not trust Garibaldi as a hero of the people. He wished to use Garibaldi's popularity to unite Italy, but he wanted to avoid antagonizing the French in Rome or the Austrians in Venetia. At the same time, Cavour was not enthusiastic about joining the poor, backward south of Italy to Piedmont-Sardinia.

4. A

Choice (C) occurred during the Franco-Prussian War. Answer (B) was an indirect result of the Seven Weeks War but not Bismarck's primary goal. (D) is false because this conflict was not about relationships with France; and (E) is inaccurate because the formation of the Zollverein and the exclusion of Austria occurred prior to 1866.

5. B

(A) and (E) are true of romanticism, which preceded realism and naturalism. (C) and (D) are exaggerations; (C) is too pessimistic and (D) too optimistic.

6. B

Freud emphasized the power of the id, the unconscious, over human behavior, making (A, D, and E) untrue. Although he was Jewish, this was generally not an issue.

7. E

Monet, Renoir, Degas, and Pissarro, (A and B), were impressionists. Seurat and Gauguin, (C), were post-impressionists, as were Kandinsky and Munch, (D).

8. A

All three scientists proposed ideas about subatomic particles, which behaved very differently from the visible universe of Newton's laws. Their ideas had no connection to those of Darwin, (D), and they were too complex to be readily understood even by fellow scientists, (C).

9. C

The Boxer Rebellion occurred at the turn of the 20th century, about 50 years after the opium wars, (E), and the Taiping Rebellion, whose object was to overthrow the Manchus, (B). The main goal of the Boxers was to rid China of foreign meddling, including Christian missionaries. Democracy, (A), and trade, (D), were not issues.

10. E

The Kruger Telegram was from William II of Germany to Paul Kruger, the Afrikaner governor of the Transvaal, congratulating the Boers on their initial victory over the British in the Jameson Raid. Although the English went on to win the Boer War, they were sharply criticized by other nations, who saw the Boers as the underdogs against a big bully, England. This war was in South Africa, making (B) untrue, and many years after the search for Livingstone, (D). The incident reflected not so much international rivalries in Africa, (A), as German antipathy toward the British.

11. B

(A) is tempting here because the English Fabians did include some literary people like G. B. Shaw; however, the realism makes (A) incorrect. The primary goal of the Fabians was social reform; they were part of the push behind the founding of the British Labour Party.

12. C

The Boers (descendants of the Dutch in South Africa) were farmers who resented the gold and diamond fortune hunters around the turn of the century, (A). Their ancestors had retreated from the British about 70 years earlier, (B). After the Boer War, the Boers (Afrikaners) did not at first accept British rule, but eventually they asked to be part of the Union of South Africa, (D) and (E).

13. D

(A) and (B) are simply untrue. So is (C); the British force was led by General "Chinese" Gordon, who had successfully put down the Taiping Rebellion in China. However, Gladstone's government was slow to respond to the threat from the Mahdi. Gladstone was fundamentally opposed to colonialism. Thus, when the British were defeated and Gordon was killed, the British Liberal government was blamed.

14. B

This doctrine did not claim divinity for the papacy, (A), but it did say that when the pope spoke from his position, he was above error. (C) is true but not related to the doctrine. (D) and (E) are untrue; the papacy isolated itself from Italian government and certainly opposed democracy.

15. E

Choices (A) through (D) all refer to domestic policy, where Louis Napoleon was very successful. His goal was to meet people's social and economic needs; he claimed that the form of government didn't matter. Generally, Louis Napoleon failed in foreign policy, most especially in the French disaster with Maximilian in Mexico.

16. D

Edwin Chadwick was a public health officer who wrote about sanitary conditions in housing of the poor and in factories. His work resulted in tougher laws and paid inspectors. He was not connected with the issues of the other answers.

17. B

The Dual Monarchy preserved the status quo and favorable conditions for the upper classes of Bohemia, Austria, and Hungary, (A, C, and E). The government was tightly connected to the Catholic Church; most citizens were Catholic. The people left out were the Slavic ethnic minorities, who had no voice.

18. B

The Austrians did not have authority in Rome, (C). When Garibaldi's red shirts advanced from the south, (A), the Piedmontese army met them and carefully avoided a confrontation with the French in Rome, (D). The pope remained dependent on French protection, (E).

19. E

All choices are true. Impressionism was characterized by the play of light, usually outside and often on water (bridges, boats). Pissarro did Paris street scenes, and Monet painted trains. Artists sometimes included snow. Monet resided at Argenteuil; Renoir and Manet also lived there for a while.

20. A

(A) is correct because the Church stayed totally out of Italian politics. Italy never developed a two-party system, (B), and the government was not especially democratic, (E). The north continued to be far more economically advanced than the south, (D). Especially in the south, corruption remained a problem, (C).

SAMPLE FREE-RESPONSE ESSAYS

1. Through specific examples from more than one country, discuss ways in which the Catholic Church stood as (or was perceived as) a force opposing representative government and progress in the late 19th century.

Perhaps in part because of the failures of the revolutions of 1848, the Church remained a strong conservative political force in the second half of the 19th century. In the face of such challenges as Darwinism and the unification of Italy, it remained solidly unchangeable in its positions. In the eyes of many who wanted to see liberal reforms, the Church continued to represent a force in opposition to democracy and progress.

As Italy underwent the process of unification in the 1860s, the Church remained aloof. During the revolts of 1848 and 1849, the pope had been forced to flee Rome in the face of the violence and instability caused by supporters of Mazzini and Garibaldi. The newly elected Louis Napoleon of France had sent troops to restore order in Rome. The rebels were driven out, and the French troops remained in Rome for another 20 years, protecting the pope. As the combined armies of Piedmont-Sardinia and the "red shirts" of Garibaldi unified Italy, they were careful to avoid confrontation with the French in Rome. Italy was unified without Rome or Venetia (still held by Austria). When the French were finally forced to go home during the Franco-Prussian War in 1870, Rome was finally joined with the rest of Italy and made the capital of the new nation. However, the pope would have no part of it. The papacy retreated to the Vatican and condemned the new government of Italy, making it impossible for an Italian to feel patriotic zeal for his nation and loyalty to the Church at the same time. It would be decades before the pope would interact with the government of Italy.

In the meanwhile, the Church published two doctrines that seemed to be reactionary. The first was the Syllabus of Errors in 1864. In it, the pope condemned as "errors" everything connected to progress, liberalism, and modern civilization. Six years later, in 1870, the church declared the doctrine of Papal Infallibility, which insisted that when the pope spoke from his official position on religious issues, he spoke for God and, therefore, could not err. Bismarck saw such views as a threat to the newly formed German Empire, in which the southern states were heavily Catholic. Bismarck began a campaign he called "kulturkampf," or battle for civilization. Germany banned the Jesuits and cracked down on Catholic education and worship. Some priests and bishops were arrested; some left the country. In time, Bismarck realized that his fears were rather groundless, and he began to court the Catholic Center party once again.

In France, anti-Church sentiment culminated in the Dreyfus affair late in the 19th century. Even though the Third Republic had formed at the end of the

Franco-Prussian War, the Church had continued to oppose republican government. When the Jewish army officer Dreyfus was convicted of treason, the result was a great outburst of controversy. The French Church sided with the extreme right, even demanding that citizenship be taken away from Jews. Eventually, Dreyfus was pardoned by the president and his rank was restored, but not before the case had dragged on for 12 years. The whole affair made the Church look bad and shifted French politics away from Church influence. In 1906, France officially declared a separation of church and state. Increasingly, all over the Western world by the early 20th century, governments were becoming totally independent of religious influence.

2. Analyze three arguments that people and nations of the late 19th century used to justify imperialism.

In the last two to three decades of the 19th century, a second wave of colonialism swept across Europe. All "respectable" nations simply had to acquire colonies. Not all European citizens were immediately enthusiastic about claiming and maintaining ownership of foreign lands thousands of miles away, but their voices were drowned in the general clamor of others to establish ownership of distant places.

Some of the pro-colonial arguments stemmed from the philosophy of the social Darwinists. These people saw Western Europe as the center of the fittest of humanity, destined to rule the globe. They then felt a patriotic duty to take the blessings of civilization to the more backward parts of the earth, mainly in Africa and Asia. Thus, missionaries were sent out to spread Christianity (the only true religion, in their eyes) and to take education and medical knowledge. The Europeans also felt totally justified in setting up new governments and justice systems and insisting on the use of their European languages and customs in foreign lands.

More realistic were the economic arguments. Many of the claimed lands simply had things the British wanted—tea, coffee, jute, coconut oil, cotton. In a kind of neo-mercantilist philosophy, nations felt that they had to have such things and colonies must supply them. The colonies were also supposed to serve as markets for the manufactured goods of Europe; thus, colonies were not allowed to make for themselves things that would compete with the sales of the mother country. Some promoters claimed that the factory workers of England or the continent would starve without the overseas markets for European-made goods. (This argument was rather false; in reality, most native peoples could not afford to buy anything beyond the necessities of life.) The modern adaptations of steam power and steel made all of this possible, and driving it all was the motive for profit. European investors expected to make money on their ventures.

The whole colonial venture of the late 19th century turned into a mad race to claim territory before one's neighbor took it. Nations carved out empires with little regard for the native population, which they kept under control with small numbers of troops and modern weaponry (the machine gun). Administrators were sent out from Europe for stated periods of time (almost no one went as a permanent settler), and some private citizens became wealthy. Parts of Asia and Africa were modernized to some degree.

However, there was never equality between the European and the native African or Asian, and the result would be complex and long-term animosities that would last throughout the 20th century and beyond. Ironically, the compulsion to own as much foreign territory as possible to enhance one's status among the nations of the earth became shameful by the middle of the 20th century, as Western nations began to recognize the rights of all people to self determination.

CHAPTER 23: WORLD WAR I

LONG-TERM CAUSES

The **Great War** (it would not be called World War I until there was a World War II) began in June 1914 in **Sarajevo** in Bosnia, when the Austrian crown prince **Archduke Francis Ferdinand** and his wife were assassinated. Their murderer was a member of a Serbian secret society called the **Black Hand**. Ironically, the archduke was known to favor concessions to the Slavs. Though Bosnia, Serbia, and even Austria-Hungary were rather minor nations, their alliances soon dragged much of the world into their conflict.

Behind all this was a sort of major expectation of war; for most of the early 20th century, everyone had thought that war was inevitable. European states at the time had the largest peacetime armies in history, with some countries requiring one to three years of compulsory military service of almost all young men. There were thousands of trained reservists apart from the standing armies.

Once Germany united, it instantly became an industrial giant, with continued huge growth in manufacturing, finance, shipping, and population. By 1900, it produced more steel than England and France combined. The Germans desired a place in the sun, which they felt they'd never had. They envied the British for their industrial strength and their naval power. The British, on the other hand, saw Germany as a threat to British foreign markets. After the turn of the century, Britain viewed Germany as a naval threat as well. The French, meanwhile, had not forgiven or forgotten the loss of Alsace and Lorraine in 1870 (Franco-Prussian War). After 1870, Bismarck fought no more wars, but he wished to keep Germany prepared. This he accomplished in part by forming alliances (discussed next). Another German move was to build a railroad from Berlin to Baghdad. Germany and France competed for colonial interests in Africa and the Middle East.

In Eastern Europe, the various Slavic groups remained dissatisfied and looked to Russia as their protector. Russia was interested in the Balkans for possible expansion and continued to support pan-Slavism. The Ottoman Empire had been disintegrating for a long time. As it showed signs of falling apart, the British wished to sustain it. All of Western Europe wanted to keep the Bosporus and Dardanelles (straits into the Black Sea from the Mediterranean) out of the hands of Russia. Among the discontented ethnicities of the Austro-Hungarian Empire, the unhappiest were the Serbs. Besides having a different language, many Serbs were Orthodox Christians in opposition to the Catholics of Austria-Hungary.

In the early 1870s, Bismarck had managed to maintain an agreement with both Austria and Russia against radical movements. Called the Three Emperors League, this was a touchy treaty to hold together because Austria and Russia both vied for influence in Eastern Europe, but Bismarck's diplomatic skills kept it in place. After Bismarck was forced into retirement, William II had no interest in continuing the alliance.

Germany, meanwhile, established a military alliance with Austria-Hungary in 1879, adding Italy in 1882. According to this **Triple Alliance**, if any of the three members found itself at war with two or more other countries, the other alliance members would come to that country's aid. The third member of the Alliance, Italy, was not a great power, though it wanted to be. Its conservative leadership was more attracted to authoritarian power than to representative government. Italy meddled in North Africa, where it competed with France, resenting the earlier French takeover of Tunisia in 1881. The danger of the Triple Alliance was that it put Russia at odds with Austria-Hungary, as it had been, and with Germany, as it had not been in the past.

France became increasingly friendly with Russia in the late 19th century, providing it loans and armaments. Tsar Alexander III visited the Paris Exposition (a world's fair featuring the newly constructed Eiffel Tower) in 1889, where he bared his head to "La Marseillaise," the French national anthem. Not all the French were enthusiastic about Russia, however; they saw Russia as backward and brutal and were embarrassed to be associated with it. Nevertheless, the two nations came to a formal agreement in 1894. France and Russia were grossly unlike, of course, but Russia needed French money, and France liked the idea of having a friendly power on the other side of Germany. By 1914, about one-fourth of French investments went to Russia, especially to build railroads and to develop mining.

In the 1890s, the possibility of Britain's joining the Russian-French alliance seemed remote. The French and English had been bitter rivals in imperialism, as in the Fashoda crisis in the Sudan. The British also competed with Russian influence in Persia. Traditionally, Britain had stood apart from the Continent and even felt pride in its isolation. The Boer War revealed a generally antagonistic international attitude against Britain, however, and England's lack of allies began to make her feel uncomfortable.

Open animosity between Germany and England first surfaced in the Kruger Telegram of 1896 (see Chapter 22). Then in 1898, Germany began to build a navy, which the British saw as a threat.

Germany argued that it needed a navy to protect its colonies, while the British justified their sea power as necessary for an island nation dependent on imports.

After the turn of the century, the British began actively to cultivate better foreign relations, first with the United States and then with Japan. In 1904, the French foreign minister, **Théophile Delcassé,** worked out an agreement with England in which the two nations acknowledged each other's presence in North Africa (the British in Egypt and the French in Morocco). The understanding was called an *entente cordiale*, or general statement of friendship. Three years later in 1907, with a settlement between the British and Russians in Persia, Russia also became a partner, making it the **Triple Entente**. The Entente was a less binding partnership than the Triple Alliance (Germany, Austria-Hungary, and Italy) because the British refused to make formal military commitments.

France, with England's blessing, began expanding its influence in Morocco with more police power, concessions, and loans. Feeling surrounded now by the French-Russian alliance, William II of Germany was increasingly alarmed by British-French friendliness. In vain, he put pressure on France to dismiss Delcassé. In 1905, William II suddenly arrived in Morocco aboard a German warship and made a speech supporting Moroccan independence. The next year, he demanded an international conference (at Algeciras) to consider the "Moroccan question." Actually, William cared little about Morocco; his goal was to embarrass France and perhaps upset French relations with England. The conference, however, backfired; only Austria-Hungary voted with Germany. The incident made Britain, France, Russia, and the United States see Germany as potential trouble and strengthened relations between the British and French. France witnessed a surge in anti-German sentiment.

In 1911, there was a second **Moroccan crisis**. A German gunboat (*Panther*) appeared in Morocco, demanding that France cede to Germany the French Congo as compensation for claiming Morocco. With British support, the French refused. The crisis passed, but the level of tension was raised; **David Lloyd George** (soon to be prime minister of Britain) made an inflammatory anti-German speech.

In the Balkans, the various ethnic groups generally spoke the same language, but they used different alphabets, depending on religion. The Serbs and Bosnians were Eastern Orthodox and used the Cyrillic alphabet. Croats and Slovenes were Catholics and used the Roman alphabet. Also, a large number of Bosnians were Muslim. The Dual Monarchy had no regard for any Slavs; the more radical Slavs wanted their own state, separate from Austria-Hungary. They looked to Serbia, which became the center of Slavic agitation.

Meanwhile, after her failure against Japan in Eastern Asia (Russo-Japanese War), Russia turned her attention again to coveting the straits into the Mediterranean. At the same time, Austria-Hungary wanted possession of Bosnia to control better Slavic nationalist activity. So in 1908, ministers of Russia and Austria-Hungary met secretly. Russia agreed to support an Austrian claim to Bosnia if

Austria would favor letting Russia use the straits. Immediately afterward, Austria annexed Bosnia, before Russia could act. The move also angered Serbia, which had wanted Bosnia for herself. There might have been war at this point, had not Austrian Archduke Francis Ferdinand pointed out that Austria needed no more Slavs in its territory.

Balkan Peninsula

In 1911, Italy seized Tripoli (Libya) and the Dodecanese Islands in the Adriatic, both former Turkish possessions. The next year, Bulgaria, Serbia, and Greece joined in an attack against the Ottomans to take territory. Turkey was defeated, but the victors fought over the spoils; Bulgaria wanted "too much," according to her partners in the affair. Thus, the second of the **Balkan Wars** ensued in 1912, in which Serbia, Greece, Romania, and Turkey defeated Bulgaria, forcing forfeiture of some of her former claims.

The next disagreement was over **Albania**, a tiny nation on the coast of the Adriatic (see map), desirable primarily because of its coastal location. Serbia was already occupying some of Albania; Greece claimed part of it; and Austria wanted it, mainly to keep Serbia cut off from the sea. The "great powers" made an international agreement to keep Albania independent.

For the second time, Serbia's wishes had been thwarted (the first time was when it lost Bosnia to Austria-Hungary).

The immediate cause of the war was the assassination of Austrian Archduke Francis Ferdinand and his wife Sophie while they were inspecting troops in Sarajevo in Bosnia. The assassin was a young revolutionary, **Gavrilo Princip**, a member of a secret society called the Union of Death (also known as the Black Hand). He was part of a bumbled plot that included seven other assassins, and his shooting the royal couple was almost entirely the result of chance. Serbian newspapers celebrated the assassinations. Austria-Hungary wished to punish Serbia but had no desire to annex it and add still more Slavs to the empire. Austria-Hungary asked Germany how far to proceed, and Germany said, "Be firm." This was the famous "**blank check**"—Austria felt assured of German backing, even if the matter led to war against Russia and/or France. Germany believed that the British would stay neutral.

Almost a month passed before Austria moved. In late July, Austria-Hungary served Serbia a lengthy **ultimatum**. Its most significant demands included an end to anti-Habsburg publications, including school texts; an end to all Serbian nationalist organizations; the elimination of officials and army officers that Austria-Hungary would name; and finally, the right to go into Serbia to search out threats. Austria demanded a response within 48 hours.

There was no way Serbia could win. Her small army was no match for Austria. She could submit in humiliation or die fighting, or she could turn to Russia. At the time, the French ambassador was visiting Russia, and he seemed to indicate support. Just before the 48-hour deadline, Serbia accepted all the demands except the one that would have allowed Austria to send its troops into Serbia to hunt down and punish "plots" against Austria-Hungary. Austria found this partial submission unacceptable and declared war on Serbia on July 28, claiming a Serbian attack on Austria-Hungary on the Bosnian border (which hadn't happened). England asked Germany to negotiate but made no effort to intervene with Austria-Hungary. All eyes turned to Russia. William II telegrammed Tsar Nicholas II a desire for peace, but at the same time, the German ambassador to Belgium had a sealed letter ready to deliver, demanding that German troops be allowed to pass through Belgium.

On July 30, the tsar ordered full Russian mobilization on the borders with both Austria-Hungary and Germany. The British asked for guarantee of Belgian neutrality—France agreed, while Germany ignored the question. On July 31, Germany warned Russia to back down; at the same time, Germany asked France to declare neutrality if Russia and Germany went to war. Germany also irrationally asked France to allow Germany to occupy some of the border with France. Neither France nor Russia responded to Germany, so Germany declared war on Russia on August 1. Next, Germany invaded Luxemburg (claiming an eminent French attack—untrue—and the need of Luxemburg's railroads for defense). On August 3, Germany declared war on France, and German troops entered Belgium. Great Britain declared war on Germany on August 4.

Germany's plan of war, the **Schlieffen Plan**, addressed the possibility of a two-front war. The idea was to deal with France first, defeating her before the British could mobilize, and then turn to Russia. No one anticipated a long war; there had been no long wars for the past 100 years. Historians agree that World War I began as a result of weaker powers, who had little to lose and, thus, were more reckless, drawing in the bigger powers. Austria-Hungary drew in Germany, while Russia drew in the British and French. The German/Austro-Hungarian side soon included the Ottoman Turks (fearing Russia) and, later, Bulgaria (anti-Serbian). These nations were collectively called the **Central Powers**. The British/French/Russian side was simply known as the **Allies**.

Other factors behind the outbreak of war included the way the German government was set up to make the top offices not responsible to the Reichstag, which was made up of socialists opposed to both the war and the military. Policy makers were members of the old upper class with military interests. High civilian officials wore military uniforms.

For 30 years before the war, the trend had been toward international economies but national politics. The feeling was that each nation had to take care of itself. Nations were driven by imperialism and the desire for alliances. Before 1900, English media had portrayed the French as untrustworthy and sneaky, but in the early 20th century, the enemy became Germany, which was pictured as brutal. The German press caricatured the British as bumbling but cruel toward colonial peoples.

All over Europe, there was initial excitement and enthusiasm for the war. It was expected to be over in a few months, at most, and young people saw it as full of patriotic possibilities.

MODERN WARFARE

The Schlieffen Plan assumed that Russia would take several weeks to get ready to fight. In the meantime, Germany expected to defeat the French in about six weeks. The plan ignored the British, seeing them as a small threat. The plan's originator, Schlieffen, was now dead. His successor, **Baron von Moltke**, had modified the plan to bolster German forces in Alsace and Lorraine, which subtracted from the main attack force.

The Germans attacked through Belgium, completely bypassing the Netherlands. The French had miscalculated the size and speed of the German force. The British sent troops, but the combined British/French army was forced back to within 35 miles of Paris, where they held their ground. The Germans then had to divert some troops to Eastern Europe, where the Russians were advancing faster and stronger than anyone had predicted. In September, the French pushed the Germans back to the Marne River, where both sides dug in, creating miles and miles of trenches. Germany tried to reach the English Channel, but the British prevented this.

The spade became the foot soldier's most important weapon. The trenches constructed on both sides totaled over 6,000 miles, were 6 to 8 feet deep, and existed 50–100 yards apart. They were protected by sandbags and barbed wire, and **trench warfare** became a nightmarish, psychologically scarring experience for the soldiers. Soldiers froze or fried, depending on the season, and contended with lice, rats, and flies, besides the imminent threat of death. The main weapons, machine guns, swept over the trenches, making emergence from them deadly.

The Germans introduced **mustard gas** as a horrible new weapon that destroyed the lungs. Primitive gas masks offered less than total protection. Late in the war, another frightening new weapon was the flamethrower.

Aviation was not even 15 years old. The early planes were, at first, primarily for reconnaissance, but fighter planes did develop during the war, with France, Germany, and Britain each producing about 50,000 planes.

In 1915, Germany and Austria-Hungary tried to knock out Russia. Although Russian losses were devastating (2 million people captured, killed, or wounded in 1915), Russia fought on. Britain and France turned to Constantinople in an attempt to take the straits from the Turks to get aid to Russia. This became the battle of **Gallipoli**, which dragged on until January 1916 and became a humiliating and costly defeat for the British, who were never able to dislodge the Turks from the heights.

In 1916, the action centered on France again. Two huge battles lasted for months, the battle of **Verdun** and the battle of the **Somme**. In both, the losses on both sides numbered in the hundreds of thousands. The British introduced the tank at the battle of the Somme but in such small numbers as to be ineffective. Tanks would become a factor late in the war.

Because nothing happened on land, both sides looked to the sea. The British blockaded the coast of Northern Europe. An issue was the concept of contraband versus noncontraband, which had been defined by international agreement long before the war. **Contraband** consisted of weapons and ammunition and other products conducive to war, while **noncontraband** meant food, medical supplies, and other humanitarian items not directly related to the military. The British refused to acknowledge any difference and allowed no ships to go to German ports. Neutral countries—the Dutch, Scandinavians, and Americans (until the United States entered the war)—all protested the British stand.

The Germans developed the **submarine**, as yet an unrefined but still very frightening weapon. The Germans claimed a right to use it in protest of British violation of international law. In 1915, a German submarine sank the British ship *Lusitania*, killing 1,200 people, including 118 Americans. (Germany had posted warnings in American newspapers about traveling aboard British vessels.) U.S. President Woodrow Wilson protested strongly to Germany, which toned down submarine warfare for two years.

Like the land war, the naval war proved nothing. With no victory in sight, both sides looked for new allies. Italy did not enter the war early and remained divided. Some Italians urged continued neutrality, while others saw the war as an opportunity to gain territory. The Allies promised Italy the Dalmatian Islands and perhaps more territory in Africa through the secret **Treaty of London** of 1915. Italy then joined the Allies.

Both sides attempted to meddle with minor countries and minorities to help their causes. U.S. relations with Mexico in 1916 were poor, mainly because of an American policy to pursue bandits across the border into Mexican territory. In 1917, the German secretary of state, **Alfred Zimmerman**, sent a telegram to the Mexican government promising the return of its "lost territories" in exchange for favorable alliance. The British intercepted, decoded, and published the telegram, hoping to gain American sympathy.

Generally, the Allies were more successful in manipulating minority discontent. The British worked against the Turks in the Middle East through Col. **T. E. Lawrence** ("Lawrence of Arabia"), who kept up an effective rebellion. At the same time, the **Balfour Note** of 1917 promised support for a Jewish homeland in the area, which contradicted official pro-Arab policy. The Balfour Note supported a campaign begun by Theodor Herzel in the 19th century, **Zionism**, which originated as a reaction to European anti-Semitism.

Eastern Turkey, close to the Russian border, was the home of Armenian Christians. In 1894, the Turks had executed the **Armenian massacre**. Now in 1915, the Turkish government began to fear their proximity to the enemy Russia and ordered their removal, supposedly for relocation. The result was a great and tragic disaster in which thousands of people were lost, raped, starved, and killed. The Armenian survivors became a dislocated people.

In Africa, the British seized German colonies with no intention of their return. Japan, who had joined the Allies in hopes of gaining territory, took German island colonies in the Pacific. Japan also used the war as a chance to further her position in China. In 1915, Japan forced on China a secret ultimatum of **Twenty-One Demands** and proceeded into Manchuria.

The winter of 1916–1917 passed bleakly. By December 1917, both Bulgaria and Turkey offered to talk peace. Austrian Emperor Francis Joseph died in November 1916. His successor offered a unilateral peace proposal, but he was ignored. As early as July 1917, the Reichstag passed a resolution seeking a peace settlement, but the German military command paid no attention to the measure. Germany maintained its war aims of territorial gain to both the east and west of its current boundaries.

Two big issues changed everything: the withdrawal of Russia and the entry of the United States. The war had proved increasingly costly to Russia; the Russian economy was collapsing, and the pressures for reform at home overwhelmed the tsarist government by early 1917. Nicholas II abdicated, and a provisional government was established under the leadership of

Alexander Kerensky. The new government tried to carry on the war, but it had to compete with the leadership of the soviets (councils of workers and soldiers), whose motto was "peace, land, and bread." Russian soldiers deserted in the field. After the collapse of the tsar, the Germans smuggled Lenin into Russia. Under his leadership, the Bolshevik Marxists gained power and influence and took over the Petrograd (St. Petersburg) soviet.

In the fall of 1917, six months after the tsar's abdication, Lenin and the Bolsheviks took over the government of Russia. Lenin was ready to acknowledge that Russia had lost the war, but other Bolsheviks objected because Germany was demanding so much.

In February 1918, the Germans marched back into Russia, and the Bolsheviks signed the **Treaty of Brest-Litovsk** in March 1918. Brest-Litovsk marked the end of a two-front war and ceded to Germany much of western Russia. By May 1918, the Germans were back to the Marne, about to take Paris.

By 1917, the British and French were becoming desperate. The United States had stayed out of the war until then, but it had made huge loans to the Allies and sold them large amounts of materials. In 1914, the United States had been a debtor nation to Europe; it would emerge from the war as a creditor nation. The Zimmerman telegram incident happened in January 1917. In February, the Germans renewed submarine warfare. In April, the United States declared war, making a big issue of moralistic rhetoric, with phrases like "making the world safe for democracy."

The U.S. navy was generally well prepared for combat; the army was not. The British, French, and Italians tried to hang on until the United States could effectively contribute. By the fall of 1917, the British began to use the tank on a large scale. After the settlement with Russia in early 1918, German troops poured back into the **Western front**, very effectively at first. At home in Germany, however, conditions were very hard, with high inflation and severe rationing. German civilians were beginning to revolt. The Americans, with fresh supplies, troops, and new equipment, began pushing back the Germans by the summer of 1918.

In late September, the German General Ludendorff asked Kaiser William II to form a new government responsible to the Reichstag. In this way, it would be the new civilian government that suffered the disgrace of surrender, not the military regime. An armistice took effect on November 11, 1918. (This pleased Woodrow Wilson, who preferred to negotiate with a government representative of the German people.)

William II abdicated on November 9 (he would spend the rest of his life in the Netherlands). The Austrian emperor abdicated on November 12, and Austria was declared a republic; Hungary followed the next week. Germany began forming a new government in the city of Weimar. It is significant to note that, unlike World War II, in 1918 Germany had not been invaded. Its army was still functioning intact; later, the military commanders could claim betrayal at home by civilian leaders.

The war left some 10 million people dead and another 20 million wounded. Each of the great powers (except Italy and the United States) lost 1 to 2 million people. The world was terrified of Bolshevism and threatened by a deadly influenza epidemic. In many places, revolution loomed, the Jews were pushing for a homeland, and the Japanese were advancing into China. The nations met at the Palace of Versailles outside Paris in January 1918 to begin the peace settlement negotiations.

SOCIETY DURING THE WAR

One of the changes wrought by the war was the creation of planned economies in which states tried to channel all resources into the war effort. For the most part, people everywhere supported their nations. The war brought tremendous demands for certain products and corresponding shortages and inflation. Most countries exercised wage and price controls, and people were willing to sacrifice for the war. Unions cooperated on rules, wages, and production.

Men were drafted into the military, and women took their places in the workforce. At first, the unions tended to be unreceptive to female workers, but employers gave in to government pressure for equal pay for equal work. Female nurses, as well as doctors, served at the front. Great Britain was the only country to institute a women's division of the military. The suffragettes put their campaign on hold during the war, and almost immediately after 1918, women received the franchise in Britain, Austria, and Germany.

Some complained that the war weakened morals. Definitely, women gained independence. They cut their hair, wore makeup and shorter skirts, and smoked and drank in public. Incomes for all workers rose. There was also more equality, partly because death struck all social classes. (After the war, women generally left the workforce, giving up their jobs to returning soldiers.)

Daylight saving time was used for the first time. Of all the nations involved, Germany had the most planned economy and the most advanced chemical industry. Germany successfully created an array of synthetic products, from rubber to nitrates (for fertilizer or explosives) to margarine. **Walter Rathenau**, a Jewish industrialist, headed the German program to utilize everything. Germany rationed food increasingly as the war progressed. By 1916, German males could work only in jobs geared to the war effort; women and children also worked. Great Britain also mobilized but to a lesser degree.

Before the war, writers and intellectuals had glorified struggle and violence, and their attitudes had contributed to the enthusiasm for war at the beginning. But as the conflict dragged on with all its unspeakable suffering, attitudes turned pessimistic. The English soldiers **Siegfried Sassoon** and **Wilfred Owen** wrote poetry around themes of irony and bitterness. Sigmund Freud, who lived into the 1930s, wrote about war as an endless struggle between deep irrational human drives and civilized moral standards; the negative instincts seemed to dominate.

Other writers questioned Western civilization. **Oswald Spengler** (German) published *Decline of the West* in 1918, which analyzed cyclical movements of civilization. He saw the 20th century as the declining old age of Western culture. **Thomas Mann** (also German) set his *The Magic Mountain* in a tuberculosis sanitarium where patients debated aspects of Western civilization. William Butler Yeats's (Irish) poem "The Second Coming" implied the dawning of a new, negative cycle. In general, Western Europe emerged from the war discouraged and disillusioned, having lost the optimism and belief in progress of the previous century.

THE TREATY OF VERSAILLES

Twenty-seven nations sent representatives to the peace talks, which began in January 1919, but only four countries mattered. The British prime minister was David Lloyd George, who had been in office since 1915. The elderly **Georges Clemenceau** spoke for France, and **Vittorio Orlando** came from Italy. **Woodrow Wilson** from the United States was the scholarly former college president and supreme idealist. The conference began with great faith in a "new day," a belief that an eternal peace was possible.

The weary, confused world saw Wilson as the man of the hour. Long before the end of the war, Wilson had developed his **Fourteen Points**, intended as negotiating points. At Versailles, they became demands. The British and French urged harsh terms for Germany. They believed that Germany should sign a **war guilt clause** and that Germany should pay heavy indemnities. They wanted Germany made incapable of aggression. Clemenceau originally wanted a buffer zone created between France and Germany, giving up the idea only after the United States and Britain pledged mutual defense.

The British, as usual, refused to discuss **freedom of the seas**. Russia was not present, nor was any defeated nation. The new republican government of Germany did not feel responsible for the war and wanted more consideration, but it was ignored. Above all, Wilson wanted a **League of Nations**. To get it, he had to compromise on a great many other points. Wilson believed that if he got the League, other things would work out in time.

Separate treaties were composed for each defeated nation, each named for a Paris suburb. By the Treaty of Versailles, Germany lost Alsace-Lorraine and all her colonies. Former German territory in Eastern Europe was taken to re-create Poland. East Prussia, part of Germany, was separated from the rest of the country by the **Polish Corridor**, a small strip of land from Poland up to the Baltic Sea and the city of Danzig (Gdansk). Germany lost the income from the Saar Basin for 15 years. The German army would be limited to 100,000 troops, and Germany was forbidden to make heavy artillery, aviation, or submarines. (Wilson had wanted total disarmament, but only Germany was disarmed.) Turkey was reduced to the Anatolian Peninsula, and its territory in the Middle East was divided into mandates to England and France. (The Zionist pleas for a Jewish homeland fell on deaf ears.) Austria was also reduced to a small size, divided from Hungary. Two new republics were created in Eastern Europe—**Czechoslovakia** and the **Kingdom of the Serbs, Croats, and Slovenes** (later called Yugoslavia).

France, especially, had gigantic demands for war reparations, but nobody considered how Germany would pay. Germany offered to repair physical damages in France and Belgium, but this offer was refused because it would take work away from French and Belgian citizens. The treaty contained a war guilt clause, by which Germany was forced to acknowledge responsibility for the war. The exact amount of the reparations was left undetermined in the treaty, but it was understood to be large.

The Allies had intended to seize the German fleet, but the Germans sank their ships rather than turn them over. The Chinese at the conference tried to get foreign concessions and extraterritorial rights abolished in China, but nobody listened. When the Japanese seemed to be rewarded with former German colonies, the Chinese walked out of the conference. The Italians also came away disappointed because they got very little in territorial rewards, despite the Treaty of London of 1915. Italy did receive the Dalmatian Islands, which upset the South Slavs.

AFTERMATH OF THE WAR

At the end of the war, a particularly virulent influenza swept across Europe, killing thousands more after the devastation of the war. The psychological result of the Great War was a complete reversal of the optimistic outlook of the prewar period. This change in attitude would be reflected in art, literature, and popular culture, as well as in politics. Soldiers came home mentally and emotionally damaged, and a whole generation of young European males had been drastically reduced in number.

The reaction to the treaty was mixed. In the United States, there was an extreme reaction against the war, the treaty, and Wilson's efforts to establish a League of Nations. The U.S. Senate became Republican (Wilson was a Democrat) and refused to ratify the treaty. American attitudes repudiated involvement in European politics, and the United States never joined the League of Nations, which was established at Geneva, Switzerland. Germany would join in 1926 and the Soviet Union in 1934.

Besides disappointed nations at Versailles, some individuals also left in discouragement. The major powers had brought large staffs with them to the conference. These bright young men tended to be liberal-minded intellectuals who did great amounts of research and writing, most of which was ignored. Many of them left the meeting angry and were then critical of the negotiations and the treaties. One of these was the British economist **John Maynard Keynes**, who wrote *Economic Consequences of the War*. He had argued at the conference that imposing heavy indemnities on Germany was a mistake that would slow postwar recovery for all of Europe.

The Treaty would not be successful; it proved to be too hard to enforce. The Germans from the beginning did not intend to live up to it, believing it to be *diktat*, or dictated, and the Allies were unwilling to enforce it. The war left Eastern Europe in chaos, but new republics were formed with hope for the future. The West was terrified of Bolshevism but unwilling to engage in further fighting to stop it. Japan continued to expand in China, and the shaky new governments in Europe were threatened by attempted revolts.

Economic recovery would be slow as economies switched from wartime to peacetime production and soldiers returned to the workforce. Labor unions had become more important during the war, growing in membership and influence. The eight-hour day had become common, as well as government insurance against accidents, illness, and old age. Industrial nations like England found that the disruption of the war had caused the loss of many overseas markets because customers had found other sources or developed their own production. These factors, plus overproduction and unemployment, created a postwar depression that lasted into the early 1920s. All of these uncertainties led the way to the postwar "age of anxiety."

CHAPTER 24: THE RUSSIAN REVOLUTION

RUSSIAN SOCIETY SINCE 1850

In 1850, Russia was a vast, multiethnic conglomeration of peoples in an agricultural society based on serfdom. In the Crimean War in the 1850s, Russia made a very poor showing; many said the reason for Russia's failure was the dependence on serfs to fill the army. Russian intellectuals began to see serfdom as degrading in general.

Most Russians were rural; only about 5 percent of the total population lived in towns. The middle class was small and insignificant. The Russian aristocracy owned the land, and almost everyone else was a serf on it. In Russian history, there had been two major outbreaks of rebellion among the serfs—the revolt led by Stephen Razin in the 1600s and Pugachev's Rebellion of the 1700s. Russian intellectuals had a tendency to read and think about revolt. They tended to speak French and to read foreign books. There were divided in their thinking; some were **Westernizers**, who looked to France, England, and Germany for models of industrialization and parliamentary institutions. Such people met in small groups in Moscow and St. Petersburg to discuss Western writing.

Other intellectuals were **Slavophiles**, who looked inward to Russia itself. They glorified the Orthodox Church, the village communes (**the mirs**), and the institution of tsardom. They believed in a Russian version of *volkgeist*, which would come from the common people of Russia.

The repressive Tsar Nicholas I died during the Crimean War. His successor, **Alexander II**, was more liberal, reducing censorship and granting more freedom to travel. There was an outburst of support for freeing the serfs, so in 1861, the serfs and peasants were granted freedom. **The Act of Emancipation** divided the land so that peasants received about half of it. The government bought the land from the landlords. For the lost land and services, serfs had to pay redemption money over a 49-year period. Actually, the peasants paid the government, which then reimbursed the landlords. The land did not go directly to the serfs as private property. Instead, it became the collective property of the mirs, the villages, which collected the redemption payments from individuals and then paid the government. In a sense, the mirs had replaced the landlords.

They assigned plots of land to peasants. Some peasants then farmed the land they held from the mir; some worked as day laborers. Still other peasants, the **kulaks**, bought their own land and became the best farmers.

Other reforms of Alexander II involved **judicial reform**, with the establishment of a court system with different levels. All people were equal before the law, and those accused of crimes had the right to an attorney and a public trial.

Emancipation did not increase the serfs' mobility. There were also complaints because the land assigned to the mirs did not include forests or pastures and most felt that the price was too high. There continued to be great land hunger among the Russian peasants, who could not leave the mir without permission and whose farming methods remained primitive. To end the landlords' control and police authority, the government created the **zemstvos**, elected local councils or assemblies, whose job was to address such issues as road maintenance, medical care, local finances, and scientific agriculture.

Some intellectuals laughed at the debate between the Westernizers and Slavophiles and claimed to be **nihilists**, believing in nothing. A major nihilist was the writer **Ivan Turgenev** (*Fathers and Sons*), who rejected both Western materialism and Russian tradition. Still other intellectuals said they wanted to destroy the state. These were the anarchists, the most famous of whom was Michael Bakunin. Some of the anarchists were forever plotting the overthrow of the government.

Another trend among upper-class thinkers was populism. The **populists** advocated faith in the Russian peasantry and mir. Some went into the countryside to preach revolution to the masses, but they were mostly ignored. There were also various secret societies, who schemed violence and talked revolution but actually did little. One group, the **People's Will**, eventually was successful in assassinating Tsar Alexander II with a bomb in 1881. His successor, **Alexander III**, ended reforms and cracked down on such groups, outlawing the People's Will. Alexander III kept spies everywhere, even outside Russia, watching émigrés. Revolutionaries and terrorists were exiles. Russian Jews became the victims of **pogroms**, or government-sponsored violence against them.

Another program that Alexander III instigated was **Russification**, a plan to assimilate various nationalist groups into mainstream Russian culture. The mind behind Russification was **Konstantin Pobiedonostsev**, the procurator of the Holy Synod (the lay head of the Russian Orthodox Church, appointed by the tsar). Pobiedonostsev saw the West as evil and Slavic culture as different from that of the West, and better. He spoke of Russia as a great religious commune, as **Holy Russia**.

However, the opposite happened; Russia became more European, as evidenced by the great cultural flowering in Russian music and literature in the late 19th century. The composer

Nikolay Rimsky-Korsakov based some of his creations, such as the haunting melodies of "Song of India" and "Scheherazade," on folk music, **Pyotr Tschaikowsky** created *Sleeping Beauty* and the *1812 Overture*. In drama, **Anton Chekhov** produced plays such as *The Cherry Orchard*. The great Russian novels *Crime and Punishment* and the *Brothers Karamazov* were the work of **Fyodor Dostoevsky**, and **Leo Tolstoy** published *War and Peace* and *Anna Karenina*.

Russia did experience economic growth in the late 19th century as the miles of railroads grew from 1,250 to over 15,000, making possible the export of grain. Around St. Petersburg and Moscow, some factories developed, though not so much out of private enterprise; factories tended to be built by foreign investors or by the Russian government.

A liberal, progressive political faction developed in the **Constitutional Democrats**, or **Cadets**. The Cadets pushed for a Western-style constitution and national parliament and paid less attention to the troubles of the urban workers and rural peasants. One question debated among the intelligentsia was whether Russia had to follow the historical process of the West and go through capitalism before it could become socialist. Some of the former populists (those who admired the Russian peasant and the mir) did not believe either that Russia had to go through capitalism, or that urban workers were the only revolutionary elements. These thinkers founded the **Social Revolutionary Party** in 1901.

Other populists had already founded a Marxist party in exile, the **Russian Social Democratic Party**. Its founders were **Georgi Plekhanov** and **Lyubov Axelrod**, and they soon added **Vladimir Lenin, Leon Trotsky**, and **Joseph Stalin**. The party won supporters in the 1890s.

Lenin was the pen name of Vladimir Ilyich Ulyanov, a small, intense man from the middle class. Lenin's life changed at age 17 when his brother was executed for being part of a plot to assassinate Alexander III. Lenin's writing got him in trouble with the authorities, and he was kicked out of the university and, in 1897, exiled to Siberia for three years. There, he interacted with other political prisoners, and after being released in 1900, he went to Switzerland, where he lived until 1917. In 1902, Lenin wrote a pamphlet, "What Is To Be Done?" which became the basis for a revolutionary party. Refusing all compromise with liberals and other reformers, Lenin believed that only a small minority of workers was needed to understand and join intellectuals to create revolution.

In 1903, the Russian Social Democratic Workers' Party met in Brussels and London. Here, a split occurred between the **Bolsheviks** ("majority") and **Mensheviks** ("minority"). Lenin's ideas governed the Bolsheviks.

Lenin saw the role of the intellectual as supplying the brains to the workers' brawn, molding the workers' movement, and making the workers class-conscious and revolutionary.

DIFFERENCES IN POLICY

Bolsheviks	Mensheviks
Party controlled by small elite	Larger party involvement
Purge of those who disagree	Cooperation with liberals and others
No compromise—class struggle	Reconciliation of differences

After 1900, there was growing unrest in Russia. Peasants occasionally trespassed on gentry land, and there were uprisings against landlords and tax collectors. Although strikes were illegal in the factories, workers sometimes refused to work. However, so far, none of these actions had connection to any political group.

REVOLUTION OF 1905 AND AFTERWARD

Alexander III died in 1894 and was followed by **Nicholas II**, the last tsar. Having been tutored by Pobiedonostsev (see Russification above), Nicholas was very narrow-minded. He regarded questioning of anything as "un-Russian." For a while, his chief minister was **Vyacheslev Plehve**, who advised the war against Japan as a way to get support for the government. Then, when the Russians were so soundly defeated, there was great shame and more criticism of the government. (Plehve was assassinated by a bomb in 1904.)

Then came the incident of **Bloody Sunday** in January 1905. A Russian priest, **Father Gapon**, had been allowed to go among factory workers, hear grievances, organize them, and compile a petition to the tsar, whom the workers revered as "Little Father." Approximately 200,000 people marched before the Winter Palace in St. Petersburg on a January Sunday. They were peasants without weapons, and they were unaware that the tsar was not in residence. The troops guarding the palace panicked and fired on the crowd, killing about 1,000 people.

The incident caused outbursts of violence throughout the country. People demanded more representation. The St. Petersburg workers' council, or soviet (comparable to the zemstvos in rural areas), called for a great strike, which paralyzed the country. With the government seemingly on the verge of collapse, Nicholas appointed **Sergei Witte** as his chief minister. Witte persuaded the tsar to end most of the redemption payments on the land (dating back to the emancipation of the serfs in 1861). The Poles and Lithuanians received the right to use their own languages, and political trials moved from military to civilian courts. The government also relaxed persecution of Jews.

Witte got Russia on the gold standard, making it easier to convert foreign currency, and began construction of the Trans-Siberian railroad. Witte also constructed a telegraph system, built post offices, and increased imports and exports.

To stop the great strike, Nicholas issued his **October Manifesto**, which promised a constitution and a **Duma**, a national parliament. These promises soothed the demands of the liberals (the Cadets), but outbreaks of violence continued. The first Duma convened in April 1906 and was made up mostly of Constitutional Democrats because both socialist groups, the Social Revolutionaries and the Social Democrats (Marxists), refused to participate. The Duma proceeded to debate land reform, but Nicholas created a State Council, an upper assembly with members from the clergy and army; the Council superceded the Duma. Nicholas then dismissed Witte and dissolved the Duma.

There were four different Dumas between 1906 and 1916. They did little because they had little power. The tsar had no faith in the Dumas and gave them no say over foreign policy, budget, or government personnel. In addition, the Dumas were opposed by the far right, the church and nobility, who organized terrorists to frighten the peasants. On the far left, both the Mensheviks and Bolsheviks ignored the Dumas.

The last attempt at reform came from Nicholas's minister, **Peter Stolypin**, who served 1906–1911. Stolypin believed in private property. He supported the zemstvos but disliked the mirs. He dissolved the remaining redemption payments and allowed peasants to leave the mirs, creating a mobile labor force. The peasants could now buy land, which Stolypin encouraged. About 25 percent of the peasants did so, becoming kulaks, but the mir remained solidly in place. Nicholas supported the Stolypin reforms, somewhat grudgingly, but then Stolypin was shot (as Plehve earlier had been killed by a bomb—perhaps by tsarist police). Despite all this, Russia was making progress on the eve of World War I, and the revolutionary groups, especially the Bolsheviks, were losing support.

THE FEBRUARY REVOLUTION

When World War I came, the peasants marched off to fight, but they went without personal conviction. There were many dissatisfied minorities—Poles, Ukrainians, Jews, and others. The middle class did feel patriotism, but they found themselves dismayed by the incompetence of the Russian government and military. In the Duma, the socialists (who had now joined the political process after initially refusing to participate) opposed the war and were jailed. (Note: In 1914,

Nicholas changed the name of St. Petersburg, a German name, to its Russian counterpart, Petrograd. It would become Leningrad in 1924; today, the city is St. Petersburg once more.)

The war brought staggering problems:

- Isolation—Russia's only ports were **Archangel and Murmansk** on the White Sea and Vladivostok on the Pacific. Until 1917, there was no railroad to Archangel.

- Transportation—If the government moved troops by railroad, there were food shortages.

- Authority—Authority was not delegated. The rather incompetent tsar insisted on controlling everything.

- Horrible losses—There was much criticism of munitions supplies. Soldiers went into battle without guns—they were told to seize guns from the dead.

- Alexandra—The tsarina opposed all reform and hated parliaments. In 1915, Nicholas took direct command of the armies, leaving the government to her and Rasputin (see below).

Alexandra was German and a descendant of Queen Victoria. Very devoted to Nicholas, she had given birth to four daughters and a son, the **Tsarevitch Alexei**, who had inherited hemophilia. The tiniest injury had the potential to be deadly. The strange "holy man" **Rasputin** obtained Alexandra's total faith because he could stop the child's bleeding. At the same time, the Russian people hated the tsarina as a foreigner; some even said she was a German spy.

The Russians also hated Rasputin, an ignorant, illiterate clergyman known for wild drunken orgies and sexual escapades. Russians in high places saw him as an embarrassment, yet at the same time, they were envious of the power he wielded. In late 1916, Rasputin was brutally murdered by members of the aristocracy, and Alexandra was devastated.

Nicholas kept dismissing capable ministers and replacing them with weak and sometimes corrupt men who could be manipulated. There was heavy criticism of how the war was being managed, especially from the Duma. There, the Social Revolutionary leader **Alexander Kerensky** denounced the war and demanded a government responsible to the Duma.

The winter of 1916–1917 was horribly cold, and the war went badly for Russia. There were massive strikes and food riots in the cities. In March (February on the Western calendar), a strike shut down Petrograd, and soldiers and sailors mutinied. Nicholas ordered the Duma to dissolve, but it simply met elsewhere and created a provisional committee. When Nicholas was unable to rally military support, he abdicated in favor of his brother, who refused the throne. At the same time, a soviet of workers and soldiers' deputies organized itself in Petrograd.

The Duma declared equality before the law and freedom of religion, speech, and assembly, and it legalized unions and strikes. By May, a provisional government was functional, with Kerensky at its head. The provisional government had to compete with the Petrograd soviet for popular support. The soviet was housed in the same building as the Duma, and it published a newspaper, *Pravda* ("truth"). The soviet proclaimed its famous **Army Order #1**, which said that army officers no longer had authority and that soldiers should organize and elect committees. Immediately, military discipline collapsed, and soldiers deserted for home. The countryside turned into anarchy as the Soviets preached **peace, food, and land**—the things the peasants most desired.

The provisional government lasted from March (February) until October (November—Western calendar) and was, in general, a total failure. The people in charge had no experience in government, and they existed on a very different plane than did the common people. The provisional government was also greatly hampered by the war. It had no way to enforce any measures nor any way to suppress opponents. It had taken a few concrete stands, advocating independence for Poland, an end of religious persecution, and an eight-hour day, but on most issues, the provisional government remained vague. Thus, it was fairly easy for Lenin and the Bolsheviks to take over the Revolution.

THE OCTOBER REVOLUTION

The Germans smuggled Lenin into Russia two months after Tsar Nicholas abdicated. Lenin and the Bolsheviks proposed four stands:

1. Withdrawal from the war

2. No support for the provisional government

3. A call for revolution in other countries (international Marxism)

4. Peasant seizure of the large states

In July, Lenin tried to seize power and failed, so he fled briefly to Finland. Meanwhile, in August, there was a failed coup against Kerensky when the head of the military, General Kornilov, tried to take over. The Bolsheviks opposed Kornilov, fearing that he would suppress the **soviets**, through which the Bolsheviks were working. Throughout the summer of 1917, the Bolsheviks gained support and influence until they had a majority in the Petrograd soviet.

Lenin's assistant was Lev Davidovich Bronstein—**Leon Trotsky**. It is said that Trotsky planned the Bolshevik takeover on the night of October 6. The Bolsheviks took Petrograd first by occupying government buildings; seizing control of the railroads, phones, and electrical system; and aiming a warship at the Winter Palace where Kerensky was headquartered. Kerensky fled. Using the Congress of Soviets then meeting in Petrograd, the Bolsheviks had the Congress declare that all power had passed to the soviets and named Lenin as head of the new government.

The Bolsheviks took Moscow next. Germany all the while was financing Bolshevik activity, including support for the newspaper *Pravda*. Outside the cities, the takeover came more slowly, and Russia plunged into civil war for the next three years.

THE RUSSIAN CIVIL WAR

The Bolsheviks first called their government "provisional" and promised elections. When these elections were held, the Bolsheviks only received 25 percent of the vote; the winners were the Social Revolutionaries, the more moderate socialists. However, the Bolsheviks then ignored the elections. A constitutional assembly met for only one day in January 1918, when armed Bolshevik sailors shut it down. These events helped to spur division and civil war. The Bolshevik army was called the Reds and its opposition, the Whites.

The **White Army** was made up of soldiers from various parts of southern Russia, the Ukraine, and Siberia and from different social groups, united only in their hatred of the Reds, without any central command. Still, for a while the Whites did well. Various independent regional governments set up to compete with Lenin in Moscow. (The Bolsheviks had moved the capital inland, thinking Petrograd was too exposed to the West.)

Meanwhile, Trotsky trained the **Red Army**. The Bolsheviks changed their party name to **Communist** in 1918. Because there were food shortages and famine everywhere, the communists seized food from the kulaks, which made them anti-communist. The communists also nationalized major industries. In the summer of 1918, the Reds moved the tsar and his family to the town of Ekaterinburg in the Urals, where they were executed.

The British and Americans made some feeble effort to help the White armies. British and Canadian forces landed at Murmansk and the Americans at Archangel (Arctic seaports), but the war in Europe was over, and the West simply wanted to go home. Czech troops were left inside Russia at the end of the war. The communists demanded that they disarm, but the **Czechs in Siberia** took the Siberian railroad to Vladivostok, seizing some towns in western Siberia for a while. However, by 1920, the White armies had failed. Ranging from one extreme to another, the Whites were never able to unite politically. The territory they held was always on the periphery, never in central areas. The peasants did not support the Whites for fear that they would have to return the land they had taken. Generally, help from the Allies was puny, and even then, it "looked bad" to some as the work of foreign meddlers.

During the Civil War, Russia experienced a **Red Terror** similar to the Terror in France in 1793–1794 but much worse. Thousands became victims. Mensheviks and others fled to Western Europe with tales of horror.

There was peace by 1922 in a Russia that had lost much territory—Finland, Estonia, Latvia, and Lithuania, all of which stayed independent. Romania and Poland now contained land that had once belonged to Russia. The nation became the **USSR** (Union of Soviet Socialist Republics) in 1922 with four republics. The USSR would last almost 70 years, until the late 20th century.

CHAPTER 25: EUROPE BETWEEN THE WARS

THE "AGE OF ANXIETY"

The economic disruption of World War I did not end when the war ended. Throughout Europe, there was extreme unemployment and inflation. All nations had borrowed heavily during the war, and afterwards they printed paper money to help repay loans, which contributed to the already high inflation. Everywhere, prices were several times what they had been before the war, with the most severe conditions in Austria and Hungary.

Owners of business and government officials had come to like the economic planning of the war years and would have liked to see the trend continue. But against such elitist tendencies stood the more powerful parliamentary bodies and universal suffrage, which now included women.

The Russian Revolution emphasized more than ever the differences between Marxism and reform socialism. To the communists, the poor economic conditions following the war seemed to prove that capitalism was dying. The **Third Communist International** came into existence in Moscow in 1919 with the purpose of developing communist parties in other countries. Efforts to develop a British communist party fell totally flat; the communists were more successful in France, where a communist party soon became as large as the socialist party.

In England, the growing Labour Party appealed to the newer voters from the lower economic classes. In 1924, **Ramsey MacDonald** led the first Labour ministry, but he was soon discredited by the publication of what was called the "Red Letter," or **Zinoviev Letter**, supposedly from the head of the Communist International, containing instructions for a communist takeover. Although the letter was a forgery, the reaction it caused allowed the Conservatives to return to power. In 1926, when workers all over Britain walked out in support of a miners' strike, the government was not sympathetic. After the strike was broken, Parliament passed the **Trades Disputes Act**, forbidding sympathy strikes.

In France, conservative politics also prevailed, except for a brief time in the middle of the 1920s when a coalition of socialists controlled the government. The socialist coalition fell after proposing a tax on capital, and the conservatives, led by **Raymond Poincaré**, returned. To try to stabilize the economy, Poincaré raised taxes on goods, which raised the value of French currency. Poincaré was credited with "saving" the franc. The working class, however, felt cheated and remained discontent.

Disillusionment from the war experience, followed by uncertainty in politics and the economy, was reflected in the arts and in philosophy. In Germany, existentialist philosophy became widespread among university students. Existentialism spread to France, where it became very popular a few years later, during and after World War II. The ideas of this philosophy were somewhat influenced by the late 19th-century German nihilist, Friedrich Nietzsche. **Existentialism** covered a wide range of concepts, some of which contradicted each other. Generally, the existentialists saw the world as a place of terror and uncertainty, where humans searched for moral values. Most, but not all, proponents of the philosophy were atheists. Humans, they felt, were very alone, facing despair and meaninglessness. They could see no God, no reason, no progress. The French existentialist **Jean Paul Sartre** said that humans still had to act; they had to make choices and be responsible for their own behavior. This, according to Sartre, was the only way to address the absurdity of life.

The war had a tremendous effect on writers, artists, and thinkers. **T. S. Eliot**, an American writer who became a British citizen, used titles such as *The Wasteland* and "The Hollow Men" to describe a world of isolation, alienation, and hopelessness. **Franz Kafka** used the theme of the helplessness of the individual against hostile forces in his *The Metamorphosis*. **Gertrude Stein**, an American living in Paris after the war, called the expatriot Americans who gathered around her the "lost generation." Some novelists experimented with the **"stream of consciousness"** technique, in which a narrator recorded a monologue of ideas and emotions; James Joyce (Irish) and Virginia Woolf (English) are examples.

In art, the Dadaists tried bright colors and a jumble of images (discussed in Chapter 21). Paul Klee (Swiss) and Piet Mondrian (Dutch) were among the Dadaists. Another art movement was **surrealism**, in which realistic images appeared in dreamlike settings. **Salvador Dali** (Spanish) became the most famous surrealist.

In architecture and design, the new principle was **functionalism**, based on the idea that everything should serve a purpose. Fancy decoration was discarded in favor of clean lines and practical efficiency. After the war, **Walter Gropius** in Germany merged a school of fine arts with one of applied arts and opened the **Bauhaus** in Weimar. Stressing functionalism, the Bauhaus was very influential in design between the wars. Its creations were criticized by traditionalists, but it remained very popular until the Nazis shut it down in the 1930s.

In music, composers arranged sounds devoid of recognizable harmonies and with rhythms described as dissonant. The ballet of **Igor Stravinsky**, *The Rite of Spring*, was first presented by the Russian Ballet Company in Paris in 1913 and almost caused a riot. Its sensuality struck some as pornographic. The Austrian composer **Arnold Schoenberg** also created music that seemed strange in its atonality and lack of harmony. The average person did not understand or appreciate this type of music or comprehend the abstract nature of modern art.

For the common people, radio and movies became standard entertainment. While Europe fought the Great War, the United States cranked up its film industry. Germany began to develop film in the early 1930s, but the United States so superseded it that German talent went to Hollywood. At first, the Americans monopolized the industry. Movies became the entertainment of the masses, the "great escape" during the Depression years of the 1930s.

Radio had become possible after Marconi's invention of the vacuum tube in 1904, but it was not widespread until after 1920. Soon, every country had a national network, most prominent of which was the British Broadcasting Corporation (BBC). Before the Second World War, almost every household in England and Germany had at least one radio.

Radio and movies both had tremendous propaganda potential. Dictators, such as Mussolini in Italy and Hitler in Germany, used this power, as did leaders in democratic countries (Churchill in England during World War II, Franklin Roosevelt's "Fireside Chats" in the United States in the 1930s).

TOTALITARIANISM IN THE SOVIET UNION

The USSR adopted a constitution in 1924 with the stated aim of spreading communism and uniting the workers of the world. The government operated on a federal principle, designed to address the problems of nationalism and the multiplicity of ethnic groups. In actuality, the republic of Russia, with one-half the population and three-fourths of the territory, dominated the USSR. There was no substance to the claim that each republic had the right to secede. At the same time, it was an accomplishment to have united so many different people, while allowing some degree of self-expression.

The Soviet government and the Communist Party were closely intertwined. There were elections and seemingly democratic institutions. However, only the Communist Party was permitted to exist. The controlling force was the **Central Committee**, which numbered about 70 members in the 1930s. Above the Central Committee was the **Politburo**, a group of about 12 people. Above all was the office of General Secretary, which Stalin dominated and which ultimately controlled all decisions.

The Party started out quite small with about 70,000 members. By 1930, there were 2 million, and by the 1980s, some 19 million. Lenin's idea was to have a small, highly disciplined party whose members intensely studied Marxism and took orders without question. Party members were privileged and, consequently, had a vested interest in the system. They were allowed open discussion and differing opinions within the party but only to a limited point; in the end, all had to conform.

Under the constitution, women received equal rights, including the franchise (though that was meaningless). They were allowed to divorce and to seek birth control and abortion (later outlawed). At first, there were no actual changes in gender roles, but in time, there would be more education for girls and more opportunity for women.

Russia under Lenin

By 1921, conditions were terrible in the USSR: famine, crippled industry and agriculture, and revolt. People were cultivating perhaps 62 percent of the land, and farming was made worse by drought and a breakdown of transportation. Hard times led some to call for "soviets without communists" along with liberal demands like free speech and the secret ballot. Leon Trotsky put down rebellion with the Red Army.

To relieve the economic crisis, Lenin developed the **New Economic Policy (NEP)** because, he said, the government had tried to socialize too rapidly. Under the NEP, peasants were allowed to practice capitalistic farming again. They had to turn over a portion of what they raised, but they could keep the rest. With the profit motive restored, production did improve toward previously normal levels. The NEP was extended to small manufacturers and businesspeople, but the government held onto heavy industry. The plan favored individual farmers and the commercial class, but the communists disliked the NEP and persecuted the program and those involved in it. Still, they didn't dare wipe it out at first.

All art forms—art, literature, and science became vehicles for political propaganda. Favored creators received rewards. Many artists, especially early, rallied to the communist cause. An example was the filmmaker **Sergei Eisenstein**, who made very innovative and skillful movies, such as *Potemkin* (1925). Ironically, though, the Russian writers who achieved the most fame in the 20th century were anti-communist—Boris Pasternak and Alexander Solzhenitsyn.

Soviet Union under Stalin

In 1922, Lenin began to have strokes. He died two years later in his 50s. Immediately, Lenin became a symbol. His body was embalmed and kept on display at the Kremlin, and the city of Petrograd became Leningrad. But even before Lenin's death, not all Party members agreed with his policies, especially the NEP. Trotsky advocated long-range planning, an end of the NEP, mechanization of agriculture, rural cooperatives, and world revolution. A power struggle developed between Trotsky and Joseph Stalin. Shortly before his death, Lenin had quarreled with Stalin and wanted him out, but it was too late.

Nikolay Bukharin, editor of *Pravda*, liked the NEP and opposed Trotsky. Stalin used *Pravda* to discredit Trotsky, but once he was gone, Stalin turned on Bukharin as well. (Trotsky fled the country, and in 1940, was murdered in Mexico.) Almost immediately after driving Trotsky out, Stalin began to adopt Trotsky's ideas. Stalin had been commissar of nationalities, a position that allowed him to build up support from local Bolshevik leaders and to have access to thousands of bureaucrats; thus, he was able to draw from a broad base of approval.

Stalin introduced the first **Five-Year Plan** 10 years after the original communist takeover. A possible reason for the time lapse in developing an economic plan was that Marx and Engels had left no concrete ideas on the topic and there had been no agreement over what steps to take. The Five-Year Plans were administered by the Gosplan, which made the decisions about who would produce how much of what. It regulated raw materials, resources, and workers. The first Five-Year Plan ran 1927–1932. Although the Soviets did not achieve their goals, they nevertheless announced success and moved into the second Five-Year Plan. The third was underway at the beginning of World War II. All the plans emphasized heavy industry—steel, electric power, concrete, oil, and coal. Certainly, the economy progressed, not counting the human costs, which are estimated at thousands of lives sacrificed.

All the plans were state-run; there was no individual freedom of choice. If a worker resisted, he or she was sent to a labor camp. Trade unions existed, but these were also government controlled. Strikes were forbidden; the unions' purpose was to promote efficiency and production.

The first Five-Year Plan called for agricultural revolution through **collectivization** of farms. Each farm consisted of several thousand acres to be worked collectively by those assigned to it. The kulaks resisted, slaughtering their livestock and destroying their tools and equipment rather than handing them over. Consequently, the kulaks were liquidated; thousands of people were killed or sent to labor camps in Siberia. By 1939, on the eve of World War II, 96 percent of the farms had been collectivized. Farmers received tractors and other modern equipment and were expected to produce quotas of products, but results were poor. Agriculture remained the weakest area in the Soviet system.

There was more success in industry, especially in iron and steel production. The Soviets developed industry—mines and factories—east of the Urals and in Siberia, which would prove very beneficial in World War II.

SOVIET SOCIETY

In the mid-1930s, Stalin had many of the old Bolsheviks arrested and subjected to very public trials with foreign reporters present, at which the accused confessed to all manner of crimes. The number of people executed from these **purge trials** was estimated by the West to be in the hundreds of thousands. Many skilled professional people, including military leaders, were eliminated. By 1938, almost all the old Bolsheviks were gone.

Austerity became a way of life in the Soviet Union. Everyone worked for low pay, and few consumer goods were available. Always, there was the promise of better conditions in the future— the promise of better housing, food, and clothing and of more leisure time—after basic industry was built up. Propaganda kept workers inspired. They accepted the program, taking pride in quotas and figures. They did not question. There were social and economic differences among people because the government favored high officials, managers, engineers, and certain artists and intellectuals. No one could leave. Religion had no place in the new order, though it survived to some degree in the countryside in both Orthodox Christian and Islamic traditions. Jews continued to be harassed. The agency **TASS** controlled the flow of all information.

Conformity was the social standard. Art, literature, and science were used for propaganda. Literature was important because it could influence people, so the government smiled upon writers who produced material along party lines, including Five-Year Plan novels. The Soviets rewrote history. For instance, Catherine was no longer "the Great"; instead, she became labeled as "dissolute" and "criminal."

Some people outside the Soviet Union looked upon the Revolution with admiration. In fact, shortly after World War I, there were attempted social revolutions in Germany and Hungary, which Lenin and the Bolsheviks tried to aid. During the 1920s, the Soviet stand was opposition to socialists in any country who were not Marxists. However, by the 1930s, as fascism became a threat, the USSR allowed Marxists to join with other socialists into popular fronts.

The biggest influence of the USSR was its long-term, persevering existence. Many people from all over the world went there to study revolution and communism. The idea of a socialist republic gave hope to repressed peoples. Communist parties formed in many countries. The material progress that the USSR accomplished convinced many international observers of the possible results of economic planning.

FASCIST ITALY

RISE OF MUSSOLINI

It was not disturbing when nations like Russia or China did not advance as democracies. Such countries were considered backward, so they "didn't count." The first big shock to democracy came in Italy, which had had parliamentary government since 1861, when **Benito Mussolini** seized power in 1922.

The ideas of what we now call *fascism* were born before the Great War. In 1912, an avant-garde group had praised danger, energy, rashness, and struggle, glorifying war as the "only cure" for the modern world. After the Great War in Italy, times were bad. Unemployment was extremely high; returning soldiers could not find work. There was also widespread anger; Italy felt cheated because she received so little after the hints and promises of the Treaty of London (1915).

Benito Mussolini was born to a working-class family; his father was a blacksmith. Named for the Mexican revolutionary Benito Juarez, Mussolini grew up a loner and a bully. After a stint in the

Italian army, he edited *Avanti*, the newspaper of an Italian socialist party. In 1912, he protested Italy's war to annex Libya. When World War I began, he advocated Italian neutrality at first, but by 1915, he decided that war might bring social revolution. Other socialists disagreed with him.

Mussolini soon joined other ex-socialists, who called themselves syndicalists. They chose as a symbol a bundle of sticks to represent an association—*fascio* in Italian—hence, **fascists**. When Italy entered the war in 1915, Mussolini rejoined the army. After receiving a slight wound in 1917, he returned to journalism. By 1919, he founded his own fascist group, the National Fascist Party.

After the war, inflation soared in Italy, and agriculture was depressed. Italy had lost 600,000 lives in the war but received little territory as compensation. Wilson had refused to acknowledge the Treaty of London, and both Britain and France had ignored Italy. Italians now faced indebtedness, depression, unemployment, and unrest. The poor wanted land. Some formed "red leagues" and simply seized property, resulting in a great fear of communism among the landowners. Meanwhile, the government proposed a graduated income tax and a tax on war profits; it also legalized peasant land seizures and seemed unable to control the violence.

Bands of fascists, who called themselves **black shirts**, attacked the peasants and communists, and the landowners and urban wealthy secretly provided them with money and weapons. Mussolini loudly boasted about having his own army, and he denounced parliamentary government.

In 1921, Mussolini and other fascists were elected to the Italian parliament. King **Victor Emmanuel III** was weak—a small, shy, indecisive man—and he had difficulty getting a coalition to hold together to form a government. In late 1922, Mussolini got himself and other fascists named to cabinet posts. Declaring a state of emergency, Victor Emmanuel turned to Mussolini to form a new government. The fascists held only a few seats in the lower house of the Italian parliament, but Mussolini persuaded Parliament to give him full emergency powers because he promised to restore order. In the elections of 1924, the fascists came out the majority party (some said the election was rigged).

When a socialist minister named **Giacomo Matteotti** publicized incidents of fascist violence and fraud, he was soon found murdered. After loud protests, Mussolini claimed readiness to punish those responsible, but then he moved to eliminate opposition. Within a few years, the Parliament had no power, and the government censored the press, forbade strikes, and reduced labor unions to nothingness. The fascists were the only political party permitted.

Mussolini developed a cultlike following, using the media—films, books, and rambling radio speeches—for propaganda. Writers were required to capitalize pronouns referring to the dictator, and all adults had to take an oath of loyalty. Mussolini even had press agents overseas. Many were favorably impressed, including the English dramatist George Bernard Shaw; Sigmund Freud in Austria; and an American poet living in Italy, Ezra Pound. Mussolini appeared on the cover of *Time* magazine eight times! People said, "He made the trains run on time."

Mussolini's method of leadership was to strut, boast, and make thundering speeches. He wore a military uniform and was photographed reviewing troops or playing sports. Some historians have noted, however, that in reality, Mussolini was rather lazy, and little real military training occurred. Subordinates tended to tell Mussolini what he wanted to hear.

ITALIAN SOCIETY

In domestic matters, Mussolini made peace with the Church. By the **Lateran Agreement of 1929**, the Vatican became independent of Italy. The papacy finally acknowledged the existence of Italy, and Mussolini agreed to religious instruction in schools and conformity to Church pronouncements on obscenity and the use of contraceptives.

Unlike communism (which declared sexual equality), fascism saw women as second-class citizens, expected to stay at home and produce large families. Actually, the concept of large families was illogical; Italy was already overpopulated and had massive unemployment.

In economics, Mussolini ended up dividing all aspects of the economy into 22 areas, called **corporations**. Private ownership remained, but the government dictated working conditions, industrial policies, wages, and prices. Members of the controlling group were not elected but appointed by the government. The fascists claimed that this was an improvement over democracy. Social unrest ceased under tight government control, which had outlawed unions and strikes.

During the Depression, Mussolini developed a large public works program. Because Italy did not have coal, there was a big push to develop hydroelectric power. Another aim was to increase food production by reclaiming swamps. In general, Italian peasants were untouched by fascist programs. The great gulf between them and the wealthy continued. Beyond the peasants, the communists, socialists, labor leaders, and liberals also despised the fascists.

THE WEIMAR REPUBLIC

EARLY YEARS

In January 1919, the German provisional government held postwar elections. Three political parties emerged—the Social Democrats, the Center Party, and the German Democratic Party—all "middle" groups. The Social Democrats, who had a majority in the Reichstag, were revisionist socialists, whose membership included trade union officials and industrial managers; the party tended to be cautious and nonrevolutionary.

Also in January 1919, there was a brief uprising backed by Russian communists and led by **Karl Liebknecht** and **Rosa Luxemburg**. The event was called the **Spartacist Revolt**, and for a short time, it appeared that Germany might turn communist under a dictatorship of the proletariat.

However, the provisional government put down the revolt by recruiting former army officers. Liebknecht and Luxemburg were arrested and shot in police custody.

A new constitution was adopted in July 1919 in the city of Weimar (thus, the government was called the **Weimar Republic**). It would last until 1933, when Hitler came to power. A year after the Spartacist uprising, there was a *putsch*, or armed revolt led by angry army officers, who tried to take control of the government. They were stopped by Berlin workers, who turned off the public utilities. A weakness of the new republic was its lack of firmness against such agitators and armed bands—Adolf Hitler would soon be one of these.

The Weimar Republic was democratic but not socialist. No property was nationalized, and there were no land reforms. Old statutes from the past remained in place. The army, now limited by the Treaty to 100,000 troops, remained a strong though miniature version of its former self. Unfortunately, how Germans accepted postwar democracy was tied to how they accepted the Treaty. The general view of the Treaty was that it was unjust and, perhaps, not final. The war guilt clause was extremely offensive.

The reparations were determined by a committee after the peace treaty. The final figure of 132 billion gold marks ($35 million) seemed impossible, even in the eyes of non-German economists. The German foreign minister Rathenau tried to help inflation by making reparations payments in goods, rather than in gold. In 1922, to the shock of Britain and France, Rathenau negotiated the **Rapallo Treaty** with the USSR (Russia had had no part in the Treaty of Versailles). Russia got technical assistance from Germany and training for the Russian army, which helped Germany maintain its military readiness despite Versailles limitations. Germany agreed to repudiate Russian tsarist debts, and Russia renounced future reparations payments. Two months later, Rathenau was murdered by right-wing nationalists.

RUHR CRISIS

By late 1922, the value of the German mark had sunk to the point that Germany told the Allies it could not meet the reparations payments. Meanwhile, Britain and France were under pressure to repay their war debts to the United States but could not without the German money. They insisted that Germany could pay in coal and natural resources. French Premier Raymond Poincaré accused Germany of doing this deliberately to get out from under the Treaty; he threatened military occupation of the **Ruhr Basin**, site of major German mining and steel manufacturing.

Germany then ordered Ruhr miners and factory workers to quit work, and in January 1923, French and Belgian troops occupied the Basin; the British disagreed with this move and refused to participate. The German workers now had no income, so the Weimar government printed paper money to support them. The result was horrible, incredible inflation. Those who were hardest hit were people on fixed incomes, creditors, and people with small savings. Prices soared for all goods.

The German middle class became poor and discouraged, feeling themselves on the same plane as lower-class laborers. Feeling hopeless, they were more inclined to turn to Marxism.

By the fall of 1923, a new government under **Gustav Stresemann** got the miners back to work and persuaded France and Belgium to withdraw troops. The government quit printing paper money, calming inflation. In 1924, a commission of the League of Nations, headed by the American banker Charles G. Dawes, developed the **Dawes Plan** (even though the United States wasn't a League member), which reworked the German payment plan and arranged for Germany to secure foreign loans. At the same time, the United States reduced the debt Europeans owed it, and economies began to improve.

ECONOMIC RECOVERY AND POLITICAL AGREEMENTS

As prosperity developed, the mid-1920s saw a period of international calm. Although the League of Nations was never a strong body, it did provide a forum in which statesmen could meet and talk. In 1925, Germany signed the **Treaty of Locarno** with France and Belgium, guaranteeing their borders unconditionally. Germany did not guarantee its eastern borders but did agree that any change would come after discussion and agreement or arbitration.

France made treaties with Poland and Czechoslovakia, promising military aid if they were invaded by Germany. France also favored the **Little Entente** among Czechoslovakia, Yugoslavia, and Romania. Britain promised to back France and Belgium if either were invaded by Germany. England felt she would be threatened only if Germany moved west, not if she moved east. People then talked about the "spirit of Locarno" as a metaphor for international cooperation.

In 1926, Germany joined the League. Two years later came the **Kellogg-Briand Agreement**, developed by the United States and France. Sixty-five nations signed the document, condemning war as a way to solve problems. It should be noted that the agreement specified no means of enforcement.

By the late 1920s, economies seemed recovered. Everywhere, production was up; by 1929, world trade had tripled from prewar statistics. One big reason for progress was the automobile industry. Cars were still relatively rare in 1914, but they became mass produced in the 1920s, fostering a number of supporting industries (petroleum, rubber, and steel). All of this was about to be shattered by the worldwide Great Depression, which permitted the emergence of a militant nationalism in Germany and a new military assertiveness in Japan.

THE GREAT DEPRESSION

Despite the appearance of prosperity and economic progress in the late 1920s, there were underlying problems. Industrial expansion was largely built on credit. Wages lagged behind profits and dividends, so mass purchasing power was limited. The whole decade also witnessed a global agricultural depression; farmers could not pay debts, nor did they have purchasing power.

Outside of Europe during the war, farmers had increased wheat production, often going into debt to do so. After the war, when European producers returned, grain prices plummeted. Farming was also becoming increasingly mechanized, and science contributed to raising per-acre productivity. Thus, the world wheat market was glutted, and prices were the lowest they had been in 40 years. Cotton, corn, coffee, and cocoa were in similar situations of overproduction and low prices. When the depression hit, it was worsened by the already bad agricultural situation; people had no money in reserve.

The **Great Depression** officially began with the crash of the U.S. stock market in October 1929. Prices of stocks had been driven up by excessive speculation. Many ordinary people had bought stock, often with borrowed funds. Investors took loans from brokers, and brokers borrowed from banks. The stock market crash set off an avalanche of selling, and within a month, stock prices fell 40 percent. Over the next three years, the average value of industrial stocks on the New York Stock Exchange fell from $252 to $61, and 5,000 banks shut down. Americans suddenly quit investing in Europe and buying foreign goods. Bankruptcies mushroomed, factories slowed down or closed, world industrial production fell by 40 percent, and world trade decreased by two-thirds. All countries had tremendous unemployment, which exacted a great psychological toll in addition to the economic strain.

National reactions to the catastrophe were unilateral, with goals of national security. Socialism and the welfare state grew. Where democracy was already established, it continued, with governments taking steps to help its citizens. In other nations, where democracy was new and/or weak, the Depression paved the way for dictatorship. Desperate people wanted a leader who would act— make decisions, inspire confidence, and restore national pride. This was already Mussolini's position in Italy; it would soon also be the situation in Germany.

The Depression worsened problems Britain already had after the war—loss of overseas markets and rising tariffs in other countries. In the early 1920s, Parliament had established unemployment insurance, pensions, medical aid, and government-subsidized housing. England had recognized the Soviet Union and promised loans in return for purchase of British goods.

When the Depression broke, Ramsey MacDonald (Labourite) was prime minister. The government cut back spending, using such terms as *belt-tightening* and *entrenchment*. These measures helped somewhat, but as in the United States, the economy would not fully recover until World War II. All the while, Britain was also dealing with demands for independence in India. In Palestine, which England held as a "mandate" following the war, there was conflict between Arabs and Jews. Despite economic and political troubles in Britain, neither the communists nor the fascists were able to develop a following there.

France was less affected by the Depression for several reasons. There was less large-scale manufacturing and less dependence on foreign markets. Production of goods tended to come from smaller, local operations. Also, France faced the Depression with sizable gold reserves. In the 1930s, a financial scandal tainted the government and aided fascist groups calling for an end to the republic. The result was a coalition of various socialist groups and French communists into a **Popular Front**, led by **Leon Blum**. The Front only lasted about a year, but it established a program of far-reaching social legislation with a 40-hour week, vacations with pay, collective bargaining, and reorganization of the Bank of France. The government aided farmers by purchasing agricultural products and maintaining price controls.

The Popular Front fell apart by 1938, and the conservative **Edouard Deladier** took over. No Western nations fully recovered from the Depression until World War II. The birth rate fell to the lowest on record. By the late 1930s, there was a notable shortage of middle-aged men, the survivors of the Great War.

TOTALITARIANISM IN NAZI GERMANY

RISE OF HITLER

Adolf Hitler was born in Austria to a lower-middle-class family. He grew up a strange child, an outcast and bully (like Mussolini). Failing to finish high school, Hitler moved to Vienna, where he was denied admission to an art school. He earned a meager income as a paper hanger, and he painted and sold postcards. In Vienna, the anti-Semitic rhetoric of the mayor influenced him to adopt excessive race consciousness.

By the advent of World War I, Hitler had moved to Munich. He joined the German army and was wounded and decorated. Even though he was rejected for officer training, Hitler gloried in the war. For the first time in his life, he was "somebody." When Germany surrendered, he felt it had been betrayed by Marxists and Jews. Like others after the war, he was restless and lost. He remained in the army and was returned to Munich to watch over a new radical group, the **German Workers' Party**. Soon, Hitler joined the group as its leader. He changed its name to the National Socialist German Workers' Party (Nazi) and began to be referred to as **Fuhrer**—leader. (In Italy, Mussolini was now called **Duce**.)

Like Mussolini, Hitler cultivated people with money who provided cash for propaganda and guns, especially for a paramilitary branch of the organization who called themselves **brown shirts** or **storm troopers**. They were not the only organization of this type at the time. Many of the members were disillusioned former soldiers. They were eager to practice violence and saw Hitler as a war veteran, a man of action. Already, he was promising to rearm Germany and expand its military.

Mussolini had already staged his coup in Italy, so in 1923, Hitler and his supporters tried to do something similar in Munich, the **beer hall putsch**. The attempt failed, and Hitler was arrested. At a big public trial, he was able to do a lot of grandstanding, primarily denouncing the Treaty. A lenient judge sentenced Hitler to five years in prison. He only served one, but he used the prison time to write *Mein Kampf* (*My Struggle*), published in 1925. It became a best seller, despite being a mishmash of ravings on various topics.

The second half of the 1920s saw excellent economic recovery in Germany after the Ruhr Crisis, and National Socialism lost support. Then, Stresemann died in 1929, and almost immediately, the Depression hit. Germany suffered perhaps more than any other nation. For the second time in less than 10 years, the middle class lost faith in the economic system. To the working class, communism seemed appealing. The middle classes and upper classes feared communism and looked for a savior from it.

The Depression reawakened German hatred of the Treaty as something to blame. Hitler used propaganda to inflame these issues. He labeled the Treaty a national humiliation and harshly criticized the Weimar government. He lashed out at communists and, in every way, denounced Jews, who were a minority of only about 600,000 in the whole country and, therefore, "safe" to criticize.

In the election of the fall of 1930, the Nazis got 18 percent of the vote; communists gained as well. Then in 1932, Hitler ran against Hindenberg for the presidency. Hitler lost, but he received 13.5 million votes to Hindenberg's 19 million. Still without majority support, Hitler did have the support of conservatives—big industrialists, Junker landowners, and army officers, who seemed to think they could "use" Hitler. After two unsuccessful chancellors in 1932, Hindenberg, at the urging of powerful people, named Hitler as chancellor. Thus, Hitler's ascension to high office in early 1933 was entirely legal.

Nazi Ideology; Nazi Society; Anti-Semitism

Part of Hitler's appeal was youth. In 1929, Hitler was 40, while President Hindenberg was 80. Forty percent of the party was under age 30, two-thirds under age 40. The ideas of national recovery, rapid change, and personal advancement were very appealing.

In 1933, the Reischstag building burned, and Hitler loudly blamed the communists (the Nazis may have set the fire themselves). He used the incident to get passed the **Enabling Act**, which suspended individual rights, such as for those accused of crimes. Hitler appointed **Hermann Göring** to create an auxiliary police force. The new order Hitler termed the **Third Reich**. (The First Reich had been the Holy Roman Empire, and the Second had been the age of Bismarck.)

The **Nuremberg Laws of 1935** defined *Jewish* as having at least one Jewish grandparent. The **swastika** became the official symbol of Germany. Jews had to wear a yellow Star of David prominently. All public places displayed signs forbidding Jews, and marriage between Jews and non-Jews was forbidden. By 1938, most Jewish businesses were closed, and Jews were excluded from professions and occupations. Next, they had to turn over all assets to the government. Some Jews (the lucky ones) fled Germany as soon as Hitler came to power. After Jews were no longer allowed to attend or teach in universities, a number of scholars went to the United States. By 1938, the Nazi government was launching violent attacks on Jews, and neighboring countries tightened immigration restrictions or totally closed their borders.

To ensure absolute control, Hitler purged old Nazi leaders. The government set up concentration camps where thousands were sent without trial or sentence. No one dared oppose the regime. The **National Labor Front** replaced labor unions and outlawed strikes. To provide jobs during the Depression, the government sponsored public works: reforestation, swamp drainage, housing, highway construction, and rearmament. Consumer goods, especially radios, became more plentiful. A program called **Strength through Joy** provided vacations, even for the lower middle class.

The German chemical industry continued to thrive, producing artificial rubber, plastics, synthetic textiles, and many substitute products. Clergy were not allowed to criticize the government, which discouraged religious schools and international religious ties. Unlike Mussolini, who made peace with the Church, the Nazis favored anti-Christian pagan movements.

The government sponsored youth movements in schools and universities. As in Italy, women were regarded as inferior. They were required to give up industrial jobs, nor could they work in public service or education. It was permissible for women to do farm work or traditional textile or handicraft work at home. The government provided financial benefits to families with children. Despite the rhetoric, as more men were drafted into the army, more women worked in factories. Later, during the war, Germany would use prison labor.

Paul Joseph Goebbels became minister of propaganda. The Nazis censored the theater and burned books by Jews, communists, and socialists. Before this regime, the Bauhaus of design had sought to join art and industry. It had attracted many foreigners and espoused modernism, which Hitler hated; he closed the Bauhaus. "Approved art" celebrated being German. In music, Jewish composers, such as Schoenberg and Mahler, were condemned, while the music of **Richard Wagner** was glorified, not only because Wagner had expressed anti-Semitism but also because of the stirring, militaristic sound of his compositions.

In Hitler's Germany, life was better for the masses, with the exception of Jews, Slavs, gypsies, Jehovah's Witnesses, communists, and homosexuals. Prior to the 1930s, class division had been rather rigid; now, suddenly, young, poorly educated dropouts like Hitler could rise rapidly. Many found comfort in excessive nationalism, in security of numbers, and in a sort of mindless enthusiasm and mob mentality. Hitler's most effective method of support was the mass rally, consisting of songs, slogans, and demonstrations to build anticipation of Hitler's arrival. Then he worked the crowd into a wild frenzy with attacks on the Versailles Treaty, the Jews, and, in the early days, the Weimar Republic.

There was resistance, but it was never unified, and enemies were dealt with quickly and harshly. Attempted coups in 1938, 1942, and 1944 all failed. There was some protest from Protestants and Catholics in defense of religion, but for the most part, churches did little.

SPANISH CIVIL WAR

Spain was ruled by the Bourbons after 1713 (end of the War of Spanish Succession). During the 1920s, Spain became very unsettled politically and economically, and in 1931, King Alfonso XIII was forced to abdicate. Spain established a republican government and attempted some reform. Church and state were separated, the government dissolved the Jesuits and seized their property, and schools became secular. Catalonia on the northeast coast, bordering the Mediterranean, had long wanted self-government, which was now granted. The government broke up some of the large estates and allotted land to peasants.

For many, the government seemed to be doing too little; strikes and uprising broke out, especially in Barcelona. By 1933, right-wing extremists seized the government, which they ran poorly. Spanish miners revolted, and their uprising was violently quashed. In 1936, there were new elections. The leftist elements united in a popular front against the old order military and Spanish fascists—the right-wing extremists were called **Falangists**. When the left won the elections, the military revolted under the leadership of **Francisco Franco**. The leftists were called the republicans or **loyalists**.

A horrible civil war then raged throughout Spain for the next three years, resulting in some 600,000 deaths. Both sides committed atrocities. The republicans hoped for aid from the French, British, and Americans. The British and French stayed out, in fear that the conflict might escalate into a general war. They also went so far as to get 27 nations to sign a document agreeing to abstain from the conflict. The United States had neutrality laws in place that forbade shipping arms to the Spanish republicans, though many Americans favored the idea. Instead, the USSR sent planes, tanks, and military advisors, accusing Franco's side of being part of an international fascist movement.

Italy and Germany aided Franco, claiming the republicans were Bolsheviks, and their joint effort cemented a military friendship between Mussolini and Hitler that hadn't existed previously. A number of nations sent observers, and in one sense, the war became a proving ground for new military technology that would soon be used on a grander scale. One of the fascist practices was **saturation bombing** to wipe out whole towns. One of the victims was **Guernica**, made famous by Pablo Picasso's huge abstract painting of that name. Its disjointed images—a dead fighter's hand clutching a broken sword, a speared horse dying in anguish, a mother with a dead child (like a Pietà)—evoked the agony of total war.

After Franco's fascists won the civil war in 1939, Britain and France recognized his government. Some loyalist refugees fled the country; those who stayed faced bloody reprisals. Franco proved wise enough not to attempt expansion and stayed neutral in World War II. His government was based on the army, the Church, and wealthy landowners. Unlike Germany, Spain allowed the Church to stay powerful. Franco would rule Spain until his death in 1975, after which Spain finally became a constitutional monarchy.

CHAPTER 26: WORLD WAR II

FAILURE OF COLLECTIVE SECURITY

In the 1930s, Germany, Italy, Japan, and the USSR were all discontented with the Treaty of 1919, so dissatisfied that they were willing to risk war to make changes. England, France, and the United States were content with the Treaty in that they could see no benefit to changing it. At the same time, however, they'd lost faith in it and were unwilling to fight to uphold or enforce it. The Western democracies waited, while the dissatisfied nations destroyed the terms, borders, and conditions agreed upon in 1919.

Western nations had come to see the Great War as a big mistake. They ceased to blame Germany as much as they had and felt that perhaps the Treaty had been too harsh. Some even rationalized that countries like Italy and Germany needed "room to grow," saying that perhaps democracy was not for all nations. Hitler ranted about living space for the **Aryan race**, a term he made up to mean the Germanic peoples.

France put faith in the **Maginot Line**, an elaborate system of fortifications along her eastern border from Switzerland to Belgium (but not expanded to the coast). France in the 1930s was a mix of conflicting ideologies. Many on the right feared socialism and its Popular Front and admired Mussolini and Hitler; others on the far left admired the USSR. There was similar controversy in the United States and Britain but to a lesser degree. The United States remained rigidly isolationist. Congress forbade loans, export of munitions, and the use of American ships to help any nation involved in a recognized war.

Resentment in the USSR went back to the great losses of territory from World War I and the *cordon sanitaire* (see Chapter 23) created at Versailles. The Soviets maintained the goal of international revolution and were paranoid about the world's fear and hatred of communism. In Hitler's *Mein Kampf* and in his speeches and other writing, he claimed he would "obliterate Bolshevism." In 1934, the USSR joined the League of Nations and even began to urge communists in other countries to work with the socialists. In 1935, the Soviets signed a pact with both France and Czechoslovakia. Nevertheless, most remained afraid of the Soviet Union and wanted nothing to do with it.

GERMAN EXPANSION

REJECTION OF THE VERSAILLES TREATY

Hitler soon found a method that worked in his dealings with the West. He ranted and demanded, then took a little of what he wanted and calmed down, giving the West a false sense of security—until he raged again and began the cycle anew. In 1933, Germany withdrew from the League of Nations. Then in 1934, Hitler signed a nonaggression pact with Poland. Later that year, the leader of Austria, **Engelbert Dollfuss**, was assassinated in an attempted Nazi coup. Hitler demanded that Austria form a union with Germany. Western nations did not act beyond a verbal protest, but Mussolini, who had not yet become Hitler's ally, sent Italian troops to the Austrian border. (Mussolini coveted Austria also.) Mussolini's action kept Germany out of Austria for four more years.

In 1935, Hitler announced the expansion of the German army to a half million troops, a blatant violation of the Treaty. Military service became compulsory, and Germany began to rebuild an air force. France remained divided, and the British were unwilling to make any moves. Also in 1935, Germany signed a naval agreement with Britain, which shocked and upset France, partly because it happened with no warning. According to the agreement, Germany would have 35 ships to every 100 English vessels.

In 1936, German troops invaded the Rhineland, which according to the Treaty was supposed to be demilitarized. This move was a test to see if the French or British would react; they did not. At home, Hitler's popularity soared because he was reversing the Treaty, as he had promised. At this point, England began to modernize her military, while Germany spent huge amounts on rearmament.

The next year, 1937, passed quietly. Then in 1938, everything began rapidly moving toward war. Mussolini, meanwhile, was using Italy's discontent over the Treaty for propaganda purposes. Because of its lack of raw materials, Italy had to import coal, rubber, and copper. The government did increase hydroelectric production and fostered Italian auto manufacturing. In 1935, Italy invaded Ethiopia (Italy was still embarrassed over its humiliating defeat there in 1896—see Chapter 22). Because Ethiopia was a member of the League of Nations, its emperor, **Haile Selassie,** pleaded in Geneva for help. The League set up some sanctions forbidding the sale of armaments or raw materials to Italy, but oil, which Italy needed most, was still allowed. Even then, England feared that the West was "going too far" and worried that the sanctions might provoke Italy to war. The West did not feel threatened by Italy's attack on an African nation, so Ethiopia was disregarded, as China would be in 1937. Italy then added Ethiopia to its colonies of Somaliland and Eritrea and continued to meddle in Albania across the Adriatic.

THE *ANSCHLUSS*; JAPANESE READINESS

The Spanish Civil War made Mussolini willing to sacrifice Austrian independence. Believing that German military strength could further Italian aims, Mussolini signed an agreement with Hitler in October 1936, forming an **Axis**. After Mussolini visited Germany in the fall of 1937, Italian soldiers began to march like Nazis. Previously, Mussolini had not expressed animosity toward Jews, who were a small minority in Italy and well assimilated into society. In fact, Mussolini had support from the Jews and had a Jewish mistress. But now, in 1938, the Italian government began a campaign against Jews, which many Italians found troubling.

Across the world, Japan had radically transformed itself in less than 100 years. In the late 19th century, its government fell into the hands of a military regime, which began to expand territorial interests and defeated Russia in 1905. During World War I, Japan sided with the Allies while she slowly and covertly advanced into China. Then in the early 1930s, Japan openly seized Manchuria. (Japan had no natural resources at home.) Fearing possible competition in China from the Soviets, Japan signed a friendship treaty with Germany, an anti-communist agreement. Japan was also involved in a major buildup of its navy, including the construction of aircraft carriers. In 1937, Japan began a big, open invasion of China and soon controlled most of the country. The United States did not invoke its neutrality laws because no "official" war existed but, instead, loaned money and sold steel, oil, and scrap metal to China. In Britain, the new prime minister was **Neville Chamberlain**, who was so conservative that he had called Nazism a "great social experiment." Knowing this, Hitler felt confident as he proceeded to annex his neighbors. Chamberlain feared that antagonizing Germany would invite Italy and Japan to go after British possessions in Africa and Asia, respectively.

In March 1938, Hitler sent German troops into Austria, claiming to defend German citizens there. This time, Mussolini did not protest, and the Germans were greeted as liberators. The unification of Germany and Austria, forbidden in the Treaty, was called the *Anschluss*. The British and French protested but did nothing more.

CZECHOSLOVAKIA

Czechoslovakia was a Slavic state created in 1918. It was made up of a number of minorities without a national majority of any group. A democracy, it had the highest standard of living east of Germany, and it maintained alliances with France, Romania, and Yugoslavia. The Czech army was well trained, and the country possessed a munitions industry. Czechoslovakia was fortified against Germany but only in **Sudetenland**, in the western end of the country, where a large percent of the population was German (see map).

Sudeten Germans listened to pro-Nazi agitators and to Hitler's argument that all Germans should be part of the Fatherland. Rumors spread that a German invasion was imminent. The frightened British and French suggested that Czechoslovakia offer Sudetenland self-government. The Soviets urged taking a stand, but the West distrusted Stalin as much as it feared Hitler. War seemed about to break out when Hitler invited Chamberlain (British) and Daladier (French) to talks in Munich. The Soviets and Czechs were not included.

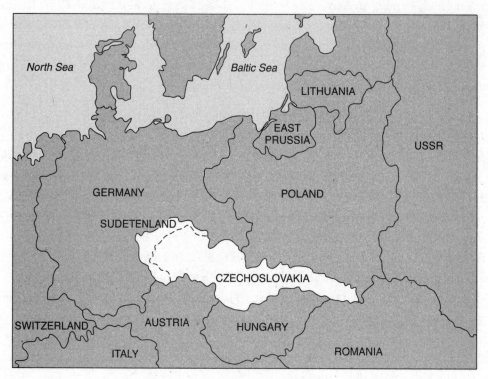

Sudetenland

The **Munich Conference** in 1938 became the ultimate in appeasement. Hitler got what he wanted because the British and French were scared of war. France dumped its agreement with Czechoslovakia and with the Little Entente, even though the USSR had vowed to defend the Czechs. Chamberlain and Daladier agreed to let Hitler take the Bohemian end of Czechoslovakia (Sudetenland), which contained the country's defenses; Britain and France promised to defend the remainder. The agreement was praised in the West because it prevented war. Probably, there was nothing concrete that England and France could have done; neither country was militarily prepared, while Germany now had the best army in Europe. The principle of self-determination from the World War I era could be cited as an excuse for the sacrifice. At the same time, the British and French were also relieved to have Hitler moving east instead of west. After the Munich crisis, both Hungary and Poland lopped off small portions of Czechoslovakia closest to their borders, and again, nothing happened.

POLAND

Six months after Munich, in March 1939, Hitler marched into Czechoslovakia and took the rest of the country. His next seizure was the Lithuanian city of Memmel; he also demanded Danzig and the Polish Corridor (which separated East Prussia from the rest of Germany), promising support against the Soviet Union in exchange.

Italy was also busy, taking over Albania, which was forcibly "Italianized," including instituting the Italian language in schools. In Africa, Italy made Somalia into a military base with great cruelty, destroying villages and killing residents. In Libya, Italy introduced mustard gas and conducted public hangings. In response, the British and French instituted a military draft, and England turned out fighter planes as fast as they could be manufactured.

Poland was not in good shape to face German demands. The dictator Józef Pilsudski had died in 1935, and the government was unstable. The West had tried to arrange for Soviet backup, but the Poles didn't trust a Soviet military presence. France and England sent negotiators to the USSR in the summer of 1939, but they were poor diplomats who offended the Soviets. The Soviets suspected that the West wanted the USSR to take the brunt of Nazi aggression, and they were angry that Britain and France had not sent their prime ministers to Moscow, as they had to Munich. They were also mindful of Polish seizure of Soviet territory since 1918. Thus, in August 1939, the Soviet Union signed a **nonaggression pact** with Germany, which shocked the West. Nazis and communists were supposed to be enemies!

On September 1, 1939, Germany invaded Poland, using the technique called *blitzkrieg*, or "lightning war." This meant a fast-rolling ground force of tanks and personnel supported by air attack. Ill-prepared, Poland was conquered in a month. The Soviets then occupied territory in eastern Poland that had once been Russian and proceeded into Estonia, Latvia, Lithuania, and Finland. When Finland resisted, Russia attacked in November. The League expelled the USSR for this act of aggression, and Britain and France sent aid to Finland. It seemed that Russia was using Germany's attack on Poland as an excuse to grab territory.

Still, nothing had happened in the West, unlike in World War I, when Germany had overrun France during the first month. The winter of 1939–40 was quiet; some began to refer to events of the previous fall as a "phony war." But in April, Germany attacked Norway (which fought back, briefly) and Denmark, which was neutral and defenseless. In May, the Nazis invaded the Netherlands, Belgium, and Luxemburg and rolled into France with tanks and bombers, bypassing the Maginot Line, which had never been extended to the sea.

The Dutch and Belgians surrendered immediately, as did much of the French army. The British were backed up to **Dunkirk** on the English Channel, which necessitated a huge evacuation, done in part by English civilians. Much military equipment had to be abandoned on the French coast.

Germany turned south in June. France surrendered on June 22, 1940, after holding out just over a month.

A French government formed in London headed by **Charles De Gaulle**, who led the **Free French**. In France, two-thirds of the country was under German occupation. The unoccupied southern third of the country was governed by Frenchmen, **Pierre Laval and Marshal Petain**, who collaborated with the Nazis. Once France was secure, Mussolini attacked it in June 1940. Then the Italians moved into Greece and North Africa, where they did poorly and had to have German aid. Hitler's plan was to commandeer the resources of Europe for the benefit of Germany. In every country, Germany cultivated collaborators, called **quislings** after a Norwegian traitor by that name. At this point, only Britain remained free; all of Western Europe was conquered, Italy was an ally, and the Soviet Union was a friendly neutral.

TURNING POINTS OF THE WAR

THE BATTLE OF BRITAIN—SUMMER/FALL 1940–1941

Germany tried to gain air control over Britain with its **Luftwaffe** before making an amphibious landing by heavily bombing British factories and airfields. The Germans were unable to attempt this attack until they had control of bases closer to England. The British, however, had an excellent air force with light fighter planes capable of round trips to Berlin (the **Spitfire** and the **Hurricane**). England also had a strong antiaircraft defense system, and the British developed **radar** early in the war. The English had superior intelligence as well. Although the British suffered heavy losses, they did not give in, even when the Germans bombed indiscriminately, trying to break British morale.

By late fall, Hitler gave up on Britain and turned his attention to the USSR. Apparently, Hitler had strange feelings about England, hating it and admiring it at the same time. He seemed also to think that German submarines could disrupt British shipping and starve out the country. English industrial power was not destroyed, nor was civilian morale broken. **Winston Churchill**, who had replaced Chamberlain as prime minister, said of England's fighter pilots, "Never in the field of human conflict was so much owed by so many to so few." German mines and submarines did affect British shipping, but radar proved extremely helpful. In May 1941, the British sank the German battleship *Bismarck* and, thereafter, had surface control of the seas. Submarines remained a problem.

WAR IN THE USSR

The German-Soviet nonaggression pact was not popular in either country. It "bought time" and let the Soviets take back territory Russia had lost in World War I. Latvia, Estonia, and Lithuania were converted to Soviet states, and then the Soviets took a Romanian province. This move toward the Balkans alarmed Germany, which wanted the agriculture of Eastern Europe. By early 1941, Romania, Bulgaria, and Hungary had joined the Axis powers.

What Hitler wanted most was the grain heartland of the Ukraine, so Germany invaded the USSR in June 1941. The attack took Stalin by surprise. The Nazis did well at first, pouring 3 million men along a 2,000-mile front. By October, the Germans surrounded Leningrad (St. Petersburg), had conquered the Ukraine, and had Moscow under siege. The Russians, however, held out, despite terrible loses. Hitler eventually gave up on Moscow and shifted to the south, where Germany did better, advancing to within 100 miles of the Caspian Sea.

There, the **Battle of Stalingrad** began in August 1942 with an assault by over 250,000 troops. It raged for six months. Within a month, the Germans were inside the city. Stalin ordered his namesake held "at all costs." Eventually, house-to-house fighting produced frightful losses on both sides. The Soviets lost more men at Stalingrad than the United States did in the entire war. The German losses were so great that only 100,000 troops were left to surrender in February 1943.

PEARL HARBOR AND ITS AFTERMATH

In 1940, Japan grew closer to Germany and Italy. Once France was occupied, Japan began seizing French bases in Indochina. Finally, the United States stopped shipping raw materials to Japan. The Japanese Prime Minister **Tojo Hideki** had representatives in the United States for negotiations at the time of the Japanese attack on **Pearl Harbor** (December 7, 1941). The United States declared war on Japan on December 8 and on Germany and Italy three days later. Japan had great success at first, on both land and sea, taking Singapore, British Malaya, the Philippines, the Netherlands Indies, and New Guinea and threatening Australia. The Japanese felt they were ridding themselves of European imperialists. From their conquests, the Japanese had access to oil and rubber. At first, the United States was rather helpless against the Japanese because its Pacific fleet had been so badly crippled at Pearl Harbor. Neither the Japanese nor the Nazis would have major losses until 1942.

1942—THE "BLEAKEST YEAR"—IN NORTH AFRICA AND THE PACIFIC

In early 1941, the British went into Libya (Italian possession) and took possession of Ethiopia. But then, Germany sent General **Erwin Rommel** to take over the Axis armies in North Africa. Rommel reorganized his forces and drove the British back into Egypt—twice—with extremely heavy losses on both sides. In the end, the British kept the canal and finally held the Germans at **El Alamein** in mid-1942, 70 miles from Alexandria.

> Rommel was a rare Axis commander in that he was admired by the Allies. In 1944, he fought at Normandy, and the next year, he advised Hitler the cause was lost. Hitler accused Rommel of treason and began a trial, but Rommel poisoned himself.

In Europe, Hitler was planning a vast East European empire, enslaving Ukrainians and Russians. He spoke of replacing local populations in conquered territories with German peasants. Prisoners of war were sent to work in Germany under such horrible conditions that about 80 percent died. By early 1942, some 26 nations had formed a Grand Alliance against Germany and Japan, vowing no separate peace agreements. The decision was to defeat Germany and Italy first and then to deal with the Pacific.

In the Pacific, U.S. forces under General **Douglas MacArthur** retreated to Australia and, from there, addressed the South Pacific. Admiral **Chester W. Nimitz** commanded the entire Pacific fleet. At about the same time as Allied victory in Egypt, the United States had some initial Pacific victories at the Battle of Midway and the Battle of the Coral Sea. The Pacific war then became a matter of **island hopping**, one island or group of islands at a time, usually involving an **amphibious landing** and, sometimes, jungle combat.

NORMANDY INVASION—1944

Russia demanded a second front long before the British and Americans were able to invade. The United States had to mobilize first; also, it was difficult for ships to cross the Atlantic because of German submarines. In the meantime, American and British bombers did much damage to Germany—something that had not happened in World War I.

After winning in North Africa, the Allies took Sicily and invaded Italy. Mussolini was overthrown and fled north to be reinstated there in a puppet government, answering directly to Hitler. Here, he held out until near the end of the war, when Italians caught him fleeing the country and executed him.

By 1943, the Allies were on the offensive as they planned an invasion of Europe. They had made amphibious landings in Africa, Sicily, and the Pacific islands, but attacking Europe was more dangerous because roads and railroads offered the enemy the possibility of rushing in reserves at any point. The invasion was planned carefully, incorporating some 4,000 ships and 10,000 planes. The chosen site was the Normandy coast, but the Germans were led to believe that the invasion would occur near Calais. The French resistance helped spread this fake intelligence and disrupted railroads and roads. The invasion included British, American, and Canadian forces with the American General **Dwight Eisenhower** in command. Over a million men poured into France during the first month; the Allies freed Paris in August and arrived at the German border by September.

ADVANCE ON BERLIN

The Soviets drove the Germans out of the Ukraine and White Russia first, then from the Baltic States and eastern Poland. They were in Warsaw by August 1944. At that point, the Polish underground rose up against the Germans, but the Soviets did not aid the Poles. The Russian agenda was to have the Polish resistance and its leadership destroyed so Russia could establish its own collaborators. Therefore, after an appalling German slaughter of Poles, the Russians took Warsaw. After Warsaw, the Soviets bogged down in Poland, so they shifted south toward Romania and Bulgaria, which had converted from Axis affiliation.

In Yugoslavia, guerrilla forces under **Josip Broz (Tito)** had fought effectively and kept the Germans occupied in Eastern Europe. Now, Tito's forces moved north toward Germany. The West reached Berlin by April 1945. There, they waited for the Soviets to catch up from the other side, as a good-will gesture in recognition of their sacrifices. The Red Army met Western forces at the Elbe River on April 26. Hitler committed suicide on May 7, and the war ended in Germany.

VICTORY IN THE PACIFIC

The Allies had decided early in the war to defeat Germany first. In the Pacific, the Americans began with the Solomon Islands and advanced slowly northwest toward Japan. The war put many tiny places on the map—Guadalcanal, the Gilberts, the Marshals, the Carolines, the Marianas—in addition to New Guinea and the Philippines.

The great final battle was **Okinawa**; this island was taken simultaneously with the Allied taking of Germany in late spring 1945. Once the Americans had Okinawa, **Iwo Jima** (famous for the flag-planting photo and, later, the monument), and others, they could better launch bombing missions on Japan in addition to those from carriers. The aim was to destroy Japanese industry and finish off its navy. The USSR wouldn't declare war on Japan until Germany was defeated. Britain had fought Japan on mainland Asia earlier, and Australia helped in the Pacific fighting.

The decision to use the atomic bomb was a unilateral one made by U.S. President Harry Truman, who succeeded **Franklin Roosevelt** at his death in April 1945. The bomb's development was partially owed to refugee scientists and had been top secret. The decision to use it was based on the hope of saving American lives and shortening the war. Another motive may have been to flex American muscle before the Soviets, whose postwar ambitions were uncertain. Flying the *Enola Gay*, the Americans dropped the first bomb on **Hiroshima** on August 6. The second bomb was dropped on August 9 on **Nagasaki**. Japan surrendered three weeks later.

DIPLOMACY DURING THE WAR

Early in the war, before Pearl Harbor, Churchill asked the United States for arms and supplies. At the time, Americans were divided between isolationists, who seemed to feel that Europe was doomed and the cause hopeless, and the interventionists, who urged aid. Franklin Roosevelt was interventionist. American neutrality legislation, the ban on arms sales, was repealed in November 1939.

In a speech, Roosevelt emphasized the **Four Freedoms**: freedom of speech, of worship, freedom from want, and freedom from fear. Then the American administration agreed to sell the British American destroyers in exchange for American bases in Newfoundland, Bermuda, and the British Caribbean. In 1941, the U.S. Congress established the **Lend-Lease** program to provide arms, food, and raw materials to countries fighting the Axis powers. At first, Britain was the primary recipient, getting the greater part of about $50 billion worth of arms and equipment. However, trucks, planes, and munitions also went to the USSR. After 1943, Lend-Lease was officially extended to the Soviets; clothing, food, and many other supplies were delivered to Russia via the Persian Gulf and the Arctic ports.

The peace terms were worked out gradually through a series of conferences. The first was between Roosevelt and Churchill in August 1941, when they met off the coast of Newfoundland. The result was the **Atlantic Charter**, which was a statement of high ideals, somewhat reminiscent of Wilson's Fourteen Points.

In January 1943, the two leaders met again at **Casablanca** in Morocco. Here, they concluded that there must be unconditional surrender—that is, no unilateral "deals." Later the same year (December), Roosevelt, Churchill, and Stalin (included for the first time) met in **Tehran** to discuss plans for the postwar occupation and demilitarization of Germany. Here also they began to plan for a new international organization, the **United Nations**. Churchill pushed for an Allied invasion through the Balkans because he was worried about what the Soviets would do after the war, but Roosevelt overrode this idea, and the invasion was planned for France in the spring of 1944. Stalin pledged an eastern front at the same time.

The last conference Roosevelt attended was at **Yalta** on the Black Sea in February 1945 (two months before his death of a massive brain hemorrhage). The Allies made agreements about Poland and Eastern Europe and the future of Germany, the war in Asia, and the United Nations. In exchange for a promise of help against Japan, Russia was promised possession of Sakhalin Island and the Kurile Islands. In regard to postwar Germany, there was settlement on four **occupation zones** (British, French, American, and Soviet). Another proposal was the Morganthau Plan to return Germany to an agricultural economy, but this idea was dropped. The Soviets expressed great expectation of reparations—this would later work out to be $10 million, partly in industrial equipment.

The last war conference was in July 1945, after the defeat of Europe. Truman, Stalin, Churchill, and France gathered at **Potsdam** (a suburb of Berlin). Stalin made territorial demands for not only part of Germany but also the Turkish straits. The USSR was already occupying the Baltic countries, parts of Poland, East Prussia, Romania, Czechoslovakia, and Finland.

EUROPEAN SOCIETY DURING THE WAR

GREAT BRITAIN

England mobilized a workforce of much of its female population under age 40. Women worked in factories, in civil service, and on farms as "land girls." They carried on gardening projects to grow food—called digging for victory. The civilian population suffered food shortages throughout the war, and there was rationing. Such food items as bacon, sugar, eggs, and fats became almost impossible to obtain.

Early in the war, during the Battle of Britain, the civilian population kept up its morale. Churchill frequently addressed the nation via the BBC, and during air raids, people took refuge in the subway system. Local brigades were organized to put out fires and clean up debris from the bombings.

Throughout the war, England maintained a planned economy, and people supported it, as they supported all aspects of government policy at the time. Tank and aircraft production went up approximately 400 percent, in part because of the female labor force. Also, the government interned all German citizens, including Jewish refugees.

FRANCE

The German victory over France spelled the end of the Third Republic; even the slogan of "Liberty, Equality, and Fraternity" was banned. The northern three-fourths of the country was directly under Nazi control, and the southern third was **Vichy France**, under puppets of the Germans. The war years were times of great misery for the French—with terrible shortages of food and other necessities and terrible living conditions under the eye of the much-despised Germans. The Nazis rounded up thousands of young French men and women and shipped them to Germany as slave labor, where many died. Vichy France was the only part of Europe not directly controlled by the Germans that deported Jews to the concentration camps of Eastern Europe.

Some French collaborated with the Nazis during the war. However, more joined one of the underground resistance movements and carried out secret missions of smuggling and sabotage. All the while, Charles de Gaulle maintained a French government in exile, first based in London, and after North Africa was freed in Algeria, and he would emerge as the leader of France following the war.

SOVIET UNION

As in World War I, there were horrible Russian losses among both soldiers and civilians, and food was so scarce that people resorted to eating rats, cats, and dogs. Some starved. In places of heavy fighting, there were also housing shortages. The economy was strictly controlled by the government. As in England, women and girls went to work in industry, the mines, the railroads, and agriculture. Russian women were the only females who served as combatants in the war; there were women snipers, aircrews in bombers, and even female pilots.

To save factories and equipment from the invading Germans, a number of operations were totally dismantled and moved into the central part of the country, east of the Urals. All metal and machinery went into the war effort, which meant that much civilian labor, such as agricultural work, reverted to human and animal power. As a result, farm production fell by almost half during the war.

However, despite all the hardships, losses, and suffering, the Russian people came through the war with a great sense of pride and patriotism. This positive outlook was very different from the disillusionment Russian citizens experienced late in World War I.

GERMANY

For much of the war, Hitler refused to convert production from consumer goods to armaments. Apparently, he feared revolt from the German people if they were forced to live under great hardships. Instead, Hitler's plan was to take food, armaments, and other supplies from conquered territories and ship them into Germany and to raise production levels through efficiency. Total mobilization was not implemented until 1944, when the government closed schools, theaters, and cafés. However, by then it was too late to make a significant difference.

Likewise, the Nazi plan was not to allow women to work outside the home. The number of German women employed in factories didn't change very much. Extra labor needs were met through the use of prison slave labor. Late in the war when there was labor conscription for women, most found ways around it.

THE HOLOCAUST

Persecution of the Jews began in a twofold manner. The first idea was emigration from Germany. One plan in the fall of 1939 called for their removal to Madagascar, which proved logistically impossible. The next action was forced removal to ghettos, taking away jobs and possessions and resulting in starvation. Some were herded together, forced to dig burial pits, and shot.

Then came the **Final Solution**, the elimination of the Jews, a mission to be carried out by Heinrich Himmler and the SS (*Shutzstaffel*, the largest paramilitary organization under Hitler's regime). Perhaps a million were initially rounded up and shot by the **Einsatzgruppen**, or mobile death units. Six extermination camps were established by 1943 in Poland, the largest of which was **Auschwitz-Birkenau**. Jews were shipped to the camps from all over Europe. On their arrival by train, more than half of the total number of prisoners—women, children, the elderly—were gassed immediately, and their bodies were burned in specially built crematoria. Approximately 30 percent were not killed immediately but sent to live in unspeakable conditions in the labor camps. Besides being worked and starved to death, many fell victim to inhumane medical experiments. By the end, the Germans had eliminated approximately 90 percent of the Jews of Poland and other parts of Europe. In addition, they also singled out and murdered gypsies and homosexuals. These deaths were in addition to all the Slavic peoples killed and other victims of slave labor.

AFTERMATH OF THE WAR

World War II left Europe in shambles. Cities, highways, airports, railroads, bridges, public buildings, and private housing had been destroyed. The Continent was crawling with displaced persons—orphans, former prisoners, homeless peoples. The first problem was simply finding food. After that came the question of rebuilding, finding jobs, and repairing lives. In general, the economic and political power of Europe had been shattered so that two superpowers emerged from the ashes of World War II: the United States and the USSR.

Eastern Europe, which had been liberated by the Red Army, was under Soviet domination. Although Stalin had promised free elections in these countries, the Soviets would not allow this, fearing anti-communist results. Only military force could have changed the situation, and the Allies were anxious for conflict to end. Thus, the stage was set for Soviet control of all of Eastern Europe.

Germany was divided into four occupation zones controlled by the United States, Great Britain, France, and the USSR. The French, British, and American sections would soon be rejoined. Berlin, the former German capital, was within the Russian zone, so the city itself was also divided into four occupation zones, which would soon lead to trouble.

By the end of the war in Europe, it was clear that relations were strained between the United States and the USSR. In early 1946, Winston Churchill, speaking in the United States, referred to the division into two hostile camps as an **iron curtain** that had fallen between East and West. This contest of superpowers would shape international politics for most of the rest of the 20th century.

Yugoslavia, which had been freed from the Nazis by the guerrilla forces of Marshall Tito, would also become a communist state but one not under Soviet domination. Meanwhile, overseas colonial possessions were almost all beginning to demand independence.

If anything good can be said to have come from the war, it was advances in medicine and technology, including the use of blood transfusions and antibiotics and the invention of the jet engine.

UNIT SIX REVIEW QUESTIONS

1. The main goal of the first Five-Year Plan was to

   (A) unite Russia under communist rule.

   (B) eliminate the kulaks.

   (C) give women equality.

   (D) build up heavy industry.

   (E) increase the size of the Soviet army.

2. Peter Stolypin

   (A) guided Russia into World War I.

   (B) pushed for peasants to own their own land.

   (C) worked through the mir.

   (D) encouraged the Russo-Japanese War.

   (E) worked to expand the railroads.

3. Before it disbanded, the Versailles peace conference did all the following EXCEPT

   (A) set a very high amount of reparations payments.

   (B) limited the Germany army to 100,000 troops.

   (C) established the nations of Czechoslovakia and Kingdom of the Slavs (Yugoslavia).

   (D) created the League of Nations.

   (E) made Germany sign a war guilt clause.

4. The main concern of Bauhaus design was

   (A) beauty of line.

   (B) use of ornamentation.

   (C) implementation of the unusual.

   (D) bold, bright color.

   (E) functionalism.

5. A major difference between the two World Wars was that

   (A) alliances were not a factor at the beginning of World War II, as they had been in World War I.

   (B) the German civilian population suffered greatly in World War II, as it had not in World War I.

   (C) Germany was heavily bombed in World War II; it had escaped physical damage in World War I.

   (D) Russia suffered terrible losses in World War II but not in World War I.

   (E) women worked in factories in World War II but not in World War I.

6. Most existentialists would generally agree with all the following EXCEPT

   (A) there is nothing human beings can do for themselves.

   (B) life is meaningless.

   (C) there is no progress.

   (D) human beings are very alone.

   (E) God does not exist.

7. The forces of the White Army failed in 1918–1921 in part because

   (A) the Allies gave them no aid.

   (B) they controlled only the urban centers.

   (C) they had the support of the tsar.

   (D) they did not have the support of the peasants.

   (E) the Russians were tired of conflict.

8. After the 1937 Italian invasion of Ethiopia, the League of Nations

    (A) showed a sympathetic attitude toward Italy.
    (B) ineffectively tried to apply sanctions.
    (C) referred the dispute to the World Court.
    (D) refused to take any action.
    (E) expelled Italy from the League.

9. Hitler argued that Germany should annex Sudetenland to

    (A) protect its German-speaking population.
    (B) reduce French influence in Central Europe.
    (C) gain control of more munitions factories.
    (D) prevent communist seizure of the area.
    (E) reduce the military threat of Czechoslovakia.

10. Weapons and equipment that were used in World War I included all EXCEPT

    (A) radar.
    (B) the flame thrower.
    (C) mustard gas.
    (D) the machine gun.
    (E) submarines.

11. The factor that cemented the friendship between Hitler and Mussolini was

    (A) Mussolini's visit to Germany in 1937.
    (B) Hitler's seizure of Austria, making his empire border Italy.
    (C) collaboration with Franco in the Spanish Civil War.
    (D) membership in the League of Nations.
    (E) a mutual animosity toward France and Russia.

12. The Ruhr Basin crisis began with the

    (A) German printing of paper money.
    (B) German claim of inability to make reparations payments.
    (C) strike by German workers.
    (D) occupation by Belgian and French troops.
    (E) ruinous inflation in Germany.

13. Which of the following describes the fascist concept of women's place in society?

    (A) Women should take the place of soldiers in the workforce.
    (B) Women deserve equal pay for equal work.
    (C) Women can stay at home, support their husbands, and produce large families.
    (D) Women can work as secretaries or teachers of small children.
    (E) Women deserve the right to vote.

14. The union of Austria and Germany in the late 1930s was called the

    (A) Anschluss.
    (B) Ausgleich.
    (C) Axis powers.
    (D) Central powers.
    (E) Teutonic League.

15. The Treaty of Rapallo came about because

    (A) Russia had not participated in the Treaty of Versailles.

    (B) Germany was willing to forgive tsarist debt.

    (C) Russia was willing to forgive future reparations payments.

    (D) Germany could stay militarily alert by training the Soviets.

    (E) of all the above.

16. The resistance movement had the greatest impact in

    (A) France.

    (B) Italy.

    (C) Norway.

    (D) Yugoslavia.

    (E) Germany.

17. One reason the provisional government of Russia failed in 1917 was that

    (A) the tsar kept trying to interfere, even though he had abdicated.

    (B) Kerensky wanted to take Russia out of the war.

    (C) the provisional government was tied to the Soviets, who were unpopular.

    (D) the Red Army opposed the provisional government.

    (E) the provisional government would not address the demand for land reform and lost peasant support.

18. Dadaist art featured

    (A) realistic objects in a dream setting.

    (B) geometric shapes overlaid upon each other.

    (C) nonsense.

    (D) abstract color and form.

    (E) dabbing brush strokes simulating the interplay of light on objects.

19. After the Lateran Agreement of 1929, Mussolini

    (A) launched a campaign of antipapal propaganda.

    (B) recognized the Vatican as an independent state.

    (C) removed religious instruction from the schools.

    (D) placed taxes on the Italian clergy.

    (E) fostered pagan religious tendencies.

20. In music, composers like Stravinsky and Schoenberg

    (A) were immensely popular.

    (B) abandoned traditional harmony and tonality.

    (C) were generally unpopular after World War II.

    (D) were unlike modern painters.

    (E) were favored by the Nazis.

For the following questions, write an essay that

- has a relevant thesis;
- addresses all parts of the question;
- supports a thesis with specific evidence; and
- is well organized.

Plan your essays and write them on your own paper.

1. Describe and analyze methods that Hitler and Mussolini used to obtain and maintain popularity.

2. List and describe factors that led to the downfall of tsardom in 1917.

_____

_____

_____

_____

_____

_____

_____

_____

_____

_____

_____

_____

_____

_____

ANSWERS AND EXPLANATIONS

1. D

Above all else, the USSR felt the need to increase greatly the output of mining, steel, concrete, and other heavy industry. Although sexual equality, (C), and military strength, (E), were also goals, they did not fall under the Five-Year Plans, which were concerned with production. Answer (A) had already occurred in the early 1920s; the Five-Year Plans originated in 1927.

2. B

Stolypin was the last important minister Nicholas II had before World War I. His main push was to let the peasants buy land and become kulaks, which meant that he opposed the mir, (C). Stolypin was assassinated before World War I (A). The earlier Russian minister Witte had expanded the railroads, (E), and Plehve had advised the Russo-Japanese War (D).

3. A

The amount of reparations was set after the conference by a committee it appointed. Delegates at the conference understood that the amount would be very large. All the other items here were part of the agenda passed by the delegates.

4. E

The Bauhaus's driving focus was the idea of function—that is, to design things in a way that combines beauty and usefulness. Thus, lines were simple, devoid of decoration, (B). While lines might be seen as attractive, beauty was not the primary concern, (A). Some of the creations were indeed unusual, (C), but again, this was not the first intention. Color, (D), was another issue secondary to function.

5. C

World War I was fought in France, Russia, and northern Italy but not in Germany itself. At the beginning of World War II, Germany's alliance with Italy formed the fascist Axis of power, (A). Answers (B) and (D) are true of both wars—the people of both Germany and Russia suffered greatly from deprivation, mainly of food.

6. A

Existentialists drew much of their philosophy from the nihilists: the meaninglessness of life, (B), and the absence of progress, (C), and of God, (E). They agreed that human beings were very alone, (D). Despite all these ideas, they said that human beings must act; they must be responsible for their own behavior.

7. D

The White Army did not have peasant support because they feared they might have to give back the land they had taken. Answer (A) is not true because both the British and Americans briefly tried to offer aid by coming into Russia through the northern ports of Archangel and Murmansk. The opposite of (B) is true—the Whites never took major urban centers. The tsar was not involved with either side, though rumors spread that the Whites would try to rescue the royal family.

8. B

The League took what punitive action it could take against Italy, which was to apply sanctions. However, oil—the import Italy needed most—was not included, so the sanctions were meaningless.

9. A

Sudetenland had a large German population, which listened to Hitler's pro-German rhetoric. The area did have a munitions industry, (C), but although this was a nice bonus for Hitler, his primary goal was to seize the region for the sake of German expansion; he used the argument of self-determination as an excuse.

10. A

Radar was developed early in World War II by the British and helped in defense against submarines. All the other answers were used in World War I.

11. C

Prior to the Spanish Civil War, Mussolini had opposed Hitler's seizure of Austria. After 1936, Italy and Germany became allies. Mussolini did go visit Germany, (A), and *after* becoming allies, Mussolini no longer objected to Hitler's seizure of Austria (B).

12. B

The Ruhr crisis was set off by Germany's claim that she could not make the next reparations payment. Then, in quick succession, the German government ordered the workers to strike and printed paper money to support them. Meanwhile, Belgian and French troops moved into the region to occupy it. The paper money then resulted in ruinous inflation, (E).

13. C

In fascist Italy and Germany, women were second-class citizens, forbidden to work outside the home. (However, in reality, Germany was forced to allow some women to work in factories.) Mussolini preached large families, an illogical idea because Italy was already overpopulated.

14. A

The *Ausgleich* was a 19th-century term for the Dual Monarchy of Austria and Hungary, (B). Axis referred to the union of Germany and Italy in World War II; the Central Powers were Germany and Austria in World War I, (D). (E) is meaningless.

15. E

All are true. The German-Soviet treaty surprised the West, but it was mutually advantageous to both Germany and the USSR. In addition to the answers (A) through (D), Russia agreed to buy German goods, which also helped both nations.

16. D

Italy and Germany did not have much in the way of resistance movements. France did, and at times the French resistance did aid the Allies, especially in preparations for D-Day. Norway also had a resistance movement that accomplished subtle goals from time to time. However, the biggest effect of a resistance movement was seen in Yugoslavia, where Tito's guerrilla army kept the Nazis occupied and eventually drove them out.

17. E

The Russian peasants in 1917 were sick of war; they wanted land and peace. The provisional government tried to carry on the war (B) and refused to discuss land reform. The Red Army, (D), was not a big factor until 1918. The provisional government had to compete with the Soviets, (C), which had the support of the people because they were preaching "peace, land, and bread."

18. C

The term *dada* meant "hobby horse" in French—in other words, it had no meaning. This post–World War I development in art and literature reflected the loss of faith in society. Answer (A) refers to surrealism, answer (B) to cubism, answer (D) to 20th-century art in general, and (E) to impressionism.

19. B

The Lateran Agreement was a settlement with the Church by which Mussolini allowed religious instruction in the schools, (C), and Catholic preference in society. The Vatican was recognized as an independent state, and for the first time, the Church acknowledged the Italian government.

20. B

Common people had no understanding or appreciation of atonal, nonharmonious, early 20th-century music. Such composers would not be well accepted until *after* World War II, (A and C). They were like modern painters in their abstract, nontraditional approach, (D). The Nazis disapproved of both modern art and modern music, (E); they also banned Schoenberg because he was Jewish.

SAMPLE FREE-RESPONSE ESSAYS

1. Describe and analyze methods that Hitler and Mussolini used to obtain and maintain popularity.

Both Hitler and Mussolini were from working-class backgrounds. Neither had an extensive education, and from their early adult years, they were both extremists. Given these common beginnings, it seems unlikely that either man would have become a leader. Certainly, had conditions not fallen apart in Italy and in Germany, neither would have been able to gather a following.

Mussolini took over in Italy in the early 1920s, shortly after the Great War. The situation in Italy was dismal at the time. The economy had been seriously disrupted by the war, and unemployment ran rampant. Returning soldiers were unable to find jobs, and inflation was skyrocketing. Likewise in Germany in the early 1930s, economic conditions resulting from the Great Depression were frightening, reminiscent of the Ruhr crisis of the mid-1920s. As in Italy, there was high joblessness and inflation. In both places and times, people were desperately seeking some change that would give some degree of security.

In both countries and times, the middle classes and upper classes feared the desperation of the poor, which led the poor to land seizures in Italy and, in both countries, to an attraction to Marxism, which was alarming to the wealthy. Both Mussolini and Hitler courted people of power and money, suggesting that they and their followers (who were often unemployed former soldiers) could keep these elements under control. People of the upper classes gave money to Mussolini and Hitler in hopes that they could restore law and order, because the governments' efforts seemed to fail. The middle class, meanwhile, was anxious for a leader who would promise change. In both countries, people in power thought they could use these self-made heroes.

Mussolini and Hitler were both former soldiers who were disappointed in the results of World War I. Mussolini believed Italy had been shortchanged by the Allies, and Hitler felt Germany's civilian government had surrendered the country to the great indignities of the Versailles Treaty. Both men promised to restore national pride.

Once in office, Mussolini and Hitler used the media for propaganda purposes, especially the radio. They wore military uniforms and reviewed troops. They made ranting speeches that appealed to the mob mentalities of huge public rallies. Both heavily censored the press.

In both countries, there was a semblance of reorganization and efficiency. Mussolini's government divided all aspects of the economy into "corporations," which were tightly controlled. Ownership remained in private hands, but manufacturers were told what and how much to produce, and the government set prices and wages. Both developed public works programs during the Depression to give people employment.

Most Italians were Catholic and, therefore, were pleased by Mussolini's settlement with the Church. Both governments created youth movements with military overtones, and there was an overall appeal of youth, energy, excitement, and newness. Both governments glorified motherhood and family (though in both countries, women were considered inferior), and Hitler's government offered vacations to even working-class families.

Above all, in both Italy and Germany there loomed the promise of restored glory, possibly through foreign conquest. This direction, of course, would soon produce World War II.

2. List and describe factors that led to the downfall of tsardom in 1917.

The backgrounds of both Nicholas II and Alexandra contained influences that made them antagonistic to reform. Nicholas had been educated by Pobiedonostsev, the author of the "Russification" policy. Nicholas was rigid in his outlook, unable to delegate, and distrustful of reform. When the Bloody Sunday incident forced his government into creating a Duma, Nicholas had no sympathy for or appreciation of a representative body and did his best to undermine it. Thus, he was totally opposed by liberal-minded Russians.

The Bloody Sunday fiasco had caused the peasant class to lose faith in the idea of the tsar as "Little Father," friend of the poor. They were further disillusioned when they were sent off to war, often to die, with no sense of patriotism and, sometimes, without weapons.

Alexandra supported Nicholas in his arrogance and intolerance. Her whole outlook was one of superiority; she urged her husband never to submit to the demands of anyone. The Russian people disliked Alexandra from the beginning, regarding her suspiciously as a foreigner (she was German). When their son Alexei was born with hemophilia, Alexandra became dependent on Rasputin, a strange, ignorant, so-called holy man. Because the monk could somehow control the tsarovitch's bleeding, he gained much power at court, to the dismay and jealousy of powerful Russians. The result was the brutal murder of Rasputin.

However, by the time this occurred, there was much disillusionment among the upper classes, because Rasputin and Alexandra seemed to be in control of the government after Nicholas took field command of the armies. The liberals were further disgruntled by the restrictions on the Duma and Nicholas's lack of willingness to work with it. They had long felt shame and discouragement over the backwardness of their nation, which had been made apparent in its defeat by the Japanese early in the new century.

The war brought horrible suffering to the Russian people. Moving troops by train meant that agricultural products did not move; the result was hunger and even starvation. The loss of life from the war was staggering, and the peasants had felt no patriotism in the beginning. By 1917, soldiers were in mutiny, and his inability to command obedience from the army prompted Nicholas to abdicate in favor of his brother, who had no desire to take on the difficulties of the war or the government. A provisional committee from the Duma was already at work.

CHAPTER 27: IMMEDIATE POSTWAR ISSUES

EUROPEAN RECOVERY

Europe in 1946 was incredibly devastated. Because of air power and the much broader physical scope of the war, the destruction was much worse than it had been in World War I. Simply finding food after the war was a terrible problem. Industry, transportation, and farms had been heavily damaged or destroyed. Even by 1947, Germany was still described as refugee clogged and on the verge of total collapse. However, by 1948, things began to turn around. Even in shambles, Europe still had great potential in its people and resources. The Marshall Plan (discussed below) produced good results. Economic recovery combined with the promise of military aid through the Truman Doctrine (also discussed below) seemed to ensure that Western European countries would not turn to communism.

The political leadership that emerged from the war in Western Europe tended to be **Catholic Center** or **Christian Democrats**—all middle-of-the-road parties. In Eastern Europe, the Soviets had already set up pro-communist governments administered by Moscow-trained politicians. There seemed to be no stopping Stalin, except with military force, and no Western nation wished to continue the conflict. The United States ended aid to the USSR. Although the Soviets pressed for joint control of the straits into the Black Sea, the British navy helped Turkey prevent this. The Soviets cranked up anti-Western, anticapitalistic propaganda, and large communist parties thrived in Italy and France.

To try to avoid the economic trouble that had occurred between the wars, nations began to plan even before the end of World War II. In 1944, the United States hosted an international conference at Bretton Woods, New Hampshire. Here, nations pledged to reduce trade barriers and to work for stable currencies. In 1948, the **General Agreement on Tariffs and Trades (GATT)** urged reduction of tariffs; 23 nations subscribed to the agreement. GATT became somewhat of a forerunner for the **World Trade Organization**, which was founded later in the century.

During the Great Depression, countries had abandoned the gold standard, and this created an unstable international currency exchange. The Bretton Woods conference tried to establish a similar standard, which worked up until 1970 or so. Two new international creations were the **International Monetary Fund (IMF)** and the **World Bank**. The IMF made loans to governments to help them manage temporary balance of payments difficulties and to reduce the need to devalue currencies. The World Bank's task was to make long-term loans to governments for economic development. The roles of both institutions grew with time.

The postwar German economy was led by **Ludwig Erhard**, who believed strongly in a free market system. He removed rationing and price controls, and economic recovery was rapid. West Germany especially excelled in steel production, precision tooling, instrumentation, and the auto industry. By the late 1950s, Germany was producing the **Volkswagen Beetle**. The German economy was so successful that it had to import labor from its neighbors—Turkey, Greece, Yugoslavia, Spain, Portugal, and Italy. Throughout Europe, there was a huge market for consumer goods to which Europeans had not previously had access because of the Depression and then World War II. There was a great demand for electric appliances and automobiles.

European prosperity led to the establishment of the **Common Market**. West European democracies saw themselves as fragile and vulnerable compared to the super powers, the United States and USSR. Because they also feared being used as pawns, they desired unity for strength. The first attempt was a political approach through the Council of Europe in 1948. This was a sort of European parliament, but it was not very successful. Nations would not cooperate; each was unwilling to relinquish individual power or rights.

However, in 1948, Belgium, the Netherlands, and Luxemburg created the customs union, or free trade area, called the **Benelux**. Two years later, the French planners **Jean Monnet** and **Robert Schuman** presented a plan for the free movement of coal and steel through the **European Coal and Steel Community**. Six nations joined: Italy, West Germany, Belgium, the Netherlands, France, and Luxemburg. The agreement did away with old political rivalries, especially between France and West Germany. The British refused to join, a decision they would soon regret.

In 1957, the same six nations signed the **Treaty of Rome** to create the **European Economic Community (EEC)**, or Common Market—today, the European Union (EU). Tariffs within the group were removed, and capital and labor could move freely from country to country. The member nations also shared atomic research and technology. From the beginning, the EEC was a tremendous success. Trade among members grew at a rate double that of outside countries. When the British witnessed the Union's prosperity, Britain tried to join in 1963, but de Gaulle kept it out. England was not able to join the EEC until 1969, after de Gaulle's retirement. The prosperity of Europe throughout the second half of the 20th century has been one of the great success stories of recent world history.

The economic theories of John Maynard Keynes, which had been practiced during the Depression, continued to be part of government policies. This meant government spending to stimulate the economy and to create jobs during periods of economic decline. Britain, France, and Italy all nationalized key sectors of the economy, including utilities and transportation. In England, the Labour government nationalized the Bank of England, coal mines, electricity and gas, and iron and steel—about one-fifth of the country's industry. The tendency across Europe was toward a welfare state, paid for with increased taxes. Britain expanded its social insurance program to cover unemployment and old-age pensions and created a national health service. Most of Western Europe saw an influx of immigrants. England received people from India, Pakistan, and the West Indies; France, from North Africa, especially Algeria; the Netherlands, from Indonesia. A postwar baby boom also increased populations.

THE RESTRUCTURING OF EUROPE

One of the first things that happened following the war was the trial of war criminals in Nuremburg, Germany (1945–1946). Hitler, Himmler, and Goebbels were already dead. The **Nuremburg Trials** sentenced 12 men to death and many others to prison.

Political reconstruction was necessary in much of Europe. Only Spain and Portugal had dictatorships into the 1970s. At the end of the war, England voted out the Conservatives (Churchill) in favor of the Labourites (Clement Atlee). Later in the 1970s, the voting age was reduced to 18 all over Europe.

The Americans and British saw the economic reconstruction of Germany as vital to the recovery of all of Europe. France and the USSR objected to the rebuilding of Germany. France, of course, feared German power, while the Soviets wanted to use German resources for their own rebuilding. They took food and machinery stripped from German factories; the Western Allies refused to allow such plunder in their zones. By the summer of 1948, the United States, Britain, and France united their occupation zones into the Federal Republic of Germany (West Germany) with a capital at Bonn. The Allies reformed the currency into a new German Deutschmark. The Soviets established a communist government in the Peoples' Republic of Germany (East Germany). Berlin, the former capital, was inside East Germany and divided into four parts. When the West united its zones into West Germany, the Soviets blockaded Berlin by closing roads and railroads through East Germany into Berlin. The West responded with the **Berlin Airlift**. For almost a year, the West dropped supplies from planes to the residents of West Berlin. Finally in May 1949, the Soviets lifted the blockade.

The occupying powers encouraged each of the ten states in the three zones to set up state governments. Then, representatives of the states met in a constitutional convention to create a new national government for West Germany. The new constitution, called the Basic Law, created a government headed by a chancellor with a cabinet, both responsible to the Bundestag, the lower house of the national parliament. The Christian Democratic Party controlled the government until 1969, first under the leadership of **Konrad Adenauer**, followed by Ludwig Erhard in 1963. After 1965, Chancellor **Willy Brandt** worked on better relations with the Soviets and East Germany. He did not attempt reunification of the two Germanies, but Brandt's administration did try to reduce Cold War tensions, a process termed **détente**.

After the war, Italy voted to abolish the monarchy, which had worked with Mussolini. A new, democratic constitution set up a legislature elected through proportional representation. **Alcide De Gasperi**, who had been a librarian in the Vatican during the war, led the government and kept Italy in the Western camp. However, the communists were the second largest political party in Italy, and at first, they were part of De Gasperi's cabinet until they sponsored strikes in 1947. After De Gasperi left the political scene in 1953, Italian politics continued to have ups and downs, including a number of scandals and charges of corruption.

In France immediately after the war, **Charles de Gaulle** became provisional president. No one wanted to return to the Third Republic; therefore, the French elected an assembly to write a new constitution. Because right-wing parties had disgraced themselves by collaborating with the Nazis, the left surged forth—communists, socialists, and a Catholic party. The Nazi collaborators were tried and executed.

The new Fourth Republic was not very different from its predecessor, the Third Republic. The office of president was rather ceremonial; the real power remained with the premier and a cabinet responsible to the National Assembly. De Gaulle disliked the new constitution and the interparty rivalries and resigned in late 1946. The Fourth Republic proved rather unstable, with cabinets lasting only a few months. The Fourth Republic ended up lasting only 12 years (the Third Republic had existed for 70 years).

Still, some good things happened. Jean Monnet's economic leadership emphasized a plan involving government, management, and labor. This worked so well that between 1946 and 1966, French production tripled. The biggest drain on the Fourth Republic was the French colonial empire. Immediately after the war, a revolt broke out in French Indochina and lasted until 1954. The opposition was led by Ho Chi Minh, who had the support of the USSR and the communist Chinese. After a major communist victory at **Dien Bien Phu** in 1954, France withdrew, and Vietnam was divided at the **17th parallel** between North Vietnam (communist) and South Vietnam.

Almost immediately, France faced a second rebellion, this time in Algeria. **Morocco and Tunisia** received independence in 1956, but France tried to hang on to Algeria, where she had been more deeply involved for a longer time. European settlers there and army leaders strongly opposed France's leaving Algeria. In 1958, a military coup seized control of Algeria, and de Gaulle came out of retirement. A new constitution created the **Fifth Republic**, which included seven-year terms for the office of president, the seat of power. De Gaulle became the new president in 1958, and he stabilized the government. In the first 10 years of the Fifth Republic, there were only 3 cabinets; there had been 25 during the 14 years of the Fourth Republic.

De Gaulle worked out a step-by-step independence plan for Algeria, which the French approved in a national referendum in 1962. In the meantime, France had freed all its sub-Saharan colonies, so France gave up all its empire. The nation went on to excellent prosperity, becoming the world's fifth industrial power, behind the United States, USSR, West Germany, and Japan.

TRUMAN DOCTRINE, MARSHALL PLAN, UNITED NATIONS, NATO

TRUMAN DOCTRINE

Immediately after the war, the Soviet Union expanded its anti-Western propaganda. The United States reduced its army to 1.5 million troops by September 1947, while the Soviet army remained at about 6 million troops. Soon after the war ended, civil war broke out in Greece between communist and noncommunist sides. Consequently, in 1947, President Truman announced a military policy, the **Truman Doctrine**, under which the United States promised aid to all nations to prevent government takeover by a "minority party" (i.e., communist).

The United States helped make a difference in Greece: the communist guerrilla forces were defeated by 1949, and democracy was securely re-established. The USSR also dropped its demands on Turkey (for the straits), withdrew from Iran (which it had occupied during the war), and gave up its blockade of Berlin.

MARSHALL PLAN

Also in 1947, the United States established a program of broad economic aid for European countries to help with recovery from the war. Assistance was open even to Soviet satellites in Eastern Europe, had the USSR permitted them to participate. The **Marshall Plan** made a huge difference, bringing Europe back from the brink of collapse. By 1948, things were turning around, and as a result, there was little danger that Western Europe would turn communist. By the early 1950s, the general economy of Europe was off to phenomenal growth, ensuring that there would be no economic depression like the one that had followed the First World War.

UNITED NATIONS

Plans for a new international organization were drawn up in San Francisco in 1945. The organization was to have economic and political purposes with the goals of keeping the peace and providing international security. It would have numerous agencies and two main bodies, the General Assembly and the Security Council. All members of the **United Nations** would have an equal vote in the General Assembly. The main purpose of the **Security Council** was preserving peace. It was composed of 15 members—five of whom were permanent and 10 who rotated for two-year terms. The rotating members were chosen by the **General Assembly**. The permanent members were the United States, USSR, England, France, and Nationalist (noncommunist) China. Each permanent member had veto power. There was much criticism of the veto power, but historians agree that the USSR and the United States wouldn't have joined the UN without it.

Fifty-one nations became the charter members of the United Nations, whose headquarters were established in New York. The ongoing problem of the UN was enforcement; even small countries would refuse to abide by UN judgments. Seldom or never would a nation give up any power in the interest of the whole. The organization had more influence, perhaps, in developing countries, those classed as third-world nations, where the UN helped mediate regional disputes and served in peacekeeping missions.

NATO

The **North Atlantic Treaty Organization (NATO)** was formed in 1949, mainly as an anti-communist group to protect Western Europe from possible Soviet attack. Its formation emphasized still further the division between the Soviets and Western nations. As a result, large numbers of American troops were stationed in West Germany. Under the NATO agreement, Germany was allowed to rebuild its army but not to develop nuclear weapons. (This regulation is still in place.) NATO's headquarters were located in France until de Gaulle forced it out in the 1960s.

CHAPTER 28: THE COLD WAR

1940s

The term **Cold War** meant the diplomatic, political, and ideological clash between the two superpowers, the United States and USSR, following World War II. All of Eastern Europe, which had been liberated late in the war, stayed under Soviet domination with new governments headed by Moscow-approved politicians. The Chinese civil war between the communist forces of **Mao Zedong** and the **Guomindang** (Nationalists) had been put on hold while the Chinese fought Japan. In 1945, the civil war resumed, and the Soviets continued to back Mao's forces, which won the war in 1949. (The Nationalists then retreated to Taiwan.)

The United States proposed international supervision of atomic weapons. This agreement would have meant that inspectors could check for violation and enforce sanctions not subject to veto by the Security Council. The Soviets said no and proceeded with research. By 1949, the USSR had nuclear capability. In the Security Council, the Soviets used the veto frequently: 75 times between 1945 and 1955, while the United States cast 3 vetoes.

Prior to World War II, Korea had been ruled by Japan since 1910. In 1945, the USSR occupied the northern part of Korea down to the 38th parallel and established a communist government there. The United States occupied the southern part. In 1947, a UN commission attempted to hold nationwide elections, but the USSR refused to let the North take part. When both the United States and the Soviet Union withdrew their occupation forces, the Soviets left behind a strong North Korean army. Meanwhile, the USSR boycotted the UN Security Council to protest the failure of an attempt to have Communist China replace Nationalist China as a permanent member. When North Korea invaded South Korea in 1950, the Soviets were not present to vote, and the Security Council condemned the invasion and authorized countermeasures.

1950s

After the invasion of South Korea, the United Nations sent troops, most of whom were American. The Soviets aided North Korea, which did well early in the war. Then, the UN forces under the command of American General MacArthur pushed them back. Europe meanwhile feared another global war. The conflict, the **Korean War**, was short, with a cease-fire in 1951 and an armistice in 1953. Korea remained divided at the **38th parallel**, with a demilitarized zone in between. The United States kept troops stationed in South Korea. South Korea developed economically; the North did not—this remains the case today.

To the dismay of many Soviet citizens, who had developed a sense of unity and patriotism during the war, greater freedom did not materialize afterwards. Instead, Stalin's dictatorship clamped down, claiming a threat of war from the West as an excuse. Stalin had earlier demanded the return of Soviet citizens living outside the USSR, and Roosevelt and Churchill had assented. There was renewed censorship of artists and writers; the composers **Sergey Prokofiev** and **Dmitry Shostakovich** were condemned, and there were renewed attacks on Jews. The concentration on heavy industry and military production continued, while consumer goods, housing, and agriculture were neglected. In 1952, wages bought 25 percent to 40 percent less than they had in 1928. Those who opposed the system in any way found themselves in prison work camps in Siberia—the gulags.

As the Soviets took over Eastern Europe, they banned all political parties except the communist and imposed Soviet indoctrination—attacks on religion, nationalization of industry, Five-Year Plans, and attempted collectivization of agriculture (which varied from country to country). When Stalin died in 1953, the USSR experienced shortages of food and consumer goods, as well as faced a solid Western bloc of opposition.

The next major Soviet leader was **Nikita Khrushchev**, who began to denounce the crimes of Stalin. The economy shifted somewhat toward the production of more consumer goods. **De-Stalinization** led to a burst of creativity among intellectuals and writers, perhaps most notably **Boris Pasternak**, whose novel *Dr. Zhivago* was published outside the USSR in 1956. When Pasternak was awarded a Nobel Prize for literature, he was forbidden to leave the country to accept it. Another aspect of de-Stalinization was changing the name of Stalingrad to Volgagrad. (Stalin's body was removed from the mausoleum in Red Square, where it had lain next to Lenin's.)

The postwar Soviet Union put heavy emphasis on science. After achieving the atomic bomb in 1949, the country had a hydrogen bomb in 1953 and began to accumulate a nuclear arsenal. In 1957, the Soviets launched the first artificial satellite, **Sputnik**, and by 1961, they put the first man into orbit around the earth. The Soviet Union's space program continued to overshadow the American's for several years. Khrushchev boasted that the Soviet Union's economy would surpass that of the United States. However, the big achievements in industry and science came at a price to ordinary people; life for the average Soviet citizen remained hard. Often in manufacturing, the emphasis was on quantity, while quality was neglected.

In 1955, the Soviet Union gathered its satellites in Eastern Europe into the **Warsaw Pact**, which was a military alliance. The Soviets saw the United States bolstering Europe through the Marshall Plan, Truman Doctrine, and NATO as a "hostile act." The Warsaw Pact was the Soviet response.

Stalin's death seemed to invite more rebellion in satellite countries, first with a **revolt in Poland** in 1956 and then a **revolt in Hungary**, also in 1956. The revolt in Poland began with riots, which resulted in the release of over 9,000 political prisoners. The Poles also got the collectivization of agriculture halted. Poland would continue to be contentious with the Soviets from time to time.

Inspired by Poland, the Hungarians also rioted, so severely as to threaten to destroy the communist government. Khrushchev sent in the Soviet army and tanks to get things under control. The former head of the Hungarian government was executed and replaced with a new, tougher communist.

1960s

Khrushchev continued at the head of the USSR until the early 1960s. In agriculture, he tried to expand farming to land not previously cultivated, which often resulted in crop failure. He also tried unsuccessfully to set term limits for high party office holders. Mainly, though, Khrushchev's failures were in foreign policy. Because of mass defections from East Germany to the West inside the divided city of Berlin, Khrushchev ordered the Allies to evacuate West Berlin. When they stood their ground, he constructed the famous **Berlin Wall**, which remained in place until the collapse of the Soviet Union in 1989.

After the Berlin Wall came the incident of the **Cuban Missile Crisis**, which occurred after the Soviets placed nuclear warheads on the now communist island of Cuba (following the coup of Fidel Castro in 1959). The United States blockaded Cuba and forced the Soviets to remove the missiles. After the crisis, Khrushchev resigned in 1964; he was replaced by Leonid Brezhnev, an old Stalin supporter. The government quit talking about Stalin's crimes, as policies clamped down once more. Agriculture remained the weakest area of the economy, as the peasants worked reluctantly on collective farms. Industry did grow tremendously, but consumer goods continued to be neglected.

Brezhnev was intent on building the USSR's military and naval strength to compete with the United States. At the same time, the Soviets wished to avoid confrontation. Meanwhile, Josip Broz Tito of Yugoslavia maintained a communist government in his country but one independent of Moscow.

The next satellite crisis came in 1968 in Czechoslovakia, where the Czech leader **Alexander Dubcek** tried to create a new sense of freedom and openness. For about eight months, the Czech people enjoyed freedom of expression, especially in the arts and also in business initiative. The Czechs embraced the new policies with great enthusiasm, calling the movement **Prague Spring**.

Suddenly, however, Brezhnev sent in tanks and the military, and Prague Spring ended. Dubcek was removed from office. Moscow then issued the **Brezhnev Doctrine**, which declared that the Soviets would intervene in satellite nations if communism were threatened. In other words, Soviet bloc countries were allowed only a very limited amount of freedom. The West was highly critical of this move in Czechoslovakia; even communist parties in Western Europe criticized it.

Brezhnev's regime did not get along well with China. Thus, in the early 1970s, when the United States became friendly with China, the Soviets were pressured into détente, or a lessening of tensions.

1970s

In 1972, the United States and USSR signed the **SALT I** treaty (SALT is the acronym for Strategic Arms Limitation Talks). Both nations agreed to reduce their antimissile defense systems and work toward equality in offensive weapons.

Then in 1975, an international conference in Finland produced the **Helsinki Accords**. The signers pledged to work for peace, economic and cultural cooperation, and protection of human rights. They also ratified territorial boundaries established since the end of World War I.

In 1979, the **SALT II** agreement addressed equality between the two superpowers on long-range nuclear missiles. But before it could be ratified in the United States, the Soviets invaded **Afghanistan**. The United States condemned the invasion as an act of aggression and placed an embargo on the sales of grain and technology to the Soviets. At home, the United States increased military spending and renewed draft registration.

1980s AND THE REVOLUTION OF 1989

An ironbound dictatorship remained in place until Brezhnev's death in 1982. During this time, the standard of living rose slowly but never to a level of plenty. People who were extremely ambitious or who possessed certain desirable skills (that benefited the state) might enjoy more consumer goods, more comfort, or more opportunity to travel. Russian patriotism grew, mainly around a dominant group from the heartland and Siberia. These people feared that greater rights could lead to rebellion of the non-Russian parts of the USSR (excluding the satellite countries).

While Brezhnev was in power, any nonconformity or any form of protest was severely punished. Being blacklisted meant no job. For those who were well-known, such as the novelist **Alexander Solzhenitsyn** (who had published, outside the Soviet Union, *The Gulag Archipelago,* a novel about a Stalinist labor camp), nonconformity translated into exile. (Solzhenitsyn came to the United States.) As the population became more urban, old peasant ways disappeared, and people had more education and better job skills. Many jobs had become highly specialized. Specialization and education paved the way to more freedom of thought. Educated people read, discussed, and formed opinions, even though they had to be careful about publicly expressing their ideas.

At the time of Brezhnev's death, there existed much apathy among the Soviet people. There seemed to be no reason for initiative. The masses had no reason to care, and well-educated persons were becoming less inclined to obey and cooperate. Brezhnev was followed by **Yuri Andropov**, who was not especially successful. Andropov lived for only two years in office. Then came **Mikhail Gorbachev** in 1985.

Gorbachev was a smart, tough lawyer who had worked his way up through the Communist Party ranks. His wife was a professor of Marxian thought. Both believed in communism and saw it failing; they wanted to improve it fundamentally. One goal was to form better relations with the West, because the arms race was too costly and a major reason for the low standard of living. Gorbachev targeted corruption, incompetence, and alcoholism. He instituted *perestroika*, a restructuring of the economy to make it freer from government control. State enterprises received more independence, and private cooperatives could make a profit for the first time. At first, these changes brought excitement, but then came shortages.

Another change was less control of the media. The new policy of openness called *glasnost* became evident to the West in 1986 after the Chernobyl nuclear disaster. The incident was announced to the world, reported, and investigated, and foreign experts came to aid. Formerly forbidden writing became the rage, including much anti-Stalin material. *Glasnost* went further and faster than Gorbachev had planned. The first free elections since 1917 were held.

The USSR then withdrew its troops from Afghanistan and repudiated the Brezhnev Doctrine, which paved the way for satellites to overthrow their communist governments. Everywhere, states established provisional governments with the promise of democratic elections and human rights. Nationalism surged. Poland took the lead with elections on July 4, 1989, to select a minority of parliament. Hungary came next, opening its border to East Germany in early 1990; refugees poured in.

The infamous Berlin Wall fell, and East Germany had elections in which the communists became a fringe party. German economic unity came first and then political unity in an agreement signed by Gorbachev and West German Chancellor Helmut Kohl in 1990. Germany agreed not to develop nuclear weapons and to loan money to the USSR, which needed cash. Communism died peacefully in Czechoslovakia in 1989. Romania, however, experienced some violence as the old communist forces tried to hang on. By the early 1990s, though, change had occurred everywhere except Albania and the USSR.

FALL OF THE SOVIET UNION

In 1990, the USSR faced multiple problems. Lithuania, Estonia, and Latvia were declaring their independence, as were various Russian republics. A civil war had begun between Armenia and Azerbaijan. At this point, the old-line communists went after Gorbachev, attempting a coup in late summer 1991. They had Gorbachev and his family arrested while the family was on vacation, but then the communists faced opposition from **Boris Yeltsin** and his supporters, and the coup failed. The Communist Party was then outlawed. Yeltsin and his backers withdrew Russia from the Soviet Union, and other republics followed suit. Gorbachev's term ran out in December 1991, and he returned to private life.

On January 1, 1992, the USSR ceased to exist. It transformed into a loose union of 21 republics called the **Russian Federation**. Many aspects of the transformation were not easy, especially the change to a market economy. At first, there were problems of unemployment, because the government no longer provided and guaranteed jobs. Other difficulties included shortages, inflation, and decline in living standards. Short-term revolts and violence erupted in some republics, but the only secessionist revolt occurred in **Chechnya** in the oil-rich Caucasus in the southwest, where the population was mostly Muslim. Eventually in 1994, Russia invaded Chechnya to try to restore order, and the result was a guerrilla war that dragged on until 1996. Russia then withdrew the military, but in Russia itself, the economy continued to flounder. Yeltsin had to face a run-off election against an old-line Communist Party candidate. In 1998, the International Monetary Fund and Western banks had to step in to prevent bankruptcy of the government.

Throughout the 1990s, Yeltsin's health declined, and his government was accused of corruption. New violence related to Chechnya erupted in 1999 with mysterious bombings in Moscow and other cities that killed about 300. Chechnyan terrorists were blamed. Yeltsin's prime minister **Vladimir Putin** launched a full-scale air and military attack on Chechnya, destroying the capital, killing about 4,000 people, and making about 100,000 refugees. This move was popular in Russia but condemned elsewhere. Yeltsin suddenly retired in 1999, naming Putin as his successor and leaving a mixed record. By the time he left office, he was under heavy criticism, but he did leave Russia with a working constitutional government.

CHAPTER 29: NATIONALISM

DECOLONIZATION

ASIA

A major factor in the first 20 years after World War II was decolonization. In some places, the European masters withdrew quietly; in others, there were nasty wars. The process seemed to result from two causes: the first was simply a growing opposition to imperialism in the West, and the second was economics—nations could no longer afford to maintain and defend empires.

India became one of the first nations to achieve independence. The movement toward this goal had been growing since the 1930s, led by **Mohandas Gandhi**. For a long time, India's government had been conducted by a British trained civil service of native Indians. During the war, India had supported the British, with the promise of independence afterwards. After the war, the Labour Party controlled the British government, and it was determined to escape the financial burden of empire.

Perhaps the biggest problem related to Indian independence was the division between Hindus and Muslims, who had long been organized into two political groups, the **Indian Congress** and the **Muslim League**. The Muslims insisted on having their own state, so the British established Pakistan as a Muslim nation in two parts, **East Pakistan** and **West Pakistan**, separated by the Hindu state of India. There were still many Muslims in India, as well as Hindus in Pakistan, and migrations sometimes resulted in bloody riots. In addition, the two countries disputed control of the border state **Kashmir**.

Gandhi was assassinated on the eve of independence. His follower Nehru led India until his death in 1964. India faced problems of economic development and, at times, political instability. Ongoing difficulties have been poverty, disease, and malnutrition. India developed nuclear power in the 1980s, and later, when Pakistan did the same, there was (and still is) world concern over their rivalry.

Although Pakistan had a constitution and parliamentary forms, it existed as a dictatorship. The division of East and West remained a serious problem. East Pakistan (much poorer, more highly populated, and subject to devastating typhoons and tidal waves) declared its independence as **Bangladesh** (Bengali Nation) in 1971. West Pakistan sent an army, but India intervened and forced Pakistan to withdraw. Bangladesh has remained one of the poorest nations in Asia.

Pakistan, meanwhile, became important to the United States as an avenue through which to channel aid to Afghanistan during its occupation by the Soviets after 1979. In 1999, a military coup led by General **Pervez Musharraf** seized power. Since the 2001 terrorist attack on the United States and the challenge of **al-Qaeda**, Musharraf has been even more important to the West.

Two other British possessions in Asia were Burma and Malaysia. Burma had been invaded by Japan during the war, and after 1945, it received independence. In 1989, Burma renamed itself **Myanmar**. It has continued under a repressive military government. After independence, the city of **Singapore** withdrew from Malaysia and has thrived on its own. Malaysia has prospered as well, with raw materials such as tin, rubber, and lumber and, since the 1980s, a high-tech industry.

Hong Kong, like Singapore, remained a thriving city, but Hong Kong was "leased" to Great Britain. The agreement returned ownership to China in 1997. The fears that this transfer would destroy the extremely successful economy have not materialized.

Indonesia, formerly a Dutch colony, was conquered by Japan during the war. Under the leadership of Sukarno, Indonesia declared its independence before the Dutch came back. The Dutch tried to stop the movement but ended up granting independence in 1949. Sukarno was a dictator who cultivated friendship with the USSR and China. In 1965, he was overthrown by a military coup led by General Suharto, who ruled for the next 32 years. Indonesia tried to take over Christian **East Timor** in 1975. After a long fight, Timor finally received independence in 2000. Financial collapse helped bring about Suharto's end in the 1990s. Some still worry that Indonesia could succumb to Muslim extremism.

AFRICA

The population of North Africa has been predominantly Arabic and Muslim. Sub-Saharan Africa, on the other hand, is mostly black, with a mixture of Islam, Christianity, and traditional African religions. The Allies granted Libya (formerly an Italian possession) independence in 1951. The French freed Morocco and Tunisia in 1956 and, after a conflict, Algeria in 1962. Former French colonies generally remained loosely associated with France. The nations of West Africa have tended to be very poor with high unemployment. The countries immediately south of the Sahara (Mali, Chad, and Niger) have suffered greatly from drought, as the desert climate seems to be migrating southward.

In sub-Saharan Africa, independence came rather suddenly. In 1940, there were almost no independent countries, and by the 1960s, all were becoming independent. Almost all countries had diverse groups of people because the Europeans had divided the continent without regard to tribes, languages, or ethnic backgrounds. The independence of North African states in the 1950s inspired the colonies of Southern Africa. The British led the way in 1957 by granting independence to the Gold Coast, which changed its name to **Ghana**. Ghana became a republic in 1960 and a member of the British Commonwealth of Nations. Ghana became known as the largest producer of cocoa.

Britain's biggest sub-Saharan colony after the war was Nigeria, which was composed of four ethnic groups, the **Hausa, Fulani, Yoruba**, and **Ibo**. The British granted independence in 1960, and Nigeria became a republic in 1963. In 1967, the Ibo tried to secede into an independent state of **Biafra**. After two and a half years of terrible fighting and starvation, the attempt failed. Because of its oil, Nigeria experienced prosperity in the 1970s; however, the common people experienced few benefits. Instead, the nation has suffered from drought and a corrupt government.

Jomo Kenyatta led the independence movement in Kenya in West Africa. The British granted independence in 1963. Like other new African nations, Kenya had a façade of democracy, but in reality, the government remained autocratic, even after Kenyatta's death in 1978. The early 21st century finds Kenya with a fragile democracy and in need of economic reform.

In 1964, the colonies of Tanganyika (formerly German East Africa) and Zambia were merged into **Tanzania**. For many years, the government had a Marxian orientation. After 1995, its biggest problem was an influx of refugees from its neighbors.

Kenya's neighbor, landlocked Uganda, was the nation Winston Churchill had called the "pearl of Africa." Uganda became independent in 1962, but after civil war, it was taken over by the unstable dictator **Idi Amin**, who wreaked much destruction on the country. Amin was driven out in 1979 by an army from Tanzania; he fled to Libya, where he was sheltered by Libya's ruler Qaddafi.

In the early 1960s, Northern Rhodesia became Zambia, with a black majority government, and was merged four years later with Tanganyika into Tanzania. Southern Rhodesia became **Zimbabwe**. There, the white minority (descendants from European settlers) tried to stay in power, declaring independence from Britain in 1965. Guerrilla war followed, which led to a black majority government in 1980. Within a few years, the extremist dictator **Robert Mugabe** seized power. Conditions have continued to be bad, with land seizures from the prosperous farmers and general destruction of the country's resources.

In South Africa, white descendants of Dutch and English settlers made up 20 percent of the population; they owned and controlled everything. The Dutch descendants spoke Afrikaans, which had developed out of Dutch, and they did not get along with the British descendants. They tended to be more conservative and more inclined to racial discrimination. In 1948, the Afrikaners took control of the government and instituted the policy of apartheid, or extreme racial separation and discrimination. Because South Africa was a member of the British Commonwealth of Nations, the English Parliament condemned apartheid; South Africa then withdrew its membership from the Commonwealth. Apartheid was also opposed at home by the **African National Congress**, which **Nelson Mandela** led. Mandela was sentenced to life in prison, but violence and uprisings continued.

Real change began in South Africa in 1989 under President **F. W. de Klerk**. De Klerk released Mandela in 1990, and apartheid was repealed in 1991. Democratic elections took place in 1994, and Mandela became president. The country adopted a new constitution in 1996. To overcome some of the horror of its past, South Africa conducted **Truth and Reconciliation Hearings**, moderated by Anglican Archbishop **Desmond Tutu**. South Africa remains a country of great contrasts, rich with gold and diamond mines but plagued with great poverty among much of the population.

Of all European countries, Belgium left one of the worst situations in Africa. Having never governed well there, Belgium simply departed the Congo, leaving it with little preparation for self-government. The result was anarchy, chaos, and violence. For a while, United Nations forces tried to establish order; then the dictator Mobutu took over and ruled for over 30 years. The name **Congo** became **Zaire** (both country and river), and the capital **Leopoldville** became **Kinshasa**. In 1996, forces from neighboring Rwanda and Angola swept through Zaire, forcing Mobutu to flee. The country became the Democratic Republic of the Congo. A military dictator took control but was assassinated. The Congo remains one of least developed areas in Africa, though it is rich in copper, cobalt, and diamonds.

In 1974, the United Nations declared **Southwest Africa (Namibia)** independent. Afterwards, neighboring South Africa and Angola fought for control of Namibia, mainly because Namibia has diamonds. For a while, Cuban troops and Soviet advisors aided Angola, while South Africa received support from the United States. Only in the 1990s did foreign countries withdraw.

The Horn of Africa, the northeastern part of Africa (Sudan, Somalia, Ethiopia, and Eritrea) has witnessed much warfare over the last 50 years. For a while, the Soviet Union exerted considerable influence. After years of fighting, Eritrea got its independence from Ethiopia in 1993. For some years, beginning in 1977, Somalia fought Ethiopia, which was aided by the Soviets and Cubans. In the 1990s, Somalia descended into anarchy, where things remain very unsettled. The situation has been worsened by drought and famine.

The general trend in postcolonial Africa has been toward authoritarian governments, in which leaders often have cared more about accumulating and hanging onto personal power and wealth than developing their countries. There does seem to be some hint of change in recent years. However, Africa remains the poorest, least developed continent on earth. Half its population survives on less than one dollar per day. Drought and famine are rampant in many areas. Its nations are burdened by severe indebtedness and exploitation by various corrupt leaders. Africa is also deeply affected by disease, especially malaria and AIDS. Stability and peace are indeed scarce throughout Africa.

THE MIDDLE EAST

Homeless survivors of the Holocaust sought a homeland in the Middle East, which they felt they'd been pledged in World War I (Balfour Declaration of 1917). During the war, the British, who controlled the mandate of Palestine, tried to limit immigration, but many came illegally. In 1947, the British turned over the problem to the United Nations, which created **Israel** in 1948 out of former Palestinian territory.

Meanwhile, Arab states tried to create an Arab bloc. Syria, Jordan, and Lebanon (with a largely Christian population) had come out of the old Ottoman Empire in 1919 and became independent after 1945. Iraq had been independent since 1937. In 1945, the **Arab League** formed with seven members (Egypt, Iraq, Syria, Jordan, Lebanon, Saudi Arabia, and Yemen). By the 1980s, there were 22 members (some of them tiny).

When Israel was created in 1948, it immediately had to fight its neighbors. There would be more **Arab-Israeli wars** in 1956, 1967, 1973, and 1982. The United States supported Israel, while the USSR aided the Arabs. At first, Israel created an advanced nation in a very poor part of the world (before the big oil discoveries). Israel had industry and scientific farming with irrigation.

In the most serious of the wars, Israel seized the Sinai Peninsula, the West Bank of the Jordan River, the Golan Heights (next to Syria), and the Gaza Strip. This action led to much future controversy. Meanwhile, displaced Palestinians founded a government in exile, the **Palestine Liberation Organization**, which functioned as if it were a country under the leadership of **Yasir Arafat**. Even though Israel has now returned much of the Arab territory it seized in 1967, and even though Palestine is now a state once more and Arafat has died, the controversy between Israel and its neighbors continues.

In 1956, Britain withdrew from the Suez Canal Zone, presuming to continue to operate the Canal, which was more important than ever to Europe because of Middle Eastern oil. Egypt's leader **Abdul Nasser** had ties to the Soviet Union, which aided in the construction of the Aswan High Dam on the Nile. When the Egyptians tried to seize the Canal, the British sent troops with French aid. However, the United States wouldn't support this policy, and England withdrew, leaving Egypt in control of the Canal.

Libya became a major oil producer after its discovery of petroleum in 1959. In 1969, the country came under the military dictatorship of **Muammar al-Qaddafi**, who became a spokesperson for extremist Arab nationalism and a loud voice in the **Organization of Petroleum Exporting Countries (OPEC)**, formed in 1960. After Qaddafi seemed to have sponsored the terrorist bombing of a plane over Scotland in the 1990s, the West applied sanctions, which only recently have been lifted as Qaddafi has mellowed a bit.

Iran became the new name of Persia in 1935. Its language was not Arabic but Persian, and its religion was Shiite Islam (nine-tenths of the Muslim world is Sunni). Religious leaders in Iran launched the extreme Islamic movement that has spread and caused so much trouble in recent years. After World War II, the United States maintained a heavy influence, working with the corrupt Shah until his overthrow in 1979.

Between 1980 and 1988, the **Iran/Iraq War** raged with horrible deeds on both sides. The United States backed Iraq under **Saddam Hussein**. Both sides used poison gas; Iraq also used the gas on its Kurdish minority, accusing it of collaborating with Iran. The extremist religious leader of Iran, the **Ayatollah Khomeini**, died in 1989. Afterwards and until very recently, Iran had a more moderate government. Most recently, a radical government threatens nuclear development and more Islamic extremism in the already unstable region.

Iraq, meanwhile, attacked Kuwait in 1990, resulting in the brief **Persian Gulf War**, in which the United States and its allies forced Iraq to back down. After the terrorist attack on the United States in 2001, the West, led by the United States and Britain, engaged in a second war in Iraq, this one much criticized on the world scene.

Despite the threat of Islamic radicalism, there have been some less-discussed developments against it. Turkey has maintained a secular government and a developing economy. Egypt recently reformed some of its family law, allowing a woman to divorce her husband without his consent. Even Saudi Arabia has shown some loosening of its strict laws.

NATIONALISM IN WESTERN EUROPE

Charles de Gaulle remained bitter toward the United States and Britain, feeling that he had been snubbed during the war. In 1966, he withdrew France from NATO and forced NATO to remove its headquarters from France. He insisted that France develop atomic power and refused to cooperate with the Americans and the British in treaties over sharing nuclear research; the French tested a hydrogen bomb in 1968. Although de Gaulle did not favor communism, he worked on a friendship with the Soviet Union. A lot of discontent brewed in France as older political parties felt left out. A reorganized socialist party reached out to the middle class. When 10 million French workers went on strike in 1968, they were joined by disgruntled students who rioted (see Chapter 30). De Gaulle had to use the military to get things back under control. The next year, de Gaulle lost a popular referendum and then retired.

The 1970s brought a worldwide economic decline. In Britain, **Margaret Thatcher** became the first female leader of a Western nation in 1979. Thatcher's government backed away somewhat from the ever-growing welfare state, returning one-third of nationalized industry to private ownership by providing credit for buyers. In 1982, Thatcher's popularity was at its height after the British navy prevented Argentina from taking the British-controlled Falkland Islands off the coast of South America in the brief **Falkland Island War**. Thatcher was succeeded by John Major, also a Conservative, but in 1997, political power shifted to the Labour Party and Tony Blair. Blair adopted a "middle" or "third way" (like Clinton in the U.S.) by combining pro-business policies, while attempting to maintain many social and welfare programs. His popularity as a British statesman allowed the government to make constitutional changes that devolved the power of Westminster, creating a new parliament in Scotland and a legislative assembly in Wales that managed internal issues.

In France in the 1980s, **Francois Mitterrand** tried to use Keynesian economic practices to ease the depression, with less than favorable results. France entered into a political practice dubbed cohabitation, in which the president and prime minister came from opposing political parties. By the 1990s, the economy improved (as it did everywhere), but unemployment remained a problem. **Jacques Chirac**, who had been Mitterrand's prime minister, was elected president in 1995. During Chirac's presidency, in cohabitation with Lionel Jospin, France privatized many state-owned industries and reduced the presidential term to five years. In Chirac's second term, he worked toward promoting European unity, while still facing problems of unemployment at home.

The second half of the 20th century witnessed renewed dispute and violence over Northern Ireland. Ireland had received its independence from Britain following World War I, but the United Kingdom had kept the northern area of Ulster, which had a large Protestant population, and it became Northern Ireland. Ireland, meanwhile, cut all ties with Britain by withdrawing from the British Commonwealth in 1949. The Irish Republican Army (IRA) practiced violence against Protestants and the British both in Northern Ireland and in England. Irish Protestants responded with more acts of violence. In recent years, the economy of Ireland has greatly improved. Ireland became one of the few spots on the globe where there has been a lessening of violence, rather than an intensification, in the early 21st century.

In Spain, **Basque separatists** violently attacked army and government facilities. Although support for the movement declined in the 1980s, occasional terrorist incidents continue to be attributed to the Basque movement. Elsewhere in Europe, small minorities publicized nationalist movements here and there from time to time, but most were short-lived. To stem separatist opposition in Scotland, Tony Blair's Labour government gave the Scots their own parliament (and a legislature to Wales, as well). In the late 1990s and early 21st century, violent outbreaks of extreme nationalism in Western Europe have been in opposition to immigration from Africa and Asia.

In general, the trend in Europe at the end of the 20th century was toward a more unified front, especially through the European Union. What had begun as the European Economic Community became the European Community in 1965. In 1992, the 12 members of the European Community signed the **Treaty of European Union**, which had been agreed upon in Maastricht in the Netherlands at the end of 1991. The agreement proposed a central banking system and a single European currency, the **euro**, which went into effect in 1999. Most but not all (notably, Great Britain) of the EU readily adopted the euro. Through the 1990s and into the 21st century, membership in the EU has expanded to the outer edges of the Continent and even beyond.

NATIONALISM IN EASTERN EUROPE

The biggest story of nationalism in Eastern Europe involved Poland and contributed to the end of the Soviet Union. Poland had long given the Soviets trouble. The revolt in 1956 forced the Soviets to back down on collectivization, so most land remained in private hands. The other big factor was the Roman Catholic Church, which the Soviets could not dominate. The Polish economy did poorly, especially in the 1970s, when a recession hit worldwide.

Then in 1978, a Polish cardinal became **Pope John Paul II**. The next year, the enormously popular pope toured Poland and inspired the people. In 1980, a great shipyard strike in Gdansk (formerly Danzig) led to the formation of the trade union **Solidarity**, which was supported by the Church. Intellectuals joined, and **Lech Walesa** led the Union. Solidarity could claim over a million members. It employed a staff of 40,000 and was capable of calling a nationwide strike.

Even though it possessed tremendous power and many Poles were impatient for change, Solidarity did not try to seize political control. However, in 1981, the Soviets suddenly cracked down on Poland, outlawing Solidarity and arresting its leaders. The Soviets declared martial law in Poland. Solidarity simply went underground.

Eight years later, when the USSR repudiated the Brezhnev Doctrine, Poles took the lead in working out an agreement with the existing communist government for free elections on July 4, 1989, for parliament seats. Solidarity won every contested seat. A week later, the editor of the Solidarity newspaper became the prime minister. In late 1990, Lech Walesa became Poland's president. However, Poland experienced difficult times after gaining its independence. As in all formerly communist countries, the transition to a free market economy was not easy. Unemployment and shortages were common, creating widespread discontent. In 1995, Lech Walesa was voted out and replaced by a former communist; this trend became common in former satellite nations. The country has also been divided by multiple political parties and by pressure from the Church to implement religious education and to reform abortion laws.

In Czechoslovakia, the communist government collapsed in 1989, and **Vaclav Havel** emerged as the new leader. Havel was a playwright and prominent in a dissident group, **Chapter 77**, which had formed in the 1970s. In 1990, Havel traveled widely and spoke out for democracy in Eastern Europe. However, ethnic issues continued to cloud the political scene. In January 1993, Czechoslovakia split into the **Czech Republic**, led by Havel, and **Slovakia**. The Czech Republic established a model for the transition to democracy, and after an initially difficult economic adjustment, the country, like most other former Soviet satellites, has become prosperous again.

Elsewhere in Eastern Europe, economic unrest and political instability have made the transition to democracy less than easy. Within the former Soviet Union, various conflicts have risen out of ethnic division. The Chechnyan revolt has been discussed in Chapter 28. Other conflicts developed between Azerbaijan and Armenia, based on religious and cultural differences. Unrest and fighting within Georgia have also threatened its relationship with Russia and the Federation. The most troubling and most violent scene of nationalist division, however, occurred in Yugoslavia, discussed next.

YUGOSLAVIA

After World War II, Tito set up a federal republic in Yugoslavia composed of six republics: Serbia, Bosnia, Croatia, Slovenia, Montenegro, and Macedonia, plus two autonomous provinces, one of which was **Kosovo** (see map). Tito tightly controlled any threat of separation and made Bosnian Muslims equal to Serbs and Croats.

Former Yugoslavia

After Tito's death in 1980, his successors had difficulty holding the country together. When communism collapsed in Eastern Europe in 1989, Yugoslavia also fell apart. The former communist leader **Slobodan Milosevic** was left with only Serbia and Montenegro, as the other states declared their independence. Despite immediate recognition of the new states by the international community, the Serbs attacked their neighbors. The worst fighting occurred in Bosnia, where the Serbian military committed atrocities against the Muslim population, even though Serbs and Croats had lived together peacefully there for generations. The Serbs practiced **ethnic cleansing**, at one point leaving some 8,000 Muslim men in a mass grave.

The United Nations became involved in the mid-1990s and worked out an agreement in Dayton, Ohio, by which Serbia accepted new boundaries of Croatia and Bosnia and the presence of UN peacekeepers.

Meanwhile, a separatist movement began in Kosovo, still technically a province of Serbia. The separatists came from the majority population of ethnic Albanians, who were Muslim. Milosevic seemed bent on a repeat of the ethnic cleansing Serbia had carried out in Bosnia. After warnings from the UN went unheeded, NATO finally launched bomb attacks against Serbia until Milosevic relented two and a half months later. Milosevic was arrested and put on trial for crimes against humanity at the World Court in the Hague (Netherlands). In 2005, in the middle of his long, ongoing trial, Milosevic was found dead in his cell. The survivors of the tiny nations of the former Yugoslavia are now trying to put their lives back together.

CHAPTER 30: POST–WORLD WAR II SOCIETY

CLASS STRUCTURE

In the second half of the 20th century, economic and technological changes helped break down old European class barriers. Ownership of property or business or being a doctor or lawyer no longer defined the middle class, which came to include managers and experts in various fields who could serve the public's needs. Thus, the middle class grew as never before. Ability and training, rather than family background, became the determining factors in advancement.

There were also changes among the lower classes. Throughout the 20th century, but especially in the second half, there was a massive exodus from the farms to urban life. Here were more employment opportunities, but jobs tended to require more education and specialization. All countries provided more social benefits, including socialized medicine in some nations. The overall results included a generally higher standard of living and many more consumer goods. Ownership of cars and home appliances, often through installment buying, became available to all classes. Travel and vacations also became more widely accessible. Overall, by the early 21st century, living standards in Western Europe equaled those of the United States and, in some nations (Scandinavia, in particular), exceeded them.

GENDER ISSUES

The struggle for sexual equality dated to the 18th century and had spokeswomen such as Olympe de Gouges (French) and Mary Wollstonecraft (English). The movement became more organized in the late 19th century, but it was not until after World War I that women were permitted to vote. Within communist countries, sexual equality was a fundamental principle, though not always practiced.

In most Western countries, women had worked outside the home during World War I only to give up those jobs at war's end. After World War II, however, more women stayed in the public workforce, and their numbers mushroomed in the second half of the 20th century.

A **women's movement** was firmly underway by the late 1960s. For the first time in history, reliable birth control was possible, so women in the West were able to control their reproduction. With more education and the benefits of technology, which made housekeeping less time-consuming, women began to view employment as lifelong rather than as a prelude to marriage and children.

One influence on the movement was the voices of feminist intellectuals who wrote and spoke out. In 1949, the Frenchwoman **Simone de Beauvoir** (companion to Sartre for many years) published *The Second Sex*. In it, she argued that male-dominated society relegated women to an inferior position of what she called "Other," where they held lesser jobs, earned less pay, and were reduced to second-class status. In the United States, **Betty Friedan** wrote *The Feminine Mystique* (1963) and founded the **National Organization for Women**. A similar group sprang up in Europe. Women demanded equal pay for equal work and pushed for maternity leave and reliable, affordable daycare for their children. They wanted reform of divorce and abortion laws and advocated for the needs of single parents and for protection from rape and abuse. The women's movement brought dramatic changes in some countries.

YOUTH

The late 1950s witnessed an emergence of a counterculture among Western youth that became a major force by the 1960s. Its sources came perhaps in part from the influence of mass communication—television, films, and above all, music. The **baby boomers**, the post–World War II youth, had not experienced the Depression or world war. People born in 1945 were age 20 in 1965. They had more purchasing power because of their numbers; jobs were plentiful, so there was less need to conform to the older generation. Perhaps they were too comfortable, perhaps bored. The 1960s brought a burst of romanticism and idealism, accompanied by rebelliousness and disillusionment with Western society. English was rapidly becoming a universal language, and popular music of the times came from **The Beatles** and, later, from The Rolling Stones and other British rock groups, all of which were tremendously influential. The older generation condemned the dress, language, sexual freedom, and implication of drugs in the music.

In the United States, a big focus was opposition to the Vietnam War. Europeans also criticized the war—Jean Paul Sartre, especially. But European youth saw other causes for radicalism and student rebellion. Here, young people revolted against a society they perceived as materialistic and flawed; many joined the Communist Party. Much of the discontent was related to higher education. In 1950, about 22 percent of U.S. citizens received education beyond high school, while in Europe at the same time, only 3 to 4 percent went to college or university. European universities had remained very traditional in their course offerings, with the intention of passing on culture and pure science to the elite.

During the 1950s and 1960s, the number of European college students grew tremendously. More scholarships enabled more opportunity for the middle and lower classes. **Curriculum reform** began to occur, as well, incorporating more technology and applied science alongside the traditional liberal arts. For many, the changes did not happen quickly enough, and intense overcrowding led to competition. Students everywhere demonstrated and rioted, especially in France in 1968, when student riots combined with a massive workers' strike to threaten the foundations of de Gaulle's regime.

By the 1970s, the atmosphere calmed through Europe and the United States. The rioters of the 1960s usually found their way into established society. But the changes forced on higher education remained in place, and young people everywhere influenced their cultures because of their sheer numbers and their buying power.

IMMIGRATION

Since the 1980s, there has been a huge influx of immigrants to Western Europe. As the Cold War ended, refugees streamed from Eastern Europe and later from the violence in the former Yugoslavia. Where there had been **guest worker** programs, as in Germany, many workers settled in to stay. Thus, for instance, Turkish Muslims became part of Germany. In addition, thousands of immigrants came from other parts of the world. Britain's newcomers originated in Asia, Africa, and the Caribbean, while France drew from North Africa and Southeast Asia.

Immigration has not always been accepted peaceably. Traditional Europeans fear losing their culture because, in some places, foreigners seem about to outnumber natives. There have been incidents of discrimination and violence. During recent recessions, Europeans by birth have blamed immigrants for unemployment. The problems have spawned extremist groups throughout Europe: **neo-Nazis** in Germany, **neo-fascists** in Italy, the **skinheads** in Britain, and **Jean-Marie Le Pen's National Front** in France. Such groups have continued to fan the flames of racism and intolerance, despite the end of the Cold War.

RELIGION

Early in the 20th century, in response to science, Christianity tended to de-emphasize miraculous and dogmatic religious ideas, going more in the direction of a **social gospel**, tending to the immediate needs of society. But after the disillusionment of World War I, a reaction against social gospel as too optimistic turned again to an interest in revealed religion. Mid-20th-century theologians returned to the teaching of the 19th-century Danish religious thinker **Soren Kierkegaard** and his emphasis on a commitment to religious experience.

A dialog began among different branches of Protestantism and also between Roman Catholic and Eastern Orthodox leaders. The new **ecumenical movement** produced some unification and agreements. Recent major issues throughout Western Christianity have included ordination of women and, more recently, ordination of homosexuals and the question of same-sex unions.

In 1947 in Jordan, Bedouin shepherds chanced to find one of the greatest archeological discoveries of centuries—the **Dead Sea Scrolls**. Although their origins are still somewhat a mystery, the Scrolls include the earliest record of most of the Old Testament canon. Study of the Scrolls has affected translation of scripture in the late 20th century.

The liberal **Pope John XXIII** came into office in 1958 and summoned the first international Church council since 1870. Called the **Second Vatican Council**, it met 1962–1965 and, according to some, was the most important Church gathering since the Council of Trent in the 1500s. Pope John XXIII died in 1963 while the Council met, but its work continued. The Council spoke out for peace and human rights and called on rich nations to share their wealth with the world—messages the Church has continued to emphasize.

The Council revised the liturgy to allow **Mass in the vernacular**. It relaxed the dress requirements for priests and nuns and absolved the Jews from **deicide** (murder of God—this issue had been used as an excuse for violence against Jews in past centuries). At the same time, the Council stood firm on other issues: celibacy of the clergy, condemnation of birth control, and an all-male priesthood.

In 1978, John Paul II of Poland became a very popular pope, traveling the world. He apologized for erroneous Church stands of the past, such as the Crusades and the Inquisition, the condemnation of scientists, and persecution of the Jews. On matters of Church doctrine, however, he remained strictly conservative, giving no ground on the issues of clergy celibacy, women priests, birth control, and homosexuality. Pope Benedict XVI, a close follower of John Paul II, became his successor. However, many speculate that such troubling problems as the scandals over sexual abuse of children by clergy and the scarcity of candidates for the priesthood may force still more changes in the future. Problems of overpopulation and the AIDS epidemic may also lead to changes in Church doctrine.

UNIT SEVEN REVIEW QUESTIONS

1. In addition to the world's opposition to imperialism, the other main reason European countries gave up overseas empires was

    (A) student riots and demonstrations in opposition.

    (B) outspoken native leaders, such as Nelson Mandela of South Africa.

    (C) the fact that colonies cost too much to maintain.

    (D) that in many places, raw materials had been depleted.

    (E) that the papacy called on rich nations to share their wealth.

2. By the 21st century, which of the following was no longer an issue in the Catholic Church?

    (A) Ordination of women

    (B) Mass in the vernacular

    (C) Homosexuality

    (D) Birth control

    (E) Abortion

3. The assertion of nationalism in recent years that has been most troubling to Russia has been in

    (A) Georgia.

    (B) Yugoslavia.

    (C) the Basque area of Spain.

    (D) Chechnya.

    (E) Azerbaijan and Armenia.

4. Post–World War II Europe did not experience economic depression as it did after World War I mainly because

    (A) the Russians were stopped from dismantling East German factories.

    (B) the damage was less severe than after World War I.

    (C) of the formation of the Common Market.

    (D) of the Marshall Plan.

    (E) of the Berlin Airlift.

5. Stalin was able to make most of Eastern Europe into Soviet satellites mainly because the Red Army had liberated these countries and also because

    (A) the West wasn't willing to use force to prevent a Russian takeover.

    (B) Eastern European nations voted for communist governments.

    (C) Poland felt betrayed by the West during the war.

    (D) the Soviet Union was closer and, therefore, could control this territory more readily.

    (E) the Communist Party was the biggest political force here.

6. Which of the following was Gorbachev's act that paved the way for the collapse of the Soviet Union?

    (A) *Perestroika*, or a more open, consumer-based economy

    (B) *Glasnost*, a relaxation of censorship and information control

    (C) More honesty in history and literature

    (D) Withdrawal from Afghanistan

    (E) Rescission of the Brezhnev Doctrine

7. Slobodan Milosevic was accused of crimes against humanity in the "ethnic cleansing" his army practiced in Kosovo and against Muslims in

   (A) Albania.
   (B) Slovenia.
   (C) Bosnia.
   (D) Montenegro.
   (E) Macedonia.

8. When Simone de Beauvoir spoke of the "Other," she meant

   (A) the right to vote.
   (B) the right to own property.
   (C) being able to instigate divorce.
   (D) the second-class status of women in a male-dominated society.
   (E) all of the above.

9. Bangladesh received its independence after

   (A) a great tidal wave destroyed the low-lying coastal area.
   (B) the Indian army prevented Pakistan from forcing Bangladesh into submission.
   (C) a peaceful agreement was worked out with Pakistan.
   (D) the poverty of Bangladesh proved to be such a burden.
   (E) the British worked out the agreement before they left in 1948.

10. A failed revolt against the Soviet Union took place in 1968 in

    (A) Czechoslovakia.
    (B) Hungary.
    (C) Poland.
    (D) both Poland and Hungary.
    (E) all three nations.

11. Which of the following has been the general trend among sub-Saharan African nations getting their independence?

    (A) Constitutions and parliamentary government
    (B) Careful use of resources
    (C) Prosperity and modernization
    (D) Dictatorships
    (E) Loans and repayments to European nations

12. All the following occurred in the Soviet Union under Khrushchev EXCEPT

    (A) the Cuban Missile Crisis.
    (B) revelation of Stalin's crimes.
    (C) lack of freedom for writers and artists.
    (D) the Berlin Wall crisis.
    (E) scientific achievement.

13. In the late 20th century, the Suez Canal remained important to Europe as a

    (A) quicker connection to Asian empires.
    (B) channel for transporting Persian Gulf oil to Europe.
    (C) British connection to Australia and New Zealand, members of the Commonwealth.
    (D) convenient route for NATO to the Persian Gulf and the Indian Ocean.
    (E) route by which all of the above were true.

14. In 1949, South Africa withdrew from the Commonwealth of Nations mainly because of

    (A) British criticism of the practice of apartheid.
    (B) a British attempt to control the gold and diamond industries.
    (C) sympathy for the Irish withdrawal from the Commonwealth.
    (D) international condemnation of fighting with Angola.
    (E) Afrikaner opposition to Britain.

15. The greatest achievement of Boris Yeltsin was

    (A) his strong stand against Chechnya.
    (B) his revitalization of the Russian economy.
    (C) the establishment and preservation of a constitutional government.
    (D) continuation of the Cold War.
    (E) reintegration of old communist diehards into the new system.

16. The creation of the European Economic Community was preceded by

    (A) the Council of Europe.
    (B) Benelux.
    (C) the European Coal and Steel Community.
    (D) the Treaty of Rome.
    (E) all of the above.

17. Where did the communists fail to take control following World War II?

    (A) Yugoslavia
    (B) Czechoslovakia
    (C) East Germany
    (D) Greece
    (E) Poland

18. The Warsaw Pact of 1955 was a(n)

    (A) attempt by the West to give economic aid to Eastern Europe.
    (B) Soviet plan for economic improvement in Eastern Europe.
    (C) Soviet military alliance in response to the perceived threat of NATO and the Truman Doctrine.
    (D) cultural exchange program among the nations of Eastern Europe.
    (E) attempt to unify East Germany and Poland.

19. All the following happened in the Soviet Union in the 1970s and 1980s EXCEPT

    (A) improvement in agricultural production.
    (B) continued shortage of consumer goods.
    (C) mass migration to the cities.
    (D) higher levels of education.
    (E) a growing class of people who spoke among themselves and wanted change.

20. The Russian writer Alexander Solzhenitsyn was forced into exile after he

    (A) denounced the Soviet system in his novel *Animal Farm*.
    (B) wrote about the Stalinist prison camps in *The Gulag Archipelago*.
    (C) described the Marxist takeover in *Dr. Zhivago*.
    (D) tried to defect to the West and was caught.
    (E) wrote about World War II in *Sophie's Choice*.

For the following questions, write an essay that

- has a relevant thesis;
- addresses all parts of the question;
- supports a thesis with specific evidence; and
- is well organized.

Plan your essays and write them on your own paper.

1. Identify characteristics of youth culture in the second half of the 20th century and describe their impact on society.

2. Describe the challenges facing religion in the 21st century and explain some of the responses to those issues.

_____

_____

_____

_____

_____

_____

_____

_____

_____

_____

_____

_____

_____

_____

_____

ANSWERS AND EXPLANATIONS

1. C

Choices (A), (B), and (D) all occurred, but they weren't as influential as the sheer cost of continuing to maintain colonies scattered throughout the globe. (E) did not occur until later and, even then, often fell on deaf ears.

2. B

The Second Vatican Council of the 1960s dropped the requirement that Mass be said only in Latin. The other answers here are issues on which many have hoped that the Church might change its policy, but so far, that has not happened.

3. D

Violence in Yugoslavia (B) and the Basque separatist movement in Spain (C) have not concerned Russia directly. Issues with Georgia (A) and with Azerbaijan and Armenia (E) are of more interest because all are members of the Russian federation. However, the most brutal and ongoing area of revolt has been in Chechnya, where much violence and death have occurred.

4. D

The Marshall Plan invested millions of dollars in Western Europe for a quick economic recovery from the devastation of the war. (B) is untrue; damage following World War II was more extensive because the war had not been confined primarily to France, as in World War I, and because of the use of aircraft bombers. The Russians did dismantle German industry, (A), in their occupation zone. The Common Market was formed more than 10 years after the war, (C). The Berlin Airlift happened in 1948–49 (E), but it affected mainly the Germans living there and the competition between the West and the Soviet Union.

5. A

There were no free elections in Eastern Europe after the war (B). (C) and (E) are untrue. While the Soviet Union was physically closer than Western Europe, (D), the main factor was that only military force could have stopped Stalin's takeover, and Western nations were anxious to leave the war.

6. E

All the other answer choices occurred as part of Gorbachev's reform efforts, but the end of the Brezhnev Doctrine allowed satellite states to withdraw from the Soviet Union without repercussions.

7. C

Milosevic's goal seems to have been the elimination of Muslims in Bosnia and Kosovo. His predecessor, Tito, had kept the different ethnic and religious groups under control and treated them equally. The other countries here from the former Yugoslavia do not have a significant Muslim element.

8. D

(A), (B), and (C) had all been granted in earlier years. De Beauvoir believed that women had been made unjustly inferior in every way by cultural perceptions and mores.

9. B

Britain created East Pakistan and West Pakistan to solve division between Hindus and Muslims. West Pakistan tried to use military force, (C), to prevent East Pakistan's secession, but India used her military to prevent this. Bangladesh remained subject to terrible poverty, (D), and the ravages of typhoons and tidal waves, (A), but these were not factors in getting independence.

10. A

This was the Prague Spring, championed by Vaclav Havel. It lasted from January until August 1968, when the Soviets used their military to stop it. Revolts in Hungary and Poland, (B, C, and D), had occurred in 1956.

11. D

In most new African nations, a ruling power has kept control for personal benefit. There has been little democracy, (A), or prosperity or modernization, (C). Africa is blessed in many areas with great natural resources; these have been ignored in some places, exploited in others, (B). Most nations have accumulated heavy debts, which they cannot pay, (E).

12. C

Khrushchev did allow more freedom of expression among writers. This was also a time of more scientific achievements, (E), about which Khrushchev boasted to the West. His failures were in foreign policy, with the Cuban Missile affair, (A), and the failed ultimatum in Berlin, which led to the Wall, (D). Khrushchev openly discussed Stalin's crimes, (B).

13. B

Europe buys oil from the Middle East, much of which is exported through the Persian Gulf, Suez Canal, and Mediterranean Sea. (A) is wrong because the colonial empires were defunct by the late 20th century. British interaction with Australia and New Zealand was less dependent on sea transport, (C). The Persian Gulf is beyond NATO jurisdiction, (D).

14. A

In the 1940s, the white population of Dutch descent (the Afrikaners) in South Africa outnumbered those of British descent and took control of the government. When the British Parliament objected to their racially discriminating policy of apartheid, the Afrikaners withdrew from the Commonwealth.

15. C

The best thing that can be said of Yeltsin is that he maintained of the constitutional system; democracy still has a chance in Russia. Yeltsin disappointed both the West and the citizens of Russia. Although Russians approved of his hard line against Chechnya, the rest of the world was critical, (A). The Cold War died with the Soviet Union, (D), and most old-line communists were left behind, (E). The economy of Russia has not thrived, (B).

16. E

The first attempt at European unity after the war was the Council of Europe, which was a failed try for political solidarity, (A). Next came the trade agreement Benelux, (B), among the Netherlands, Belgium, and Luxemburg. These three then joined France, West Germany, and Italy in the Coal and Steel Community, (C), which led to the Treaty of Rome among the same six to create the EEC, (D).

17. D

Immediately after the war, Greece fell into a civil war in which Marxist forces tried to take control. The United States passed the Truman Doctrine in 1947, which provided military assistance to defeat the communists by 1949. All the other nations named here became part of the Soviet Union's Eastern bloc of satellite nations.

18. C

The Soviet Union saw the Marshall Plan, Truman
Doctrine, and NATO as hostile action by the West.
Thus, the Warsaw Pact was a military alliance of its
Eastern satellites in the face of Western aggression.
The Marshall Plan had offered aid to Eastern
Europe, but the countries under Soviet domination
weren't allowed to accept it. (A), (D), and (E) did not
exist.

19. A

Throughout its existence, agriculture remained the
weakest area of the Soviet system. (B), (C), (D), and
(E) all happened and led to Gorbachev's reforms in
the late 1980s.

20. B

Solzhenitsyn spent time in a Soviet gulag, so his
novel in answer (B) was written from firsthand
experience. (D) is not true. The other choices are by
other writers: (A) by British writer George Orwell,
(C) by Russian Boris Pasternak, and (E) by an
American, William Styron.

SAMPLE FREE-RESPONSE ESSAYS

1. Identify characteristics of youth culture in the second half of the 20th century and describe their impact on society.

People in their late teens and early 20s in the 1960s had grown up in a different era than their parents. They were born at the end of World War II, so they knew not the hardships of war or the Depression of the 1930s. Education and jobs were readily available. Life was good; young people had leisure time.

A major influence on their lives was rock music. Elvis and other music of the 1950s were temporarily forgotten in favor of The Beatles and other members of the "British music invasion." Young people copied the appearance of their idols—long hair and strange clothes became the rage. The language of the young changed, with new slang, more profanity, more sexually explicit phrases—these, too, were a reflection of popular music. Drug use became more prevalent, and song lyrics were primary evidence (and, some claimed, a cause). All culture seemed to become radically casual. The young of the 1960s had reliable birth control for the first time in history, which also had a profound effect, permitting more sexual freedom to the dismay of the older generation.

Rebellion against the establishment became common. In the United States, this took the form of protest against the Vietnam War, in marches, sit-ins, and demonstrations. At the same time, many American young people rebelled in a different way against society. They joined the Peace Corps or worked in the civil rights movement. In Europe, a major protest was focused on discontent with European universities because of overcrowding and limited curriculum. Protesting students demanded and received changes, and the results helped to break down traditional class barriers. They also became vocal in politics, sympathizing with striking workers or joining the Communist Party, especially in Italy and France.

It was impossible for the establishment to ignore the youth movement. For one thing, baby boomers made up a large portion of the population. For another, they had buying power, so advertisers and consumer marketers needed to appeal to them. Television, radio, and film made the world smaller and spread ideas and music. Everywhere in the West, the general outlook became more global.

What happened to the rebels of the 1960s? Many became more conservative as they aged. Some continued to champion causes and promote awareness of societal problems. Western society's overall vision of itself remained youthful, perhaps because the young continued to be major consumers. The trend toward casualness in dress, language, and lifestyle continued, especially the influence of more open expression of sexuality and what many regarded as a decline in the moral standards of past generations.

2. Describe the challenges facing religion in the 21st century and explain some of the responses to those issues.

In the late 20th century, there developed worldwide a division between traditional and fundamentalist religion and more liberal visions of faith. This trend has been true for both Islam and Christianity. In the face of violent and extremist Muslim governments of such nations as Iran and Afghanistan under the Taliban, it has been difficult to hear the voice of moderate Muslims. Often, they find themselves judged and discriminated against because of the behavior of fundamentalist extremists half a world away. The same division has occurred in Christianity, if not to the violent degree that Islam has experienced. Both Protestants and Catholics disagree among themselves over such issues as abortion, birth control, female clergy, and homosexuality. In both Islam and Christianity, the more fundamentalist and more radical voices seem to be the loudest and the ones who are dominating.

The Catholic Church has been shaken in recent years by widely publicized cases of sexual abuse of children by ordained clergy. At the same time, the Church has refused to budge on the issue of celibacy of the priesthood, and a result has been a steady decline of candidates for ordination. Among Protestants, some denominations (the Episcopalians and Methodists, for instance) have ordained women for some time, while other branches of Protestantism (Baptists, in particular) refuse to consider the possibility.

In Europe, even staunchly Catholic countries, such as Italy and Ireland, have legalized abortion, despite the protests of the Church. In the United States, the conservative "religious right" still fights to reverse abortion legislation. However, in recent years, even more explosive and divisive issues have been those related to homosexuality. The Anglican Communion worldwide condemned the American Episcopal Church when it ordained an openly gay priest as a bishop. In other Protestant denominations, clergy have lost their positions by revealing that they were homosexual. Related to the question of ordination of gays and lesbians is the issue of same-sex unions. A few very liberal branches of Christianity have embraced the concept, while others are vehemently opposed. At the same time, some private companies, as well as some state legislatures, have granted medical and legal rights to gay and lesbian relationships.

Throughout Europe and, to a lesser degree, in the United States, a serious challenge facing most branches of Christianity is a general disenchantment with organized religion. In many places, the majority of the population does not claim any religious faith or belong to any group of believers. At the other end of the scale, the more fundamentalist, more conservative churches seem to be growing in membership. This seems to be a trend worldwide and contributes to the creation of a radically different world from that of a millennium ago, when almost no one existed outside of religious influence.

| Part Four |

PRACTICE TESTS

HOW TO TAKE THE PRACTICE TESTS

This section of the book contains two practice tests. Doing them under testlike conditions will give you an idea of what it's like to sit through a full AP European History exam. You'll find out which areas you're strong in and where additional review may be required. Any mistakes you make now are ones you won't make on the actual exam, as long as you take the time to learn where you went wrong.

The two tests are both full-length; allow a total of three hours and five minutes to do one test. Each includes 80 multiple-choice questions, a document-based essay question, and 6 free-response essay questions (you will do 2 of the 6). You will have 55 minutes for the multiple-choice Section I. The questions are designed to measure your knowledge of European history from the High Renaissance to the present.

Section II, the essay section, begins with a *mandatory* 15-minute reading period, followed by Part A, in which you write an essay based on the question and documents of the document-based question (DBQ). You should spend approximately 45 minutes writing the essay. Plan to divide the remaining 70 minutes approximately equally between the two free-response essays of Parts B and C.

You must choose one essay from the three questions of Part B and one from the three of Part C. You are advised to spend 5 minutes planning and 30 minutes writing each of these thematic essays. Thematic questions are grouped to cover a range of historical periods; grouping is often not chronological. At the beginning of Section II, you are advised to spend the 15-minute reading period analyzing the documents for the DBQ, outlining your essay, and considering the choices of questions in Parts B and C. (Note: It is okay to do one of the free-response essays before you do the DBQ, but it is not a good idea to leave the DBQ until last.) On the actual exam, it is up to you to decide which essay to write first and to plan your time carefully.

Before taking a test, find a quiet place and a time when you can work uninterrupted for just over three hours. Bring blank paper for your essays. You will receive a 16-page booklet for the real thing. Time yourself and make use of all the time allowed for each section. Take a five-minute break between Sections I and II. Use the reading and planning time before you begin the essays.

Pace yourself. Note the different types of questions and what strategies seem to work for you. Afterward, read the detailed explanations that follow. Focus not only on questions you miss but also read explanations for the ones you get right—you may learn additional information.

You may want to review the information on essay writing in Chapter 1 before you take the test. The sample DBQ essay and the sample free-response essays are intended to model how an informed student might approach the questions.

Good luck!

HOW TO COMPUTE YOUR SCORE

SCORING THE MULTIPLE-CHOICE QUESTIONS

There are 80 questions in Section I. To compute your score, calculate the number of questions you got right; then multiply that number by 1.125 to find your weighted score. Unanswered questions neither earn nor lose points.

If you got six questions wrong, for instance, your score would be $74 \times 1.125 = 83.25$.

SCORING THE ESSAY QUESTIONS

Multiply your score for the DBQ essay (out of 9) by 4.5. Multiply your score on each of the two FRQs (out of 9) by 2.75. Add these three weighted scores together to find your total weighted essay score.

Add your weighted multiple-choice and essay scores together to find your composite score (out of 180).

Conversion Chart

Composite Score Range	AP Score
119–180	5
100–118	4
71–99	3
60–70	2
0–59	1

The DBQ essay is scored by a standard rubric—see Chapter 1. Free-response essays are scored holistically by standards established at the reading. A good essay has a thesis, addresses all parts of the questions, and offers specific examples that illustrate points and that are chronologically accurate. Each question here is followed by a sample essay, which is intended to model good writing that covers the question well.

Do not take any score on the practice test too literally. There is no way to determine precisely what your AP grade will be. Conditions under which you take the practice test will not exactly mirror real test conditions. The multiple-choice answers are scored by computer, but essays are evaluated manually by high school teachers and college professors. For more information on how scores are computed, see Chapter 1.

Practice Test 1 Answer Grid

1. Ⓐ Ⓑ Ⓒ Ⓓ Ⓔ   15. Ⓐ Ⓑ Ⓒ Ⓓ Ⓔ   29. Ⓐ Ⓑ Ⓒ Ⓓ Ⓔ
2. Ⓐ Ⓑ Ⓒ Ⓓ Ⓔ   16. Ⓐ Ⓑ Ⓒ Ⓓ Ⓔ   30. Ⓐ Ⓑ Ⓒ Ⓓ Ⓔ
3. Ⓐ Ⓑ Ⓒ Ⓓ Ⓔ   17. Ⓐ Ⓑ Ⓒ Ⓓ Ⓔ   31. Ⓐ Ⓑ Ⓒ Ⓓ Ⓔ
4. Ⓐ Ⓑ Ⓒ Ⓓ Ⓔ   18. Ⓐ Ⓑ Ⓒ Ⓓ Ⓔ   32. Ⓐ Ⓑ Ⓒ Ⓓ Ⓔ
5. Ⓐ Ⓑ Ⓒ Ⓓ Ⓔ   19. Ⓐ Ⓑ Ⓒ Ⓓ Ⓔ   33. Ⓐ Ⓑ Ⓒ Ⓓ Ⓔ
6. Ⓐ Ⓑ Ⓒ Ⓓ Ⓔ   20. Ⓐ Ⓑ Ⓒ Ⓓ Ⓔ   34. Ⓐ Ⓑ Ⓒ Ⓓ Ⓔ
7. Ⓐ Ⓑ Ⓒ Ⓓ Ⓔ   21. Ⓐ Ⓑ Ⓒ Ⓓ Ⓔ   35. Ⓐ Ⓑ Ⓒ Ⓓ Ⓔ
8. Ⓐ Ⓑ Ⓒ Ⓓ Ⓔ   22. Ⓐ Ⓑ Ⓒ Ⓓ Ⓔ   36. Ⓐ Ⓑ Ⓒ Ⓓ Ⓔ
9. Ⓐ Ⓑ Ⓒ Ⓓ Ⓔ   23. Ⓐ Ⓑ Ⓒ Ⓓ Ⓔ   37. Ⓐ Ⓑ Ⓒ Ⓓ Ⓔ
10. Ⓐ Ⓑ Ⓒ Ⓓ Ⓔ   24. Ⓐ Ⓑ Ⓒ Ⓓ Ⓔ   38. Ⓐ Ⓑ Ⓒ Ⓓ Ⓔ
11. Ⓐ Ⓑ Ⓒ Ⓓ Ⓔ   25. Ⓐ Ⓑ Ⓒ Ⓓ Ⓔ   39. Ⓐ Ⓑ Ⓒ Ⓓ Ⓔ
12. Ⓐ Ⓑ Ⓒ Ⓓ Ⓔ   26. Ⓐ Ⓑ Ⓒ Ⓓ Ⓔ   40. Ⓐ Ⓑ Ⓒ Ⓓ Ⓔ
13. Ⓐ Ⓑ Ⓒ Ⓓ Ⓔ   27. Ⓐ Ⓑ Ⓒ Ⓓ Ⓔ   41. Ⓐ Ⓑ Ⓒ Ⓓ Ⓔ
14. Ⓐ Ⓑ Ⓒ Ⓓ Ⓔ   28. Ⓐ Ⓑ Ⓒ Ⓓ Ⓔ   42. Ⓐ Ⓑ Ⓒ Ⓓ Ⓔ

43. Ⓐ Ⓑ Ⓒ Ⓓ Ⓔ   56. Ⓐ Ⓑ Ⓒ Ⓓ Ⓔ   69. Ⓐ Ⓑ Ⓒ Ⓓ Ⓔ
44. Ⓐ Ⓑ Ⓒ Ⓓ Ⓔ   57. Ⓐ Ⓑ Ⓒ Ⓓ Ⓔ   70. Ⓐ Ⓑ Ⓒ Ⓓ Ⓔ
45. Ⓐ Ⓑ Ⓒ Ⓓ Ⓔ   58. Ⓐ Ⓑ Ⓒ Ⓓ Ⓔ   71. Ⓐ Ⓑ Ⓒ Ⓓ Ⓔ
46. Ⓐ Ⓑ Ⓒ Ⓓ Ⓔ   59. Ⓐ Ⓑ Ⓒ Ⓓ Ⓔ   72. Ⓐ Ⓑ Ⓒ Ⓓ Ⓔ
47. Ⓐ Ⓑ Ⓒ Ⓓ Ⓔ   60. Ⓐ Ⓑ Ⓒ Ⓓ Ⓔ   73. Ⓐ Ⓑ Ⓒ Ⓓ Ⓔ
48. Ⓐ Ⓑ Ⓒ Ⓓ Ⓔ   61. Ⓐ Ⓑ Ⓒ Ⓓ Ⓔ   74. Ⓐ Ⓑ Ⓒ Ⓓ Ⓔ
49. Ⓐ Ⓑ Ⓒ Ⓓ Ⓔ   62. Ⓐ Ⓑ Ⓒ Ⓓ Ⓔ   75. Ⓐ Ⓑ Ⓒ Ⓓ Ⓔ
50. Ⓐ Ⓑ Ⓒ Ⓓ Ⓔ   63. Ⓐ Ⓑ Ⓒ Ⓓ Ⓔ   76. Ⓐ Ⓑ Ⓒ Ⓓ Ⓔ
51. Ⓐ Ⓑ Ⓒ Ⓓ Ⓔ   64. Ⓐ Ⓑ Ⓒ Ⓓ Ⓔ   77. Ⓐ Ⓑ Ⓒ Ⓓ Ⓔ
52. Ⓐ Ⓑ Ⓒ Ⓓ Ⓔ   65. Ⓐ Ⓑ Ⓒ Ⓓ Ⓔ   78. Ⓐ Ⓑ Ⓒ Ⓓ Ⓔ
53. Ⓐ Ⓑ Ⓒ Ⓓ Ⓔ   66. Ⓐ Ⓑ Ⓒ Ⓓ Ⓔ   79. Ⓐ Ⓑ Ⓒ Ⓓ Ⓔ
54. Ⓐ Ⓑ Ⓒ Ⓓ Ⓔ   67. Ⓐ Ⓑ Ⓒ Ⓓ Ⓔ   80. Ⓐ Ⓑ Ⓒ Ⓓ Ⓔ
55. Ⓐ Ⓑ Ⓒ Ⓓ Ⓔ   68. Ⓐ Ⓑ Ⓒ Ⓓ Ⓔ

PRACTICE TEST 1

SECTION I: MULTIPLE-CHOICE QUESTIONS
Time—55 Minutes
80 Questions

Directions: Each of the questions or incomplete statements below is followed by five suggested answers or completions. Select the one that is best in each case and then fill in the corresponding oval on the answer sheet.

1. In which of the following artistic movements did Pablo Picasso participate?

   I. Impressionism
   II. Cubism
   III. Expressionism
   IV. Surrealism

   (A) II and IV
   (B) II only
   (C) II and III
   (D) I and II
   (E) All four

2. Which of the following policies did Napoleon I of France and Peter the Great of Russia both use?

   (A) Codification of the law
   (B) Promoting individuals, based on talent
   (C) Balancing the budget
   (D) Reforming social practice at court
   (E) Coming to an agreement with the papacy

3. The most inclusive and influential of the early Protestant reformers was

   (A) Luther
   (B) Zwingli
   (C) Calvin
   (D) John Knox
   (E) Michael Servetus

4. Early English explorers of the coast of North America were searching for a northwest passage because they

   (A) wanted to get to the west coast of North America.
   (B) wanted to establish safer inland colonies that were still accessible by sea.
   (C) had heard rumors of El Dorado, a city of gold.
   (D) wanted to get past the Americas and on to the spice islands of the East.
   (E) wanted to do all of the above.

5. All the following were characteristic of the 1920s EXCEPT

   (A) women in shorter skirts, wearing makeup.
   (B) women in the workforce.
   (C) households in England and Germany with radios.
   (D) more widespread ownership of automobiles.
   (E) movies as a form of entertainment.

GO ON TO THE NEXT PAGE

6. During the Interregnum, English Puritans outlawed blood sports such as bearbaiting because the

   (A) Puritans opposed cruelty to animals.
   (B) public saw the sports as entertaining.
   (C) sports violated the teaching of scripture.
   (D) sports drew people away from the theaters.
   (E) sports invited sinful gambling and drinking.

7. _____ was the biggest medical advancement of the 18th century.

   (A) Germ theory of disease
   (B) X-ray
   (C) Smallpox inoculation
   (D) Surgery under anesthesia
   (E) The humane treatment of the mentally ill

8. Napoleon's Continental System was aimed at

   (A) achieving political and economic unity of his empire.
   (B) destroying the British economy by boycotting British goods.
   (C) developing agriculture to be self-sufficient.
   (D) spreading the blessings of the French Revolution, such as the metric system.
   (E) uniting Europe behind the Catholic Church.

9. After the War of Austrian Succession, Maria Theresa was disappointed because

   (A) Austria lost the Southern Netherlands, which she had owned since 1713.
   (B) Austria was forced to pay indemnities to Prussia.
   (C) the nations of Europe turned on Austria and allied with Frederick of Prussia.
   (D) Frederick kept Silesia, which he had seized in 1740.
   (E) Hungary revolted against Austria.

10. The principles of laissez-faire advocate that

    (A) a country should have colonies for raw materials.
    (B) a country's wealth is counted in its gold and silver.
    (C) all tariffs should be eliminated.
    (D) countries should be self-sufficient.
    (E) governments should control wages and prices.

11. To Europeans, the most important result of the American Revolution was that it

    (A) proved that the British could be defeated.
    (B) weakened France financially.
    (C) proved that Enlightenment ideals could become reality.
    (D) provided impressions of American life to those Europeans who fought.
    (E) opened possibilities for immigration.

GO ON TO THE NEXT PAGE

12. _____ developed a large cash crop out of tulip cultivation.

    (A) The Netherlands
    (B) Belgium
    (C) France
    (D) Germany
    (E) Switzerland

13. Yugoslavia in the 1990s differed from Yugoslavia in the 1960s in all of the following ways EXCEPT

    (A) Yugoslavia broke up into separate nations.
    (B) Milosevic practiced ethnic cleansing against the Muslims in Bosnia and Kosovo.
    (C) civil war waged.
    (D) Yugoslavia no longer answered to the Soviet Union.
    (E) Tito's presence no longer prevailed.

14. Sculpture in the Southern Renaissance differed from sculpture of the Middle Ages in that it featured

    (A) free-standing forms rather than bas-relief.
    (B) nude figures.
    (C) the human form portrayed more realistically.
    (D) Pietàs—sculptures of Mary holding the body of the crucified Christ.
    (E) all of the above.

15. In the early 20th century, before World War I, what France most resented about Germany was

    (A) its buildup of a naval force.
    (B) its seizure of Alsace and Lorraine in 1871.
    (C) the militaristic attitude of William I.
    (D) competition for colonies in Africa.
    (E) the big increase in Germany's armed forces.

16. The 16th-century Spanish conquistadors were able to overcome large numbers of Native American people primarily because the

    (A) Americans had no resistance to European diseases such as smallpox.
    (B) Spanish greatly outnumbered the Americans.
    (C) Native Americans thought the Spanish were gods.
    (D) Native Americans had never seen horses.
    (E) Spanish made use of the wheel, which was unknown to the Americas.

17. The 18th-century agricultural revolution included all the following EXCEPT

    (A) rotating crops with nitrogen-fixing plants and root plants.
    (B) enclosure of the common land.
    (C) better animal breeding practices.
    (D) new crops, such as potatoes and turnips.
    (E) the use of chemical fertilizers.

18. Which of the following events occurred during the Directory period of the French Revolution, 1795–1799?

    (A) Napoleon set up the Cisalpine Republic in northern Italy.
    (B) The Reign of Terror occurred.
    (C) The Revolutionary calendar renamed the months and days.
    (D) France adopted the metric system.
    (E) Louis XVI and Marie Antoinette were executed.

GO ON TO THE NEXT PAGE ▷

19. England did not accept the Gregorian calendar of 1582 until the middle of the 18th century primarily because

    (A) English astronomers disagreed with the math behind it.

    (B) Protestants refused to accept a Catholic calendar.

    (C) the old Julian calendar fit better with English tradition.

    (D) the King and Parliament could not agree.

    (E) all the above are true.

20. The English Corn Laws primarily benefited the

    (A) working class.

    (B) big merchants.

    (C) Chartists.

    (D) large landowners.

    (E) clergy.

21. After the assassination of Francis Ferdinand in 1914, Serbia agreed to all of Austria's demands EXCEPT

    (A) ending anti-Habsburg publications.

    (B) allowing Austria to enter Serbia to search out threats.

    (C) bringing an end to Serbian nationalist organizations.

    (D) the elimination of certain officials and army officers.

    (E) responding within 48 hours.

22. Lenin and the Bolsheviks found support among the Russian peasants primarily because they (the Bolsheviks)

    (A) called for the execution of the tsar.

    (B) promised land and peace.

    (C) worked with the Russian Duma, the parliament.

    (D) promoted the mir.

    (E) promised a revision of the legal system.

23. The art movement between the world wars, one that reflected a world that no longer "made sense," was

    (A) surrealism.

    (B) impressionism.

    (C) Dada.

    (D) expressionism.

    (E) cubism.

24. The Warsaw Pact was a(n)

    (A) military alliance of the USSR's satellites in Eastern Europe.

    (B) declaration that the Soviet Union would intervene in any satellite country if communism were threatened.

    (C) American offer of economic aid after World War II.

    (D) alliance of Eastern Europe against the USSR.

    (E) secret, anti-communist organization in Eastern Europe.

25. Renaissance humanism was a contradiction of the Middle Ages in that it

    (A) denied Church doctrine, including the Trinity.

    (B) promoted art, especially painting.

    (C) ignored the authority of the Church.

    (D) emphasized the goodness of the present and the power of humanity.

    (E) sought a logical explanation for the outbreak of plague in the 14th century.

GO ON TO THE NEXT PAGE ⟩

26. Henry VIII converted England to Protestantism mainly because he

   (A) resented the authority of Rome.

   (B) wanted his marriage annulled so he could marry Anne Boleyn.

   (C) had sincere Protestant convictions.

   (D) feared leaving the throne to his only child at the time, a daughter.

   (E) disagreed with the Archbishop of Canterbury.

27. In *The Leviathan*, Thomas Hobbes said that government is a contract

   (A) between the ruler and those governed; those being ruled should turn over all authority to the ruler to ensure security and order.

   (B) between the government and people to protect the rights to life, liberty, and property.

   (C) among the people, determined by the general will.

   (D) between an elected parliament and a ruler for peace and justice.

   (E) among the nobility and the monarch to provide best for the kingdom.

28. In the Thirty Years War, Cardinal Richelieu sided

   (A) with the Holy Roman Empire because he was a Catholic clergyman.

   (B) with the armies of Wallenstein.

   (C) with the Protestant side against the Austrian Habsburgs.

   (D) against the English.

   (E) with no one; he kept France neutral.

29. During World War I, Japan

   (A) sided with the Allies.

   (B) advanced its claims in China.

   (C) became increasingly militaristic.

   (D) secretly issued its Twenty-One Demands.

   (E) did all of the above.

30. A major difference between Mussolini and Hitler was that Mussolini

   (A) did not dress in a military uniform.

   (B) did not personally hate Jews.

   (C) had not been in World War I.

   (D) was not involved in aiding other fascist movements.

   (E) did not court the financial powers of the country.

31. Writers from the school of naturalism described a world in which

   (A) nature is positive and in accord with the human spirit.

   (B) all things that happen are part of a broad scheme of things.

   (C) God is master of the universe.

   (D) reason and natural law prevail.

   (E) things happen entirely by chance.

32. The Zollverein was

   (A) the unification agreement between Austria and Hungary in the late 19th century.

   (B) the German attempt to lure Mexico into World War I against the United States.

   (C) a trade union among the German states.

   (D) the military agreement between Hitler's Germany and Austria.

   (E) an attempt to discredit a British Labour government in the 1920s through publication of a supposedly communist letter.

GO ON TO THE NEXT PAGE ▷

33. Greece gained her independence in 1832 with the help of

    (A) France and Britain.
    (B) Russia.
    (C) the revolutionary leader Ypsilanti.
    (D) a peaceful agreement with the Ottoman Empire.
    (E) Piedmont-Sardinia.

34. Which country is INCORRECTLY matched with a royal family in 1550?

    (A) England—Tudors
    (B) Spain—Habsburgs
    (C) France—Bourbons
    (D) Austria—Habsburgs
    (E) All are accurately paired.

35. Frederick II of Prussia proved himself an enlightened monarch in all the following ways EXCEPT

    (A) introducing new crops and scientific agriculture.
    (B) hosting Voltaire at Potsdam.
    (C) composing music for the flute.
    (D) establishing total religious toleration.
    (E) eliminating torture and establishing appellate courts.

36. After the Seven Years War, which ended in 1763, England received

    (A) Gibraltar.
    (B) French sugar islands in the Caribbean.
    (C) the *asiento*, or slave trade to Spanish America.
    (D) Canada.
    (E) the Louisiana Territory in North America.

37. All the following were results of the Irish potato blight in the 1840s EXCEPT

    (A) reforms to benefit the Irish peasants.
    (B) starvation and disease.
    (C) Irish immigration, mainly to the United States.
    (D) repeal of the Corn Laws.
    (E) continued severe poverty in Ireland.

38. The German fairy tales published in the 19th century by the brothers Grimm were something of a by-product because

    (A) they never intended the stories for publication.
    (B) they were really scholarly historians.
    (C) they were linguists who traveled throughout the German states, studying dialects.
    (D) the stories were taken from a work of philosophy on the German *volkgeist*.
    (E) they were really recorded by one of Napoleon's occupation soldiers.

39. The *Communist Manifesto* of 1848

    (A) helped bring about the revolutions of 1848.
    (B) urged the middle class to unite against the nobility.
    (C) claimed that events in history happened erratically by chance.
    (D) was written for the Communist Party of Russia.
    (E) had no influence on the revolutions of 1848.

GO ON TO THE NEXT PAGE ⇨

40. The *philosophes* were primarily

    (A) early scientific experimenters.

    (B) journalists and popularizers of the Enlightenment.

    (C) philosophers of the Enlightenment.

    (D) experimenters in new agricultural methods.

    (E) astronomers such as Galileo and Kepler.

41. The purpose of Metternich's Carlsbad Decrees of 1819 was to

    (A) stifle revolutionary activity.

    (B) keep a close eye on German university students and professors.

    (C) outlaw the Burschenschaft.

    (D) maintain the status quo.

    (E) do all of the above.

42. The Bauhaus school of design in Weimar, Germany, closed in the mid-1930s because

    (A) of the Great Depression.

    (B) people were no longer interested in functionalism.

    (C) its designs ceased to sell.

    (D) its main designers were lured to America.

    (E) Hitler and the Nazis saw it as degenerate.

43. The main focus of groups such as the neo-Nazis and neo-fascists has been

    (A) African and Asian immigrants to Europe.

    (B) members of the Communist Party.

    (C) Jews.

    (D) trade unions.

    (E) conservation of natural resources.

44. Which of the following African countries is incorrectly matched with the European country that dominated it in the late 19th century?

    (A) Kenya—Britain

    (B) Morocco—France

    (C) Libya—Italy

    (D) South Africa—the Netherlands

    (E) Congo—Belgium

45. The main contribution of the religious reformer Zwingli was

    (A) services in the vernacular.

    (B) the concept of salvation by faith.

    (C) removal of art, decoration, and music from the church and service.

    (D) marriage of the clergy.

    (E) congregational government.

46. Louis XIV of France accomplished all the following EXCEPT

    (A) religious unification by elimination of the Edict of Nantes.

    (B) reform of the tax system.

    (C) reliance on a number of advisors.

    (D) control of the nobility.

    (E) establishment of the scientific academy.

47. The English scientist William Harvey became known for his experiments that led him to write about

    (A) circulation of the blood.

    (B) the discovery of capillaries.

    (C) accurate human anatomy.

    (D) the digestive system.

    (E) the respiratory system.

GO ON TO THE NEXT PAGE ⟩

48. Maria Theresa's father, Charles XII of Austria, spent much of his reign

    (A) trying to establish the Ostend, an overseas trading company, out of the Austrian Netherlands.

    (B) ensuring the solidity of Catholicism in his empire.

    (C) getting European nations to sign the Pragmatic Sanction guaranteeing his daughter's inheritance.

    (D) securing an acceptable marriage for Maria Theresa.

    (E) controlling the rebellious Magyar nobles.

49. The *scientific method* may be defined as

    (A) moving from the general to the specific.

    (B) moving from the specific to the general.

    (C) reading widely from the work of others.

    (D) inventing new instruments such as the microscope.

    (E) being part of the new scientific academies.

50. The British Navigation Acts of the 17th century were aimed at trade competition from the

    (A) French.

    (B) Spanish.

    (C) Belgian Ostend Company.

    (D) Dutch.

    (E) Scandinavians.

51. The ecumenical movement of the late 20th century was aimed at

    (A) finding common ground among different religious denominations.

    (B) encouraging free trade among the EU countries.

    (C) fostering new openness in Eastern Europe.

    (D) establishing a common currency in Western Europe.

    (E) saying Catholic Mass in the vernacular.

52. One postwar similarity between World Wars I and II was

    (A) extensive damage to Germany.

    (B) economic depression and inflation.

    (C) recovery from damage and deprivation in Russia.

    (D) a dangerous outbreak of influenza.

    (E) recovery from trench warfare.

53. Hitler's beer hall putsch in Munich in 1923 was geared toward

    (A) creating publicity for his book *Mein Kampf*.

    (B) foiling a communist plot.

    (C) taking over the government as Mussolini had in Italy.

    (D) keeping the government from reining in his renegade practices.

    (E) getting attention for his National Socialist Party.

54. The impressionist painters of late 19th-century France were most interested in

    (A) creating dreamlike images.

    (B) overlaying geometric shapes.

    (C) using bright colors and simple lines.

    (D) experimenting with the effects of light.

    (E) forming abstract images.

GO ON TO THE NEXT PAGE

55. The Pretender generally refers to

    (A) Louis Napoleon, who became Napoleon III and ruled France in the mid-19th century.

    (B) the son of Louis XVI, who died in prison during the French Revolution.

    (C) Richard Cromwell, who tried to carry on the Interregnum after the death of his father, Oliver Cromwell.

    (D) Catherine the Great of Russia, who was actually a rather minor German princess.

    (E) James II and his descendants, who fled England in 1688 in the wake of the accession of William and Mary.

56. The main consequence of the Dreyfus Affair in late 19th-century France was

    (A) an overhaul of the justice system.

    (B) immediate restoration of the soldier's rank.

    (C) negative images of the Church and separation of Church and state in 1906.

    (D) the closing of harsh prisons such as Devil's Island.

    (E) the suicide of Alfred Dreyfus.

57. Any ambition that Catherine the Great may have had to reform serfdom in Russia fell by the wayside after

    (A) Diderot visited her in Russia.

    (B) Pugachev staged his rebellion in 1773–1774.

    (C) she met with delegates to consider codifying Russian law.

    (D) she got involved with the partitions of Poland.

    (E) she was preoccupied with her various lovers.

58. The Chapelier Law in France originated during the Revolution and remained in place for many years. The Chapelier Law

    (A) established wage and price controls.

    (B) made it illegal for women to participate in political clubs.

    (C) declared labor unions and strikes illegal.

    (D) established equal taxation.

    (E) made all citizens equal before the law.

59. The influential theory of 20th-century British economist John Maynard Keynes was that

    (A) harsh war reparations are a mistake that backfires later.

    (B) international free trade should prevail.

    (C) immigration should be regulated.

    (D) governments should stimulate the economy and create jobs in difficult economic times.

    (E) welfare states are necessary.

60. In England, the first country to industrialize, the first industry to implement machinery was

    (A) mining.

    (B) textiles.

    (C) iron production.

    (D) ship building.

    (E) railroads.

61. During the French Revolution, the Thermidorean Reaction was

    (A) the beginning of the Directory.

    (B) Year One of the Republic.

    (C) the end of the Reign of Terror.

    (D) the execution of Louis XVI.

    (E) the coup d'etat of 1797.

GO ON TO THE NEXT PAGE ⟩

62. In the early 16th century, one's religion was determined by

(A) one's ruler.

(B) one's personal conscience.

(C) the bishop of the diocese.

(D) one's parents.

(E) God.

63. The 18th century in England was a time when Parliament was able to strengthen its power over the monarchy, mainly because

(A) of the documents William and Mary had to sign in 1689.

(B) rich merchants and landowners controlled the House of Commons.

(C) Parliament controlled the government's purse.

(D) the first two Hanover kings hardly spoke English and were unconcerned with English affairs.

(E) Parliament was elected by universal male suffrage.

64. Calvinism spread to all these areas EXCEPT

(A) the North American British colonies.

(B) Scotland.

(C) Paris.

(D) Holland.

(E) South Africa.

65. The Battle of Gallipoli in 1915 was

(A) an Allied attempt to break into the Black Sea and connect with Russia.

(B) an Allied attempt to break the stalemate of trench warfare in France.

(C) a famous sea battle involving submarines.

(D) the last battle in which Russia played a decisive role.

(E) a battle in the Alps of northern Italy.

66. Lenin instituted the New Economic Plan (NEP) to

(A) win support of the kulaks.

(B) give Stalin and Trotsky common ground of agreement.

(C) increase the supply of food and other products.

(D) get Russia out of World War I.

(E) reconcile with the Mensheviks.

67. Following World War II, the general attitude of Russian civilians was

(A) grinding despair over the war's hardship and suffering.

(B) great patriotism and optimism.

(C) anger and revolt against the communists.

(D) disillusionment as people asked, "What now?"

(E) a revival of faith in the Russian Orthodox Church.

68. Under a NATO agreement, Germany was not allowed to

(A) rebuild its army.

(B) join NATO.

(C) participate in the Common Market.

(D) have military bases on its soil.

(E) develop nuclear weapons.

69. The first Russian leader to discuss the crimes of Stalin was

(A) Brezhnev.

(B) Gorbachev.

(C) Yeltsin.

(D) Andropov.

(E) Khrushchev.

GO ON TO THE NEXT PAGE

70. The Schlieffen Plan in place in Germany on the eve of World War I

    (A) warned Germany to beware of the English.

    (B) said to attack and destroy Russia first, then deal with the West.

    (C) advised a naval war using submarines.

    (D) had been altered to bolster Alsace and Lorraine.

    (E) did all of the above.

71. The Church practice that spurred Luther to revolt was

    (A) simony—buying or selling church offices.

    (B) indulgences—forgiveness of sin or escape from purgatory in exchange for a monetary gift.

    (C) absenteeism—clergymen who did not live in their dioceses.

    (D) nepotism—giving church positions to relatives.

    (E) pluralism—holding more than one church position at the same time.

72. The Society of Friends (the Quakers) originated in 17th-century England and advocated

    (A) more equality in property ownership.

    (B) a broader franchise.

    (C) a communal society.

    (D) many rules against various sins.

    (E) toleration and peaceful living.

73. The biggest difference between the British colonies in the Americas and those of the Spanish and French was that the

    (A) British women and families came.

    (B) British tended to farm.

    (C) ambition of the British was not necessarily to get rich.

    (D) British who came were less connected to religion.

    (E) English didn't have as much trouble with the Native Americans.

74. The British seemed to profit LEAST in 1713 from the settlement of the War of Spanish Succession in which of the following ways?

    (A) They got Gibraltar.

    (B) They got the *asiento*, the slave trade with Spanish America.

    (C) The Southern Netherlands went to Austria.

    (D) The throne of Spain went to the Bourbons.

    (E) They got Newfoundland and Nova Scotia.

75. Tycho Brahe's biggest contribution to astronomy was his

    (A) observatory on the coast of Denmark.

    (B) telescope that he built.

    (C) 20 years of records documenting naked-eye observations.

    (D) mathematical formulas.

    (E) correspondence with Galileo.

GO ON TO THE NEXT PAGE

76. The English clergyman John Wesley was part of a movement called the Great Awakening, which emphasized

    (A) personal, emotional religious experience.
    (B) public confession of sins.
    (C) caring for the poor, the sick, and prisoners.
    (D) outdoor, evangelical services.
    (E) all of the above.

77. During the French Revolution, the Civil Constitution of the Clergy required

    (A) the conversion of churches into "temples of reason."
    (B) the clergy's swearing an oath of loyalty to the Revolution.
    (C) that the Church turn over its property to the government.
    (D) that the Church no longer collect the tithe.
    (E) that nuns renounce their vows.

78. The Frankfurt Assembly of 1848–49 failed to unite Germany for all the following reasons EXCEPT

    (A) it did not have the support of the military.
    (B) it did not have the support of the peasants.
    (C) the delegates could not agree on a Constitution.
    (D) Frederick William IV would not accept a position as a constitutional monarch.
    (E) it had no real authority or power.

79. In the German states after 1850, the term *realpolitik* implied

    (A) an optimistic, emotional outlook on the future.
    (B) a hopelessness and sense of doom.
    (C) a glorification of the powers of human reason.
    (D) a belief in liberalism and reform.
    (E) science, facts, law and order, and hard work.

80. Rudyard Kipling's "White Man's Burden" seemed to indicate that

    (A) Europeans had a duty to civilize other peoples.
    (B) imperialism meant hard work but great rewards.
    (C) service to one's country was patriotic duty.
    (D) peoples of Africa and Asia, given a chance, could achieve as much as the Europeans.
    (E) democracy must be established worldwide.

IF YOU FINISH BEFORE TIME IS CALLED, YOU MAY CHECK YOUR WORK ON THIS SECTION ONLY. DO NOT TURN TO ANY OTHER SECTION IN THE TEST.

STOP

SECTION II

Part A

(Suggested writing time—45 minutes)

Percent of Section II score—45

Directions: The following question is based on the accompanying Documents 1–12. The documents have been edited for the purpose of this exercise.

This question is designed to test your ability to work with and understand historical documents. Write an essay that does the following:

- Provides an appropriate, explicitly stated thesis that directly addresses all parts of the question and does not simply restate the question.

- Discusses a majority of the documents individually and specifically.

- Supports the thesis with appropriate interpretations of a majority of the documents.

- Analyzes the documents by explicitly grouping them in at least three appropriate ways.

- Takes into account both the sources of the documents and the authors' points of view.

You may refer to relevant historical information not mentioned in the documents.

1. What were some of the major perceptions of the Falkland Islands War between Great Britain and Argentina in 1982?

Historical Background: The Falkland Islands, called the Malvinas by Argentina, lie in the extreme South Atlantic off the southern tip of South America. The British took the islands from Argentina in 1833 and maintained a colonial administration over them after 1842. Argentine nationalism after World War II developed a sense of offense at British occupation. Colonialism everywhere was dying, and the islands were of little economic or military significance to either country. However, the Falkland population of approximately 1,800 people in 1980 considered themselves British; they were adamantly opposed to being transferred to Argentina.

In 1981, a new military regime seized power in Argentina under President Leopoldo Galtieri. Galtieri's government needed glory and a distraction from domestic problems. British Prime Minister Margaret Thatcher's Conservative government also needed a patriotic boost in popularity. On April 1–2, 1982, Argentina invaded East and West Falkland under the plan of Navy Admiral Jorge Anaya. Britain soon sent a task force to retake the islands. After several battles in terrible winter weather and almost 1,000 casualties (two-thirds of them Argentine), Argentina surrendered in June 1982.

Please use separate paper to write your answers.

GO ON TO THE NEXT PAGE ⇨

Document 1

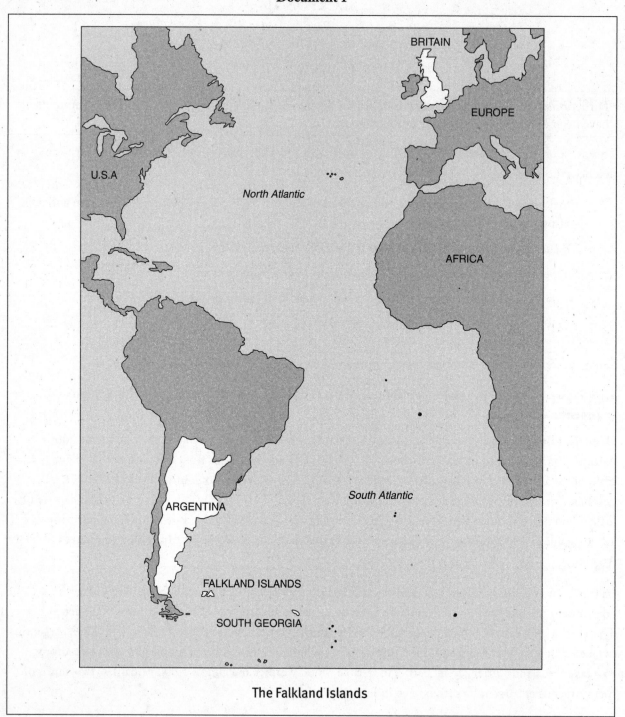

The Falkland Islands

GO ON TO THE NEXT PAGE ⇒

Document 2

Source: Aldous Huxley, *Brave New World*, 1932

"I should like a thoroughly bad climate," Helmholtz answered. "I believe one could write better if the climate were bad. If there were a lot of wind and storms, for example…"

The Controller nodded his approbation. "What about the Falkland Islands?"

"Yes, I think that will do," Helmholtz answered.

Document 3

Source: The Franks Report. Commissioned by the British Government after the Falklands War, published January 1983.

At the beginning of 1982 there was evidence from several sources that Argentina, and particularly the new government of President Galtieri, was committed to achieving success in its Malvinas policy in a much shorter timescale than most previous Argentine Governments had envisaged.

Document 4

Source: "The Falklands, 1982" by British poet Gavin Ewart
This must have been more like the Boer War
than anything seen in our lifetime,
with the troopships and the cheering,
the happy homecoming…

Document 5

Source: Lt. David Tinker, secretary to the captain of the British warship *Glamorgan*, in a letter to his parents, early April 1982

Today we have heard the news that we are off to the Falkland Islands to bash the Argentines . . . . Of course, the whole thing may blow over in a week, but the thrill of some real confrontation in a "colonial war" is quite exciting compared to the routine of exercises and paperwork. The captain is of course delighted; he may be able to finish his career in a blaze of glory.

GO ON TO THE NEXT PAGE

Document 6

Source: American Aide to Secretary of State Alexander Haig, April 1982

Like two schoolboys itching for a fight. They'll not be satisfied until there's some blood on the floor.

Document 7

Source: An Argentine ex-patriot now living in the United States

The military were very discredited at that time and they played with one of Argentina's fairy tales: the Malvinas are ours. I hear the voice of many fanatics (including my father) refute what I state. However, I believe that none of them would give up the comfort of living in continental Argentina to move to the islands.

Document 8

Source: Pope John Paul II, speaking in Coventry, England, May 1982

The scale and horror of modern warfare make it totally unacceptable as a means of settling differences between nations.

Document 9

Source: Argentine soldier, June 1982

No one really told us where we were going. We weren't prepared psychologically. In my company we all had secondary education at least, but in A, B and C companies, who were the ones most in the front line, there were boys who didn't even know what the Malvinas were.

Document 10

Source: British Lt. David Tinker, letter, May 1982

At times the situation seems so absurdly silly. Here we are in 1982, fighting a colonial war on the other side of the world; 28,000 men going to fight over a dreadful piece of land inhabited by 1800 people.

GO ON TO THE NEXT PAGE

Document 11

Source: Senior Argentine Official, speaking after the war

We never dreamed for one minute you would send a task force. Had we known what we know now, the skeptics would have powerful evidence to counter [Admiral] Anaya's proposals for invasion.

Document 12

Source: Max Hastings and Simon Jennings, British journalists. Hastings accompanied the task force to the Falklands. *The Battle for the Falklands*, 1983

The Falklanders' spontaneous enthusiasm for their deliverance seemed to die very quickly. Instead of a vast alien army of Argentinians camped all around them, there was now a scarcely less alien British army. Just as many Falklanders made clear their impatience to be left alone once more, so the British did not conceal their burning anxiety to be gone from the islands, to go home to enjoy their triumph among their own people. They had done what they came to do. By the end of June, most of the men who fought were gone. Gone too were many of the ships of the battle group, to be replaced by other men and other ships, with the thankless task of holding those barren, unlovely islands for Britain, without the prospect of the glory.

GO ON TO THE NEXT PAGE

Part B
(Suggested planning and writing time—35 minutes)
Percent of Section II score—27½

Directions: You are to answer ONE question from the three questions below. Make your selection carefully, choosing the question that you are best prepared to answer thoroughly in the time permitted. You should spend five minutes organizing or outlining your answer.

Write an essay that

- has a relevant thesis;

- addresses all parts of the question;

- supports a thesis with specific evidence; and

- is well organized.

2. **Compare and contrast the art of the Southern Renaissance with that of the Northern Renaissance, showing how each reflected its time and place.**

3. **Discuss the economic theories of Adam Smith and those of the Physiocrats of the French Enlightenment, showing how they were both alike and different.**

4. **Analyze the successes and failures of Louis Napoleon Bonaparte of France, 1849–1870.**

Please use separate paper to write your answers.

GO ON TO THE NEXT PAGE

Part C
(Suggested planning and writing time—35 minutes)
Percent of Section II score—27½

> **Directions:** You are to answer ONE question from the three questions below. Make your selection carefully, choosing the question that you are best prepared to answer thoroughly in the time permitted. You should spend five minutes organizing or outlining your answer.

Write an essay that

- has a relevant thesis;

- addresses all parts of the question;

- supports a thesis with specific evidence; and

- is well organized.

5. **Describe the factors involved in the naval aspects of World War I and assess their effectiveness.**

6. **The work of such scientists as Charles Darwin, Sigmund Freud, Ivan Pavlov, Albert Einstein, Max Planck, Ernest Rutherford, and the Curies changed people's outlook on the world and on themselves. Explain the effects of the ideas of at least three of these thinkers.**

7. **Evaluate three challenges the Western world faces in the early 21st century, showing the connections of these problems to events in the 20th century.**

Please use separate paper to write your answers.

IF YOU FINISH BEFORE TIME IS CALLED, YOU MAY CHECK YOUR WORK ON THIS SECTION ONLY. DO NOT TURN TO ANY OTHER SECTION IN THE TEST.

STOP

Practice Test 1: **Answer Key**

1. C	15. B	29. E	43. A	57. B	71. B
2. B	16. A	30. B	44. D	58. C	72. E
3. C	17. E	31. E	45. C	59. D	73. A
4. D	18. A	32. C	46. B	60. B	74. D
5. B	19. B	33. A	47. A	61. C	75. C
6. E	20. D	34. C	48. C	62. A	76. E
7. C	21. B	35. D	49. B	63. D	77. B
8. B	22. B	36. D	50. D	64. C	78. C
9. D	23. C	37. A	51. A	65. A	79. E
10. C	24. A	38. C	52. C	66. C	80. A
11. C	25. D	39. E	53. C	67. B	
12. A	26. B	40. B	54. D	68. E	
13. D	27. A	41. E	55. E	69. E	
14. E	28. C	42. E	56. C	70. D	

PRACTICE TEST 1: ASSESS YOUR STRENGTHS

The following tables show how the Practice Test is broken down by time period. If you need help with the free-response questions or document-based questions, refer back to Chapter 2: Strategies for Success.

Time Periods	Questions	If you missed these questions, study these chapters.
1450 to the French Revolution	2, 3, 4, 6, 7, 8, 9, 11, 12, 14, 16, 18, 19, 25, 26, 27, 28, 34, 35, 36, 40, 45, 46, 47, 48, 49, 50, 55, 57, 58, 61, 62, 63, 64, 71, 72, 73, 74, 75, 76, 77	Chapter 3: The Renaissance Chapter 4: The Reformation and Religious Wars Chapter 5: Discovery, Expansion, and Commercial Revolution Chapter 6: The Age of Absolutism—Western Europe Chapter 7: The Age of Absolutism—Eastern Europe Chapter 8: Constitutionalism in England and the Dutch Republic Chapter 9: The Scientific Revolution Chapter 10: The Enlightenment Chapter 11: 18th-Century Economics and Politics Chapter 12: The French Revolution
19th Century (and very beginning of 20th century)	1*, 10*, 15, 17*, 20, 31, 32, 33, 37, 38, 39, 41, 44, 54, 56, 60, 78, 79	Chapter 13: The Industrial Revolution Chapter 14: Conservatism (1815–1848) Chapter 15: The Rise of Liberalism (1815–1848) Chapter 16: The Rise of Nationalism (1815–1848) Chapter 17: Romanticism Chapter 18: The Age of Realpolitik (1848–1914) Chapter 19: The Rise of Socialism Chapter 20: The Age of Mass Politics (1871–1915) Chapter 21: Intellectual Movements (1850–1914) Chapter 22: The New Imperialism
20th Century (and very beginning of 21st century)	5, 13, 21, 22, 23, 24, 29, 30, 42, 43, 51, 52, 53, 59, 65, 66, 67, 68, 69, 70, 80	Chapter 23: World War I Chapter 24: The Russian Revolution Chapter 25: Europe Between the Wars Chapter 26: World War II Chapter 27: Immediate Postwar Issues Chapter 28: The Cold War Chapter 29: Nationalism Chapter 30: Post–World War II Society

* Question 1: Cubism is a 20th century development but is typically framed along with major shifts in art that occur at the end of the 19th century and into the early 20th century.

Question 10: The principle of *laissez-faire* emerges out of Enlightenment economic ideas of the 18th century, but it has become part of policy in the 19th century.

Question 17: Although the Agricultural Revolution is associated with 18th century developments in England, it is typically framed as a precursor to the Industrial Revolution.

Chapters and Topics	Number of Questions	Answered Correctly
1450 to the French Revolution	41	
19th century (and very beginning of 20th century)	18	
20th century (and very beginning of 21st century)	21	

ANSWERS AND EXPLANATIONS

SECTION I: MULTIPLE-CHOICE QUESTIONS

1. C

Picasso, with Georges Braque, was one of the pioneers of cubism, and later he practiced expressionism. The impressionists predated Picasso. Though Picasso's contemporary Salvador Dali adhered to surrealism, it was not Picasso's style.

2. B

Both rulers promoted men based on their abilities. Napoleon alone codified the law, (A), balanced the budget at first, (C), and signed the Concordat with the papacy, (E). Peter the Great forced better social skills on the Russian nobility, (D).

3. C

Calvin wrote his theology in Latin, the international language of scholarship and religion, while Luther (A) addressed the German people by writing in German. Zwingli, (C), was Swiss, and his career was short-lived because he was killed in violence against Catholics. John Knox, (D), took Calvinism to Scotland, and Servetus, (E), was a Spanish physician who was executed by Calvin for his denial of the trinity.

4. D

The earliest explorers viewed North America as an impediment, a barrier to their ambition to get to the Far East, where one might get rich from the spice trade. It was primarily the Spanish who searched for El Dorado, (C), and it was they who reached the Pacific, (A). The first English adventurers were more concerned with making immediate money than with founding colonies, (B).

5. B

Radios and film became popular diversions, (C and E), in the 1920s. More people owned cars, (D). Women wore short hair, short skirts, and makeup, (A), but they did not stay in the workforce after the war.

6. E

The Puritans enforced many rules to attempt to reduce what they regarded as human sin. The 1600s predate concern for animals, (A). The Puritans closed the theaters, along with other venues of public entertainment, (D). Jokes have been made in relation to choice, (B), the idea that Puritans opposed behavior that gave pleasure, but this is not true. Choice (C) is also irrelevant.

7. C

Edward Jenner published his findings in the 1790s after 20 years of study and experiments. Germ theory, (A), was the brainchild of Louis Pasteur in the 19th century. X-rays, (B), appeared in the early 20th century. Surgery with anesthesia, (D), and kinder treatment of the insane, (E), both developed after the 18th century.

8. B

When Lord Nelson destroyed the French fleet in 1805, Napoleon gave up his plans for an invasion of England and, instead, ordered all his conquered territory not to trade with the British. He hoped to destroy England financially. (A), (C), and (E) simply aren't true. Napoleon did spread the metric system (D) and other principles of the French Revolution, but this was unrelated to the Continental System.

9. D

In 1848, following the War of Austrian Succession, Austria was given back the Southern Netherlands, (A), which was not particularly desirable, but Frederick kept Silesia. Most of Europe, which had been against Austria in the war, now reversed allegiances and opposed Prussia, (C). Neither (B) nor (E) happened. In fact, Maria Theresa courted the favor of the Hungarian Magyars quite successfully.

10. C

Laissez-faire meant free trade without tariff barriers. The theory was that each entity would produce what it could best provide and that markets would adjust accordingly. Wealth was counted in a nation's productive capability, (B), and international exchange of goods was expected, (A and D). Choices (A), (B), and (D) are principles of mercantilism. Choice (E) is not a part of either mercantilism or laissez-faire.

11. C

Choices (B) and (D) are certainly true, but the biggest impact was the proof that Enlightenment principles could work. No doubt, some countries enjoyed seeing the British defeated, (A), but this was not a major issue. The war did not greatly affect immigration one way or the other.

12. A

During the 1600s, the Dutch developed a strong agricultural base, primarily from dairy products and from tulip cultivation. Belgium, (B), developed as an industrial nation. France and Germany had agriculture, (C and D), but tulips weren't the focus. Switzerland, (E), was too mountainous to be a commercial agricultural producer.

13. D

Choice (D) is correct because even under Tito, Yugoslavia had never been a Soviet satellite; it was communist but independent. The other choices accurately describe the nation after Tito's death.

14. E

Choices (A) through (D) are all true of Renaissance art—for example, Michelangelo's *David* or Cellini's

Perseus. Artists knew more about the human body (some, like Michelangelo, had dissected cadavers), and they were perhaps influenced by the new perspective in paintings that resulted in greater realism, (C). The Pietà, (D), was a popular form for Michelangelo and others.

15. B

The French never forgave Germany's taking Alsace and Lorraine in the Franco-Prussian War. Not being a naval power, (A), France was less concerned than Britain about the buildup of the German navy. France's colonial competition in Africa, (D), was more with England than with Germany. All of Europe was disturbed by choices (C) and (E), France no more so than other nations.

16. A

The earliest conquistador, Cortez, was driven back at first, but some months later, after European disease had wiped out thousands of Aztecs, Cortez was able to conquer with a rather small force, (B). This scenario was repeated elsewhere. Choices (C), (D), and (E) are true, but (A) remains a better reason for the relatively easy conquest.

17. E

Farmers used fertilizers, but they were mostly animal manures; this was before the days of chemical fertilizers. All the other choices were part of the agricultural revolution in Western Europe in the 1700s.

18. A

Napoleon received the commission to Italy partly through Josephine's connections to the Directory (they married in 1796). Choices (B) and (E) took place in 1793–94. The metric system replaced France's hodgepodge of weights and measures early in the Revolution, (D), and the Revolutionary calendar went into effect in 1792.

19. B

England refused the calendar revisions for so long because they were considered papist, which the ardent Protestants adamantly opposed. The other choices here are all fictitious.

20. D

The Corn Laws were tariffs on imported grain, which kept English grain prices high, benefiting the big farmers. The expensive grain hurt the working class, (A), because of high bread prices. The merchants and clergy were not affected, (B and E). The Chartists were a reform movement who campaigned against the Corn Laws, among other things.

21. B

All the choices here were part of the Austrian ultimatum presented to Serbia almost a month after the murder. Serbia agreed to all except allowing Austria into Serbia to search for offenders; this was unacceptable.

22. B

The Bolsheviks worked through the Soviets in 1917 under the campaign of land and peace. The peasants had been land-hungry since emancipation in 1861, and they felt no patriotism toward the war. Russian civilians had suffered greatly. The Bolsheviks opposed the Duma, (C), which backed the provisional government. Although the Reds executed the tsar and his family in 1918, (A), there was no publicity beforehand or afterward. (D) and (E) are irrelevant.

23. C

Choices (B), (D), and (E) predate World War I. Surrealism is of this time period, and it featured realistic images in unrealistic settings, (A). However, it is the dada movement that truly implied nonsense.

24. A

In 1955, feeling threatened by the Marshall Plan, Truman Doctrine, and NATO, the Soviet Union proclaimed a communist military alliance in Eastern Europe. (B) is a description of the Brezhnev Doctrine, (C) sounds like the Marshall Plan, and (D) and (E) never existed.

25. D

The humanists saw people as good and life as exciting and enjoyable, not as mere preparation for the afterlife. The humanists did foster art, but so had the Middle Ages, (B). Their thinking and lifestyle did not deny the Church, (A), or ignore Church authority, (C). When the plague struck, all sought answers, but this did not relate to humanism, (E).

26. B

Henry had fallen in love with 26-year-old Anne Boleyn when he was 40 and his wife Catherine was 46 and barren. He did want a son, which Catherine had not been able to produce, but probably this was more of an excuse for disposing of her, (D). (C) and (E) are not true. Henry resented papal authority, (A), only in the sense that the pope was unwilling to annul his marriage.

27. A

Hobbes had experienced the English Civil War and believed that a strong, absolute monarchy was necessary to ensure law and order. (B) describes the beliefs of John Locke, and (C) is attributable to Rousseau. (D) and (E) are unrelated.

28. C

Even though Richelieu was a Catholic cardinal and France was a Catholic country, enmity toward the Habsburgs dictated alliance with the Protestants, not the Catholics, (A). Wallenstein was the mercenary general hired by the Holy Roman Emperor, (B).

The English were not involved in the Thirty Years War, (D). France participated in most of the war, especially in the last phase, (E).

29. E

After the turn of the 20th century, Japan built her military, (C), and looked to the mainland for power, control, and natural resources, (B). During World War I, Japan sided with the Allies, (A). But covertly, while the West was busy fighting, Japan pushed demands on China (D), trying to establish a protectorate over it.

30. B

Until Hitler and Mussolini came to an understanding as they both aided Franco in the Spanish Civil War, (D), Mussolini had no special dislike for Jews; he had even had a Jewish mistress. Both men were veterans of World War I, (C), both dressed in military uniforms, (B), and both sought money from the rich and powerful, (E), claiming the ability to control the communists.

31. E

The naturalists went a step beyond the realists. In naturalist works, humans were at the mercy of chance, and the universe was neutral or even hostile, (A, B, and D). There was little or no discussion of God or religion, (C).

32. C

Most of the German states except Austria belonged to the free trade union, which Bismarck used to isolate Austria. Choice (A) refers to the Ausgleich, (B), to the Zimmerman telegram of World War I, choice (D) to the Anschluss, and (E) to the Zinoviev letter.

33. A

In the early 1820s, a Greek revolutionary Ypsilanti, (C), tried to lead a Greek revolt against the Turks, hoping to get help from Russia, (B), but this attempt

fell apart. In the late 1820s, France, England, and Russia agreed to support Greek independence, but Russia did little except try to take other Turkish territory, which was condemned by France and England. The French and English destroyed the Turkish fleet, (D), before the Ottomans granted independence. (E) is irrelevant.

34. C

The Bourbons did not take the throne until the late 1500s, with Henry IV (of Navarre). In 1550, the French royal family was Valois.

35. D

Frederick did everything here except (D). He built a Catholic Church in predominantly Lutheran Prussia, but he continued to discriminate against Jews (unlike Joseph of Austria, who instituted total religious freedom).

36. D

In the American part of the Seven Years War, the French and Indian War, England gained control of the Ohio River Valley and Canada. (A) and (C) refer to the War of Spanish Succession earlier (1713). Louisiana went to Spain, (E), which would later lose it to Napoleon, to be sold to the United States. England took French sugar islands during the war but returned them at the peace settlement, (B).

37. A

The failed potato crop convinced Prime Minister Peel that if the Corn Laws (grain tariffs) were not repealed, there would be an uprising, (D). The repeal did little to help the Irish, however. They starved and suffered, (B), some left Ireland, (C), and general Irish poverty continued, (E).

38. C

The Grimm brothers learned the stories accidentally as they studied German dialects. They were not historians, (B), or philosophers, (D), although the stories are an expression of *volkgeist*, or spirit of the people. (E) is untrue.

39. E

The *Manifesto* was written for a tiny, insignificant secret party in France; at the time, there was no Russian Communist Party, (D). It addressed the working class, (B). It said that history was predetermined and that the age of the worker was yet to dawn, (C). It had no influence on the revolutions of 1848, (A).

40. B

Except for a few Enlightenment thinkers, like Voltaire and Montesquieu, most of the 18th-century French *philosophes* were writers who popularized science and Enlightenment thought, though they themselves were not scientists, (A). Diderot, who edited the *Encyclopedia,* is an example. As such, they also spread new ideas about agriculture without actually experimenting themselves, (D). The early astronomers, (E), had lived and worked before the days of the *philosophes.*

41. E

The Carlsbad Decrees were an extremely conservative attempt to prevent change, (D). Metternich of Austria suspected that the German student organization Burschenschaft might be plotting revolution, (A and C). He placed observers within the universities to spy on students and professors, (B).

42. E

The Nazis disapproved of all modern art and shut down the Bauhaus. The other choices simply aren't true.

43. A

Although traditional fascism campaigned against communists and Jews, (B and C), their modern revivals have targeted immigrants.

44. D

Although the Dutch were the first Europeans to settle in South Africa in the 1600s, the British took the colony in the early 1800s. The controversy between the descendants of the two European groups led to the Boer War at the turn of the century.

45. C

Zwingli was a trained organist, but he became convinced that there was no place for music, stained glass windows, paintings, or sculpture in churches because such things were not mentioned in scripture. (A), (B), and (D) were already established by Luther. After Zwingli, Calvin and his followers practiced congregational government.

46. B

The inefficient tax system remained the bane of French monarchs and government. The nobility paid few taxes. Louis resorted to selling titles and positions to raise money. Louis did both, (A) and (E). He also had learned, from his mother's dependence on Mazarin, to place his reliance on more than one advisor, (C). The revolt of the nobility, the Fronde, during Louis's childhood led him to distrust the nobility and to devote much effort to keeping a tight rein on them, (D).

47. A

Through vivisection, Harvey understood and wrote about the circulation of blood, contradicting the much earlier work of Galen. Capillaries, (B), were discovered by the Italian Malpighi. None of the other answers apply.

48. C

Because he had no sons, Charles feared that other nations would challenge Maria Theresa's inheritance. He gave up the Ostend to please the British, (A). Catholicism was not in doubt, (B). The Magyars were troublesome, (E), but less of an issue than the Pragmatic Sanction.

49. B

The scientific or empirical method means drawing conclusions (general statements) only after many experiments (the specific). This is inductive reasoning. Its opposite, (A), is deductive reasoning. (C), (D), and (E) are all results of the movement in science, but they do not actually define *scientific method*.

50. D

Throughout the late 1500s and early 1600s, Dutch navigation and trade boomed and competed with that of the British. No other nation mentioned here had naval strength compared to that of the Dutch and English. The Navigation Acts were effective in hurting Dutch international trade.

51. A

Ecumenism involved talks between Roman Catholics and Eastern Orthodox Christians and among various Protestant denominations about issues on which they might agree. (B) and (D) refer to moves within the EU. Choice (E) refers to Vatican II in the 1960s. New openness, (C), could refer to Gorbachev's Soviet policy of the late 1980s.

52. C

In both wars, there was fighting in Russia and terrible suffering, including starvation. (D) and (E) refer to World War I. Answer (A) refers to World War II because of the bombing. (B) didn't occur after World War II as it had after World War I, partly because of the Marshall Plan.

53. C

Hitler had operated in Munich in a way similar to Mussolini in Italy. In 1923, he prematurely tried to stage a coup and failed. He had not yet written *Mein Kampf*, (A)—it would be a product of his year in prison. The Weimar government seemed powerless to control groups like Hitler's, (D). Certainly, Hitler wanted attention for his party, (E), and he used the threat of communism to generate support, (B), but the beer hall incident was specifically designed to seize power.

54. D

The impressionists played with the shimmering effects of light; for example, on water or falling snow. (A) refers to the surrealists, (B) to the cubists, (C) to the fauves, and (E) to the expressionists.

55. E

The Pretenders were the deposed Catholic James II and his son Charles ("Bonnie Prince Charlie"), who fled to France and continued to claim the English throne. There were a couple of attempts to invade England to retake the throne, but these both failed.

56. C

Because the Church promoted anti-Semitism in the Dreyfus affair, after Dreyfus's innocence had been established, the Church and its meddling were seen negatively. (A), (D), and (E) didn't happen. Dreyfus's rank, (B), was restored but not until 12 years after the original trial.

57. B

Pugachev led a violent serf revolt, which scared Catherine into giving noble landlords more complete control over their serfs. The other choices reflect events in Catherine's life, but they are not related to serfdom.

58. C

The Chapelier Law forbidding unions and strikes stayed in place well into the 19th century. The other choices were also part of the revolution, (A) for a short time, (D) and (E) permanently.

59. D

Keynesian theory was practiced by the governments of the United States and European countries during the Depression and later. Keynes also spoke against the reparations required of Germany after World War I, (A), but no one listened. (B) and (C) are irrelevant. (E) became increasingly true but was not Keynesian theory per se.

60. B

In the days of hand production and cottage industry, England had produced great amounts of woolen cloth, which was sold domestically and abroad. By the 1700s, especially after the invention of the cotton gin, cotton cloth seemed to offer even more possibilities. Before the refinement of the steam engine, textile mills applied waterpower to spinning machines and looms. The advent of the steam engine enhanced production still more. (A), (D), and (E) were revolutionized by the steam engine, and iron production, (C), developed independently and a bit later than textiles.

61. C

The Thermidorean Reaction came with the execution of Robespierre and an end of the Reign of Terror; this was in July 1794. (A) occurred the next year, 1795. Louis XVI was executed in January 1793, (D), and Year One began in 1792, (B).

62. A

In the early 16th century, personal religious choice was as yet unknown. If a ruler (prince or king, depending on the area) became Protestant, all his subjects were considered Protestant as well. If he remained Catholic, then everyone stayed faithful to Rome. The Latin term was *cuius regio eius religio*— "whose the region, his the religion."

63. D

When Anne, the last Stuart monarch, died in 1714 without surviving children, the crown went to royal Protestant relatives in the German state of Hanover. George I and George II were more German than British and were uninterested in English affairs. While answers (B) and (C) are true, they are not the primary reasons for Parliament's ascendancy. William and Mary had to agree to the Bill of Rights and other restrictions on royal authority, (A), but again, (D) is a more relevant answer. Answer (E) was not true until the late 19th century.

64. C

The city of Paris remained so solidly Catholic that Henry IV had to renounce his Protestant faith to enter the city as king. The English Puritans took Calvinism to North America, (A). The Scots became Presbyterian Calvinists, (B). The Dutch established their Reformed Church, (D), and took it with them to their colony in South Africa, (E).

65. A

The Battle of Gallipoli involved the straits from the Mediterranean into the Black Sea. A large number of Australian and New Zealand soldiers joined the British here. The battle dragged on for months until finally, in January 1916, the Allies gave up. The Turks held on to the straits.

66. C

By 1921, there was great famine in Russia and shortages of everything. The NEP returned ownership of production to the people in hopes that the profit motive would increase supplies. It was a temporary measure. Answer (D) had occurred earlier, in 1918. Lenin had no desire to win over the kulaks, (A), or to reconcile with the Mensheviks, (E). By the time the disagreement between Stalin and Trotsky was evident, (B), Lenin was dying.

67. B

Russian citizens took pride in their war effort. They banded together and saw sacrifice as patriotic duty. They emerged with a feeling of national solidarity (which would be quashed by Stalin's new restrictions). Therefore, (A), (C), and (D) are not true. As for (E), traditional Christianity survived to some degree in rural areas, but urban workers found little place for it in their lives.

68. E

Germany was allowed to do all the things listed in (A) through (D) but was forbidden to develop nuclear weapons.

69. E

When Khrushchev came to power in the 1950s, he lightened the whole atmosphere of the USSR, allowing more economic and creative freedom. He made public speeches denouncing the wrongs of Stalin. Brezhnev and Andropov, (A and D), were old-line communists who never criticized Stalin. Only later, in the 1980s and 1990s, did Gorbachev and Yeltsin (B and E) voice negative ideas about Stalin.

70. D

The Schlieffen Plan originally did not mention Alsace and Lorraine, German holdings that might prove vulnerable. The plan was adjusted to provide German backup here, which took troops away from the main attack force. It ignored the British, seeing them as a small threat, (A). The plan was to attack France first, defeat it in about six weeks, and then address Russia, (B). The plan did not discuss a war at sea, (C).

71. B

Luther was upset when a begging friar named Tetzel sold indulgences in the German states to raise money for construction of St. Peter's in Rome. The indulgences were said to lessen a soul's time in purgatory. Luther saw no mention in scripture either of purgatory or indulgences, so he concluded that both ideas were false. The other answers name other abuses, but Luther was less concerned about those.

72. E

Answers (A) and (B) refer to another contemporary group, the Levelers, and (C) refers to the Diggers. Choice (D) refers to the Puritans, who were in charge at the time—the Interregnum. The Quakers preached peace and tolerance.

73. A

Few French women came to Canada, and few Spanish women went to Central and South America, but from the beginning, English women and children came. The Spanish established large plantations and farmed, as did the British, (B). Many Englishmen did come to get rich, (C), and many, like the Puritans, Catholics, and Quakers, came to escape religious persecution, (D). The English had many conflicts with the Native Americans, (E).

74. D

The passing of the throne of Spain to the Bourbons was of less importance to England than the other benefits listed here. Controlling the Mediterranean was so important, (A), that the British still have Gibraltar. Britain would gain wealth from the *asiento*, (B), and getting land at the edge of Canada, (E), would add to the Empire. The English were also pleased to see the southern Netherlands pass to Austria, (C), which was too far away to be a threat.

75. C

Brahe had no telescope, (B), knew little math, (D), and was a generation before Galileo, (E). A year before Brahe's death, his patron king died, and Brahe left his observatory in Denmark, (A), and went to Prague, where he left meticulous records of his 20 years of nocturnal sightings to his young assistant, Johannes Kepler.

76. E

Wesley and his followers left the traditional confines of the Anglican Church and conducted emotional outdoor services that emphasized confession of sin for salvation. Wesley took his message to mining towns, to prisons, and to the British American colonies.

77. B

The Civil Constitution of the Clergy required oaths of loyalty to the Revolution. Some clergy refused, believing that swearing would violate their loyalty to Rome. The Revolutionary government had already seized Church land, (C), and the Church had ceased to collect tithes, (D). Later, some churches were made into "temples of reason," which conducted rather non-Christian rituals, (A).

78. C

All the statements are true except (C). The Assembly did write a constitution, but Frederick William would not accept it because he feared Austria's reaction and it would have lessened his authority under a constitutional monarchy.

79. E

(A) refers to the period of romanticism, which had occurred earlier. (C) and (D) refer to the Age of Reason of the previous century. (B) is a nihilistic idea. Realpolitik followed the failed revolutions of 1848; it expressed a practical, unsentimental approach to life and government.

80. A

Kipling's poem advocated imperialism as a thankless obligation that Europeans owed the rest of the world. He discussed sacrifice rather than rewards, (B), or patriotism, (C). The poem is racist, describing foreign peoples as "half devil and half child."

SECTION II: PART A

SAMPLE DOCUMENT-BASED QUESTION SAMPLE ESSAY

The Falkland Islands War of 1982 between England and Argentina seems in many ways to have been an illogical war caused by nationalistic rivalries. It was a very brief war, beginning in April 1982 and ending less than three months later. Some people condemned the war; some experienced patriotic glory from it; and some saw the conflict as unnecessary. How the war benefited the people of the Falklands is open to question.

The Falkland Islands are located in the far South Atlantic, very close to the tip of Argentina and many thousands of miles from their owner, Great Britain (Map, Doc. 1). Argentina has always felt that the islands, which she calls the Malvinas, are rightfully Argentine. The islands themselves are rather barren and subject to bad weather (Doc. 2). Their residents number fewer than 2,000 people, and they consider themselves British, rather than Argentine.

Several factors probably contributed to Argentina's decision to seize the Falklands in 1982. One was the general trend since World War II of European countries giving up their overseas possessions. In 1982 Argentina had been taken over by a military regime under President Galtieri. The Franks Report, commissioned by the British government after the war, acknowledged that Argentina was bent on recovery of the islands (Doc. 3). An Argentine expatriot, living in the United States after the war, verified this determination (Doc. 7). This speaker claimed that Argentines really had no desire to move to the Falklands. He implied that the military government wanted the glory of conquest. One wonders if this speaker felt shame or bitterness over the event because he is an "expatriot" and calls those who supported the war "fanatics."

Argentina started the war by invading the Falklands in early April 1982. Britain then hastily put together a military task force to go retake the islands. The trip began with excitement. British poet Gavin Ewart described the "troopships and the cheering" (Doc. 4) and compared the mood to that of going off to the Boer War at the turn of the century. A British Lieutenant Tinker wrote to his parents about the "thrill of some real confrontation" (Doc. 5). Of course, this was before he had seen any actual fighting, so his naïve excitement is to be expected. Later, his attitude was more questioning (Doc. 10), when he wrote about the absurdity of sending 28,000 men to fight over a "dreadful piece of land inhabited by 1,800 people" (Doc. 10). No doubt, these words were written after Tinker had experienced battle.

Not everyone approved of the war. An aide to American Secretary of State Alexander Haig called Argentina and Britain "two school boys itching for a fight" (Doc. 6). Of course, as an American, he was speaking as an outside observer who had no interests at stake in the affair. During the war, Pope John Paul II visited England and spoke out against the conflict, condemning it as a means of "settling differences among nations" (Doc. 8). Throughout his papacy, John Paul II condemned war, as one would expect from a Christian leader.

After a few battles, Argentina was obviously getting the worst of the war. The Argentine soldier in Doc. 9 spoke of the ignorance of many ordinary soldiers who "didn't even know what the Malvinas were." His words hint of disillusionment and suffering. An official of the Argentine government claimed later that Argentina had no idea that the British would defend their sovereignty of the islands so fiercely (Doc. 11). These words came after Argentina's defeat, so perhaps they are merely an excuse or "sour grapes."

Argentina surrendered on June 20, 1982, after less than 90 days of fighting. According to British journalists who had accompanied the task force, the British were as anxious to get home as they had been to go to the Falklands in early April (Doc. 12). The journalists claimed that the islanders seemed not to care; they only wished to be left alone. Their report seems believable as a firsthand account. The British soldiers and sailors could go home heroes, and even the Argentines could claim that they had defended their country's honor. One must wonder, however, if the price of nearly 1,000 lives was worth the war. And afterwards, what questions had been solved? The British had upheld their national honor, which benefited the party in power, the Conservatives, but they were left to continue to supply and defend territory very far away and rather unimportant to Great Britain.

SECTION II: PART B

[Note: Answers to the FRQ essay questions may vary somewhat. The following sample essays are intended to suggest what a good essay *might* include. The two most important things in answering an FRQ essay question are to answer all parts of the question and to give ample, accurate examples to illustrate the points you are making.]

SAMPLE ESSAY RESPONSE QUESTION 2

The idea and practices of the Southern Renaissance drifted to Northern Europe by the 1500s. Visual art was very much a part of the expression of both cultures, primarily painting. The Northern Renaissance did not develop sculpture, as did the South. In both areas, the methods of creation were somewhat similar, but there was considerable difference in subject matter.

Artists in both Italy and Northern Europe painted in oils and employed the principles of perspective to create more realistic art. The human form was depicted more three-dimensionally. However, there were differences. Italian artists often painted nude figures, as in Botticelli's *Birth of Venus*, while Flemish masters and others of Northern Europe never painted nudes. Some of the Southern painters, such as Da Vinci and Michelangelo, specialized in frescoes—painting scenes into wet plaster on walls or ceilings. However, in the North there were no frescoes because the colder, damper climate didn't allow proper drying of the wet plaster.

The subjects of Southern Renaissance art were usually either religious figures or characters from mythology. Even though the Italians had become quite secular in their outlook, their art became a great showy, elaborate celebration of religion, as in Michelangelo's *Sistine Chapel*. Another Southern Renaissance painter was Rafael, who made a specialty out of painting Madonnas. The Church became a major patron of the arts, commissioning frescoes and other types of art to decorate churches. This celebration of religious art became even more elaborate during the Counter-Reformation a few years later.

In Northern Europe, there were also a number of great artists who also worked primarily on commission, but usually the church was not a patron. Instead, rulers or wealthy merchants had their portraits done by artists like Holbeins or Hals. Some, like Rembrandt, might do group portraits of members of a guild. The paintings also reflected the lifestyle of the North by showing the comfortable interiors of homes. The new interest in trade and exploration is evident in details such as globes or rich tapestry. Vermeer's *The Geographer* stands thoughtfully, holding a compass, which was evidence of new technology.

Another Northern painter who took a different approach was Breughel, who created busy scenes of peasant life. Instead of close-up portraits of individual figures, Breughel painted village scenes teeming with various people. Still another Northern painter who chose different subject matter was Bosch, whose work featured distortions and ironic twists to his human figures.

Ironically, even though Northern art tended not to focus on religious topics, the people of Northern Europe remained personally more religious. For some, religion became a more personal, private affair, an attitude that led to the Reformation, while the showy demonstration of religion in the South seemed the opposite of the very secular attitudes of the culture.

SAMPLE ESSAY RESPONSE QUESTION 3

The Physiocrats in 18th-century France were the first people to be called "economists" (meant as an insult at the time). They developed ideas about manufacturing and trade that differed sharply from the mercantilist policies of the past. At about the same time, a Scottish professor, Adam Smith, published *Wealth of Nations*, which advocated a similar philosophy. Both Smith and the Physiocrats spoke out for free trade, but they differed in their ideas about the role of government and how a nation's wealth should be counted.

The Physiocrats were among the most influential men of France at the time. They believed that the nation would become more prosperous if all tariffs, price controls, and guild regulations were eliminated. (French trade still was hampered by internal, as well as external, tariffs.) The term that came to be applied to such an economic policy was laissez-faire—or "let it go as it will." To achieve these needed changes, the Physiocrats said strong government was necessary to override all the current regulations and barriers to free trade. They also wished for a government that would provide incentives and other support for new manufacturing.

Adam Smith also strongly argued for free trade, but he differed with the Physiocrats on the role that government should play. Smith believed that government should be limited to providing an atmosphere where business might flourish. This meant an environment of security and justice. Beyond that, Smith felt that government should stay totally out of manufacturing and trade.

Smith believed that the impetus behind all business activity should be self-interest. He said that left alone, markets would regulate themselves. When a commodity was in short supply, its price would rise, prompting more people to make that good or provide that service. As it became more plentiful, the price would fall, and some people would move in another direction. Smith described a pin factory as an example. In it, no worker produced a whole pin; each completed only one part of the process. The result was that more pins were produced and at a lower cost than when each worker made complete pins. Smith applied his example to nations, insisting that each should produce what it could do best, which would lead to wholesome trade, better quality, and cheaper prices.

Smith claimed that empire and colonies were not necessary for a healthy economy. To him, a nation's wealth was measured in the labor of its people. The Physiocrats agreed that wealth was not counted in gold or silver, as it was in mercantilist practice. The Physiocrats counted a nation's wealth in its soil and agricultural production.

Both outlooks moved permanently away from the mercantilism of earlier times. However, very seldom have nations been willing or able to abolish tariffs and risk the totally free trade advocated by the Physiocrats and Adam Smith.

SAMPLE ESSAY RESPONSE QUESTION 4

Louis Napoleon Bonaparte was elected president of France in 1848, winning primarily because of "name recognition." Also, prior to the election, Louis Napoleon had written a pamphlet called "Elimination of Poverty." The French people had high hopes that their new leader would help France's depressed economy. Louis Napoleon ruled for just over 20 years. He was successful in social and economic issues; his failures were political, both domestically and internationally.

Louis Napoleon was first elected to a four-year term, but he soon got this extended to 10 years, and after that, he declared himself Emperor Napoleon III. There was little democracy now in France. The National Assembly was left with very little power. Louis Napoleon insisted that economic and social improvements mattered more than the forms of government. He let the Church regain control of French schools.

Internationally, Napoleon III supported the construction of the Suez Canal by de Lesseps, but in other foreign endeavors, he was less impressive. Almost immediately after coming to power, Louis Napoleon sent troops to Rome to defend the pope against insurrections there. These troops stayed during his entire time in office as a barrier to total Italian unification. Briefly, he lent aid to Cavour of Piedmont-Sardinia in his efforts to drive the Austrians out of northern Italy. To get Louis Napoleon's help, Cavour had offered Nice and Savoy. Napoleon grabbed the ceded territory, but after a couple of successful battles against Austria, he made a secret separate peace and withdrew. He had been pressured by the Church and by Prussia to get out.

The worst site of Louis Napoleon's failure was Mexico. During the American Civil War, France installed an Austrian archduke as ruler. When the American Civil War ended, the United States demanded France's removal from Mexico. The archduke Maximilian was executed. The affair discredited France and Louis Napoleon.

At home, however, Louis Napoleon had many successes. He renovated and modernized Paris by improving the water supply and sewer system. The old narrow, winding streets were replaced with wide boulevards, and the city abounded in parks, trees, and public buildings. Louis Napoleon established banks and built railroads. France's old wooden sailing ships were replaced with modern steamships. The government built hospitals and asylums and gave medicine to the poor. Even labor unions and strikes finally became legal again. All of the construction projects created jobs and helped the economy.

The French army wasn't up to fighting Prussia in 1870–71, and Prussia easily won. The Prussians captured Louis Napoleon as he tried to flee the country. But despite his military and foreign failures, Louis Napoleon had modernized France and the city of Paris and improved the economy. Banking, transportation, and medicine were effectively modernized. Overall, it can be said that Louis Napoleon benefited France economically and socially.

SECTION II: PART C

SAMPLE ESSAY RESPONSE QUESTION 5

For the most part, World War I was a land war, fought primarily in the trenches of France. There was also fighting in northern Italy and on the "Eastern Front" in Russia until early 1918. But in addition to the land war, there were several events at sea, including submarine warfare and the use of blockade, all with limited effectiveness.

Once both the Allies and the Germans were bogged down in the stalemate of trench warfare in France, the Central Powers concentrated on Russia. The hope was to force Russia to surrender or to withdraw from the war. Russian losses were tremendous, but she kept fighting. The British wished to get more aid to Russia, but transportation was a problem. The Ottoman Empire entered the war on the side of Germany and Austria-Hungary. The Turks then closed the straits from the Mediterranean into the Black Sea, which shut down this route for the Allies to Russia. Another British concern was for the Suez Canal and the fear that the Turks might try to seize it and cut off Britain from her colonies in East Africa and Asia. In the spring of 1915, the British navy and a force of Australians and new Zealanders attacked Gallipoli at the entrance to the straits. The battle dragged on until January 1916, with heavy losses to both sides, but the Allies were unable to dislodge the Turks from Gallipoli.

For at least 20 years before the war, Germany had built up her naval power, resulting in a British perception of competition and threat. The two countries even established a ratio of German ships to British ones that both could accept. When the war came, Germany made use of a frightening new naval weapon, the submarine. Its invisibility made it shocking. The Germans justified submarines by claiming that the British were violating international law.

Britain was using her navy to blockade the coast of Northern Europe, ignoring the concepts of "contraband" and "noncontraband." International agreements prior to the war had determined that no nation should stop the flow of food, medicine, and nonmilitary supplies to countries at war. The United States and other nations protested the blockade until the United States joined the Allies. After that, the idea was ignored.

The Germans used their submarines in 1915 to sink a British vessel, the Lusitania, killing a number of Americans. U.S. President Wilson protested (because the United States was neutral in 1915). This scene was repeated with the sinking of the Sussex in 1916, again with loss of American lives, but Germany did step down her submarine warfare until 1917. Its resumption was a factor in the U.S. entrance into the war.

The one great sea battle of the war was called the Battle of Jutland (Denmark) in 1916. The Germans had tried to break the blockade by luring away smaller groups of British ships. An almost accidental encounter here led to a two-day battle, in which the British lost more men and ships than the Germans but the blockade held.

Overall, the war at sea proved little because neither side gained decisively. When the United States entered the war in 1917, its navy began heavily escorting convoys of men and supplies to Europe, and these were able to get through and help finally bring the conflict to a close the next year.

SAMPLE ESSAY RESPONSE QUESTION 6

The second half of the 19th century was a time of far-reaching scientific advancement, with such inventions as the electric light bulb, internal combustion engine, and the typewriter revolutionizing daily life for many. The work of still other scientists, however, was more troubling because it called into question traditional ideas about humankind, the universe, and religion. The writings of Darwin, Freud, and Pavlov shifted people's opinions about themselves and their world, and the "new" physicists, such as Einstein and others, seemed to discredit long-accepted scientific concepts.

Charles Darwin's theory of evolution, natural selection, and "survival of the fittest" implied that there were no constants in the universe and that everything was in an ongoing state of change. Nature itself, which the first half of the 19th century had viewed as benign and in relationship to humanity, now seemed indifferent or even hostile. Changes occurred by chance. Where, then, were standards of morality or truths about religion?

The Austrian Sigmund Freud seemed to prove that human beings really had little control over their actions. Instead, a lot of human behavior was dictated by the unconscious, instinctive part of the brain. People were driven by selfish desires for power and sex. Where, then, was there room for charity and altruism?

The Russian scientist Ivan Pavlov did experiments with dogs, food, and a bell. He rang the bell each time the dogs were fed. Eventually, he only rang the bell, and the dogs salivated, or reacted the same as they had at the sight of food. Pavlov proved that reactions can be conditioned in animals and implied that the same happens to humans. The overall result of the work of Darwin, Freud, and Pavlov was a sense that human beings seemed to have very little control over their lives and their world.

At about the same time, Pierre and Marie Curie and Lord Rutherford studied radioactivity. Max Planck proved that atoms emitted and absorbed energy and that energy and matter were not different from each other. Albert Einstein then produced his famous equation to show the relationship of energy, space, and time. He said that space and time were "relative" to human perception, not absolute factors, as Newton had said. Thus, in the subatomic world, Newton's laws seemed not to apply. It seemed impossible for the general public, and even for some scientists, to grasp the implications of such new theories. Human conception of the universe seemed to be permanently altered. Gone were the old comforts and certainties of a rational world. There seemed to be more questions than answers.

SAMPLE ESSAY RESPONSE QUESTION 7

The 21st century has not begun with great optimism. Everywhere, it seems that humanity faces insurmountable challenges. Many of these problems have grown out of events, trends, and practices of the 20th century. Three of the most troubling issues are world poverty, religious extremism, and the ongoing threat of nuclear weapons. No one of these issues exists in isolation; all are intertwined with each other and with numerous other disturbing questions.

One of the biggest global problems is poverty. While wealthy nations become richer or, at least, hold on to their high standards of living, the poor of the earth seem only to become poorer. Nowhere is this more manifest than in Africa. When colonialism ended in the 1950s and 1960s, European nations left most African countries poorly equipped to govern themselves or to maintain a thriving economy. Although many parts of Africa are rich in natural resources, more often than not, these lie undeveloped, or they have been abused in destructive ways that have enriched a few and ignored or impoverished the majority.

The desert climate on Northern Africa has shifted southward, bringing drought and starvation in its wake. Unemployment is rampant. Some countries, such as parts of Sudan, have fallen into anarchy as various warlords contend for dominance. Government instability and poverty are coupled with the worst outbreak of AIDS on the planet. Even nations that possess some stability of government are over-whelmed by the consequences of this debilitating and deadly disease.

Another seemingly unsolvable threat is religious extremism in the Middle East. This trend began in the late 1970s when the U.S.-backed Shah of Iran was driven out and replaced with the Muslim extremist, the Ayatollah Khomeini. For the next 10 years, extreme fundamentalist Islamic law dominated Iran. Women became non-citizens, and everything Western was condemned. After the Ayatollah's death in 1989, Iran seemed to move in a more moderate direction until its government came under new and irrational extremist leadership again in 2005. Meanwhile, Islamic fundamentalism spread to other parts of the Middle East, especially in the Taliban takeover of Afghanistan when the Russians left in the late 1980s. Terms like jihad (holy war) and suicide bomber became familiar to the West. Much Islamic hatred is focused on Israel, the Jewish state created out of Arab land in 1948.

All the problems of Islamic extremism are further complicated by the fact that the Middle East controls much of the world's oil reserves. Europe and the United States are the major buyers and, thus, have great financial interest in the stabil-ity of the region. The stateless radical groups such as al-Qaeda, dedicated to the perpetuation of violence, threaten not only the security of the Middle East but that of the West as well.

When the United States used two atomic bombs at the end of World War II, the nuclear arms race began. Within a few years, France and the USSR had nuclear capability. As the 20th century progressed, a number of less likely nations also acquired nuclear weapons, including India and Pakistan, which are hostile to each other, and China. When the Soviet Union collapsed, a big question was what would happen to its nuclear arsenal. Would Russia, which needed cash, sell weapons to the highest bidder? Since the new millennium began, the possibility of nuclear threat has loomed in such renegade governments as Saddam Hussein's Iraq, North Korea, and the new extremist regime in Iran.

There seem to be no answers at present to any of the above questions. Perhaps there might be hope if, somehow, economic prosperity could be developed in these troubled regions of the world. The end of the 20th century witnessed such a change in Ireland, produced in part by a successful economy. But how this could happen elsewhere is still very much in question.

**PRACTICE TEST 2 ANSWER GRID
ON THE NEXT PAGE.**

Practice Test 2 Answer Grid

1. Ⓐ Ⓑ Ⓒ Ⓓ Ⓔ   15. Ⓐ Ⓑ Ⓒ Ⓓ Ⓔ   29. Ⓐ Ⓑ Ⓒ Ⓓ Ⓔ
2. Ⓐ Ⓑ Ⓒ Ⓓ Ⓔ   16. Ⓐ Ⓑ Ⓒ Ⓓ Ⓔ   30. Ⓐ Ⓑ Ⓒ Ⓓ Ⓔ
3. Ⓐ Ⓑ Ⓒ Ⓓ Ⓔ   17. Ⓐ Ⓑ Ⓒ Ⓓ Ⓔ   31. Ⓐ Ⓑ Ⓒ Ⓓ Ⓔ
4. Ⓐ Ⓑ Ⓒ Ⓓ Ⓔ   18. Ⓐ Ⓑ Ⓒ Ⓓ Ⓔ   32. Ⓐ Ⓑ Ⓒ Ⓓ Ⓔ
5. Ⓐ Ⓑ Ⓒ Ⓓ Ⓔ   19. Ⓐ Ⓑ Ⓒ Ⓓ Ⓔ   33. Ⓐ Ⓑ Ⓒ Ⓓ Ⓔ
6. Ⓐ Ⓑ Ⓒ Ⓓ Ⓔ   20. Ⓐ Ⓑ Ⓒ Ⓓ Ⓔ   34. Ⓐ Ⓑ Ⓒ Ⓓ Ⓔ
7. Ⓐ Ⓑ Ⓒ Ⓓ Ⓔ   21. Ⓐ Ⓑ Ⓒ Ⓓ Ⓔ   35. Ⓐ Ⓑ Ⓒ Ⓓ Ⓔ
8. Ⓐ Ⓑ Ⓒ Ⓓ Ⓔ   22. Ⓐ Ⓑ Ⓒ Ⓓ Ⓔ   36. Ⓐ Ⓑ Ⓒ Ⓓ Ⓔ
9. Ⓐ Ⓑ Ⓒ Ⓓ Ⓔ   23. Ⓐ Ⓑ Ⓒ Ⓓ Ⓔ   37. Ⓐ Ⓑ Ⓒ Ⓓ Ⓔ
10. Ⓐ Ⓑ Ⓒ Ⓓ Ⓔ   24. Ⓐ Ⓑ Ⓒ Ⓓ Ⓔ   38. Ⓐ Ⓑ Ⓒ Ⓓ Ⓔ
11. Ⓐ Ⓑ Ⓒ Ⓓ Ⓔ   25. Ⓐ Ⓑ Ⓒ Ⓓ Ⓔ   39. Ⓐ Ⓑ Ⓒ Ⓓ Ⓔ
12. Ⓐ Ⓑ Ⓒ Ⓓ Ⓔ   26. Ⓐ Ⓑ Ⓒ Ⓓ Ⓔ   40. Ⓐ Ⓑ Ⓒ Ⓓ Ⓔ
13. Ⓐ Ⓑ Ⓒ Ⓓ Ⓔ   27. Ⓐ Ⓑ Ⓒ Ⓓ Ⓔ   41. Ⓐ Ⓑ Ⓒ Ⓓ Ⓔ
14. Ⓐ Ⓑ Ⓒ Ⓓ Ⓔ   28. Ⓐ Ⓑ Ⓒ Ⓓ Ⓔ   42. Ⓐ Ⓑ Ⓒ Ⓓ Ⓔ

43. Ⓐ Ⓑ Ⓒ Ⓓ Ⓔ   56. Ⓐ Ⓑ Ⓒ Ⓓ Ⓔ   69. Ⓐ Ⓑ Ⓒ Ⓓ Ⓔ
44. Ⓐ Ⓑ Ⓒ Ⓓ Ⓔ   57. Ⓐ Ⓑ Ⓒ Ⓓ Ⓔ   70. Ⓐ Ⓑ Ⓒ Ⓓ Ⓔ
45. Ⓐ Ⓑ Ⓒ Ⓓ Ⓔ   58. Ⓐ Ⓑ Ⓒ Ⓓ Ⓔ   71. Ⓐ Ⓑ Ⓒ Ⓓ Ⓔ
46. Ⓐ Ⓑ Ⓒ Ⓓ Ⓔ   59. Ⓐ Ⓑ Ⓒ Ⓓ Ⓔ   72. Ⓐ Ⓑ Ⓒ Ⓓ Ⓔ
47. Ⓐ Ⓑ Ⓒ Ⓓ Ⓔ   60. Ⓐ Ⓑ Ⓒ Ⓓ Ⓔ   73. Ⓐ Ⓑ Ⓒ Ⓓ Ⓔ
48. Ⓐ Ⓑ Ⓒ Ⓓ Ⓔ   61. Ⓐ Ⓑ Ⓒ Ⓓ Ⓔ   74. Ⓐ Ⓑ Ⓒ Ⓓ Ⓔ
49. Ⓐ Ⓑ Ⓒ Ⓓ Ⓔ   62. Ⓐ Ⓑ Ⓒ Ⓓ Ⓔ   75. Ⓐ Ⓑ Ⓒ Ⓓ Ⓔ
50. Ⓐ Ⓑ Ⓒ Ⓓ Ⓔ   63. Ⓐ Ⓑ Ⓒ Ⓓ Ⓔ   76. Ⓐ Ⓑ Ⓒ Ⓓ Ⓔ
51. Ⓐ Ⓑ Ⓒ Ⓓ Ⓔ   64. Ⓐ Ⓑ Ⓒ Ⓓ Ⓔ   77. Ⓐ Ⓑ Ⓒ Ⓓ Ⓔ
52. Ⓐ Ⓑ Ⓒ Ⓓ Ⓔ   65. Ⓐ Ⓑ Ⓒ Ⓓ Ⓔ   78. Ⓐ Ⓑ Ⓒ Ⓓ Ⓔ
53. Ⓐ Ⓑ Ⓒ Ⓓ Ⓔ   66. Ⓐ Ⓑ Ⓒ Ⓓ Ⓔ   79. Ⓐ Ⓑ Ⓒ Ⓓ Ⓔ
54. Ⓐ Ⓑ Ⓒ Ⓓ Ⓔ   67. Ⓐ Ⓑ Ⓒ Ⓓ Ⓔ   80. Ⓐ Ⓑ Ⓒ Ⓓ Ⓔ
55. Ⓐ Ⓑ Ⓒ Ⓓ Ⓔ   68. Ⓐ Ⓑ Ⓒ Ⓓ Ⓔ

PRACTICE TEST 2

SECTION I: MULTIPLE-CHOICE QUESTIONS
Time—55 Minutes
80 Questions

> **Directions:** Each of the questions or incomplete statements below is followed by five suggested answers or completions. Select the one that is best in each case and then fill in the corresponding oval on the answer sheet.

1. In the 1600s, the Dutch Republic differed from its neighbors in all the following ways EXCEPT that it had

   (A) no king.
   (B) a high standard of living.
   (C) religious toleration.
   (D) a thriving textile industry.
   (E) reliable banking.

2. The 18th-century deists

   (A) were atheists.
   (B) were part of the Great Awakening, an evangelical Christian movement.
   (C) believed in a rational world that operated according to natural law.
   (D) were reformers in the Church of England.
   (E) were similar to the pietists of Germany.

3. The July Revolution of 1830 in France

   (A) was a response to Charles X's July Ordinances.
   (B) produced Delacroix's *Liberty Leading the People*.
   (C) was led by republican forces—workers, students, and intelligentsia.
   (D) caused Charles X to abdicate.
   (E) did all of the above.

4. Much of the agenda of the 19th-century Chartist movement in England involved voting reform. The Chartists wanted

   (A) numerically balanced electoral districts.
   (B) female suffrage.
   (C) elimination of the House of Lords.
   (D) reduction of the voting age to 18.
   (E) all of the above.

5. Which of the following Italian Renaissance writers is INCORRECTLY paired with his work?

   (A) Machiavelli—*The Prince*
   (B) Castiglioni—*The Book of the Courtier*
   (C) Petrarch—sonnets
   (D) Dante—*Divine Comedy*
   (E) Boccaccio—*Praise of Folly*

6. Which of the following is LEAST likely to be government controlled to some degree in a "welfare state"?

   (A) Public utilities
   (B) Small businesses
   (C) Medicine
   (D) Education
   (E) Old-age pensions

GO ON TO THE NEXT PAGE ⇒

7. Napoleon's forces and reforms were generally welcomed in both the German states and northern Italy, primarily because

(A) they brought more unity and a better organized government than those regions previously had.

(B) the French imposed the metric system of standard weights and measures.

(C) new native people had greater chances to rise politically.

(D) the Church lost some of its influence and control.

(E) the French brought more modern agricultural practices, which meant better and more plentiful food.

8. In the 19th century, France exported more money to Russia than did Great Britain or Germany mainly because

(A) it was more profitable to invest in Russia.

(B) Russia produced natural furs for France's luxury trade.

(C) France wanted a friendly power on the other side of Germany.

(D) Russia had a booming mining industry.

(E) of all the above.

9. What ultimately happened to the Dutch colony of New Amsterdam in the New World?

(A) It was abandoned because it was unprofitable.

(B) The British seized it in the mid-17th century.

(C) It was incorporated into the Belgian Ostend Company after 1830.

(D) It was destroyed in the Indian wars.

(E) Its residents voted to join the English settlers nearby.

10. According to John Locke, the purpose of government is to protect

(A) life, liberty, and the pursuit of happiness.

(B) freedom of thought and religion.

(C) economic security.

(D) life, liberty, and property.

(E) an uncensored press.

11. Leonardo da Vinci was not considered a forerunner of the scientific revolution because his

(A) ideas and drawings were too far-fetched to be creditable.

(B) work went unpublished and unknown until the 20th century.

(C) life predates the early scientists.

(D) art interested the public more than his science.

(E) work and life included all of the above.

12. The Spartacists in Germany

(A) tried to create a communist revolution there.

(B) were prominent in 1919.

(C) tried to overthrow the Weimar Republic.

(D) were led by Rosa Luxemberg and Karl Liebneckt.

(E) were all of the above.

13. In mid-20th-century France, the colony whose liberation stirred the most controversy was

(A) Morocco.

(B) French Indochina.

(C) Algeria.

(D) Tunisia.

(E) Senegal.

GO ON TO THE NEXT PAGE

14. Bismarck's main purpose instigating the Franco-Prussian War was

   (A) a desire to defeat Louis Napoleon.
   (B) a plan for a European empire.
   (C) scaring the remaining south German states into unity with Germany.
   (D) creating patriotism and unity at home.
   (E) proving Prussia to be mightier than Austria.

15. The worldwide recession of the 1970s was made worse by

   (A) the fear of nuclear war.
   (B) the threat of communism.
   (C) Islamic extremism.
   (D) British rock music.
   (E) sharply rising oil prices.

16. Generally, the only major changes enacted by the Council of Trent related to

   (A) the language of the liturgy.
   (B) closer supervision and higher standards for clergy.
   (C) the closing of convents.
   (D) indulgences and purgatory.
   (E) financial accountability.

17. During World I, British Col. T. E. Lawrence worked against the Central Powers by

   (A) helping Arabs revolt against the Ottoman Empire.
   (B) uncovering the plot of the Zimmerman telegram.
   (C) encouraging Jewish migration to the Middle East.
   (D) urging the Irish to ignore German scheming.
   (E) negotiation with the United States to enter the war.

18. The early Industrial Revolution was detrimental to skilled craftsmen primarily because

   (A) wages went down drastically.
   (B) they were forced to move to the big cities.
   (C) the guilds disappeared.
   (D) the new jobs were for unskilled labor.
   (E) of all of the above.

19. Around 1700, the most valuable agricultural product coming to Europe from the New World was

   (A) cotton.
   (B) sugar.
   (C) tobacco.
   (D) tea.
   (E) cocoa.

20. The Saint Bartholomew's Day Massacre was part of which larger conflict?

   (A) French religious wars of the late 16th century
   (B) Thirty Years War
   (C) English Civil War
   (D) War of Spanish Succession
   (E) War of Jenkins' Ear

21. The greatest advantage of maintaining the gold standard (1870–1914) was that it

   (A) gave nations who possessed gold an edge over those who did not.
   (B) provided an advantage for persons and nations who were in debt.
   (C) kept prices high.
   (D) encouraged explorers to find new gold.
   (E) maintained a stable rate of currency exchange among nations.

GO ON TO THE NEXT PAGE

22. H. M. Stanley originally went to Africa to

   (A) claim land for Leopold of Belgium.
   (B) look for gold.
   (C) search for David Livingstone.
   (D) explore the Congo River.
   (E) search for Victoria Falls.

23. In his writing, Machiavelli most admired the

   (A) Medici of Florence.
   (B) leaders of the Church.
   (C) Italian merchant class.
   (D) new monarchies of the north.
   (E) Holy Roman Empire.

24. The *cahiers*, or grievance lists, prepared prior to the meeting of the French Estates General in 1789 showed that the people wanted

   (A) freedom of religion and the press.
   (B) equality before the law.
   (C) equal taxation.
   (D) equal opportunity for positions in government.
   (E) all of the above.

25. In 1849, the new Austrian emperor, Franz Joseph, restored order in Hungary by

   (A) employing the Croatian leader Jellachich.
   (B) following the advice of Metternich.
   (C) discrediting Louis Kossuth, the Magyar leader.
   (D) giving in to Hungarian demands.
   (E) getting military aid from Nicholas II of Russia.

26. The work of French artist Georges Seurat differed from that of the mainline impressionists in that Seurat

   (A) used stronger lines and brighter colors.
   (B) concentrated on painting trains and railroad stations.
   (C) did more abstract work.
   (D) used tiny dots of primary colors.
   (E) did all of the above.

27. The Irish Republican Army (the IRA) had as its primary objective

   (A) Irish independence.
   (B) separation of Ireland from the Commonwealth of Nations.
   (C) inclusion of Northern Ireland in the Irish state.
   (D) an end of the Corn Laws.
   (E) recognition of the Catholic Church in Ireland.

28. In the 16th and 17th centuries, Prussia expanded its territory mainly through

   (A) marriage and inheritance.
   (B) war against its neighbors.
   (C) the building of a huge military force as threat.
   (D) papal decrees.
   (E) all of the above.

29. In the early modern Italian city-states, the term *condotierri* referred to

   (A) the wealthy merchant class.
   (B) hired mercenary soldiers.
   (C) powerful and unscrupulous popes.
   (D) cloth guilds.
   (E) ruling oligarchies of some city-states.

GO ON TO THE NEXT PAGE

30. In 1618, the Protestants of Bohemia openly defied the Holy Roman Emperor by

    (A) refusing to pay taxes.

    (B) murdering the emperor's emissaries.

    (C) attacking its Catholic neighbor Bavaria.

    (D) throwing the emperor's emissaries out a window.

    (E) making a deal with Richelieu of France for support of their cause.

31. Toussaint L'Ouverture led a second revolt in Haiti against France after Napoleon

    (A) decided to sell Louisiana to the United States.

    (B) reinstated slavery in French colonies.

    (C) moved into Spain and began the Peninsular War.

    (D) eliminated colonial representation in the National Assembly.

    (E) took away universal male suffrage.

32. The main problem that Denis Diderot encountered in the compilation of his *Encyclopedia* was

    (A) the huge investment that the multivolume work required.

    (B) getting a variety of authors to contribute.

    (C) dealing with various levels of censorship.

    (D) finding purchasers.

    (E) printing illustrations.

33. In his political commentary, the French philosopher Montesquieu most admired England for its

    (A) democratic institutions.

    (B) freedom of the press.

    (C) division of power.

    (D) power of the monarchy.

    (E) freedom of religion.

GO ON TO THE NEXT PAGE

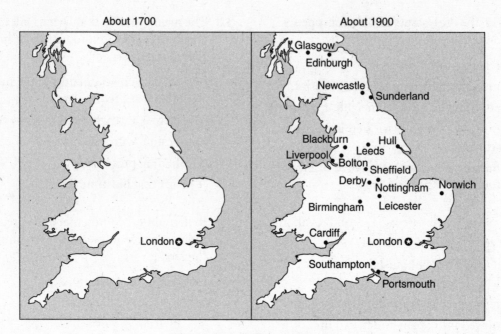

About 1700

About 1900

British Cities of Over 100,000

34. As indicated on the map above of England, Scotland, and Wales, the main reason for the change between 1700 and 1900 was

   (A) the agricultural revolution.

   (B) a decline in disease.

   (C) better diets and more food.

   (D) a higher birth rate.

   (E) the Industrial Revolution.

35. The Paris Commune of 1871 was

   (A) seen by Karl Marx as the beginning of class conflict.

   (B) in existence for a few months.

   (C) a revival of social revolution in France.

   (D) punished with arrests, imprisonments, and executions.

   (E) all of the above.

36. Theodor Herzl was a Jewish journalist who

   (A) defended Alfred Dreyfus when he was accused of treason.

   (B) fought the idea of ghettos in Russia and Eastern Europe.

   (C) wrote a book praising Jewish cultural achievements.

   (D) first pushed for the creation of a Jewish state in Palestine.

   (E) was the first president of Israel.

37. Prior to Matthew Perry's visit in 1853, Japan's main source of knowledge of the West since the early 1600s had been through

   (A) occasional Christian missionaries who were admitted.

   (B) the Dutch, who continued to engage in limited trade.

   (C) English books that were imported.

   (D) Japanese citizens who traveled abroad.

   (E) photographs of Western cities.

GO ON TO THE NEXT PAGE

38. The Fashoda Crisis in Africa resulted from tension between the

    (A) Dutch and British in South Africa.
    (B) French in Morocco and the British in Egypt.
    (C) French and British in the Sudan.
    (D) Belgians and Germans in West Africa.
    (E) Italians and native peoples in Ethiopia.

39. As a result of the Russian Revolution of 1905,

    (A) Nicholas II instituted the Duma.
    (B) the Bolsheviks gained political power.
    (C) a number of political prisoners were released.
    (D) the kulaks received more land.
    (E) the Soviets gained strength.

40. Twentieth-century writers, such as the Irish novelist James Joyce, established a style of interior monologues called

    (A) soliloquies.
    (B) asides.
    (C) stream of consciousness.
    (D) realism.
    (E) naturalism.

41. In 1938, Czechoslovakia differed from its neighbors in Eastern Europe in that it had

    (A) become communist.
    (B) a fascist dictator.
    (C) a line of defense on all sides its borders.
    (D) retained democracy.
    (E) an ethnically mixed population.

42. The major difference between England's response to the "South Sea Bubble" and France's reaction to the "Mississippi Bubble" (both in the early 1700s) was that

    (A) men in high office in France were discredited, but that did not happen in England.
    (B) France repudiated much of its debt; England did not.
    (C) the French government repaid citizens their losses; England's government did not.
    (D) the French government could more readily borrow money from its citizens.
    (E) there were not major differences; public outcry and financial loss were very similar.

43. Political problems in Poland around 1750 included all of the following EXCEPT

    (A) the nobility paid no taxes.
    (B) the king was elected.
    (C) the national diet could be shut down by the veto of any member.
    (D) the king was often a foreigner.
    (E) the king was a powerful dictator.

44. Many of the French Protestants—the Huguenots—fled to North America, Prussia, and other places after

    (A) the Council of Trent in the 16th century.
    (B) Cardinal Richelieu took away their military privileges.
    (C) Louis XIV revoked the Edict of Nantes in 1685.
    (D) many were guillotined in the French Revolution.
    (E) Napoleon's Concordat with the pope.

GO ON TO THE NEXT PAGE ⇨

45. During the 15th-century reign of Ferdinand and Isabella of Spain, the most unifying factor of the country was the

    (A) pride Spain felt in overseas exploration, such as that of Columbus.
    (B) Catholic Church.
    (C) "price revolution" that brought wealth to Spain.
    (D) Cortes, a national parliament.
    (E) unity among the Spanish nobility.

46. Probably, the biggest factor in the spread of Luther's ideas was

    (A) the fact that he wrote in German rather than in Latin.
    (B) his marriage to a former nun.
    (C) the support he got from the German nobility.
    (D) the printing press.
    (E) his great faith.

47. All the following are true of the Jesuits (Society of Jesus) EXCEPT that they

    (A) required strict and arduous training for members.
    (B) became international missionaries to distant parts of the globe.
    (C) were expelled from some countries in the 1800s.
    (D) engaged in cloistered prayer and meditation.
    (E) taught in schools and influenced society and politics.

48. After the War of Spanish Succession, which ended in 1713, Spain was ruled by the

    (A) Valois.
    (B) Habsburgs.
    (C) Bourbons.
    (D) Hohenzollerns.
    (E) Romanovs.

49. Rousseau can be considered an early romantic thinker primarily because he

    (A) saw the world as a machine.
    (B) admired the peasant and, even more, the uncivilized.
    (C) advocated reason over emotion.
    (D) directly encouraged revolutionary thought.
    (E) had faith in an absolute monarch.

50. During the 1960s–1980s, a major source of income for Great Britain was

    (A) the rock music industry.
    (B) textile manufacturing.
    (C) automobile production.
    (D) sugar refining.
    (E) tourism.

51. The German romantic philosophers and the populists of 19th-century Russia were similar in their respect for the

    (A) nobility.
    (B) middle class.
    (C) clergy.
    (D) common people.
    (E) landed aristocracy.

GO ON TO THE NEXT PAGE

52. The Stalinist purge trials of the 1930s seemed to be designed to

    (A) eliminate any opposition from the old Bolsheviks.
    (B) show the West the extent of Stalin's power.
    (C) discourage opposition to World War II.
    (D) consolidate opposition to Trotsky.
    (E) maintain strict Leninist philosophy.

53. The Soviet satellite in post–World War II Eastern Europe that seemed to exhibit the most independence was

    (A) Czechoslovakia.
    (B) Romania.
    (C) Yugoslavia.
    (D) Hungary.
    (E) Poland.

54. A major change that came to the United Nations Security Council in the 1970s was the

    (A) rescission of veto power.
    (B) expansion of the number of permanent members.
    (C) replacement of Nationalist China with Communist China.
    (D) domination of African nations.
    (E) domination of communist nations.

55. Following World War II, the Western European nation(s) that had a large Communist Party were

    (A) Spain and France.
    (B) Spain and Italy.
    (C) France and Italy.
    (D) Germany.
    (E) Italy and the Netherlands.

56. Contributing to the retirement of Boris Yeltsin in Russia was/were

    (A) Yeltsin's poor health.
    (B) the revolt in Chechnya.
    (C) Yeltsin's alleged alcoholism.
    (D) Russian financial problems.
    (E) all of the above.

57. What nationality were many of the early explorers who claimed parts of North America for their sponsoring nations—Columbus, Verrazzano, the Cabots, for instance?

    (A) Spanish.
    (B) French.
    (C) English.
    (D) Dutch.
    (E) Italian.

58. The English Parliament disagreed with all the following policies of Charles I EXCEPT his

    (A) claim of divine right.
    (B) high church religious policy.
    (C) demands for money.
    (D) authorization of translation of scripture.
    (E) refusal to call Parliament.

59. The primary advantage of growing the potato introduced from North America was that it

    (A) could be stored for many months.
    (B) could serve as food for both humans and animals.
    (C) would grow in relatively poor soil.
    (D) was inexpensive to produce.
    (E) was easy to cultivate.

GO ON TO THE NEXT PAGE ⟶

60. The biggest contribution of Johannes Kepler was

    (A) the heliocentric theory of the universe.
    (B) mathematical formulas for the elliptical orbits of planets.
    (C) the theory of gravity.
    (D) his data from 20 years of astronomical observations.
    (E) the invention of the telescope.

61. Lady Jane Grey was

    (A) a wife of Henry VIII.
    (B) the mistress of an 18th-century French salon.
    (C) a young woman whose relatives tried to seize the English throne in her name, following the death of Edward VI.
    (D) a Shakespearean actress.
    (E) a leader of the Gaelic movement in 20th-century Ireland.

62. Voltaire's greatest concern was

    (A) that governmental power be shared with the nobility.
    (B) for universal male suffrage.
    (C) for freedom of religion and press.
    (D) the rights of the poor.
    (E) the advancement of the *Encyclopedia*.

63. Before the arrival of the Europeans, Native Americans lacked all the following EXCEPT

    (A) horses.
    (B) a calendar.
    (C) metal implements.
    (D) written language.
    (E) smallpox.

64. The early Protestants stressed education, even for girls, primarily so that females could

    (A) read and study scripture individually.
    (B) be better wives and mothers.
    (C) operate shops and keep accounts.
    (D) serve in church leadership roles.
    (E) teach religion.

65. Popular culture is more difficult to trace than elite culture primarily because popular culture

    (A) involved fewer people.
    (B) had few religious connections.
    (C) tended to be destroyed by wars.
    (D) left fewer written records.
    (E) is less appealing to modern historians.

66. A major cultural change in the lives of European women in the second half of the 20th century was

    (A) the availability of reliable birth control.
    (B) equal opportunities for advanced education.
    (C) working outside the home at professional levels.
    (D) the availability of labor-saving household appliances.
    (E) all of the above.

67. Erasmus of the Netherlands (16th century)

    (A) advocated religious separation from Rome.
    (B) was a strong supporter of the papacy.
    (C) made fun of corruption and superstition in the Church.
    (D) disapproved of the Brothers of the Common Life.
    (E) lived before the northern humanists.

GO ON TO THE NEXT PAGE

68. In the early 16th century, the most powerful monarch(s) in Europe was (were)

(A) Henry VIII of England.
(B) Elizabeth I of England.
(C) Francis I of France.
(D) Hapsburg emperor Charles V.
(E) Ferdinand and Isabella of Spain.

69. John Calvin's doctrine of predestination refers primarily to the idea that

(A) only the elect, God's chosen, were destined for heaven.
(B) God selected roles for individuals before they were born.
(C) Protestants were destined to overtake Catholics.
(D) God selected special people to be ministers.
(E) societies should be theocracies, ruled by the religious leaders.

70. All of the following were late 19th-century Russian authors EXCEPT

(A) Tolstoy.
(B) Dostoevsky.
(C) Pasternak.
(D) Turgenev.
(E) Chekhov.

71. A condition of World War I warfare that was NOT present in World War II was

(A) trench warfare.
(B) women in factories.
(C) use of planes.
(D) use of submarines.
(E) rationing.

72. In 17th-century France, the *intendants* were

(A) archbishops of certain dioceses.
(B) representatives of the king who governed each district.
(C) delegates to the Estates General.
(D) judges in the parlements.
(E) Huguenot military leaders.

73. In the 1980s, Mikhail Gorbachev instituted *perestroika,* which was a

(A) tightening of Soviet control.
(B) re-Sovietization of Chechnya.
(C) return to strict Leninism.
(D) loosening of the Soviet economic and political structure.
(E) new freedom of expression and openness in government.

74. The main difficulty related to the reunification of Germany in the late 20th century was the

(A) disagreement over the form of government.
(B) destruction of the Berlin Wall.
(C) poverty and lack of development of East Germany.
(D) religious division.
(E) presence of American military bases.

75. Until the Renaissance, European moneylenders tended to be Jews because

(A) they did more traveling as merchants.
(B) they were the wealthiest citizens.
(C) they drove hard bargains with Christians.
(D) they owned all the banks.
(E) Christians were forbidden to loan money; collecting interest was considered usury.

GO ON TO THE NEXT PAGE

76. The greatest achievement of the English sailor Francis Drake was

   (A) attacking Spanish galleons and seizing gold and silver from the New World.
   (B) defending England against the Spanish Armada.
   (C) expanding British naval and commercial power.
   (D) succeeding as a favorite of Queen Elizabeth I.
   (E) becoming the second European commander to circumnavigate the globe.

77. In the French and Indian War of the 1750s, the British succeeded in all the following EXCEPT

   (A) making their colonies assume financial responsibility for their defense.
   (B) capturing French forts in the Ohio River Valley.
   (C) incorporating American colonists into their military ranks.
   (D) defeating the French in Canada.
   (E) preparing to take Canada from France at the end of the Seven Years War (1763).

78. Prior to the Revolution in France, there was great fear of a poor grain harvest because

   (A) bread was the mainstay of the working-class diet; high grain prices meant malnutrition, disease, and starvation.
   (B) factory workers would have to be paid more.
   (C) the queen had little sympathy for the poor.
   (D) there would be foreign competition.
   (E) of all of the above.

79. Slobadan Milosevic was put on trial at the World Court in The Hague for

   (A) using poison gas again the Kurds.
   (B) practicing ethnic cleansing against Muslims in Kosovo.
   (C) deliberately splitting up Yugoslavia.
   (D) bombing Serbia.
   (E) plotting with the hard-line communists.

80. The main change that came from the 1991 Treaty of Maastricht was the

   (A) formation of the European Union.
   (B) inclusion of Eastern European states in the EU.
   (C) formation of NATO.
   (D) plans for a common European currency.
   (E) removal of international tariffs.

IF YOU FINISH BEFORE TIME IS CALLED, YOU MAY CHECK YOUR WORK ON THIS SECTION ONLY. DO NOT TURN TO ANY OTHER SECTION IN THE TEST.

STOP

SECTION II

Part A

(Suggested writing time—45 minutes)

Percent of Section II score—45

Directions: The following question is based on the accompanying Documents 1–13. The documents have been edited for the purpose of this exercise.

This question is designed to test your ability to work with and understand historical documents. Write an essay that does the following:

- Provides an appropriate, explicitly stated thesis that directly addresses all parts of the question and does not simply restate the question.

- Discusses a majority of the documents individually and specifically.

- Demonstrates understanding of the basic meaning of a majority of the documents.

- Supports the thesis with appropriate interpretations of a majority of the documents.

- Analyzes the documents by explicitly grouping them in at least three appropriate ways.

- Takes into account both the sources of the documents and the authors' points of view.

You may refer to relevant historical information not mentioned in the documents.

1. What were the attitudes toward mental illness and its treatment in England in the late 18th and early 19th centuries?

Historical Background: Until the late 18th century, Europeans viewed mental illness as possession by evil spirits or as connected in some way to witchcraft. Attitudes began to change somewhat as these beliefs died out in the late 1700s. Traditionally, the mentally ill were cared for at home or confined to prisons or workhouses. Until the early 18th century, the only public asylum in England was London's Bethlehem Hospital, whose corrupted name "Bethlem" or "Bedlam" became synonymous with insanity. In the 1700s, popular entertainment included paying a small fee to laugh at the hospital inmates. There were also privately run "madhouses." Beginning in 1714, justices of the peace could authorize locking up lunatics who were considered violent or dangerous.

Please use separate paper to write your answers.

GO ON TO THE NEXT PAGE ⟩

Document 1

Source: William Hogarth, Engraving, Scene #8, *The Rake's Progress*, scene from Bethlehem Hospital, 1735, retouched 1763

Photo credit: Tate Gallery, London/Art Resource, NY

Document 2

Source: Article commenting on private madhouses, *Gentlemen's Magazine*, 1763

When a person is forcibly taken or artfully decoyed into a private madhouse, he is, without any authority or any further charge than that of a mercenary relation or a pretended friend, instantly seized up by a set of inhuman ruffians trained up to this barbarous profession, stripped naked, and conveyed to a dark room. If he complains, or asks the reasons for this dreadful usage, the attendant brutishly orders him not to rave, calls for assistance, and ties him down to a bed, from which he is not released until he submits to their pleasure.

GO ON TO THE NEXT PAGE

Document 3

Source: Diary entry, Jonathan Swift. An account of taking three hired coaches of children and nursemaids to see the sights of London, 1760s

Set out at ten o'clock to the Tower, and saw the Lions. Then to Bedlam. Then dined at the Chop-house… and concluded the night at the Puppet Show.

Document 4

Source: Visitors' Minutes, after inspection of a private madhouse in Warwickshire, 1776

And we also report that we found the said house and the apartments of all the lunaticks neat and in good condition, and the lunaticks themselves furnished with proper accommodations and under due care and management and that for the confinement of each lunatick there appears to be an order in writing duly made out under the hand and seal of a physician, surgeon or apothecary.

Document 5

Source: William Perfect, *Select Cases in the Different Species of Insanity*, 1787

A maniacal man they had confined in their workhouse….He was secured to the floor by means of a staple and an iron ring, which was fastened to a pair of fetters about his legs, and he was handcuffed. Continuous visitors were pointing at, ridiculing and irritating the patient, who was thus made a spectacle of public sport by several feats of dexterity, such as threading a needle with his toes.

Document 6

Source: Countess Harcourt, comments on King George III, 1788

The unhappy patient was no longer treated as a human being. His body was immediately encased in a machine which left it no liberty of motion. He was sometimes chained to a staple. He was frequently beaten and starved, and at best he was kept in subjection by menacing and violent language. The history of the King's illness showed that the most exalted station did not wholly exempt the sufferer from this stupid and inhuman usage.

GO ON TO THE NEXT PAGE ▷

Document 7

Source: Frenchman Charles-Gaspard de la Rive, 1798, description of the Retreat at York, founded by the Society of Friends in 1792

The insane are regarded as children who have an overabundance of strength and make dangerous use of it. They must be given immediate punishment and rewards; whatever is remote has no effect on them. A new system of education must be applied, a new direction given to their ideas; they must first be subjugated, then encouraged, then applied to work, and this work made agreeable by attractive means.

Document 8

Source: George Paul, High Sheriff of Gloucestershire, to the Secretary of State, 1806

I believe there is hardly a parish of any considerable size in which there may not be found some unfortunate human creature of this description, who, if his ill-treatment has made him phrenetic, is chained in the cellar or garret of a workhouse, fastened to the leg of a table, tied to a post in an outhouse, or perhaps shut up in an uninhabited ruin; or if his lunacy be inoffensive, left to ramble half naked and half starved through the streets and highways, teased by the scoff and jest of all that is ignorant, vulgar, and unfeeling.

Document 9

Source: John Haslan, administrator at Bedlam, 1809

Where one of the parents have been insane, it is more than probable that the offspring will be similarly affected. R. G.—his grandfather was mad, but there was no insanity in his grandmother's family. His father was occasional melancholic, and once had a raving paroxysm. His mother's family was sane. His father's brother died insane. R. G. has a brother and five sisters; his brother has been confined at St. Luke's. All his sisters have been insane; with the three youngest the disease came on after delivery.

Document 10

Source: Dr. Bryan Crowther, surgeon at Bethlem, *Practical Remarks on Insanity*, 1811

The curable patients at Bethlem Hospital are regularly bled about the commencement of June and the latter end of July. The lancet has been found a very communicative sort of instrument. I have bled a hundred and fifty patients at one time, and have never found it requisite to adopt any other method of security against haemorrhage than that of sending the patient back to his accustomed confinement.

GO ON TO THE NEXT PAGE ⟶

Document 11

Source: Samuel Tuke, grandson of the founder of the Quaker institution, the Retreat at York, *A Description of the Retreat,* 1813

Some years ago a man of Herculean size and figure was brought to the house. He had been kept chained. His clothes were contrived to be taken off and put on by means of strings, without removing his manacles. The manacles were taken off when he entered the Retreat, and he was ushered into an apartment where the superintendents were supping. He was calm. He was desired to join in the repast, during which he behaved with tolerable propriety. The maniac was sensible of the kindness of his treatment. He promised to restrain himself, and he so completely succeeded that during his stay no coercive means were ever employed towards him. In about four months he was discharged, perfectly recovered.

Document 12

Source: Godfrey Higgins, County Magistrate, investigating the York Asylum (founded in 1777), 1813

…found a series of cells about eight feet square, in a very horrid and filthy situation. The walls were daubed with excrement; the airholes, of which there was one in each cell, were partly filled with it. I went upstairs and [the keeper] showed me into a room, twelve feet by seven feet, ten inches, in which there were thirteen women who, he told me, had all come out of those cells that morning. I became very sick, and could not remain longer in the room. I vomited.

Document 13

Source: Henry Alexander, testimony before a Select Committee of Parliament, inquiring into the treatment of the insane. Alexander had made a tour of 47 workhouses in the West Country, 1815

At Tavistock lunatic patients had been removed from their cells and the cells washed. I never smelt such a stench in my life. Having entered one, I said I would go into the other; that if they could survive the night through, I could at least inspect them. The stench was so great that I felt almost suffocated, and for hours after, if I ate anything, I retained the same smell. I could not get rid of it; and it should be remembered that these cells had been washed out that morning and the doors had been opened some hours previous.

GO ON TO THE NEXT PAGE

Part B
(Suggested planning and writing time—35 minutes)
Percent of Section II score—27½

Directions: You are to answer ONE question from the three questions below. Make your selection carefully, choosing the question that you are best prepared to answer thoroughly in the time permitted. You should spend five minutes organizing or outlining your answer.

Write an essay that

- has a relevant thesis;
- addresses all parts of the question;
- supports a thesis with specific evidence; and
- is well organized.

2. Compare and contrast the religious policies of Elizabeth I of England (1558–1603) with those of Henry IV of France (1589–1610).

3. Identify and explain the characteristics of romanticism in literature. Give examples of writers and works from more than one European country, showing how each demonstrates the qualities of romanticism.

4. Analyze the long-term and short-term causes and the effects of the Boer War in South Africa (1899–1902).

Please use separate paper to write your answers.

GO ON TO THE NEXT PAGE ⇨

Part C
(Suggested planning and writing time—35 minutes)
Percent of Section II score—27½

> **Directions:** You are to answer ONE question from the three questions below. Make your selection carefully, choosing the question that you are best prepared to answer thoroughly in the time permitted. You should spend five minutes organizing or outlining your answer.

Write an essay that

- has a relevant thesis;

- addresses all parts of the question;

- supports a thesis with specific evidence; and

- is well-organized.

5. **Explain how financial problems helped create the French Revolution.**

6. **England is one of the smallest European nations, yet it has been one of the most powerful countries on earth. Evaluate at least three key factors that have enabled Great Britain to become and remain such a strong nation.**

7. **Until the late 20th century, women in Western society were denied opportunities of education and careers, yet despite the culture, some women did make significant contributions to the arts or science. Identify at least three such women—nonroyalty—from more than one country and describe the contribution of each. You must identify at least one woman in the arts and one in science.**

Please use separate paper to write your answers.

Practice Test 2: **Answer Key**

1. D	15. E	29. B	43. E	57. E	71. A
2. C	16. B	30. D	44. C	58. D	72. B
3. E	17. A	31. B	45. B	59. A	73. D
4. A	18. D	32. C	46. D	60. B	74. C
5. E	19. B	33. C	47. D	61. C	75. E
6. B	20. A	34. E	48. C	62. C	76. E
7. A	21. E	35. E	49. B	63. B	77. A
8. C	22. C	36. D	50. A	64. A	78. A
9. B	23. D	37. B	51. D	65. D	79. B
10. D	24. E	38. C	52. A	66. E	80. D
11. B	25. E	39. A	53. E	67. C	
12. E	26. D	40. C	54. C	68. D	
13. C	27. C	41. D	55. C	69. A	
14. C	28. A	42. B	56. E	70. C	

PRACTICE TEST 2: ASSESS YOUR STRENGTHS

The following tables show how the Practice Test is broken down by time period. If you need help with the free-response questions or document-based questions, refer back to Chapter 2: Strategies for Success.

Time Periods	Questions	If you missed these questions, study these chapters.
1450 to the French Revolution	1, 2, 5, 7, 9, 10, 11, 16, 19, 20, 23, 24, 28, 29, 30, 31, 32, 33, 42, 43, 44, 45, 46, 47, 48, 49, 57, 58, 59, 60, 61, 62, 63, 64, 65, 67, 68, 69, 72, 75, 76, 77, 78	Chapter 3: The Renaissance Chapter 4: The Reformation and Religious Wars Chapter 5: Discovery, Expansion, and Commercial Revolution Chapter 6: The Age of Absolutism—Western Europe Chapter 7: The Age of Absolutism—Eastern Europe Chapter 8: Constitutionalism in England and the Dutch Republic Chapter 9: The Scientific Revolution Chapter 10: The Enlightenment Chapter 11: 18th-Century Economics and Politics Chapter 12: The French Revolution
19th Century (and very beginning of 20th century)	3, 4, 8, 14, 18, 21, 22, 25, 26, 34, 35, 36, 37, 38, 51, 70	Chapter 13: The Industrial Revolution Chapter 14: Conservatism (1815–1848) Chapter 15: The Rise of Liberalism (1815–1848) Chapter 16: The Rise of Nationalism (1815–1848) Chapter 17: Romanticism Chapter 18: The Age of Realpolitik (1848–1914) Chapter 19: The Rise of Socialism Chapter 20: The Age of Mass Politics (1871–1915) Chapter 21: Intellectual Movements (1850–1914) Chapter 22: The New Imperialism
20th Century (and very beginning of 21st century)	6*, 12, 13, 15, 17, 27, 39, 40, 41, 50, 52, 53, 54, 55, 56, 66, 71, 73, 74, 79, 80	Chapter 23: World War I Chapter 24: The Russian Revolution Chapter 25: Europe Between the Wars Chapter 26: World War II Chapter 27: Immediate Postwar Issues Chapter 28: The Cold War Chapter 29: Nationalism Chapter 30: Post–World War II Society

* Although the welfare state would be more of a predominant feature of the 20th century, programs would be introduced in late 19th century Germany.

Chapters and Topics	Number of Questions	Answered Correctly
1450 to the French Revolution	43	
19th century (and very beginning of 20th century)	16	
20th century (and very beginning of 21st century)	21	

ANSWERS AND EXPLANATIONS

SECTION I: MULTIPLE-CHOICE QUESTIONS

1. D

The Dutch did not specialize in textiles as the British and Belgians did. Instead, the Dutch developed lens grinding, optics, and clock making in addition to their dairy and tulip production, fishing, trade, and banking. The standard of living was perhaps the highest in Western Europe, (B), and the Dutch practiced religious toleration, (C).

2. C

The deist conception of God was a creator of the universe, sometimes referred to as a "clockwork god." The deists believed that God had set the world to function mathematically by natural law. They did not see God as emotionally involved with daily human affairs. The deists were not atheists, (A), nor were they evangelicals, (B) and (E); they were also not religious reformers, (D).

3. E

All of these things happened as a result of Charles's attempt to take power away from the Chamber of Deputies and the upper middle class (by reducing the suffrage). He also censored the press. The Parisians revolted with riots and barricades in the streets; a panicky Charles fled the country.

4. A

The Chartists pushed for reform in the way voting districts were drawn, which had never related to population. They advocated universal male suffrage but did not campaign to give women the vote, (B). Choices (C), (D), and (E) are not true.

5. E

Boccaccio composed the *Decameron,* a series of stories told to entertain people who had isolated themselves to avoid the plague. The title implied 100 stories, but Boccaccio never completed it. *Praise of Folly* was by Erasmus of the Northern Renaissance.

6. B

The modern welfare state is most likely to control services that affect almost everyone, such as utilities, medicine, and education, (A, C, and D). They are also characterized by government-sponsored retirement/pension plans, (E). Most welfare states, however, do not alter private ownership and control of small businesses.

7. A

The old Holy Roman Empire of the German states was a strange combination of around 300 entities, many of them tiny. Napoleon combined many into fewer, larger states with better organized, more stable governments. He did the same in northern Italy, creating the Cisalpine Republic and driving out the Austrians. Answers (B), (C), and (E) are true but of less importance; answer (D) is not true.

8. C

From the late 19th century well into the 20th century, France cultivated good relations with Russia as a balance against France's powerful neighbor Germany. None of the other answers are totally accurate.

9. B

In the 1650s, as part of the Navigation Acts and the Anglo-Dutch conflicts, the British seized control of New Amsterdam and changed its name to New York. Remnants of Dutch culture are evident in place names, family names, and in the fiction of Washington Irving. The other answers here are all untrue.

10. D

These were rights Locke insisted that all people were entitled to enjoy. He said that people formed governments solely to guarantee those rights. (B), (C), and (E) might be considered parts of Locke's general theory. (A) refers to Thomas Jefferson's reinterpretation of Locke's words.

11. B

No one knew about da Vinci's amazing scientific ideas until his private notebooks were discovered and decoded in the 20th century. (A), (C), and (D) are not especially true.

12. E

All the choices are true. The revolt failed, and Luxemburg and Liebneckt were both executed (actually, shot while in police custody).

13. C

France readily relinquished control of all her colonies in the 1950s, except Algeria. Algeria had been under French control for many decades, and a number of French people lived there; therefore, some French people and the government tried to keep Algeria. A war resulted, and eventually, de Gaulle conducted a referendum in France to secure Algerian independence.

14. C

Prussia had already defeated Austria in the Seven Weeks War, (E), which had created Prussian patriotism, (D). Bismarck had no plans for empire beyond the unification of the German states, (B). He had no particular quarrel with Louis Napoleon, (A), but he needed leverage to push the remaining south German states into the German Empire.

15. E

(A), (B), and (C) were all factors of the 1970s, but they did not affect the recession. If anything,

popularity of British rock music, (D), helped, rather than hurt, the economy of Britain. Oil shortages and sharply rising fuel prices had profound economic effects, (E).

16. B

The Council ordered clergy to live in their dioceses, where they would be visited by their bishops. More seminaries were established to educate the clergy better. The Council did not alter the Latin of the liturgy, close convents, or rule on indulgences or purgatory, (A, C, and D). Finances were not a major issue, (E).

17. A

Lawrence was nicknamed "Lawrence of Arabia." During the war, he helped the Arabs of the Middle East rebel against the Ottoman Turks, often through sabotage and guerilla warfare. When the war was over, Turkey was reduced to the Anatolian Peninsula and Istanbul. None of the other answers apply here.

18. D

The new factory jobs required only unskilled labor, including that of women and children, so skilled craftsmen were left out. Wages did go down, (A), but this was because of the use of unskilled labor. The guilds would disappear in time, (C), and workers did move to the cities, (B), but again, these were the results of the displacement of labor.

19. B

Though tobacco, (C), was a cash crop from the Middle Atlantic colonies, sugar from the Caribbean was by far more profitable. Cotton, (A), did not shift into high production until after the invention of the cotton gin later in the 18th century. Tea, (D), came mainly from Asia and cocoa, (E), from Africa.

20. A

The St. Bartholomew's Day Massacre of 1572 occurred in France during the French religious wars between the Catholics and Huguenots (Protestants). The Huguenot leader, Henry of Navarre, had married the king's sister that day, in an attempt to bring a settlement to the conflict. Instead, the Catholic forces, with help from Spain, murdered Protestants, which resulted in renewed conflict.

21. E

The biggest benefit was the stable exchange, which facilitated international trade. (A) is true but not necessarily a general advantage. Prices fell worldwide, (C); those who owed money were hurt the most, (B). Wealthy lenders had the advantage because they were paid back in money that would buy more than the original amount did. As for (D), new gold was discovered in Alaska, Australia, and South Africa.

22. C

Stanley was hired by an American newspaper to look for the "lost" Scottish missionary David Livingstone. After finding Livingstone, Stanley made deals with Leopold of Belgium and explored and claimed land for Belgium, (A and D). (B) and (E) are irrelevant.

23. D

Machiavelli looked with admiration on France and England, where powerful ruling families had united their countries. This kind of unity was not happening in Italy, (A and C). Machiavelli kept religion totally out of his writing, (B), and saw nothing admirable about the Holy Roman Empire, (E).

24. E

All the choices are true. The *cahiers* revealed a deep desire for the end of special privilege and, in its place, demanded equality and freedom.

25. E

Franz Joseph finally let the Russian army put down the Hungarian revolt in 1849. The year before, he had made use of Jellachich for a while, (A). By 1849,

Metternich had fled in fear of the revolt and violence, (B). Answers (C) and (D) simply are not true.

26. D

Seurat developed a style called pointillism, which meant painting with tiny dots of primary colors placed close together so that in the eye of the viewer, the dots blurred and mixed into various hues of light and shadow. (B) refers to Monet, an impressionist. (A) and (C) refer somewhat to the fauves and expressionists.

27. C

The IRA worked in the second half of the 20th century to get Northern Ireland, part of the United Kingdom, transferred to the state of Ireland. This has not materialized, but the problem seems to have subsided with Irish economic prosperity. The other answers here refer to earlier issues.

28. A

Choice (C) may be tempting because the early Hohenzollerns did put much energy and expense into building their military. However, they almost never fought. Not until the days of Frederick II in the 18th century did Prussia attack a neighbor. Prussia's early expansion was through peaceful means.

29. B

The Italian city-states never unified and never developed a strong sense of patriotism. They tended to hire foreigners for their defense. Thus, by the early 16th century, much of Italy was overrun by armies from the powerful new monarchies of Northern Europe. All the entities of the other choices did exist in Renaissance Italy.

30. D

The act is called the Defenestration of Prague. Apparently, it was an accepted way to show defiance against authority. The emissaries fell some distance

(some texts say 70 feet!) and landed unhurt in a
manure pile. The Bohemians then turned to a nearby
Protestant prince for leadership, and the Thirty Years
War began.

31. B

L'Ouverture's first revolt had occurred during the
Revolution, when the Assembly abolished slavery in
France but not in the colonies. His revolt made an
impact, and slavery was eliminated in the colonies
in 1801. L'Ouverture then became governor of
Haiti. When Napoleon reinstated slavery in 1802,
L'Ouverture led a second revolt, which caused the
French much difficulty. As a result, Napoleon sold
Louisiana to the United States, (A).

32. C

Diderot faced censorship pressure from the Church,
the French government, and the printers' guild.
At times, publication was temporarily halted
over censorship issues. (A), (B), and (E) were not
problems, and the work found ready buyers in many
countries, (D).

33. C

Montesquieu was a member of the nobility and, as
such, believed that power should be shared among
the king, the aristocracy, and various institutions.
He did not believe in democracy, (A). It was Voltaire
who admired (B) and (E).

34. E

(A) through (D) are all partially correct in that they
can all be seen as factors in population growth.
But the main reason for the extreme growth in *city*
population was the Industrial Revolution. Jobs
became concentrated in urban areas; hence, this was
where a great many people lived.

35. E

The Paris Commune was a brief social revolution
that erupted following the Franco-Prussian War. It
was a violent protest against the establishment—
clergy and aristocrats. When order was restored, the
government harshly punished the *communards*.

36. D

Herzl was influenced by the Dreyfus Affair, (A), and
other incidents of anti-Semitism in Europe to found
the movement called Zionism. (B), (C), and (E) are
purely fictional.

37. B

When Japan shut her doors to foreigners in the early
1600s, only a few Dutch remained, and occasionally,
Dutch ships were allowed. Eventually, they brought
some Western technology, such as telescopes and
barometers. Missionaries were not admitted, (A), nor
were Japanese allowed to leave, (D). Answers (C) and
(E) are not true.

38. C

Both the British and the French claimed territory
in the Sudan. The British had an encounter with
a native revolt in 1885 at Khartoum, in which a
famous British general was killed. In 1898, the
British went further up the Nile (south), and they
defeated the natives this time. Afterwards, the British
encountered the French, and after a face-off, the
French backed down and withdrew.

39. A

After the protests following Bloody Sunday, Nicholas
II issued the October Manifesto, promising a
national legislature, a Duma. (However, Nicholas
would not give the successive Dumas much control,
so they failed.) In 1905, the Bolsheviks were
in exile, (B), and would not return until 1917.
Likewise, the soviets would not become powerful

until 1917, (E). The Russian peasants were given opportunity to acquire land through the reforms of Peter Stolypin, (D).

40. C

(A) and (B) refer to Shakespearean drama. (D) and (E) are from late 19th-century poetry and prose. The stream of consciousness style evolved in the early 20th century. An example is James Joyce's *Ulysses*.

41. D

Most of Europe's nations became democracies following World War I, but by 1938, Czechoslovakia was the only nation in Eastern Europe that retained constitutional government. (E) is true of Czechoslovakia but also true of all the nations of Eastern Europe. The country did not become communist, (A), until after World War II. Czechoslovakia had military defenses but only on its western border, (C).

42. B

Both "bubbles" were the result of highly inflated investments in overseas trading companies. When the stock prices suddenly plummeted, so did the trading companies. Definitely, England was in better position to deal with financial crisis. In both countries, people in high places were disgraced, (A). But the English government, the Bank of England, and the South Sea Company weathered the storm and repaid the losses. The government of France repudiated much of the debt, which destroyed its credit, (D).

43. E

The Polish king had little power. To become elected, (B), he had to negotiate away most of his authority. He was often a foreigner, (D), because the fractious Poles could not agree on one of their own. The national diet didn't function very well because any member could use the liberum veto to close it down, (C).

44. C

The Edict of Nantes of 1598 gave the Huguenots military privileges, which were revoked by Cardinal Richelieu in 1629, (B). However, they retained their religious freedom until Louis XIV demanded Catholic conformity. The French Revolution brought religious freedom, (D), and even Napoleon's Concordat allowed freedom of worship, (E).

45. B

In the 1400s, Spain was only vaguely united; its citizens did not think of themselves as Spanish. The only thing that united people was the Catholic Church. Overseas exploration, (A), had barely begun; the price revolution, (C), had not yet occurred. (D) and (E) are irrelevant.

46. D

Luther was a prolific writer, and he wrote in German, (A). But an even bigger factor in the spread of his ideas was the power of the printing press to produce multiple copies relatively cheaply. Answers (B) and (C) are true about his life but not major reasons for the spread of his ideas.

47. D

The Jesuits were perhaps the least confined to monasteries of all Catholics orders. Instead, they engaged in worldly affairs, often teaching the sons of the wealthy and powerful, (E), and traveling to the Americas and Asia, (B). They did undergo vigorous preparation for their careers, (A). Because they often tried to influence government, they were expelled from some countries (e.g., Maria Theresa of Austria), (C).

48. C

The peace treaty established the grandson of Louis XIV of France, a Bourbon, as King of Spain, with the stipulation that the same person could not rule both Spain and France.

49. B

Rousseau believed civilization to be corrupt; therefore, he most admired the uncivilized, such as the Native Americans (though he had never seen one—he liked the idea of living simply and close to nature). He claimed that nature was better than civilization, (A). He advocated emotion over reason, (C), *indirectly* influencing revolutionary thought, (D), and he preached the importance of the general will of the people, (E).

50. A

The British music industry brought much money to the country in the late 20th century, beginning with The Beatles in the 1960s and continuing with a number of other pop groups, such as The Rolling Stones. (B) and (D) relate to earlier times. Tourism and the auto industry (C) and (E) have contributed to the modern economy but not as much as rock music in recent times.

51. D

The German philosophers talked about a *volkgeist*, or spirit of the common people, which they believed to be the definition of a nationality. The Russian populists and slavophiles believed in the mir and the rural peasants as representatives of the Russian people.

52. A

The purge trials seemed designed to rid Stalin of all the original Bolsheviks who might create opposition. Trotsky had been forced out in the 1920s (D). Western reporters were invited to the trials, but (B) was less of a purpose than (A).

53. E

Yugoslavia, (C), is tempting here because of its independent action, but it was not a Soviet satellite. Revolts in Hungary (1956) and Czechoslovakia (1968) were violently put down, (D and A). Poland's revolt in 1956 stopped the collectivization of agriculture, kept the Catholic Church strong, and paved the way for the formation of Solidarity in the 1980s.

54. C

At its founding in 1945, one of the permanent members of the Security Council was Nationalist China. In the 1970s, Nationalist China (Taiwan) was replaced with Communist China. (A) and (B) have not occurred. More African nations have joined the United Nations, and some have served as rotating members of the Security Council, but they certainly do not dominate, (D).

55. C

The Communist Party thrived for several decades as a far-left movement in both France and Italy. It was not a major factor elsewhere in Western Europe.

56. E

All of the factors contributed to Yeltsin's retirement and the election of Vladimir Putin.

57. E

Many early explorers were Italian. Italians were the best sailors in Europe in the late 1400s and early 1500s. Some were employed to sail for other nations of Western Europe—Columbus for Spain, the Cabots for England.

58. D

The official translation of the Bible was ordered by Charles I's father, James I. It was a move that generally pleased all of the Protestant population. The other answers were all divisive issues that led to the English Civil War.

59. A

All of these choices are somewhat true, but (A) reflects the most important advantage that the potato offered. The fact that it lasted through winter storage gave the poor an excellent energy (carbohydrate) food that was cheaply and easily available. It could also be carried on long ocean voyages, and the vitamins in the potato's skin prevented conditions like scurvy.

60. B

Kepler took the records of Tycho Brahe, (D), and used his own mathematical background to work out his formulas. (A) is attributed to Copernicus, (C) to Newton, and (E) to the Dutch.

61. C

Lady Jane Grey is referred to as the "nine-days queen." Her parents plotted with another family to marry her in her teens and claim the English throne after the death of Henry VIII's son Edward VI. However, Edward's half-sister Mary garnered support and had Jane and her husband executed for treason.

62. C

Voltaire despised the religious bigotry of the Church in France and the censorship imposed by both the government and the Church. He was not a democrat, (B), and he distrusted the nobility, (A). He wrote articles for the *Encyclopedia*, (E), but so did many other people.

63. B

The Aztecs had developed a sophisticated calendar. The Spanish brought all the other answers listed here.

64. A

The primary goal of education was literacy in order to read the Bible. This, the Protestants believed, would make young women better wives and mothers, (B), and enable them to teach religious truths to their children, (E). They were not expected to run businesses, (C), except to help their husbands, nor were they allowed to serve as church leaders, (D).

65. D

Popular culture involves the social history of the common people, which included far more people, (A), than elite culture but which left few written records. Both the common people and the elite were affected by wars, (C), and religion, (B).

66. E

All the choices occurred in relation to women after 1950.

67. C

Erasmus's *Praise of Folly* (1509) was a satire that especially criticized the hypocrisy, corruption, and superstition he saw in his fellow clergy. He satirized the corrupt Pope Julius II, (B). Erasmus was brought up and educated by the Brothers of the Common Life, (D), and he was a scholarly humanist, (E). Though he saw many flaws in the church, he did not advocate separating from it, (A).

68. D

In the early 1500s, Charles V inherited Habsburg Spain, Austria, the Netherlands, claims to Central and South America, and everything included in the Holy Roman Empire. This was during the reigns of Henry VIII and Elizabeth I of England, (A and B), and after that of Ferdinand of Isabella of Spain, (E).

69. A

Although Calvinism implied the other answers here, the concept of predestination referred primarily to the idea of salvation, or admittance to heaven. Calvin taught that this was reserved for the elect, the chosen of God.

70. C

Boris Pasternak was a mid-20th-century writer, most famous for *Dr. Zhivago*. The others listed here came from the late 19th century.

71. A

Trench warfare dominated the Western Front in World War I but was not used extensively in World War II. The other answers here were part of both wars.

72. B

Cardinal Richelieu, who advised Louis XIII, sent out representatives of the king to 32 districts. These governed each district and were directly responsible to the monarchy.

73. D

Gorbachev encouraged the production of consumer goods and a relaxation of government controls. He also allowed, (E), but this was called *glasnost*. All the other choices refer to earlier times.

74. C

The inclusion of East Germany must have seemed like a family reunion with poor relatives, because the economy of East Germany was woefully behind that of West Germany. The communist system had not allowed for the degree of growth that the West had experienced. (A) and (D) did not occur. The destruction of the Berlin Wall was part of the initial celebration, (B). There were American military bases in West Germany, but they created no problem, (E).

75. E

The Church frowned upon loaning money at interest as sinful. Thus, the Jews, who did not live under such strictures, filled this economic need. Often, they were traveling merchants as well, (A), but this was not the reason for their lending. There were few actual banks, (D). (B) and (C) might have been true on occasion but were not reasons why the Jews were the moneylenders.

76. E

All the choices here are correctly things that Drake accomplished, but his greatest achievement was sailing around the world.

77. A

Militarily, the combined force of British soldiers and American militiamen, (C), defeated the French and took their fortresses west of the Appalachians. The British also defeated the French on the Plains of Abraham at Quebec, (D and E). All of this distant warfare was very expensive, and the British colonists were paying few taxes to England. When Parliament tried to increase colonial taxes after the war, the colonists revolted.

78. A

The poor feared famine when grain prices rose; grain shortages could produce riots and violence. The Industrial Revolution had not reached France before 1789, (B).

79. B

In the breakup of Yugoslavia after 1989, Milosevic was left with Serbia and Montenegro. Serbia fought the other states, especially Bosnia, where the Serbs practiced ethnic cleansing against Bosnian Muslims. Later, Milosevic and the Serbs went after the Muslims of Kosovo. Finally, NATO bombed Serbia to stop the war; Milosevic was arrested and died in 2005 during his trial for war crimes.

80. D

The Treaty of Maastricht set the stage for the euro. The EU had been formed several decades earlier, (A), as had NATO, (C). The basic Union did away with tariffs, (E), and the EU has constantly expanded, (B), without any special treaty.

SECTION II: PART A

SAMPLE DOCUMENT-BASED QUESTION SAMPLE ESSAY

By the 1700s, educated Englishmen no longer blamed mental illness on witchcraft or evil spirits. However, there was still little understanding of how to treat the insane. From paupers and criminals to kings, the victims of insanity often faced terrible abuse. Many were confined to workhouses or private asylums to exist in inhumane conditions. The few exceptions, such as the Quaker establishment, the Retreat at York, stood out as models and perhaps influenced public officials to investigate the treatment of the mentally ill.

Many viewed the insane as topics of amusement. The writer Jonathan Swift (Doc. 3) listed in his diary a series of "sights" for children in London and included "Bedlam," the public asylum for the insane, along with seeing lions and attending a puppet show. The fact that he so casually included the hospital and apparently considered it suitable entertainment for children showed the lack of understanding and sympathy that was perhaps typical of the times. The Hogarth engraving of a scene at the same hospital (Doc. 1) shows two aristocratic ladies in the background, viewing the insane for their amusement. They watch a patient "looking at the stars" through a paper tube and another playing a violin with a stick. A few years later (Doc. 5), another author described a chained "maniac" in a workhouse, who was also a "spectacle of public sport." Here, visitors were amused by the patient's ability to thread a needle with his toes.

There were, apparently, exceptions to the general practice of mistreatment. In 1776, a visitors' report of a private madhouse in Warwickshire (Doc. 4) praised the decency of the accommodations and the treatment of patients. This report also mentioned the fact that the residents had been committed by medical personnel. However, Document 2, an article about another private madhouse, implied that patients were tricked or forced into confinement. The article went on to describe their brutal treatment once they were locked up. Likewise, the Hogarth print depicts the central patient in chains.

Even royalty could not escape. When King George III became mentally ill, he was "no longer treated as a human being," according to one observer (Doc. 6). This writer claimed that the king was beaten and starved and subjected to "menacing and violent language." The writer, Countess Harcourt, called the King's treatment "stupid" and "inhuman," which showed her disapproval of it. The description of the King's mistreatment was not so different from that of the "maniacal man...confined in their workhouse" in Document 5.

Obviously, no one had any understanding of the causes of insanity. However, Document 9 (1809) by an administrator at the public asylum Bethlem (Bethlehem Hospital) observed that insanity seemed to run in families. This speaker gave an example of a patient who had various relatives who were also affected by madness.

Also at Bethlem, one method that was applied to "curable patients" was bleeding. A doctor, Bryan Crowther, in Doc. 10, described this practice, claiming to have bled 150 patients at one time. However, the doctor's attitude is defensive, making a point that he had never had to especially guard against hemorrhage. One wonders if he was responding to questioning or criticism of this procedure.

The documents seem to indicate that the treatment of the mentally ill was generally horrific. The 1806 letter from the Sheriff of Gloucestershire to the Secretary of State (Doc. 8) spoke of victims chained in cellars or garrets of workhouses or left to ramble and starve in the streets. The sheriff also mentioned others' laughing at the unfortunate persons, which recalls the earlier reactions in Docs. 1, 3, and 5. Conditions for the insane unlucky enough to be confined in a workhouse seem to have been despicable. The same was true of many asylums. One example was reported by a county magistrate (Doc. 12)—a local official like the sheriff in Doc. 8. The magistrate, Godfrey Higgins, investigated the York Asylum in 1813 and found cells where female patients were kept. These cells were so filthy with excrement that the magistrate vomited. Such a violent reaction would testify to the truth of his reported information.

Another institution at York was run quite differently. It was founded by Quakers in 1792 and was simply called "the Retreat" (Doc. 11). The fact that it was not named an "asylum" or "madhouse" was significant. Some years later (1813), Samuel Tuke, the grandson of the Retreat's founder, wrote his *Description of the Retreat* (Doc. 11), in which he gave an example of a violent patient's calm response to humane treatment. Of course, Tuke could simply be praising the work of his grandfather. However, there is another reference to the Retreat by a Frenchman who visited it in 1798 (Doc. 7). He described patients treated "as children," given immediate rewards and punishments, and given attractive work to do. Because this Frenchman was a foreign observer, his report is probably creditable.

In 1815, a Select Committee of Parliament investigated the treatment of the insane. The testimony in Document 13 was by Henry Alexander, who had toured 47 workhouses. His report resembled that of Godfrey Higgins in 1813 (Doc. 12). This investigator reported the conditions he found at a workhouse in Tavistock. Like Higgins, he used the term "cells" and emphasized the filth and sickening stench.

By the early 19th century, there appeared to be some hope of improvement in attitudes toward mental illness and its treatment. The Quaker establishment at York seemed to prove that kinder methods and care of the insane produced better results. Also, government officials, such as magistrates and sheriffs, and members of Parliament were appalled by the brutality toward the insane in workhouses and asylums. Their awareness seemed to indicate that people had begun to see the insane as fellow human beings and, as such, deserving of better treatment.

SECTION II: PART B

[Note: Answers to the FRQ essay questions may vary somewhat. The following sample essays are intended to suggest what a good essay might include. The two most important things in answering an FRQ essay question are to answer all parts of the question and to give ample, accurate examples to illustrate the points you are making.]

SAMPLE ESSAY RESPONSE QUESTION 2

Henry IV of France and Elizabeth I of England were both politiques, which means that they placed more importance on practical politics than on religion. Both came to power after times of religious dispute that had led to many deaths. Both were willing to compromise on religious issues for the purpose of restoring security and order and developing the economy. Both ascended the throne almost by default, after the death of other possible rulers.

Henry of Navarre was the sole surviving royal figure from France's religious wars of the late 1500s. In the last phase, the "War of the Three Henrys," the leader of the radical Catholics, Henry of Guise, was assassinated, followed by the murder of the king, Henry of Valois. There were no more Valois males, and Henry of Navarre had married the king's sister earlier, so he became the monarch.

However, Henry was a Huguenot, leader of the Protestants, and parts of France, including Paris, were strongly Catholic. Henry decided that he could gain acceptance and better unite the country by reconverting to Catholicism, no matter what his personal beliefs. At the same time, to protect the Huguenots, Henry established the Edict of Nantes. The Edict guaranteed religious freedom to French Protestants, allowing private worship anywhere and public worship where they were the majority. They even received the right to maintain their own armies and fortified towns (a potentially dangerous measure that would be rescinded during the reign of Henry's son, Louis XIII).

Henry's moves worked. France was reunited after all the division of civil war. The economy got back on its feet, and France began to prosper once more.

Elizabeth came to power in England in the middle of the 1500s. She also became the ruler after a period of religious conflict and after there was no one else left to rule. At the death of Elizabeth's father, Henry VIII, her half-brother Edward VI had ruled briefly, and his reign had taken England even more in the direction of Protestant practices than had Henry VIII. Then, Elizabeth's older half-sister Mary had reversed all of that by her radical attempt to re-Catholicize England by execution and imprisonment. As in late 16th-century France, people were sick of violence and conflict.

Like Henry of Navarre, Elizabeth was Protestant, but her personal religion was not the "be-all, end-all" of her existence. Unlike Henry, for her, it seemed most practical to restore Protestantism to her country. But in doing so, Elizabeth made the Church of England rather broad-based, a sort of middle road between the Calvinists and the Catholics. Services were in English, and clergy married, but much of the ritual resembled Catholic practice. Also, to avoid religious controversy, Elizabeth's government turned a "blind eye" to private religious practice, not objecting if Catholics said mass in their homes or if extreme Protestants conducted private Bible study. Unlike Henry, Elizabeth established no formal ordinance to protect religious minorities, but in practice, somewhat the same outcome occurred. In both countries, the monarch's actions were as close to religious toleration as the times would allow.

In England, as in France, the result was a time of peace, security, and prosperity. Both rulers were popular with their subjects, and in both countries people experienced economic prosperity.

SAMPLE ESSAY RESPONSE QUESTION 3

The 18th century was the Age of Reason, during which writers and thinkers looked to the ancient Greeks and Romans for models. They cared about natural law, science, and reason. By the late 1700s, some writers, like Rousseau in France or the poets William Blake in England and Robert Burns in Scotland, began to say that reason wasn't enough, that matters of the heart counted more. Thus, the Age of Romanticism rejected the mind and embraced emotion, feeling, and inspiration. Romantics viewed nature with a reverence, and they admired the peasant or even the primitive among human society. While the Age of Reason had spoken of universal law, the romantics glorified the individual. They also turned to the Middle Ages for legends and myths and admired the mysterious and supernatural.

Both Blake and Burns wrote poetry about common people. Blake championed children of poverty and the victims of all the abuses of industrialism. Burns wrote in Scottish dialect, and his characters were the rural poor. A fellow Scotsman, Sir Walter Scott, praised the individual hero. Both Burns and Scott drew on folklore and legends.

For others, like William Wordsworth, nature had an almost sacred quality that could soothe, teach, and inspire humanity, as in such poems as "My Heart Leaps Up" and "The Tables Turned." In the United States, Emerson and Thoreau also looked to nature as the source of all knowledge.

For still others, romanticism turned to the gothic, or mysterious, in poems and tales that hinted at the mysterious or even supernatural. Emily Brontë's *Wuthering Heights* features a storm-tormented atmosphere around a big, dark house and characters who seem to interact with the dead. Mary Shelley's *Frankenstein* spun a yarn about creating a monster out of human body parts. Edgar Allen Poe in the

United States used similar themes in his strange poems and stories about mystery and death.

Other romantics made heroes out of the poor and outcast, as in Victor Hugo's *Les Miserables* and *The Hunchback of Notre Dame*. The English poets Shelley, Byron, and Keats all saw themselves as misunderstood and alienated from society. They turned to nature for solace and inspiration. Shelley's "Ode to the West Wind" and Keats's "Ode on a Grecian Urn" are examples.

Romanticism in literature began to fade by the middle of the 19th century. Some writers, like Charles Dickens, would continue the romantic appeal to the emotions by focusing on the ugly realities of industrial England in his novels. But for most, the second half of the 19th century moved toward realism and naturalism, which established bleaker, less feeling world than the romantics had championed.

SAMPLE ESSAY RESPONSE QUESTION 4

The Boer War was a brief conflict in South Africa at the turn of the 20th century. It involved descendants of Dutch settlers, the Afrikaners, and the British. Part of the cause of the war can be attributed to national rivalries. Other causes related to the recent discoveries of gold and diamonds in the Transvaal area, which brought thousands of foreign adventurers to South Africa. The British won the war, but their international relations were affected. Also, the English had to work out a new relationship with their Afrikaner citizens.

The Dutch were the first Europeans to arrive in South Africa, coming in the early 17th century. There, they established two coastal colonies, Natal and Cape Colony. The Dutch settlers were farmers, or "Boers," and they brought with them their Calvinist faith in the Dutch Reformed Church. After the Napoleonic wars, in the early 19th century, the British took control of South Africa, and British settlers began to arrive. To escape from the English, the Boers retreated inland, a movement called the Great Trek. They went by covered wagon and fought the Zulu to take new land. Thus, the Afrikaners remained apart from the English and set up new, inland states, the Transvaal and the Orange Free State.

The English and Afrikaners coexisted separately but peacefully until near the end of the 19th century, when gold and diamonds were discovered in the Transvaal. This brought prospectors and adventurers from everywhere, and Johannesburg became a boomtown. The Dutch farmers hated the intruders, whom they called uitlanders, and there were acts of violence against them. To restore order, the British sent a small force into the Transvaal under the command of a man named Jameson. The Boers defeated the Raid, and the Afrikaner governor of the Transvaal received a congratulatory telegram from William II of Germany.

When the trouble did not subside, the British sent an army, which soon defeated the Afrikaners. In the process, the English interned Boer women and children in camps, where hundreds died. Almost the entire international community opposed the British in the war, seeing them as a global bully. One result of the negative press was a new effort after the war to cultivate alliances, which would help set the scene for World War I. Another contributing factor toward World War I was the German telegram to Paul Kruger, Afrikaner governor of the Transvaal on the occasion of the Raid. Germany's congratulations on the British defeat emphasized the growing enmity between Britain and Germany.

After the war, the British allowed the Afrikaners virtual self-government in the Transvaal and Orange Free State, and the English continued to dominate in the rest of South Africa. Gold and diamond mining continued to develop. In 1910, when the Union of South Africa was established, the two Afrikaner states applied for inclusion. The Union of South Africa then became a member of the British Commonwealth of Nations.

Eventually, however, the Afrikaners outnumbered the white South Africans of British descent and took control of the all-white government. When the Afrikaners established apartheid, a policy of extreme racial discrimination, the British Parliament criticized them. The result was South Africa's withdrawal from the Commonwealth. The Afrikaner government prevailed until the 1990s, when it bowed to pressure for majority control, and government by the white minority ended.

SECTION II: PART C

SAMPLE ESSAY RESPONSE QUESTION 5

From early modern times, the most troublesome aspect of the French monarchy was finance. The French nobility simply paid few taxes; in fact, paying taxes was seen as an indication of low social class. One consequence of this tradition was that the nobility assumed no responsibility for government because they had no financial commitment to it. Another result was that French monarchs had to struggle to find other ways to raise revenue; it also meant that they constantly had to borrow. Monarchs tried in vain to break the tax exemption of the wealthy. As time passed, the government's financial desperation was made worse by France's participation in the mid-18th-century wars, followed by the American Revolution. Eventually, these problems plunged France into a financial crisis that helped create the French Revolution.

Because paying few taxes was a sign of social status, it was the object of the middle class to move into the nobility. This could be accomplished with money. The king sold titles and positions. As a result, many high-ranking jobs in government and the military were filled by men who had few qualifications. There was no national parliament as in England, so most people, rich or poor, were not involved in government. Meanwhile, the poor barely survived under the huge burden of various taxes (on land, salt, and heads, for instance), as well as the required tithe to the Church.

In 1740, France went to war with others against Austria in the War of Austrian Succession. This war lasted for eight years, and then, beginning in 1756, France fought again in the Seven Years War. In both wars, France had to defend trading posts in India, and in the Seven Years War, there was also extensive fighting in North America. This part of the war, the French and Indian War, actually began in 1754 and involved defending French fortresses in the Ohio River Valley and along the St. Lawrence River against the British. France also had to fight the English over sugar islands in the Caribbean. All this warfare was very, very expensive.

France had hardly time to recover from the expenses of these wars before the American Revolution erupted in the mid-1770s. The American colonies had very persuasive emissaries to France (such as Ben Franklin), who convinced French leaders such as Lafayette to help the Americans as a way to get at their enemy, the British. After the American victory at Saratoga in 1777, the French sent men, munitions, and ships to aid the colonists. Thus, an already insolvent government accumulated still more debt.

In desperation, King Louis XV tried to bring change by abolishing the traditional parlements. These were district law courts, made up of the nobility, which insisted on the right to judge the constitutionality of new laws. Of course, they would never permit new tax laws. Therefore, Louis XV allowed his finance minister Maupeou to replace the parlements with new courts that no longer possessed this power. The new judges were to be salaried employees of the state, whose positions did not come with any special privileges. The "Maupeou parlements," as they were called, might have worked, had they stayed in place. But Louis XV died, and the new king, Louis XVI, was a weak young man of 20 who wanted to please. Under pressure from the nobility, Louis XVI dismissed Maupeou, shut down the new parlements, and returned to the old system.

By the fall of 1788, the government of France could no longer afford even the interest on the money it owed. It seemed that there was no choice left except to call a meeting of the Estates General, the national parliament, which had not convened in 175 years. The meeting began in May 1789. When Louis XVI backed the nobility in their demands to vote by estates, instead of individually, the delegates of the third estate declared itself a National Assembly and swore to meet until they had drafted a new constitution. This move marked the beginning of the French Revolution.

SAMPLE ESSAY RESPONSE QUESTION 6

Although Great Britain is a small island off the coast of Europe, it became one of Europe's leading nations by the 1700s. By the 1800s, it possessed the greatest empire in the world. Even though its overseas possessions shrank in the 20th century, England has continued to be among the world's most influential nations. England excelled over her neighbors in a number of ways, among the most important of which are its early development of Parliament and constitutional monarchy; its initiation of, first, the Agricultural Revolution, and then, the Industrial Revolution; and its dominance of the seas through its navy, merchant marine, and overseas empire.

By the 1500s, Parliament was already a strong institution in England. As its power grew, it gained increased control over taxation and national finance. While France's national assembly, the Estates General, ceased to meet and French kings were hampered by the district courts, the parlements, Britain kept its national Parliament strong. Because the members of Parliament at first were the landed aristocracy, the most powerful citizens were directly involved in government and were willing to tax themselves to maintain that control. This was very different from France, where the nobility paid few taxes and had little involvement in politics. Indeed, no other country in Europe developed a strong national legislature before the 19th century. During the 1700s, England had particularly weak kings (the German Hanovers), which enabled Parliament to gain still more power. The Reform Bills of the 19th century (1832 and 1867) broadened the franchise to allow the middle and working classes to have voice in government.

Unlike the landed aristocracy of the Continent, British landowners were directly involved in farming their estates. By the early 18th century, England was undergoing an agricultural revolution, which included the introduction of new plants such as clover, turnips, and the potato; the use of animal manure as fertilizer; and more controlled animal breeding. The formerly common lands were incorporated into the large estates, making farming an even bigger business and freeing a percentage of the rural labor force to move to cities for factory work. Profits from agriculture were also available for investment elsewhere.

Meanwhile, English inventors developed machines to greatly speed up textile production. As cloth making switched from cottage industry to mills, the now mobile labor force came to cities like Manchester and Liverpool to work. The invention of the steam engine sped up production even more and led to still more innovations in transportation—railroads and steamships. Thus, England became the first European nation to industrialize.

All the while, England had the biggest sailing fleet in the world. From the 1600s, England established colonies and trade across the globe. Although she lost her

American colonies in 1781 (excluding Canada), she took other possessions elsewhere in the 1800s, mainly in Africa and Asia. The merchant marine enabled Britain to trade worldwide, selling English cloth (first, woolens and later, cotton) and buying food and raw materials to import. For many years, Britain totally controlled the world's seas, which ensured her supremacy in both war and peace. In 1875, England gained the controlling shares of the Suez Canal, which greatly reduced sailing time to English colonies in East Africa and Asia. London became the center of world trade and international banking and insurance. English sea power enabled the Allies to blockade Germany effectively during World War I.

Great Britain lost some of her dominance following World War II, with the emergence of the two superpowers, the United States and the USSR and the process of decolonization. But despite these factors, England has maintained her position as an influential and important country on the international scale.

SAMPLE ESSAY RESPONSE QUESTION 7

Until recent years, even in the advanced countries of the Western world, women have always been second-class citizens. Girls were not given education equal to that of boys, and women were not admitted to most professions. For the most part, women did not excel in public ways. However, there were occasional women who made great contributions to the arts, such as the Brontë sisters and Berthe Morisot, and also to the sciences, such as Emilie du Chatelet and Marie Curie.

In the middle of the 19th century, female writers were almost unheard of. An exception occurred in the English Brontë family, where three sisters wrote poetry and stories. Two of them, Charlotte and Emily, wrote novels that became English classics. None of the Brontë children lived long lives, so neither sister produced more than the one great work, but each established her place in English literature with that one book. Charlotte's contribution was *Jane Eyre* and Emily's was *Wuthering Heights*, both of which are still read. Both are considered part of the 19th-century romantic tradition. *Wuthering Heights* is one of the great Gothic novels, characterized by a remote, stormy setting; a strange, isolated house; passionate characters; death; and hints of the supernatural.

There was also the occasional appearance of a great female painter. Such was the case of the impressionist French artist Berthe Morisot, sister-in-law of the famous Edvard Manet. Although Morisot never achieved as great recognition as did Manet, Monet, and Renoir, she definitely established her own niche in the art world, specializing in pastel portraits of women and children and domestic scenes. Today, Morisot's name is frequently cited among the great impressionist painters of the late 19th century.

During the scientific revolution and the Enlightenment, there were a few women who made valuable contributions and/or discoveries. One of these was Emilie du Chatelet, the wife of an 18th-century French nobleman and friend of Voltaire. In fact, Voltaire lived at her estate for some time. Chatelet's contribution was her translation of the work of Isaac Newton into French, which Voltaire then published. It can be said that French thinkers were first made aware of Newton's work because of the labors of Chatelet.

In the very early 20th century, a Polish woman and her French husband, Marie and Pierre Curie, studied radiation, which had been discovered in the late 19th century. They became the first to isolate radium as a radioactive element in 1910. Marie Curie was refused admission to the French Academy of Science because of her sex, but she went on to explore further the properties of radioactivity and won two Nobel Prizes.

Although the number of women who have achieved great things in the past has been rather limited, compared to the number of men, the contributions of these women has been quite significant. With more opportunities today for girls and women, it seems likely that future generations will produce many more women who will make great strides in a variety of areas of accomplishment.

GLOSSARY

THE RENAISSANCE

Baldassare Castiglioni, *The Courtier*

One of the greatest nonfiction literary creations of the Southern Renaissance, it described the proper behavior for Renaissance men and women.

Brothers and Sisters of the Common Life

A prominent group in the Netherlands that developed outside the traditional Church. They practiced a faith and lifestyle called Modern Devotion, in which men and women lived separately and communally but were not monks or nuns. They took no vows, wore no special clothes and could leave at will. Their teachings emphasized humility, tolerance, reverence, love of neighbor, and duty.

Bubonic plague (Black Death)

A deadly disease caused by a bacillus, which was carried by fleas living on black rats. It arrived in Italy from the Middle East in the middle of the 14th century and quickly spread throughout Europe. The disease lasted for two to three years and killed around 30 percent of the population.

Christian humanists

Christian-based thinkers and writers who were more spiritual in their outlook, less materialistic, and more focused on questions of morality and ethics

Condottieri

Foreign mercenaries who were hired for security purposes in the Italian city-states

Crusades

A series of wars fought in an attempt to capture the Holy Land from Muslim control. The Christian crusaders who survived brought back with them silks, porcelains, and spices, which introduced Europe to Asian goods. They also gained knowledge of Arabic medicine, science, and navigation, which were superior to European knowledge at the time.

Dante Alighieri

In the 1300s, this writer wrote his *Divine Comedy* in Florentine Italian.

Disiderius Erasmus, *Praise of Folly*

A clergyman from the Netherlands who believed in the goodness of humanity. He advocated the study of the Bible and the classics, emphasizing the life and teachings of Jesus and ignoring the ideas of original sin and the power of relics. His *Praise of Folly* made fun of the worldliness and superstition of the Church.

Eastern Orthodox Church

In 1054, the Christian Church formally split into the Roman Catholic Church, centered in Italy, and the Eastern Orthodox Church, centered in Constantinople.

Filippo Brunelleschi

His creation of the dome remains one of the most influential innovations in Renaissance architecture.

Flemish masters

Northern Renaissance artists who constructed realistic portraits in oil

Francesco Petrarch

A Renaissance poet who used Italian to create sonnets

Frescoes

Paintings done by mixing color into wet plaster on a wall or ceiling. Da Vinci's *The Last Supper* and Michelangelo's Sistine Chapel paintings are examples of such works.

Fugger

A family of merchants and bankers in the German states

Giovanni Boccaccio, *The Decameron*

A Renaissance writer who focused on secular tales

Gunpowder

An invention that completely changed the Western world. The development of gunpowder led to warfare conducted with muskets and cannons rather than with bows and swords.

Holy Roman Empire

All of the German states bound together under an elected emperor

Humanism

A secular conception of life adopted during the Renaissance that emphasized individualism

Inquisition

A Church court that was vigilant in enforcing religious uniformity

Leonardo da Vinci

A Renaissance artist whose extensive knowledge of the human form is reflected in his art

Madonnas

One of the religious icons depicted by Renaissance artists

Medici

Merchants in Florence who went into banking as the flow of money increased

Michelangelo

A Renaissance artist who used oil paint to create more individually lifelike images

Mysticism

The Northern Renaissance religious way of thinking, which said that individuals could commune with God without the Church

New Monarchies (Tudors, Valois, Habsburg)

Powerful ruling families who politically united large parts of Northern Europe. Henry VII became the first Tudor monarch of England in 1485 after the War of the Roses, passing laws against "livery and maintenance." The Valois monarchy of France established control of most of the countryside in the 1400s. The French king could tax his subjects without parliamentary consent and appoint bishops and abbots. The Habsburgs, the powerful ruling family of Spain, controlled the Low Countries and much of Central Europe, including Austria.

Oligarchies

Committees of the wealthy and powerful members of society who ruled the Italian city-states

Perspective

Painters of the Renaissance employed this artistic style, which gave their work depth and a sense of the three-dimensional.

Pietà

A popular Renaissance sculpture featuring Mary cradling the body of the crucified Jesus

Raphael Sanzio

A Renaissance artist who painted religious topics, including the Madonna and Child

Renaissance man

The ideal person who used his opportunities, demonstrated control, and was casually expert in many areas

Star Chamber

A royal court, established by Henry VII of England, for offending nobility. It was conducted without a jury.

The Prince

This 1513 book, written by Niccolo Machiavelli, described what effective rulers did to get what they wanted. Machiavelli saw the great political failures of the Italian city-states and admired the rising new monarchies of Northern Europe.

Thomas More, Utopia

An English scholar who described an ideal society in which the goal for all inhabitants was to develop their rational faculties. Material possessions had no value, and adults divided their time between manual labor and study.

Virtù

A wide range of skills possessed by a Renaissance man, which included the ability to dance, fight, write poetry, converse with women, or ride a horse

THE REFORMATION AND RELIGIOUS WARS

95 Theses

A theses posted on the Church door in Wittenberg in 1517 by Martin Luther that began the actual Reformation of the Christian Church

Absenteeism

Rarely or never residing in the area where one had a position

Baroque

A style of art, decoration, and music characterized by extravagant ornamentation. Its goal was to impress and inspire by overwhelming the emotions.

Cardinal Wolsey

A high English churchman who came to fill a high government position

Council of Trent

Organized by the Catholic Church as a response to the spread of Protestantism. Their meetings between 1545–1563 resulted in the general affirmation of almost all Catholic traditions.

Council of Troubles

The Duke of Alba's church court, which executed prominent nobles, seized property, and applied new taxes after the Dutch Revolt emerged in 1566. It was nicknamed the "Council of Blood."

Defender of the Faith

The name given to Henry VIII after he wrote the pamphlet "In Defense of the Seven Sacraments" in 1520

Defenestration of Prague

The first act of the Thirty Years War in which the Estates of Bohemia threw two emissaries from the Holy Roman Emperor out a window 70 feet above the ground

Edict of Nantes

To protect the Huguenots, King Henry permitted Protestants to maintain their own fortifications and armed men, hold services, and operate schools in some towns.

Edict of Restitution

The Catholic "high point" of the Thirty Years War in which church property taken by Protestants over the past 70 years was returned

Election and Predestination

A Christian concept that taught that only God could know or decide who was saved and who was damned

Institutes of the Christian Religion

In this work, John Calvin advocated faith rather than works.

Ironsides

Oliver Cromwell's Puritan army, who defeated the king's supporters

John Hus

An outspoken German critic of the Church who condemned the worldliness of Church figures in the 1300s

John Wycliffe

An English scholar and outspoken critic of the Church who insisted on salvation by faith alone

Nepotism

One of the abuses of the Church, which included giving lucrative church jobs to one's children or other relatives

Oliver Cromwell

The military leader of the Puritans who combined forces into the "New Model Army." His army defeated the king's supporters and eventually captured King Charles.

Palatinate

One of the western German states that eventually became Protestant. In 1608, the Protestant German states, led by the Palatinate, formed the Protestant Union.

Papal Index of Forbidden Books

Published by the Church to punish heresy. All Protestant writing was included.

Peace of Augsburg

Treaty that ended the dispute between Lutherans and Catholics in the German states

Peace of Westphalia

Treaty that ended the Thirty Years War

Peasant Revolt

Revolt in the mid-1520s, stemming from German grievances against social ills and abuses of the Church

Pluralism

Having more than one church position and hiring a poor parish priest to serve in the less desirable office

Politique

One willing to strike a compromise between religion and politics for the greater good

Presbyterianism

A form of Calvinism brought to Scotland by John Knox

Purgatory

According to the Church, a place between heaven and hell where souls awaited entrance into paradise

Puritans

Calvinist strand of Protestants in England who had a desire to purify the Church of England. They opposed bishops and wished to eliminate the *Book of Common Prayer*.

Re-Catholization of Bohemia

This occurred when Bohemia was reconquered and the land was taken from the nobility. The Jesuits set up schools, and there were trials and executions, effectively ridding the area of any Protestantism.

Restoration

Widespread changes that took place in 1600, when the former members of Parliament initiated new Parliamentary elections and invited Charles's son, Charles II, to return as monarch

Roundheads versus Cavaliers

Nicknames given to the Cromwell-led Puritans and the Charles I-led Anglicans. The Puritan roundheads defeated the Anglican Cavaliers in 1649.

Salvation

To be saved from the punishment of suffering and sin

Society of Jesus or Jesuits

Founded by the Spaniard Ignatius Loyola, this order grew rapidly into the "militant" arm of the Church, carrying Christianity to remote Spanish Colonies, operating schools, and advising monarchs.

St. Bartholomew's Day Massacre

A slaughter of several thousand Protestants in Paris and the surrounding countryside the night after Catherine de Medici married Henry of Navarre. It marked a turning point in the French wars of religion as it radicalized the Calvinist Protestants.

Transubstantiation and Consubstantiation

Martin Luther took the idea that in the Eucharist, the bread and wine mystically became the body and blood of Christ (transubstantiation) and changed it to the idea that the "presence" of Christ was in the Eucharist (consubstantiation).

Treasury of Merit

A "savings bank" where the extra good deeds of devout Christians were held. It was an integral part of the buying and selling of indulgences.

Union of Utrecht

A union of the 10 northern provinces of the Netherlands, formed after the Duke of Parma won back the 10 southern provinces

Unitarianism

A Protestant movement whose core belief was that God existed as the Father, Son, and Holy Spirit

War of Three Henrys

After King Henry's men assassinated Henry of Guise, a Catholic monk, in turn, killed the king. After this event, Henry of Navarre, who had capitalized on the repugnant idea of Spanish intervention, took over as the first Bourbon monarch of France.

William Tyndale

An English reformer who translated, printed, and distributed the New Testament. He was later seized by the Catholics and executed for heresy.

DISCOVERY, EXPANSION, AND COMMERCIAL REVOLUTION

Aztecs

A group of people living in Central America before Columbus's arrival. They were defeated by Hernando Cortez, one of the first Spanish conquistadors.

Bartholomew Diaz

Portuguese explorer who reached the tip of Africa in 1488

Bullionist

An economy whereby a country's wealth was measured in gold and silver

Christopher Columbus

Genoan sailor who, financed by Ferdinand and Isabella of Spain, set sail to Asia by heading west. Although he did not bring back the gold and riches the Spaniards were hoping for, he is credited with "discovering" America.

Conquistadors

Spanish soldiers and adventurers who conquered much of the Americas

Cottage industry

An attempt to avoid the guild restrictions in town, where spinning, weaving, and dying cloth were done in piecework in private homes

Creoles

American-born whites in the 1500s

East India trading companies

Trading companies held by the Dutch, French, and English in East India

Encomiendas

Large Spanish plantations in the Americas run by Indian slave labor

Ferdinand Magellan

Pursuer of a Southwestern Passage to the Pacific who took five ships down the coast of South America in 1519 across the Pacific

Francis Drake

English explorer and soldier who led the second European circumnavigation of the globe and harassed Spanish explorers

Francisco Pizarro

Spanish conquistador who conquered the Incas, a prominent Indian tribe in present-day Peru

Hernando Cortez

The first of the Spanish conquistadors, who conquered the Aztecs in Mexico

Jacques Cartier

A French navigator who first explored the St. Lawrence River. He helped the French establish a name in North American expansion.

John Hawkins

Like Francis Drake, a leader of the English naval fleet against the Spanish

Madieras and Azores

Islands in the Atlantic that were home to two of the earliest Portuguese colonies. From here, the Portuguese began inching their way down the coast of Africa.

Mercantilism

A type of economy based on importing less and exporting more, using colonies to provide raw materials, and guarding trade secrets. It focused on accumulating gold and silver.

Mestizos

A person born of mixed Indian and Spanish ethnicity. Mestizos adopted the Spanish language and religion.

Moriscos

People of Moorish decent who were often skilled farmers and craftsmen

New Amsterdam

A colony along the Hudson River that the Dutch made a brief attempt to settle. Within 50 years, the colony was seized by the English and renamed New York.

Pedro Cabral

A voyager who sailed down the coast of Africa in 1500 and was blown off course, ending up in what is now Brazil

Ponce de León

A Spaniard who explored southern North America

Prince Henry, the Navigator

Led the Portuguese during their exploration of the Atlantic in the mid-1400s

Sea dogs

Nicknames of Englishmen John Hawkins and Francis Drake, who became the bane of Spanish treasure ships during the rule of Elizabeth I

Smallpox

European disease that allowed Spanish soldiers to conquer thousands of Stone Age natives

Southwestern Passage

A path to the Pacific that Ferdinand Magellan and others attempted to explore by traveling down the coast of South America in 1519

Treaty of Tordesillas

An agreement in 1493 that "divided the world" between Spain and Portugal and allowed Portugal to claim Brazil

Vasco de Balboa

Spanish explorer who crossed the Isthmus of Panama in 1513, becoming the first European to see the Pacific Ocean

Vasco de Gama

Portuguese explorer who rounded the Cape of Good Hope in 1498 and crossed the Indian Ocean, allowing the Portuguese to begin trade with Asia

THE AGE OF ABSOLUTISM—WESTERN EUROPE

Absolutism

The theory held by most of the rulers of the European states who established themselves as absolute monarchs, which advocated taking control over taxation, the military, and religion

Anne of Austria

Served as regent of France when her son Louis XIV became king in 1643 at the age of four. She was often criticized as an outsider.

Asiento

The privilege to conduct slave trade with Spanish America

Austrian Netherlands

Name given to the former Spanish Netherlands when it came under the control of Austria

Balance of power

A type of political strategy implemented by William of Orange when Louis XIV attempted to invade the Dutch. His attempt was blocked by an alliance of the Dutch with other nations.

Cardinal Richelieu

A high-ranking clergyman who placed practical politics first. Marie de Medici and Louis XIII relied on his skills after the assassination of Henry IV in 1610. He worked to strengthen royal control through better tax collection, divided France into 32 districts, revoked portions of the Edict of Nantes, and sided against the Catholic Habsburgs of Austria and Spain during the Thirty Years War.

Charles II

The Spanish Habsburg monarch who died without an heir, willing his throne to the grandson of Louis XIV

Divine right

The theory that kings ruled by the will of God

Estates General

The body of people King Henry IV chose to ignore after 1593, thus ruling without interference. He attempted to restore peace and unity to France at the end of the religious wars and selected his councilors from the lower-ranking nobles, whom he believed to be more loyal.

Five Great Farms

A large area, free of internal tariffs, set up by Jean-Baptiste Colbert to enhance trade

Franche-Comté

A province between eastern France and Switzerland that Louis XIV captured

The Fronde

The nickname of the 1648 revolt in which the refractory nobility attempted to overthrow Jules Mazarin and give control to the nobility

Gibraltar

The region England was permitted to keep according to the Treaty of Utrecht in 1713

Grand Alliance

Led by William of Orange and others in Europe who feared a mega-monarchy of France and Spain following the death of Charles II

Jacques Bossuet

A French author who believed that kings ruled by divine right

Jansenists

A Catholic minority who pursued a doctrine of faith and divine grace similar to that of the Calvinists

Jean-Baptiste Colbert

To build France's economic strength, Louis XIV employed this man, who sponsored the development of manufactures such as silk, tapestries, and other cloth by awarding tax exemptions and monopolies.

Jules Mazarin

An Italian cardinal who led the government when Louis XIV became King of France in 1643 at the age of four

THE AGE OF ABSOLUTISM—EASTERN EUROPE

Charles VI of Austria

Became the Habsburg emperor in 1711. Since he had no male heirs, Charles spent much of his reign making deals with the other nations of Europe, the Pragmatic Sanction, by which they agreed to accept his daughter, Maria Theresa, as his successor and ruler of the Austrian territory.

Frederick

Frederick William's son, who used the War of Spanish Succession to gain even more authority. In exchange for supplying troops to the Holy Roman

Emperor, Frederick received the right to call himself King in Prussia and eventually King of Prussia.

Frederick William

Became the Elector in 1640 and used the Thirty Years War to ignore old rights of the landlords. He assumed the right to tax without their consent and used the revenue to build a large, permanent standing army.

Frederick William I

The early Hohenzollern monarch who made Prussia's army the fourth largest in Europe. He also centralized government power in order to manage the military. Historians often describe him as earthy and crude.

Great Northern War

The conflict between Russia and Sweden in which Peter the Great took the Baltic coastal areas of Latvia and Estonia around 1709

Junkers

The powerful Prussian landed aristocracy who accepted Hohenzollern authority as long as they were left alone on their own estates, where they had total control of their peasants

Kiuprili Family

Came to power in the middle of the 1600s, arousing the Ottoman Empire to attempt further conquest in Eastern Europe.

Magyars

The Hungarian nobility who accepted the Habsburg monarchy but kept local control. They maintained their own diet and did not pay taxes to Vienna.

Peter the Great

Developed absolutism in Russia in the late 17th and early 18th centuries. He wanted to develop a state and military equal to those of the Western nations. He increased the Russian army to over 200,000, placed the Russian Orthodox Church under a committee of bishops, constructed a new capital, and reorganized the country into 10 territories.

Stephen Razin

Led a large peasant rebellion in 1670–1671 that scared the nobility into clamping down on the peasantry and giving more authority to the tsar.

CONSTITUTIONALISM IN ENGLAND AND THE DUTCH REPUBLIC

Anglo-Dutch Wars

Three indecisive wars between the British and the Dutch, lasting from 1652 to 1674, in which England annexed the Dutch colony of New Amsterdam, renaming it New York.

Baruch Spinoza

A member of a refugee Portuguese family who worked as a lens grinder and wrote philosophy discussing the nature of reality and human conduct

English Bill of Rights

Reaffirmed the Test Act but allowed dissenters to worship and maintain their own schools. It also ensured the rights of Parliament, particularly financial control.

Florin

The Dutch gold coin, which became the international unit of monetary exchange.

Glorious Revolution

The name given to the bloodless regime change in 1688, when William and Mary became the unchallenged leaders of England

James II

Took over the throne of England when his brother, Charles II, died in 1685. He ignored the Test Act, dismissed Protestant ministers, and declared freedom of worship.

Navigation Acts

Required goods coming into England to arrive either in ships from the exporting country or in British vessels.

New Amsterdam

The colony established by the Dutch East India Company in North America in 1612

Stadholder

The chief executive selected by each of the seven provinces of the Dutch Republic

Test Act

Excluded non-Anglicans from military and civil office.

THE SCIENTIFIC REVOLUTION

Frances Bacon

An Englishman who believed that the path to knowledge was doing hands-on investigations and drawing conclusions. He insisted that this method of inductive reasoning would produce knowledge with a more practical application.

Galileo Galilei

An Italian mathematician who developed the laws of uniform acceleration and the laws of motion. He also concluded that the surface of the moon was uneven and announced that the Milky Way was made up of a cluster of stars.

Isaac Newton

An Englishman who put together various ideas to form the law of universal gravitation, the forces of attraction and repulsion between objects. He published *Principia Mathematica* in 1687, a work on the laws of dynamics, motion, mechanics, and how things move in relation to each other.

Johannes Kepler

An astronomer who mathematically proved that the paths of the planets were ellipses, not circles. He established mathematical laws to show that the length of time of a planet's orbit varies proportionally with its distance from the sun. He also established a formulaic relationship between space and time.

John Locke

An Englishman who rejected heredity and the Church's teaching of original sin. He claimed that humans were influenced by what they were taught and that it was possible to create a better society through education.

Nicholas Copernicus

A Polish scholar who believed in a heliocentric model; that is, the sun, not the earth, was the center of the universe. He thought that the earth moved, rather than the stars, and that the universe was much bigger than anyone had imagined.

Ptolemy

A Greek astronomer who believed that the earth was fixed and motionless (geocentric). He thought that invisible crystal spheres moved around the earth, to which attached the sun, moon, stars, and the five known planets.

Scientific Revolution

The period during the 17th and 18th centuries in which innovative thinkers and experimenters changed people's view of the universe. The scientific method became important, influencing practical human activity and social institutions.

Tycho Brahe

A Danish astronomer who believed that the planets revolved around the sun, as well as the geocentric concept

Vesalius

The founder of biological science. He dissected and studied cadavers and was the first to assemble a human skeleton.

THE ENLIGHTENMENT

Adam Smith

A philosopher who published the *Wealth of Nations* in 1776, in which he opposed mercantilism. He wanted the government uninvolved in manufacturing and trade.

Baron de Montesquieu

A French philosopher who believed in the importance of the upper class and its ability to share ruling power. His work, *The Spirit of Laws*, was a comparative study of republics, monarchs, and despotic societies. He admired the English balance of power among the king, Parliament, and an independent court system.

Deism

The religious view that explained God as the mastermind and creator of the universe. The theory held that God was not personally involved in human affairs.

Great Awakening

An evangelical movement in England and the colonies in North America. It lasted about 20 years, reaching its height in 1740.

Jean Jacques Rousseau

A French philosopher who saw government as an agreement among people. He believed that the government should honor the general will of the people.

Laissez-faire

The concept of letting the economy move freely in its own way, without tariffs or other regulatory controls

Marquis de Becarria

An Italian nobleman who believed that the state had to protect its citizens, including those accused of crimes. His position that a person was innocent until proven guilty later became a basic concept of Western law.

Natural law

An idea held by Enlightenment thinkers, who believed that there must be something inherent in the universe that is true for all people in all places and times

Pietism

A branch of evangelical Lutheranism that developed in the German states. It emphasized the "inner experience" of ordinary people seeking an "inner light."

Voltaire

A French philosopher who worked for individual liberty and equality before the law. He admired Enlightenment rulers who practiced religious toleration and encouraged the arts and sciences.

18TH-CENTURY ECONOMICS AND POLITICS

Black Hole of Calcutta

The most publicized event of the Seven Years War in which a local Muslim ruler locked 146 Englishmen in a tiny cell, where most suffocated

Common land

An area of land on which landless peasants could graze their animals, pick berries, or gather firewood. These common lands were "enclosed" (by Parliamentary decree in England) by the major landowners.

Cottage industry

This system allowed men, women, and children to work in the home. Workers often engaged in the production of woolen cloth, copper, tin, iron, and leather goods.

French and Indian War

The American phase of the conflict between France and England began in 1754 over competition for territory in the Ohio River valley and resulted in a British victory.

Pragmatic Sanction

An agreement stating that other nations would acknowledge Maria Theresa as the Queen of Austria and accept the Austrian Empire

Seven Years War

A conflict between the British and French over outposts in India

Treaty of Aix-la-Chapelle

A 1748 agreement that returned everything to prewar conditions, except for Silesia, which Frederick II of Prussia kept

Treaty of Hubertusburg

One of the treaties ending the Seven Years War in 1763. According to its provisions, Prussia kept Silesia and Austria kept the southern Netherlands.

Treaty of Paris

One of the treaties ending the Seven Years War in 1763. Canada and all of North America east of the Mississippi River went to England. Territory west of the Mississippi River went to Spain.

War of Jenkins' Ear

A brief conflict between England and Spain that resulted when an English ship captain named Jenkins asserted that he'd had his ear "pickled" by the Spaniards

THE FRENCH REVOLUTION

100 Days

The last period of fighting by Napoleon after his escape from Elba before the Congress of Vienna ended in the spring of 1815

De-Christianization

A belief brought on by the study of deism. Services were held to a "Supreme Being" and "Reason" impersonated by an actress.

The Declaration of the Rights of Man and Citizen

A document produced by the National Assembly that listed the following as basic human rights: liberty, property, security, resistance to oppression, freedom of religion, due process of law, and taxes by common consent

Jacques Louis David

A French artist of both the revolution and Napoleonic era who captured the spirit of France in such paintings as *The Oath of the Tennis Court, Oath of the Horatii,* and *Death of Marat.* He held much admiration for Napoleon and painted him on many occasions.

Marie Antoinette

The wife of King Louis the XVI was despised as a frivolous foreigner and often referred to as the "Austrian whore."

The Napoleonic Code

Napoleon's replacement of the previous French legal system that was divided into a criminal code and a civil code. Citizens were declared equal before the law, and freedom of religion was guaranteed.

National Assembly

An assembly formed when the third estate refused to act until the king ordered the other two estates to the meeting as well. The Assembly was formed with no legal precedent and, therefore, was locked out of the final meeting room. It met for the first time at an indoor tennis court where the Oath of the Tennis Court was first brought forth.

Olympe de Gouges

In 1791, she wrote *Rights of Women*, which declared woman's rights to education, to control property within marriage, and to initiate divorce. She spoke of a social contract between men and women and hinted that men were not free unless women had rights as well.

Rosetta Stone

Discovered by the French at Rosetta, this stone held the key to deciphering ancient Egyptian hieroglyphics.

The Terror

A period from 1793 to 1794, less than a year, in which the Convention sought to eliminate all enemies of the Jacobins, with more focus on the Girondins. Victims included the former Queen Marie Antoinette, Olympe de Gouges, and the French scientist Lavoisier.

THE INDUSTRIAL REVOLUTION

Alfred Krupp

A major developer in the Ruhr region who put together a thriving steelworks by the middle of the 19th century

Factory Act, 1883

This act limited the number of hours children under the age of nine could work. It also provided money for inspectors and provided procedures for enforcement.

George Stephenson

Inventor of the *Rocket*, the first steam locomotive, which traveled from Liverpool to Manchester at the roaring speed of 16 miles per hour.

Iron law of wages

David Ricardo claimed that if workers were paid more, they would produce more children, who would consume the increase. Therefore, he said, the working class would forever exist at subsistence levels.

James Hargreaves

Inventor of the spinning jenny, which has multiple spindles, enabling spinning to keep up with weaving for the first time

Laissez-faire capitalism

The belief that a natural law applied to the world of manufacturing and trade, based on Adam Smith's principle of supply and demand

Mines Act, 1842

An act passed that prohibited women, girls, and boys under ten from working in the mines.

Robert Peel

A cotton lord who, in 1802, pushed the first Factory Act through Parliament. The law attempted to regulate the conditions under with pauper children worked in factories, but it accomplished little because there was no agency to inspect and enforce it.

Thomas Malthus, "Essay on the Principle of Population"

An essay in with the English-born Malthus compared human beings to lemmings, tiny rodents whose populations exploded until they outstripped naturally occurring resources and then committed mass suicide

Zollverein

A tariff union developed by Friedrich List, which included 80 percent of the German states

CONSERVATISM (1815–1823)

Alexander Ypsilanti

A Greek who attempted to start an uprising against the established order of the Ottoman Empire. He led a group of followers from Russia to Romania, expecting Greeks to rise up, join the cause, and get Russian support.

Carbonari

A nationalist group in Italy that led the revolt against post-Vienna restored rulers

Congress Poland

A new Kingdom of Poland created out of land that Austria and Prussia had taken in the 1700s

Corn Laws

Tariffs or import limits on foreign grain. These restrictions hurt consumers because bread prices were high, and manufacturers because they had to pay their workers higher wages.

German Confederation

A continuation of the loose organization Napoleon had dubbed the North German Confederation

Holy Alliance

A document insisted upon by Alexander that referred to rulers of European nations as delegates of Providence and claimed that their actions were based on sublime truths of religion

Peterloo Massacre

In 1819, a large group of disgruntled but peaceable laborers demonstrated their unrest at the state of unemployment. They demanded universal male suffrage, annual elections for the House of Commons, and the repeal of the Corn Laws. Local authorities panicked and fired into the crowd, killing 11 and wounding around 400 more.

Pocket boroughs

In Parliament, districts said to be "in the pocket" of some wealthy landowner who was routinely reelected without opposition

Protocol of Troppau

A protocol composed by Metternich and Alexander that called for the collective international action in the interest of general peace and stability. Castlereagh and England refused to participate, but Prussia joined Alexander and Metternich.

White Terror

Returning émigrés tried to punish former revolutionaries and Bonapartists.

THE RISE OF LIBERALISM (1815–1848)

Anti–Corn Law League

One of two major liberal movements in England before 1848. Supporters of the league argued that the grain tariffs kept grain prices unnaturally high, which hurt wage earners.

Bloody June Days

After conservatives won the majority of the power in the National Assembly, violent riots took place with casualties ranging from 1,500 to 10,000.

Chartists Movement

Tied into the anti–Corn Law movement, this movement was based on the idea of the great charter, or a national petition with thousands of signatures that would be presented to Parliament.

François Guizot

Louis Philippe's much despised, excessively conservative premier, who forbade a workers' rally in support of electoral reform

July Ordinances

Four ordinances. The first dissolved the newly elected Chamber before it met, the second censored the press, the third greatly reduced the franchise to exclude the upper middle class, and the fourth called for new elections based on the revised franchise.

Legitimists

In a divided French provisional government, this group wanted the return of a Bourbon descendent.

Liberalism

A product of the Enlightenment made up of liberal-minded people who were well-educated members of the upper middle class, often professionals. They believed in constitutions and representative government that protected such human rights as freedom of expression, religion, and equality before the law.

Louis Philippe

Cousin to the king, he replaced Charles X. He was careful to downplay the royal image, dressing in the equivalent of today's business suit and carrying an umbrella. His reign lasted for 18 years and was called the July Monarchy.

Orléanists

People who favored the leadership of one of Louis Philippe's sons in the divided French provisional government

Reform Bill of 1832

Approximately doubled the number of men in England who could vote. The bill did not give numerical balance to electoral districts, but it did eliminate some of the smaller boroughs, whose seats were reallocated to the new industrial centers.

THE RISE OF NATIONALISM (1815–1848)

All-Slav Conference

A conference in 1848 wherein representatives from various Slavic groups within the Austrian Empire demanded equal recognition with other nationalities

Declarations of the Rights of the German People

One of two important documents produced by the Frankfurt Assembly that emphasized individual rights such as religion, press, and assembly. Although very similar to the American Declaration of Independence, this bill emphasized the rights of only the German people, not the rights of man.

Frankfurt Assembly

A group of delegates from all the German states who met in 1848–1849 to debate the question of a unified Germany

J. G. Herder

A protestant clergyman who published *Ideas of the Philosophy of the History of Mankind*, which focused on the idea that imitation of foreign ways was shallow and artificial and that German ways were different from those of all others

Joseph Mazzini

The spokesman for Italian nationalism. He started out as part of the secret Italian society called the Carbonari and eventually organized his own group, called Young Italy.

Leopold von Ranke

A German historian who claimed that Germans had a mission to create a purely German state. He did not feel that Western European ideals, like parliamentary government and constitutionalism, applied to Germany.

Louis Kossuth

A Hungarian national who, in response to the February Revolution, made a speech about "liberty" that was printed in German and spread to Vienna. There, workers and students revolted by putting up barricades and invading the royal palace.

Treaty of London (1827)

England, France, and Russia joined together and threatened Turkey with military action if it did not grant Greece its freedom. When the Turks rejected the proposal, the allies used a naval force to destroy the Turkish fleet.

Volkgeist

An idea created by J. G. Herder that spoke of the spirit of the German people, often found among commoners. Although Herder did not claim his German idea was better than others, it did directly oppose thinkers like Voltaire, who said that certain truths were operative for all people of all places and times, not just Germans.

William Tell

An opera presented in 1829 by Italian composer Rossini that glorified the Swiss hero who had refused to submit to Austrian rule several centuries earlier.

The work is often viewed as a metaphor for Italian patriotism against domination by Austria.

ROMANTICISM

Eugene Delacroix, *Liberty Leading the People*

A romantic painter who, in one of his paintings, idealized the July Revolution of 1830. His painting showed people of all classes following a goddesslike Liberty, carrying the tricolor flag.

Franz Shubert

An Austrian composer who drew on romantic lyric poetry and folksongs, especially Hungarian Gypsy tunes, for his operas, Masses, symphonies, piano sonatas, and quartets

Fredrich von Schiller

German romantic who spoke of the passions of the senses and of the soul, as manifested in the person of a hero

Ludwig von Beethoven

A German composer who provided a musical bridge between the classical and romantic eras. Incorporating new structures and harmonies, Beethoven was one of the first composers to achieve wealth and fame in his lifetime. He composed string quartets, symphonies, and sonatas for his new instrument, the piano.

Lyrical ballads

A collection of poems written by Samuel Taylor Coleridge and William Wordsworth that are considered the foundation of the romantic movement in literature

Robert Burns

A Scottish poet who preceded many of the romantic poets. He led a short, colorful life and drew on

Scottish folklore and wrote poetry in Scottish dialect. His subjects, most often, were the common people.

Sturm and Drang (storm and stress)

An early name for romanticism, which was emerging as part of the rebellion of the French occupation. The major emphasis was on nature, the emotions, and the individual.

Theodore Gericault

Romantic painter who painted *Raft of the Medusa*. It pictured stormy seas and skies, illustrating the fate of survivors of a shipwreck.

Victor Hugo, *The Hunchback of Notre Dame, Les Misérables*

A French novelist who wrote inspiring tales of heroic action. Both of these novels featured poor and ostracized members of society.

William Blake

An English mystical poet who spoke out for the poor, especially children. Like William Wordsworth, Blake saw industry as evil and ugly, polluting the natural landscape and dehumanizing.

THE AGE OF REALPOLITIK (1848–1914)

Camillo di Cavour

Appointed prime minister by Victor Emmanuel in 1852, he came from a liberal, aristocratic background. He worked to improve the economy with more credit, lower tariffs (to attract foreign investors), more railroads, and an improved army.

"The Elimination of Poverty"

One of two influential pamphlets published by Louis Napoleon that helped convince the majority of voters that he would do something to improve the sagging economy

Florence Nightingale

An English woman who helped organize and train a group of female nurses who traveled to the volatile region of Crimea. They found terrible conditions of filth and malnutrition, and they revolutionized field hospitals, dramatically dropping the mortality rate among the wounded.

Giuseppe Garibaldi

An Italian patriot and soldier who was said to have inherited the spirit of Mazzini. He fought in Lombardy in 1848 and in Rome in 1849.

Louis Napoleon Bonaparte

Nephew of Napoleon Bonaparte and one of four candidates for the presidential position created by the French Assembly. He won by a huge majority, most likely because of name recognition.

Needle gun

A revolutionary precursor to the machine gun. It helped the Prussians defeat the Austrians during the Seven Weeks War.

North German Confederation

Formed when Bismarck dissolved the former German Confederation and created a new union of 22 states. The new confederation had a constitution and bicameral parliament.

Otto von Bismarck

A foreign diplomat appointed by King William I as his chief minister. He was totally Machiavellian, willing to do whatever was necessary to get what he wanted. Often described as practical, opportunistic, and doggedly determined, Bismarck ignored the parliament, moving ahead with enlarging and reforming the army.

Realpolitik

The politics of reality. This approach emphasized law, order, and hard work and felt skepticism toward religion.

Ringstrasse

A grand boulevard built in Vienna that was an example of Austrian prosperity. It held the prosperous city center, public buildings, and expensive housing.

THE RISE OF SOCIALISM

Charles Fourier

A French utopian socialist who, like Saint-Simon, advocated a planned society

Communist Manifesto

A 50-page pamphlet published by Karl Marx in 1848, outlining the guidelines of the communist ideal

Dialectic materialism

A basic Marxist theory that said that all history was logical and predetermined and that all was in the process of change

Etienne Cabet

A French utopian who wrote a novel describing an ideal city with economic harmony and education. Craftsmen, especially, were attracted to Cabet's vision, some going as far as to establish various utopian settlements in the New World.

Flora Tristan

A female representative among the socialists. She fought for the equality of women in marriage and in the workplace and demanded more equitable wages for female workers.

Labor theory of value

A Marxist idea that insisted that the worth of a human-made object was determined by the amount of labor that went into its creation

Phalanxes

Part of the utopian society created by Fourier. Each consisted of exactly 1,620 individuals who had all the skills necessary to make a society function.

Robert Owen

An English cotton lord considered one of the earliest socialists. He tried to improve the lives of his employees by paying them higher wages and reducing the number of hours they worked. He also built schools, housing, and stores for his workers and tried to control drunkenness and other harmful vices.

Saint-Simon

A soldier in the American Revolution, Simon and his followers discussed a planned society in which the public owned both the capital and industrial equipment. Big public projects, they argued, would make the best use of resources and labor.

Surplus value

A Marxist idea, this was the difference between an object's cost of production and its selling price.

THE AGE OF MASS POLITICS (1871–1915)

Alfred Dreyfus

A Jewish army officer accused of selling military secrets to Germany. Supposedly, Dreyfus's handwriting made him appear to be a traitor, and he was secretly court-martialed, found guilty, and imprisoned on Devil's Island off the coast of South America.

Jules Verne

A science fiction writer who incorporated geography, science, astronomy, physics, and new transportation ideas into such works as *Around the World in Eighty Days* and *Twenty Thousand Leagues Under the Sea*

Paris Commune

A revival of ideas from the French Revolution, opposing the wealthy and the clergy and demanding government controls on various aspects of the economy (wages, prices, etc.)

Realism/Naturalism

A literary movement characterized by ordinary characters and the problems of daily existence. Topics like sex, violence, alcoholism, slums, factories, and slaughterhouses were not uncommon.

Revisionists

German socialists who worked with existing authority, not against it, even though they were still excluded from the highest positions in government

Taff Vale Act

Made unions responsible for employers' financial losses during strikes. Opposition to Taff Vale helped galvanize workers politically, and by 1906, the Labour Party elected 29 members of Parliament, which then repealed the law.

Syllabus of Errors

Published by the pope in 1864, this was a general condemnation of all things modern and progressive.

Victorian Age

The period under Queen Victoria's rule starting in 1837 and lasting for over 60 years. It demonstrated a British contentment, self-confidence, and a faith in self-reliance and progress.

William Butler Yates

A poet and member of the Gaelic League, which praised the Gaelic language and encouraged its expression

William Gladstone

Leader of the liberals, he was a very religious man who, as Chancellor of the Exchequer, sought to reduce government spending and waste. He generally disapproved of colonialism, arguing that it was too costly.

INTELLECTUAL MOVEMENTS (1850–1914)

Albert Einstein

A German mathematician who published "The Electro-dynamics of Moving Bodies," which included the famous equation $e = mc^2$. Einstein played a key role in the intellectual movement, as well as creating the foundation for the atomic age to come.

Alfred Nobel

One of the major contributors to the intellectual movement, Nobel invented dynamite in 1866, which enabled engineers to construct tunnels and large canals.

Camillo Pissaro

An impressionist painter who often painted city scenes, always striving to capture the "first impression." He strove to capture the vibrancy and immediacy of the outdoor atmosphere, especially in the interplay of light and shadow created by quick, bold brushstrokes.

Charles Darwin

An English naturalist who, after traveling to the Galapagos Islands for five years, wrote *On the Origin of Species by Means of Natural Selection*. In this book, he outlined his "survival of the fittest" and "natural selection" ideas, which rebelled against the natural, orderly, divine universe that had existed previously.

Gustave Courbet

A French painter who saw romanticism as an escape from reality. His realism was often disturbing to viewers, and his work was sometimes denounced as vulgar.

Les fauves

In English, "wild beasts." This term referred to a few early 20th-century French artists who were united by an independent style of creative experimentation.

Marie and Pierre Curie

Polish-born physicists who studied radiation and eventually isolated radium as a natural element in 1910. Marie was denied admission to the French Academy of Sciences because of her gender.

Paul Cézanne

A post-impressionist who claimed that all forms in nature were based on the cone, the cylinder, and the sphere. He deliberately distorted perspective by simplifying forms and employing dark outlines of figures. His subjects included portraits, still lifes, and landscapes.

Sigmund Freud, *The Interpretation of Dreams*

A Viennese medical doctor who believed dreams were extremely important to the unconscious mind, the entity that he believed controlled much of human behavior. He divided the mind into three parts: the id, the ego, and the super ego.

Wassily Kandinsky

A Russian who encompassed the ideals of *les fauves* and went a step further by abandoning any effort toward representation of people or objects

THE NEW IMPERIALISM

Boer War

After gold and diamonds were discovered in the late 1890s in the Transvaal, the Afrikaner Boers hated the influx of foreigners. They were often hostile, and eventually, the British sent a military force to quell the violence. The Boers fought fiercely and defeated the British.

David Livingstone

A Scottish medical missionary who, in 1841, became one of the first white men to explore the African interior

Dutch East Indies

One of the more developed colonies. It had internal business and exported more than it imported.

Evelyn Baring

In the late 1880s served as a very able British administrator. He reformed the economy to improve the lot of the peasants, while at the same time maintaining the production that the British demanded.

H. M. Stanley

Sent by the New York *Herald* to find David Livingstone after he disappeared in Africa, Stanley found Livingstone in 1871.

Jute

One of the imported goods that was in high commercial demand. It was a fiber used in burlap, twine, carpets, sacks, and rope and grown only in India.

Kruger Telegram

A telegram sent by William II of Germany to Paul Kruger, the Afrikan governor of the Transvaal, congratulating him on his victory over the British.

New Imperialism

A new version of imperialism that operated on a much larger and more complex scale. For example, Europeans built factories and warehouses, established mines and plantations, and built railroads that led to huge overseas financial investments.

Opium Wars

A series of wars that started after the British tried to smuggle opium into China

Taiping Rebellion

A 14-year civil war in the middle of the 19th century in which the Chinese revolted against the weakening Manchu Dynasty. The rebels were fighting their own government, not the Europeans, protesting poverty, exorbitant rents, and other financial issues.

WORLD WAR I

Albania

A tiny nation on the coast of the Adriatic, it was desirable during the Great War primarily because of its coastal location.

Allies

The opposition to the Central Powers was composed of Britain, France, and Russia.

Fourteen Points

Although originally intended as negotiating points for the Treaty of Versailles, they became a series of harsh demands forced on Germany.

Gavrilo Princip

Nicknamed the Black Hand, he was a member of the secret society the Union of Death, and he was responsible for the assassination of Archduke Ferdinand and his wife.

The Great War

Later called World War I, the Great War began in June 1914 after the assassination of Archduke Ferdinand and his wife.

John Maynard Keynes, *Economic Consequences of the War*

One of many people who left the Treaty of Versailles unhappy. He argued at the conference, and later in his book, that imposing heavy indemnities on Germany was a mistake that would slow postwar recovery for all of Europe.

Schlieffen Plan

The name of Germany's plan for war that addressed the possibility of a two-front war. The idea was to focus on France first, defeating her before the British could mobilize, and then turn to Russia.

Submarine

A German invention that provided Germany with a serious naval advantage. Submarines sank the *Lusitania*, killing 1,200 people, including 118 Americans.

Triple Alliance

Germany established a military partnership with Austria-Hungary in 1879 and then added Italy in 1882. If any of the three members found itself at war with two or more countries, the other alliance members would come to that country's aid.

Walter Rathenau

A Jewish industrialist who headed the German program to utilize resources at home while Germany was at war

THE RUSSIAN REVOLUTION

Act of Emancipation

An act that, in 1861, freed the serfs and peasants. It also divided the land, and peasants received about half of it.

Bolsheviks (majority)

One side of the split within the Social Democratic Workers' Party. It was characterized by control by a small elite, a purging of those who disagreed, and class struggle.

Bloody Sunday

In January 1905, approximately 200,000 people marched with a petition to the tsar before the Winter Palace in St. Petersburg. They were peasants, without weapons, and unaware that the tsar was not in residence. The troops guarding the palace panicked and fired on the crowd, killing about 1,000 people.

Mensheviks (minority)

One side of the split within the Social Democratic Workers' Party. It was characterized by large party involvement, cooperation with liberals, and reconciliation of differences.

October Manifesto

A manifesto proposed by Nicholas II that promised a constitution and a Duma, or a national parliament

Sergei Witte

Appointed by Nicholas II as chief minister, Witte persuaded the tsar to end most of the redemption payments on the land, dating back to the emancipation of the serfs in 1861.

Slavophiles

Intellectuals in the Russian Revolution who looked inward on Russia itself. They glorified the Orthodox Church, the village communities, and the institution of tsardom.

Westernizers

Intellectuals in the Russian Revolution who looked to France, England, and Germany for models of industrialization and parliamentary institutions

White Army

One side of the Russian civil war. It was made up of soldiers from various parts of southern Russia, the Ukraine, and Siberia, as well as from different social groups, united only in their hatred of the Reds and without any central command.

Zemstvos

Elected local councils or assemblies, whose job was to address such issues as road maintenance, medical care, and local finances

EUROPE BETWEEN THE WARS

Adolf Hitler

Born in Austria to a lower-middle-class family, Hitler quickly rose to the top position in the German Workers' Party. He spread his anti-Semitic and pro-Aryan ideology through books and charismatic speeches.

Great Depression

Began with the crash of the U.S. stock market in October 1929. Many banks closed, bankruptcy mushroomed, factories shut down, and world industrial production fell by 40 percent.

Guernica

A town that was destroyed by the fascist practice of saturation bombing. It was made famous by Pablo Picasso's huge abstract painting of that name.

Kellogg-Briand Agreement

Developed by the United States and France. Sixty-five nations signed the document, condemning war as a way to solve problems.

Mein Kampf (My Struggle)

After being sentenced to five years in prison, Hitler published this book in 1925. It became a best seller, despite being a mishmash of ravings on various topics, including anti-Semitism.

New Economic Policy

A policy developed by Lenin under which peasants were allowed to practice capitalistic farming again. They had to turn over a portion of what they raised, but they could keep the rest.

Paul Joseph Goebbels

Minister of propaganda for the Nazi party, he censored the theater and burned books by Jews, communists, and socialists.

Putsch

An armed revolt

Salvador Dali

Probably the most famous artist in the surrealist movement. His work was characterized by realistic images appearing in a dreamlike setting.

Treaty of Locarno

A treaty signed by France, Germany, and Belgium guaranteeing their borders unconditionally

WORLD WAR II

Axis

Formed in October of 1936 when Italy, believing that German military strength could further Italian aims, signed an agreement with Hitler.

Blitzkrieg

Nicknamed "lightning war," this style of warfare was characterized by a fast-rolling ground force of tanks and personnel, supported by air attack.

Enola Gay

The plane used to drop the first atomic bomb on Hiroshima on August 6, 1945

Four Freedoms

Part of Franklin Roosevelt's diplomacy during the war. Included freedom of speech, freedom of worship, freedom from want, and freedom from fear.

Maginot Line

An elaborate system of fortifications along France's eastern border, from Switzerland to Belgium.

Munich Conference, 1938

A pivotal conference that mainly focused on the future of Czechoslovakia, ending in a division among Nazi Germany, Poland, and Hungary

Neville Chamberlain

A prime minister of Britain who was so conservative that he called Nazism a "great social experiment." Knowing this, Hitler felt confident as he proceeded to annex his neighbors.

Nonaggression pact/Germany and USSR

A pact that guaranteed no aggression between these previously warring nations

Okinawa

The place of the final battle on the Pacific front guaranteeing an Allied victory

Pearl Harbor

U.S. naval port in Hawaii that was attacked on December 7, 1941, pushing the United States into World War II

IMMEDIATE POSTWAR ISSUES

Berlin Airlift

Series of Western supply drops that occurred for almost a year after the Soviets blockaded Berlin

Fifth Republic

Created by a new French constitution, it included seven-year terms for the office of president.

General Agreement on Tariffs and Trades (GATT)

Established in 1948, it urged reduction of tariffs. Twenty-three nations subscribed to the agreement, and the GATT became a forerunner for the World Trade Organization, which was founded later in the century.

Ludwig Erhard

Leader of the postwar German economy who believed strongly in a free market system. He removed rationing and price controls, and economic recovery was rapid.

Marshall Plan

Named after General George Marshall, this plan was designed to help rebuild postwar Europe and oppose communism.

North Atlantic Treaty Organization

Formed in 1949, mainly as an anti-communist group to protect Western Europe from possible Soviet attack, it emphasized the division between the Soviets and Western nations.

Nuremberg Trials

A series of trials held in Nuremberg, Germany, where 12 men were sentenced to death and many others to lifelong prison terms

Security Council

A part of the United Nations whose main purpose was preserving peace. It was composed of 15 members—five of which were permanent and 10 that rotated for two-year terms.

Treaty of Rome

Signed by six nations, this treaty created the European Economic Community (ECC). Tariffs within the group were removed, and capital and labor could move freely from country to country.

Truman Doctrine

A military policy under which the United States promised aid to all nations to prevent government takeover by a "minority party" (i.e., the communists)

THE COLD WAR

Boris Pasternak, *Dr. Zhivago*

A notable novelist who was able to thrive after Russia's "de-Stalinization." His novel was published outside the USSR in 1956.

Cold War

The diplomatic, political, and ideological clash between the United States and the USSR following World War II

Cuban Missile Crisis

A pivotal point in the Cold War when the Soviets moved nuclear warheads to the island of Cuba, putting them in range to fire on the United States. The United States, after mild hysteria, blockaded Cuba and forced the Soviets to remove the missiles.

De-Stalinization

A means of removing the ideals and practices of Stalin after the end of World War II that led to a burst of creativity among intellectuals and writers in Russia

Nikita Khrushchev

The next major Soviet leader after Stalin died in 1953, he began to denounce the crimes of Stalin.

Perestroika

A restructuring of the economy to make it freer from government control. State enterprises received more independence, and private cooperatives could make a profit for the first time.

Russian Federation

On January 1, 1992, the USSR ceased to exist and transformed into this loose union of 21 republics.

SALT I

Strategic Arms Limitation Talks. Both the United States and the USSR agreed to reduce the antimissile defense system and work toward equality in offensive weapons.

Sergei Prokofiev

A Russian composer who, under Stalin's strict laws, was condemned

Sputnik

The first artificial satellite, launched by the Russians in 1957

NATIONALISM

Arab League

Formed in 1945, it originally consisted of Egypt, Iraq, Syria, Jordan, Lebanon, Saudi Arabia, and Yemen. By the 1980s, there were 22 members.

Czech Republic

Formed in 1993 after Czechoslovakia split into the Czech Republic and Slovakia. The Czech Republic created a model for the transition to democracy, and after an initially difficult economic adjustment, the country became prosperous again.

Ghana

After the North African states became independent, southern African colonies were inspired to become independent as well. In 1957, the British granted independence to the Gold Coast, which was renamed Ghana. Ghana became a republic in 1960 and a member of the British Commonwealth of Nations. Ghana also became the world's largest producer of cocoa.

Hausa, Fulani, Yoruba, and Ibo

These four ethnic groups made up Nigeria, which was Britain's largest sub-Saharan colony after the war. Nigeria was granted independence in 1960 and became a republic in 1963.

Iran/Iraq War

Took place 1980–1988. The United States supported Iraq under Saddam Hussein. This war is well known for Iraq's use of chemical weapons.

Israel

Created in 1948 out of former Palestinian territory by the United Nations. After the Holocaust, many homeless survivors sought this land in the Middle East, and although the British tried to control immigration, many came in illegally.

Kosovo

One of the two autonomous provinces that was included in the federal republic of Yugoslavia set up after World War II. In the mid-1990s, a separatist movement began in Kosovo, which was still technically a province of Serbia.

Margaret Thatcher

In Britain, she became the first female leader of a Western nation in 1979. Thatcher gained most of her popularity in 1982 after the British navy prevented Argentina from taking the

British-controlled Falkland Islands off the coast of South America.

Mohandas Gandhi

He was a strong leader in India's Independence Movement. Ghandi was assassinated on the eve of independence.

Nelson Mandela

He was an part of the anti-apartheid movement and became the leader of the African National Congress. He was sentenced to life in prison, but in 1990, President F. W. de Klerk released him. Apartheid was repealed in 1991. Mandela became president in 1994, when democratic elections took place.

Pervez Musharraf

He seized power after a military coup in Pakistan in 1999.

Solidarity

Trade union, led by Lech Walesa, founded in 1980 during a great shipyard strike in Gdansk. Even though Solidarity had enough members to call for a nationwide strike, it never tried to seize political control, despite its members' desire for political change. In 1981, however, the Soviets cracked down on Poland and began outlawing Solidarity and arresting all of its leaders.

Treaty of European Union

Signed in 1992 by the 12 members of the European Community. The agreement proposed a central banking system and a single European currency, the euro, which went into effect in 1999.

Truth and Reconciliation Hearings

In an attempt to overcome some of the horrors of the past, South Africa conducted these hearings, which were moderated by Anglican Archbishop Desmond Tutu.

Yasser Arafat

Lead the Palestine Liberation Organization, a government in exile, which was founded by displaced Palestinians after the most serious of wars between Israel and the Arabs.

POST–WORLD WAR II SOCIETY

Baby Boomers

Term given to the post–World War II youth. This generation of children did not experience the Depression or world war. They had much power, experienced an abundance of employment opportunities, and therefore felt less need to conform to the older generation. As a result, a burst of romanticism and idealism in the 1960s was accompanied by rebelliousness and disillusionment with Western society.

Betty Friedan

A woman from the United States who, in 1963, wrote *The Feminine Mystique* and founded the National Organization for Women

Curriculum reform

In the 1950s and '60s, as there became an increase in the number of European college students, college curriculums began incorporating more technology and applied science, along with traditional liberal arts.

Dead Sea scrolls

In 1947 in Jordan, Bedouin shepherds found these scrolls, one of the greatest archeological discoveries in centuries. Although the origin of these scrolls is still somewhat a mystery, the scrolls include the earliest record of most of the Old Testament canon.

Deicide

The term used to describe the killing of a God. Prior to the Second Vatican Council's revision to allow Mass in the vernacular, deicide was used as an excuse for violence against Jews.

Ecumenical movement

Produced some unification and agreements between the different branches of Protestantism, the Roman Catholic Church, and Eastern Orthodox leaders.

Guest worker

The term given to someone who works in a different country from where they grew up. In Germany, many guest workers ended up staying there. There was a huge influx of immigrants to Western Europe in the 1980s.

Mass in the vernacular

The Second Vatican Council revised the liturgy to allow this. It relaxed the dress requirements for priests and nuns and absolved the Jews of deicide.

National Organization for Women

Group of women who advocated equal pay for equal work, maternity leave, and reliable, affordable daycare for their children. They also wanted to reform divorce and abortion laws, and they advocated for the needs of single parents, as well as for rape and abuse protection rights.

Neo-Nazis

An example of an extremist group formed against immigrants. This group has continued to advocate racism and intolerance despite the end of the Cold War.

Pope John XXIII

He came into office in 1958 and summoned the first international Church council since 1870.

Second Vatican Council

The first international Church council since 1870, summoned by Pope John XXIII. This council met 1962–1965, and some believe that it was the most important Church gathering since the Council of Trent in the 1500s. The council spoke out for peace and human rights and called on rich nations to share their wealth with the rest of the world.

Simone de Beauvoir

Frenchwoman who, in 1949, published *The Second Sex*. She argued that male-dominated society relegated women to an inferior position, which she called the "Other," where they held lesser jobs, earned less money, and were reduced to second-class status.

Social Gospel

The results of a shift in Christianity from miraculous and dogmatic religious ideas to reflect the more immediate needs of society. This occurred early in the 20th century in response to science.

Søren Kierkegaard

The 19th-century Danish religious thinker who emphasized a commitment to religious experience. After the disillusionment of World War I, there was a strong reaction against the social gospel as being too optimistic, so people turned again toward a "revealed" religion, including the teachings of Kierkegaard.

The Beatles

Popular band in the '60s, along with The Rolling Stones and other British rock groups.

Women's movement

By the 1960s, the women's movement was firmly underway. For the first time, birth control, more education, and the benefits of technology were made readily available to women.